THE
McGRAW-HILL
36-Hour Course

ACCOUNTING

THE McGRAW-HILL 36-Hour Course

ACCOUNTING

Fourth Edition

Robert L. Dixon
Professor Emeritus of Accounting
School of Business Administration
University of Michigan

Harold E. Arnett
Professor of Accounting
School of Business Administration
University of Michigan

Howard Davidoff
Professor of Accounting, Law and Taxation
Department of Economics
City University of New York at Brooklyn College

McGraw-Hill

New York   Chicago   San Francisco   Lisbon   London   Madrid   Mexico City
Milan   New Delhi   San Juan   Seoul   Singapore   Sydney   Toronto

The **McGraw·Hill** Companies

12 13 14 15 16 17 18 19 20   QFR   21 20 19 18 17

ISBN-13: 978-0-07-148603-3
ISBN-10: 0-07-148603-8

McGraw-Hill books are available at special discounts to use as premiums and sales promotions, or for use in corporate training programs. For more information, please write to the Director of Special Sales, McGraw-Hill, Two Penn Plaza, New York, NY 10121-2298. Or contact your local bookstore.

This publication is designed to provide accurate and authoritative information in regard to the subject matter covered. It is sold with the understanding that the publisher is not engaged in rendering legal, accounting or other professional service. If legal advice or other expert assistance is required, the services of a competent professional person should be sought.

—*From a Declaration of Principles Jointly Adopted by a Committee of the American Bar Association and a Committee of Publishers and Associations*

Library of Congress Cataloging-in-Publication Data

Dixon, Robert L.

  The McGraw-Hill 36-hour course : accounting / by Robert L. Dixon, Harold E. Arnett, and Howard Davidoff. — 4th ed.
    p. cm.
  Rev. ed. of: The McGraw-Hill 36-hour accounting course / Robert L. Dixon, Harold E. Arnett. 3rd ed. c1993.
  Includes index.
  ISBN 0-07-148603-8 (pbk. : alk. paper) 1. Accounting. I. Arnett, Harold E. II. Davidoff, Howard. III. Dixon, Robert L. McGraw-Hill 36-hour accounting course. IV. Title. V. Title: McGraw-Hill thirty-six hour course.

HF5636.D59 2007

657—dc22   2006103341

CONTENTS

PREFACE

It has been thirteen years since this book was last revised by my esteemed colleagues, and as I'm sure you know, much has happened in the world of business, finance, and accounting during that time.

Back in 1993, the business world was barely introduced to the concept of Internet communication, something we now take for granted. Instant nonstop 24-hour access via cellular phone was still quite a novelty. Heck, the Yankees hadn't finished in first place in more than a decade back then! The Clinton administration had just begun, with a tax policy aimed at "soaking the rich" by raising the highest income tax brackets in order to pay for expanded social programs like national health care (remember that failure?). Most of the "Big Eight" accounting firms were still around, and the Dow Jones Industrial Average was around the 3,000 mark.

Since 1993, our economy experienced a technological revolution that led to unprecedented economic expansion. The accounting profession prospered from industry deregulation that led to associations with the financial planning and securities brokerage industries. There was also deregulation in the financial services industry generally. Commercial banks got into the insurance and securities brokerage business. Investment companies became mortgage lenders, and depositors at local savings banks were offered opportunities to buy initial public offerings of the bank's shares at bargain prices. As the 1990s rolled on, the boom led to a bubble, the bubble burst, and financial scandals at Enron, Worldcom, and Tyco (to name a few) contributed to several developments impacting the accounting profession, including

1. The demise of one of the titans of the accounting profession, Arthur Andersen & Co.

2. The enactment, in 2002, of the Sarbanes-Oxley Act, imposing more stringent reporting and disclosure requirements on publicly held corporations and the CPA firms that undertake their financial audits.
3. An enhanced interest in the field of forensic accounting, which seeks to analyze financial statements in order to detect fraudulent or manipulative accounting techniques.

As you compare the current edition of this book to its prior editions, you will note several updates and changes. In the view of many, the most important financial statement to analyze has become the Statement of Cash Flows, which now must be presented for all publicly held corporations in addition to the Balance Sheet and the Income Statement. Accordingly, the alternative "Working Capital" funds statement has now been eliminated. A popular technique for accounting for business combinations, the pooling method, has been eliminated due to the perception that it provided advantages to the acquiring company that might mislead prospective lenders and investors. The conventional view is that added productivity has mitigated the threat of inflation and eliminated the need for inflation accounting.

The George W. Bush administration has taken the prior administration's "soak the rich" tax policy and completely reversed it by enacting sweeping tax cuts. The first cuts, known as the Economic Growth and Tax Relief Reconciliation Act of 2001, enacted soon after President Bush took office, was aimed at giving the federal budget surplus of the 1990s "back to the people." The next two rounds of tax cuts—the Jobs and Growth Tax Reconciliation Act of 2003 and the Working Families Tax Relief Act of 2004—were made in an attempt to stimulate the economy in the wake of an economic slowdown after the bursting of the "dot-com" bubble and the tragedy of 9/11. These cuts, coupled with drastically reduced interest rates by the Federal Reserve, were frequently cited for bringing the country out of a recession in 2001–2002.

Needless to say, many aspects of the Federal Income Tax law have been overhauled several times since the book was last published. The chapter on personal computers has also been completely revised in light of the fact that the accounting profession has become much more dependent on computerized systems.

THE INTENDED USER OF THIS BOOK

The goal of this book is to provide the nonaccountant with an understanding of the fundamental aspects of financial, managerial, and tax accounting concepts. Those who would benefit from this book include students, financial and managerial executives, attorneys, financial analysts, investors, engineers, small business entrepreneurs, and anyone else who would profit from an enhanced knowledge as to the inner workings of economic transactions, financial statements, tax returns, production reports, and business combinations, to name a few of the covered concepts.

PURPOSE OF THIS BOOK

This book is *not* intended as a preparation course for the CPA exam. It does not burden the reader with endless pronouncements from the Financial Accounting Standards Board (FASB), or sections of the Internal Revenue Code, or regulations of the Securities and Exchange Commission (SEC). This book *will* allow you to familiarize yourself with the ability to measure, process, and communicate financial information about an economic entity so that you can hold an intelligent discussion with an accountant, a banker, or other members of a managerial team.

FORMAT OF THIS BOOK

The first five chapters should be read in sequence before proceeding to the others, for they provide the "building blocks" of accounting. Most chapters have test problems at the end to reinforce the knowledge gained through the chapter's study. Appendix A will provide the user with the answers ... but don't peek until you have made an honest effort to answer the questions yourself! If you're truly a glutton for punishment, Appendix B will provide additional exam questions (Appendix C has those answers). A "Final Examination" has been prepared at the end of the book. If you are so inclined, take the exam and send the answer sheet to us in accordance with the instructions listed on the first page of the final exam. An official "Certificate of Achievement" will be awarded to those that pass the exam.

I would like to extend my thanks to McGraw-Hill, Inc., and specifically to Dianne Wheeler, whose help, cooperation, and patience made this work a truly enjoyable experience. I hope that you, dear reader, find this work to be informative and educational, and refer to it often throughout your business careers.

Howard Davidoff

INSTRUCTIONS AND STUDY PLAN

This is a concentrated self-instruction course that can be completed at your own pace in time segments as short as 10 minutes or as long as your schedule allows. It is designed for the intelligent person who, as an *executive*, must be able to communicate with, and understand, accountants; for the *lawyer* who is faced with client problems that are interlaced with accounting; for *engineers* who must deal with business matters and who wish to be better qualified for executive positions; for financial analysts and stockbrokers who will be far better qualified to interpret financial statements for their clients; and, of course, for the "ordinary" *investor* who wants to understand accounting statements. The course assumes the reader to have a layman's acquaintance with such terms as *accounts receivable* and *common stock*, but it also assumes zero knowledge of the accounting process at the outset.

Made up of only 36 hours of assignments, the course quickly and effectively "paints the big picture" and leaves the many small details to be filled in from daily experience and from a continuing habit of regular study which it can instill. It does not aim to qualify you either as an accountant or as a bookkeeper; perhaps its most important aim is to develop your ability to read accounting literature and to listen to and converse with the professional accountant. Then you will be able to understand what the accountant is up to and to communicate your needs.

YOUR STUDY PLAN

The serious student of this course should bear the following points in mind:

1. Be prepared to concentrate. If accounting were easy, the world would be flooded with accountants and this study would have little value.
2. Time spent on the course must be taken from other activities in your day. Sacrifice is involved (though the tuition is low!).
3. Continuity is very much to be desired. Study sessions should be scheduled from the beginning to the end of the course. This will require real determination, but a steady rate of progress through the course will repay you. If steady progress is not made, you are almost sure to lose interest and drop the course.
4. Best results are obtained if a definite hour, or other time period, is set for study sessions-the optimum, probably, is two separate sessions per week, for example, Tuesday and Thursday, 8:00 to 9:30 P.M.
5. Accounting, like law, medicine, or any other profession, is loaded with controversy. Accountants love to argue with each other. You may well find, in talking with accountants about the materials you are covering in this course, that the practitioners have contrary views. If so, listen politely but don't be persuaded that the book is dead wrong-at least not until you have finished the course. Then you should be able to size up the elements of any controversy and reach your own rational conclusion.
6. Toward the back of the book you will find a set of supplementary problems; there are two or three problems for nearly every chapter. It is not mandatory that you work these problems, and they are not included in the overall allowance of 36 hours. But if you want a deeper and more lasting comprehension of the field of accounting, it will be worth your while to work as many supplementary problems as your ambition dictates.

PROGRAM OF STUDY SESSIONS (AVERAGE ONE HOUR EACH)

LESSON 1 Read Chapter 1; work the test problem. You should have no trouble reading this chapter in an hour, but you should use most, if not all, of the hour anyway. Each of the first six sections is headed by a question (e.g., What Is a Balance Sheet?). After you have read through the chapter once, go back to these introductory sections and test your-self by seeing if you can answer each of the questions. Then, by all means, work the test problem. (Note that the author's solution to each problem appears in the appendix.)

LESSON 2 Read Chapter 2 and work the test problem. This chapter follows a format much like that of Chapter 1. You should be able to absorb its content in one session and work the test problem too. Possibly the most important principle of accounting is found under the heading The Accrual Concept. You should really concentrate on this section and, as before, be sure you have found the answers to the questions posed at the beginning of a number of the other sections.

LESSON 3 Read Chapter 3 to the middle of page 34. The chapter contains the internal organs of bookkeeping. Boring as it may be, most accounting language is related to the process of properly analyzing and recording business transactions, and you shouldn't leave this chapter until you feel quite familiar with it.

LESSON 4 Finish Chapter 3 and work the test problem. We'll make considerable use of the material in this chapter throughout the rest of the book, and the use of debit and credit sides of an account will become very familiar to you.

LESSON 5 Read Chapter 4. This chapter pulls it all together for you. The work sheet is a most useful tool for providing interim, as well as end-of-year, statements. Work the test problem in Chapter 4.

LESSON 6 Study Chapter 5. We've finished the survey of the bookkeeping framework of accounting, and now we begin study of specific areas of general interest. You'll find a large number of journal-entry illustrations of a variety of transactions. Please be sure to study the explanations that follow the transactions, and be sure you understand the logic of the debit and credit entries that have been made in each case.

LESSON 7 Work the test problem in Chapter 5. This probably won't take a full session, but do try to get each journal entry right before going on to the next one. This kind of practice is absolutely vital to your understanding of accounting. If you find that you cannot make the entries, you may need to go back over some of the earlier material.

LESSON 8 Study Chapter 6. The accounting profession has promoted the cash flow funds statement to the same level of importance as the balance sheet and income statement. The accounting profession has specified the minimum requirements for the funds (cash flow) statement-particularly the requirement of adequate disclosure. The forms shown in this chapter comply with these requirements. Since this chapter is relatively short work the test problem in Chapter 6.

LESSON 9 Study Chapter 7. The subject of inventories is always of enormous importance to companies that must carry stocks of merchandise or raw materials or work in process and finished goods. The methods of accounting for and finding the valuation of inventories have a dramatic effect upon reported earnings (as well as upon income taxes). We hope this chapter will be of value to you in pointing up (in accounting language) the critical aspects of the inventory control problem.

LESSON 10 Work the test problem in Chapter 7. This is a short assignment. After working it as prescribed (by using FIFO), you should re-work it with average cost and then by using LIFO, and compare your resulting amounts of cost of raw materials used.

LESSON 11 Study Chapter 8. Depreciation probably heads the list of controversial subjects. There is a considerable variety of methods of computing depreciation, and they, like inventory valuation methods, may have enormous impact upon reported profit figures. Each method has its logic and its advocates. You owe it to yourself to understand the reasons for each method as well as to reach some conclusion as to your own preferences.

LESSON 12 Work the test problem in Chapter 8. It calls for two methods of recording depreciation. Because you'll have a lot of time left over, you should also work the problem a third way, by using the declining-balance method.

LESSON 13 Study Chapter 9. This chapter deals with the more frequently used types of capital stock and related transactions. Corporate executives, lawyers, bankers, accountants, regulators, and tax gatherers have created a bewildering maze of corporate investment securities. We can only scratch the surface here, but that should be enough to get you started in discussions with sundry members of the groups referred to above.

LESSON 14 Work the test problem in Chapter 9.

LESSON 15 Study Chapter 10 and work the test problem. This chapter is pretty straightforward. By now you should feel entirely at home with the debit-credit concept, and you should have no trouble with either the examples or the test problem.

LESSON 16 Read Chapter 11 to the middle of page 156. This is a short reading assignment, but there's too much in the whole chapter for a single assignment. The subject of accounting for leases (under what circumstances should they be "capitalized") has evoked many years of argument and discussion. Here's hoping you can make up your own mind!

LESSON 17 Finish Chapter 11. Work the test problem.

LESSON 18 Read Chapter 12 to the bottom of page 173. This also is a short reading assignment, but the chapter needs to be split if only to have process cost accounting given extra attention.

LESSON 19 Finish Chapter 12 and work the test problem. In this section we accountants undertake the impossible, and don't ever forget it! The allocation of manufacturing (and administrative) overhead to departments, processes, cost centers, and, finally, units of product involves much that is arbitrary, pure estimate, and wishful thinking. Nevertheless, it appears that the allocations must be made if only to find the cost of goods sold and valuation of inventories. You should at least know what kinds of things the cost accountants are doing, and you should be aware of the weaknesses in their procedures.

LESSON 20 Study Chapter 13 to the top of page 186. This is a very short chapter, but it is a very important one regardless of your line of business. From it you should emerge with a familiarity with the notion of cost standards (as compared with the very misleading "actual" costs) and cost variances. The accounting involves enough complexities to justify your concentrating first on raw materials and direct labor and then on manufacturing overhead.

LESSON 21 Finish Chapter 13 and work the problem.

LESSON 22 Study Chapter 14 and work the test problem. This chapter skims over only a few of the special managerial decision aids that can be generated from a good accounting system. The six topics that are touched upon (responsibility accounting, standard costing, direct costing, differential costs, make-or-buy decisions, and capital budgeting) represent a set of fairly potent managerial activities in which the accountant should take a prominent part. We only mention operations research, which is simply the application of more or less rarefied mathematics to business problems. Any executive would be well-advised to become familiar with our six topics (as bread-and-butter items) and have at least a nodding acquaintance with the potentials of operations research.

LESSON 23 Read half of Chapter 15 on federal income tax concepts. This chapter deals entirely with the basic concepts. A familiarity with the concepts should be all that the typical businessperson needs, provided that good accountants, or tax practiceners, are available for preparation of the tax returns and to help with tax planning.

LESSON 24 Read the rest of Chapter 15 and work out the short test problems. Read Chapter 16. This is a very short chapter designed to give you some helpful general information on useful software packages. No problems are assigned in Chapter 16.

LESSON 25 Study Chapter 17 to the middle of page 241. Consolidated financial statements constitute about the toughest part of accounting; but if you apply yourself thoughtfully to the material of this chapter, you should understand the fundamentals very well and should be able to comprehend the process used in the case of the company, or companies, that you are interested in by talking them over with the accountants in charge. It has been said that every company listed on the New York Stock Exchange presents consolidated statements.

LESSON 26 Finish Chapter 17 and work the test problem. This is a continuation of Lesson 25 with special attention to consolidated balance sheets *after* the date of acquisition and to consolidated income statements.

LESSON 27 Study Chapter 18. It's the rare company nowadays that does not practice income tax allocation in some form. You should spend two study sessions on this subject even though everything appears clear to you the first time over.

LESSON 28 Work the test problem in Chapter 18.

LESSON 29 Study Chapter 19. The past few decades were notable for what might be termed "acquisition fever."

LESSON 30 Work the test problem in Chapter 19.

LESSON 31 Read Chapter 20. So many of our larger corporations are involved in foreign operations that the average business executive is quite likely to have need for insight into some of the intricacies of such operations as well as the financial statements that are forthcoming. The translation of foreign currencies presents some especially fascinating accounting problems.

LESSON 32 Work supplementary problem 20-1 in Appendix B.

LESSON 33 Take the final examination. You should allow up to two hours to do a thoughtful job. Send your solution in (see instructions on the first page of the examination) for grading.

ACCOUNTING

1

THE BALANCE SHEET

WHAT IS A BALANCE SHEET?

Imagine, first, that you have made a list of everything valuable that you own, and also the estimated dollar value of each thing, and have then added the dollar values to find their total. Second, you have made a list of the people, stores, etc., to whom you presently owe money, and also the amount owing to each party, and have determined the total of those amounts. Third, you have subtracted the smaller of the two totals from the larger to determine the dollar difference between the two lists. You now have all of the ingredients for a balance sheet.

Your first list can be labeled "assets"; your second list can be labeled "liabilities"; and the dollar difference can be termed your "net worth." If you arrange all that information in more or less orderly fashion, you will have a balance sheet. In the style customarily used by accountants, your balance sheet might appear as in Figure 1.1.

THE BALANCE SHEET—WHAT GOOD IS IT?

A balance sheet is what accountants call a financial statement. Many accountants will assert that it is the most important of the various kinds of "statements" that they prepare. However, there's much uncertainty as to just how one arrives at the dollar figures that are assigned to the various assets. This could mean that not only are the individual asset valuations unacceptable to certain users of the statements but so also is the amount that we labeled "net worth" (since it was found by subtracting the liability total from the asset total as listed).

Figure 1.1   Balance Sheet

MY NAME
Balance Sheet (date)

Assets		Liabilities	
Cash	$ 10,000	Owed to stores	$ 1,200
Stocks and bonds	50,000	Owed to bank	60,000
Clothing	2,500	Total liabilities	$ 61,200
Furniture	28,000		
House	160,000	Net worth	244,300
Land	40,000		
Miscellaneous	15,000		
Total Assets	$305,500	Total liabilities & net worth	$305,500

In spite of disagreement on the matter of the dollar valuations (e.g., is our house worth $160,000 exactly or approximately?), the balance sheet is considered to be a statement of the "financial position" of the enterprise (or of the person or any other "entity" depicted) on the date noted in the heading of the statement. It goes without saying that the dollar measures that are assigned to the various assets must all be "as of" the same date; otherwise, we would have a mishmash and the total would have no meaning.

The balance sheet does not show how the subject—let's call it the "entity reached its displayed position. It also fails to show where the entity is heading (although a series of balance sheets on successive dates can be of help in that connection). Let's pursue this line of inquiry a bit more.

DOES THE BALANCE SHEET REALLY SHOW FINANCIAL POSITION?

Your own financial position is made up of the valuable possessions, or resources, owned by you, offset by your debts. As stated earlier, the difference between the dollar measure of your resources and the dollar measure of your debts is what is commonly called your net worth. If we apply the same formula to the company with which you are associated, we might, for example, find that the company's balance sheet shows assets totaling $1,000,000 and offsetting debts of $400,000, so that its net worth is $600,000. Accountants, particularly the teacher crowd, are so impressed by the algebra of this situation that they often refer to the accounting equation as: Assets minus liabilities equals net worth, or $A - L = NW$.

The balance sheet basically consists of a reporting of the dollar amount of assets on the left-hand side and all the existing debts on the right-hand side; the two sides are then made equal by filling in enough on the right-hand side to make them equal. The amount of the filler is the net worth. So if we want to flaunt our mathematical ability a bit, we may point out that, as mentioned above, $A - L = NW$. This can just as well be written as $A = L + NW$, which is a kind of arithmetic model of the standard balance sheet in which the assets, on the left, equal the sum of the liabilities and net worth, on the right.

So far it would appear that financial position means nothing more than a pair of totals (assets and liabilities) offset to show their difference (net worth). As a matter of fact, this arithmetic pattern constitutes only a minor aspect of any analysis of a company's financial position. The asset total has some meaning; the liability total has some meaning; and the net worth has some (very limited) meaning; but these are gross concepts, to say the least. Any analysis of a company's financial position will surely take into account, and with considerably greater interest, the relationships (ratios) that exist between some of the more detailed items within the asset, the liability, and the net worth categories. Financial position, in other words, is not to be construed as a mere difference between the asset and the liability totals. We'll look at that again later.

DOES THE BALANCE SHEET ACTUALLY SHOW WHAT YOU THINK IT MAY?

We have just been commenting, with an apparent degree of confidence, on the service of the balance sheet in revealing a company's financial position. Before we become overly enthusiastic, let's slow down a bit and test our premises.

If the balance sheet does, in truth, show the current value of all the assets owned by a company and if it also shows all the company's debts, it would apparently qualify as an accurate statement of financial position—if the asset amount is correct and the liability amount is correct, then their difference, the net worth, must be correct. But now we come to the real hooker. The asset total (as well as many of the details which go to make it up) is virtually never equal to the current value of all the assets. If that isn't enough to discourage you, let us add that the real worth of a company depends on a great deal more than its list of assets and list of liabilities. You could probably imagine, in this age of leasing almost everything, a company that owns no assets at all, has some real liabilities, and, although its accounting net worth would then be a negative figure, might have a great deal of worth in the eyes of the expert investor. In other words, it takes more than tangible assets to make a company worth something—this essential ingredient is management. It would be perfectly ridiculous to expect, for example, that the stock of a company that has an accounting net worth of $100,000, with 10,000 shares outstanding, would have a market value per share that is exactly twice as much as that of another company with an accounting net worth also of $100,000 but with 20,000 shares of stock outstanding. The only time this relationship would be likely to hold true would be in case the $100,000 was in hard cash and the companies were about to be dissolved.

HOW ARE ASSETS VALUED?

Early in the preceding paragraph it was pointed out that the balance sheet fails to show true financial position, or true net worth, because the asset total is virtually never equal to the current value of all the assets owned. This admission might come as a surprise to almost everyone who has looked at a balance sheet but who has not had any experience or formal training in accounting.

The fact of the matter is that assets can be divided into two very general categories—the first being cash and claims to cash and the second being assets that have been purchased for use in the business (such as inventories, plant, and equipment). Roughly speaking, the first group is reported in the balance sheet at the amount of cash funds they represent (e.g., cash on hand, cash in bank, and amounts due from customers) and the second group is reported at the amounts invested in them (i.e., at their cost). Let's hasten to add that in making up the cost figures one must take into consideration (1) not only the amounts paid for the assets originally but also (2) the amounts (usually estimated) representing the using up of the assets. Thus, we buy a machine for $10,000, and that's its original cost. As the machine is used, it depreciates; on successive balance sheets we show the machine (probably combined with other related assets) at lower and lower amounts to reflect its inevitable depreciation or, as someone has phrased it, "its inevitable march to the junk heap."

It should be perfectly obvious that if some of the assets of the company are listed in the balance sheet as cash or near cash (such as accounts receivable) and the remainder are listed at what the company paid for them (in some cases years ago), the sum of the two groups simply won't equal the "present value" of the total assets. For purposes of discussion, let's refer to the two groups of assets as (1) the monetary assets and (2) the nonmonetary assets.

WHY ARE NONMONETARY ASSETS REPORTED AT COST?

Some accountants, particularly some of the folks in the ivory towers, sincerely believe that all nonmonetary assets should be reported in the balance sheet at their current values. It may be observed, however, that it is easier for the people in this group to tell *why* the assets should be so valued than it is for them to tell *how* current value, or current cost, is to be ascertained. They point out that the asset side of the orthodox balance sheet is a conglomerate mass of dollars representing not only the monetary but also the nonmonetary assets at costs that have been incurred sometimes over a span of 25 or more years, and they feel that these cost amounts may be far removed from current reality (the more modern expression is "irrelevant"). Certainly there's a good deal of truth to this accusation. But we must then examine the alternatives—that is, the utilization of current market value. (Some prefer to use the comparable term "current cost," or merely "current value.")

Surely no problem exists in listing cash at its current value because cash (and we're concerned here only with our domestic currency) is itself the ultimate measure of value. Similarly, marketable securities, such as the stocks and bonds that are listed on the organized stock exchanges or are traded in the over-the-counter market, can readily be listed at current values. Next, accounts and notes receivable can quite readily be listed at a close approximation of their current values—that is, at the amounts that will rather surely be collected from them within a reasonable period of time. However, when we move on to assets such as machinery and equipment—especially if those items were tailor-made for our firm—it becomes quite difficult to determine a reasonable market value. Particularly when the machinery is permanently affixed to the plant and would not conceivably be sold, the relevance of a current market value becomes pretty hard to recognize. Often the only market would be the secondhand, or junk, market. The land on which our buildings stand may have high potential value in the current real estate market. So what? Does the strength of our company lie in the fact that it could sell its site land for more than it cost, or does its strength lie in the day-to-day operations that it carries on? Needless to say, the market values of most buildings, so often designed for the special purposes for which they are being used, would be quite meaningless even if they were ascertainable. If the company is a going concern, it will not sell its building for the profit that is thus available, unless it is contemplating going out of business. Sometimes structures are appraised by a process of finding the present cost of the kinds of materials and labor that were originally expended in their construction, but such a procedure may result in a very poor representation of the current value of the structure.

Admittedly, this is only a sketchy, preliminary look at the subject of asset valuation, but it is intended to warn you, if not to soften the blow, that in most cases in dealing with accounting data we will be relying on historical cost where nonmonetary assets are concerned. The argument for cost can be expressed quite simply: First, there is no satisfactory means of determining current cost or current market value of most nonmonetary assets economically on a continuous basis; second, the essence, if not the quintessence, of profit determination lies in the matching of cost against revenue. Revenue is what we collect from the sale of something; cost is what we paid

for something. "Buy low and sell high." In other words, a cardinal principle of accounting is that profit is not earned by mere changes in the value
of things; it must be realized by actual transactions in which something is
literally sold for an amount greater than its cost.

All this leads us to another conclusion. We had better stop using the term
net worth in our balance sheets. Commonly in the balance sheets one now
finds a term such as *stockholders' equity* or *capital stock and retained earnings* to represent the difference between the total assets and the total liabilities.

BALANCE SHEET ILLUSTRATIONS

Mainly for purposes of rounding out the present chapter, a few balance
sheet illustrations will now be presented. Care is taken to exclude balance
sheet items that might be unfamiliar or might require special explanation at
this point in our study. Here we are concerned mostly with the basic concept of the balance sheet, including content and structure.

Figure 1.2 is a balance sheet that is condensed beyond all reality but
is intended to depict the skeleton structure of the orthodox balance sheet.
As shown, the balance sheet in Figure 1.2 is in so-called account form. That
is, the assets appear on the left-hand side and the liabilities and owners'
equities are shown on the right. By the simple process of showing the liabilities and owners' equities below the assets, the form becomes known as
the report form, as in Figure 1.3. Quite obviously, it makes little difference
whether the balance sheet is presented in account or in report form; the
choice may depend solely on page size and convenience.

Figure 1.4 shows the same data, rearranged a bit more significantly, in
"sequence" form. This form has a relatively small following, but it is used

Figure 1.2   Account Form

ORANGE PRODUCTS CO.
Balance Sheet
as of December 31, 20XX

Assets		Liabilities and Stockholders Equity		
Current	$ 40,000	Liabilities:		
Noncurrent	60,000	Current	$20,000	
		Noncurrent	15,000	$ 35,000
		Stockholders' equity:		
		Capital stock	$50,000	
		Retained earnings	15,000	65,000
Total assets	$100,000	Total liabilities & stockholders equity		$100,000

Figure 1.3   Report Form

ORANGE PRODUCTS CO.
Balance Sheet
as of December 31, 20XX

Assets

Current	$ 40,000
Noncurrent	60,000
Total assets	$100,000

Liabilities and Stockholders Equity

Liabilities:		
Current	$20,000	
Noncurrent	15,000	$ 35,000
Stockholders' equity:		
Capital stock	$50,000	
Retained earnings	15,000	65,000
Total liabilities & stockholders equity		$100,000

Figure 1.4   Sequence Form

ORANGE PRODUCTS CO.
Balance Sheet
as of December 31, 20XX

Current assets	$40,000
Less: Current liabilities	20,000
Working capital	$20,000
Noncurrent assets	60,000
	$80,000
Less: Noncurrent liabilities	15,000
Stockholders' equity (see Schedule A)	$65,000

Schedule A
Stockholders' Equity

Capital stock	$50,000
Retained earnings	15,000
	$65,000

Figure 1.5   Annual or Interim Report

ORANGE PRODUCTS CO.
Balance Sheet
as of December 31, 20XX

Assets

Current:			
Cash		$ 5,000	
Marketable securities (at cost; market value is $12,500)		8,000	
Receivables (after subtracting $1,000 for estimated amount uncollectible)		10,000	
Inventories (at the lower of cost or market)		15,000	
Prepaid expenses		2,000	$ 40,000
Property, Plant, and Equipment:			
Land		$10,000	
Building	$30,000		
Machinery and equipment	40,000		
	$70,000		
Less: Accumulated depreciation	25,000	45,000	55,000
Intangibles:			
Patents (at cost less $1,632 of amortization)			5,000
Total assets			$100,000

Liabilities and Stockholders' Equity

Current liabilities:			
Accounts payable		$12,000	
Taxes payable		4,000	
Dividends payable		2,500	
Miscellaneous		1,500	$ 20,000
Long term liabilities:			
Bonds payable, x%, due in 20XX			15,000
Total liabilities			$ 35,000
Stockholders' equity:			
Capital stock, par $10		$50,000	
Retained earnings		15,000	65,000
Total liabilities & stockholders' equity			$100,000

by some of the big companies. Some people feel that it is less clear than the others.

Figure 1.5 shows, in report form, a balance sheet with a few of the more common headings and explanatory notes included. This example might easily represent the balance sheet of a moderately large corporation as it would actually be presented in an annual report, or an interim report, to the company's stockholders.

BALANCE SHEET CATEGORIES

Most people with a nodding acquaintance with accounting would define "current assets" as assets that "can be converted into cash within a year." Such a definition is both out of date and wrong. In the early days, the balance sheet was prepared mainly for use in dealing with creditors— in seeking bank loans or credit from suppliers—who were mainly interested in the "liquidity" of the borrower. Accordingly, current assets have traditionally been displayed ahead of the other assets in the balance sheet; from the creditor's standpoint, assets had to be liquid in order to be current. Now, however, we view the balance sheet as a conveyor of financial information to all parties with a legitimate interest in the company—not only the creditors, but especially the owners and, at the same time, potential investors, the tax collectors, and the labor force. So, current assets now include the five classes of assets shown in Figure 1.5 on the assumption that the balance sheet should show the financial structure of the enterprise—that is, its circulating assets (current) and its relatively permanent plant assets. Thus, we toss out both the one-year rule as well as the "can-be-converted-into-cash" rule. In fact, the latter rule is nonsense from any point of view. Land, for example, is likely to be salable and in most cases could easily be "converted into cash within a year," but it is usually considered to be a leading example of the noncurrent group.

The noncurrent assets are more commonly called property, plant, and equipment and are placed under that heading.

Current liabilities can safely be defined as those that are to be paid within a year from the date of the balance sheet, although some exceptions to this rule may occasionally arise. Long-term liabilities are those debts not due for more than one year from the balance sheet date. Owner's equity for a corporation is known as stockholder's equity. Stockholder's equity is divided between two major components: capital stock, which accounts for the investments made in the corporation by its shareholders, and retained earnings, which is the accumulation of the corporation's net income over its life less dividends distributed to its shareholders (see Chapter 9 for a further discussion).

BALANCE SHEET RELATIONSHIPS

Almost inevitably, routine note of certain fundamental relationships is made by a person who scans a balance sheet. First, a rough calculation of the current ratio is likely to be made. The current ratio is the arithmetic ratio of the total of current assets to the total current liabilities. (In our example the ratio stands at 40 to 20, or 2 to 1.) A rough determination of the amount of working capital, which is the difference between the total current assets and the total current liabilities, might also be made. (In our example the working capital is $40,000 to $20,000.) These two calculations are made in order to determine the company's ability to pay its short-term debts as they become due.

Financial analysts have invented dozens of "pet" ratios in addition to the three just described. Because this is a book on accounting and not a book on corporation finance or financial analysis, we won't worry about what the various ratios should be in any given case, but you should be warned not to settle for any predigested rules or standards. The analysis of any balance sheet rests first and most importantly on a knowledge of what underlies the reported figures, a knowledge of the industry that you are dealing with, a knowledge of what kind of management rules the firm (nothing is more important than that), and a lot of other things. At best, the ratios constitute supplementary or confirmatory data, and they should never be taken as complete answers in themselves.

BALANCE SHEET TERMINOLOGY

In concluding this chapter, let's point out that different words are used by different accountants in referring to the same things. Incidentally, the very title, Balance Sheet, is often replaced by a title such as Statement of Financial Condition, Statement of Financial Position, or, simply, Position Statement. In the examples in this chapter, only the most common types of position statement items have been mentioned. This is lesson 1; we'll delve into matters such as reserves, LIFO, deferred federal income taxes, consolidated statements, and many other more complex and exciting subjects as we progress through our advanced lessons.

At this point it would be desirable for you to work the exercise that follows. It includes nothing new, and you won't know whether you're qualified for reading Chapter 2 until you have worked it. You'll find model answers in Appendix A, but, of course, you won't peek until you have finished working the problem.

TEST PROBLEM

Denton Bread Co. was organized on January 1, 20XX, when 10,000 shares of $10 par common stock were issued for cash at par. During the remainder of the year, the company succeeded in earning $12,000, and it paid dividends of $8,000. Land was purchased for $5,000 cash; a building was purchased for $50,000 cash; and machinery and equipment were purchased for $60,000 cash. To finance the fixed-asset purchases, a 20-year mortgage note for $30,000 was negotiated with the local bank. At the end of the year, assets other than those identified thus far consisted of cash $9,200, accounts receivable with a face value of $12,000, raw materials inventory that cost $5,000, miscellaneous supplies that cost $1,000, and prepaid expenses of $500. Liabilities, in addition to the mortgage, consisted of wages payable $1,600, taxes payable $3,000, and mortgage interest payable $200. Depreciation of the property, plant, and equipment (other than land) was recognized in the amount of $3,400, and it was estimated that about $500 of the receivables might prove to be uncollectible.

REQUIRED

In the solution space provided, prepare a balance sheet, as of December 31, 20XX.

TEST PROBLEM SOLUTION SPACE

DENTON BREAD CO.
Balance Sheet
as of December 31, 20XX

Assets

Liabilities and Stockholder's Equity

2

THE INCOME STATEMENT

WHAT IS THE INCOME STATEMENT'S PURPOSE?

If you were to start a business concern by investing $100,000 in cash, it is conceivable, but unlikely, that you would be willing to operate it, or assign the job to a manager, and wait until the concern was finally dissolved before any computation of your earnings was made. Actually, such a delay in reckoning the earnings would have one virtue—the difference between the amounts of cash invested during the lifetime of the enterprise and the amount *finally realized* upon dissolution comes close to being the true profit (or loss) of the venture (assuming that you make proper allowance for any dividends or other withdrawals of funds during the lifetime of the venture). Rather than that, of course, owners and other interested parties demand *periodic* information on the progress of the enterprise; in short, they require a report of net income at least annually and in a great many cases quarterly or more often. The space of time covered by such a report is known as an *accounting period.*

It would be difficult to locate any truly authoritative statement of the purpose of the income statement, and it is best perhaps not to focus on any single purpose. If we want to be theoretical, we might state that the leading purpose is to show how much the *net assets of the enterprise have increased (or decreased)* during the accounting period, always with due allowance for any dividends paid or any additional investments or withdrawals by the stockholders.

Net assets and *net worth* are synonymous terms—each refers to the arithmetic difference between total assets and total liabilities. (Remember the equation, $A - L = NW$.) Possibly the term *net assets* is to be preferred because it avoids the word *worth,* but it is less likely to be comprehended by nonaccountants.

Unfortunately, as we noted earlier, there is a wide range of opinions on the manner in which the A of the basic equation should be measured. Should the net assets reflect current *market* values, current *replacement costs*, historical costs, or historical costs translated into dollars of current purchasing power?

A more fruitful approach, it would seem, is to attribute more than a single purpose to the income statement and set out to prepare income statements that will, in fact, serve multiple purposes. This is achieved, basically, by avoiding overcondensation—*by disclosing the component elements* that go to make up the figure at the bottom of the statement rather than by limiting the report to a half-dozen or fewer figures.

The income statement is often referred to as the *operating statement*, and it should, indeed, portray the current operations of the enterprise to the degree that mere dollar figures can. The reader should be able to make some assessment of the size, growth, and perhaps the growth potential of the enterprise by analyzing the sales data. The relationship between the amount of a given expense, for example, and sales for the period may give some insight into the operating efficiency of the company. The relationship between net income and any "fixed charges" for bond interest or leasehold rents may be significant in evaluating the amount of risk inherent in making a stock investment, in lending funds to the enterprise, etc.

As in the case of the balance sheet, the financial analysts have developed a large number of "favorite" ratios relating particular income statement items to others and relating certain income statement items with certain balance sheet items. For our purposes, then, let's not think of the income statement as a mere (and possibly frail) measure of financial growth through net income for the period.

WHAT IS NET INCOME?

As you might guess, the term *net income* means different things to different accountants, so one can safely define it in a number of ways. One way relates to a possible purpose of the income statement—to show, at some point, the *earnings that management has produced during the period for all capital suppliers*. To illustrate, assume that, with assets of $100,000, management produces $10,000 of net income during a year; this is an important bit of financial information in itself. Then a separate question is, who is entitled to this $10,000 of net income? If some of the assets were acquired through the issuance of $40,000 in bonds, then the interest on the bonds, assume $3,200 of the $10,000 net income, goes to the bondholders, which leaves a balance of $6,800 properly termed Earnings of Stockholders. This amount, in turn, might be subject to cumulative dividend claims of "preferred" stockholders (let's assume an amount of $2,500), leaving a balance to be labeled Earnings of Common Stockholders ($4,300).

Net income cannot really be described clearly without employing other accounting words that we are about to examine. Net income is made up of revenues, as the positive factor, from which are subtracted the negative factors, which are the expenses, most losses, and income taxes. Take particular note of the fact that the word *cash* has not been used at any time in this discussion; the reason is that cash has nothing, or at least very little, to do with the *determination* of net income.

A more popular definition, a variant of the one just presented, holds that net income consists of the earnings *after* interest on bonds, etc., has been subtracted. Thus, in the example the net income would be $6,800 rather than $10,000.

WHAT IS REVENUE?

First, let's shower you with words: sales revenue, interest revenue, rent revenue, dividend revenue, royalties revenue, and so on. The *total* revenues of a business are the sum of all the revenues from all sources during a given period. An enterprise can have billions of dollars of revenues in a given year and yet report a net loss for that year—because the dollars of expenses, losses, and income taxes must be deducted from the dollars of revenue before the amount of net income (or net loss) is determined. Thus, the sales revenue is the *total* amount collectible from customers for the delivery (sale) of goods and services during the period. This is *not* income in any proper sense of the word—it is revenue. For example, if we sell for $100 an object that cost us $70, our revenue from the sale is $100; whether or not we earn any *income* on the sale then depends on the total costs (including the $70) of the sale. Incidentally, many (perhaps most) accountants, in this simple example, would subtract the $70 from the $100 and call the remaining $30 "gross profit," which is a real corruption of the English language. There simply cannot be any profit until *all* related costs have been deducted from revenue, and the term "gross profit" should be jettisoned.

Revenue, then, is the total amount obtained by us from the sale of merchandise or other commodities or from the rendering of services to our customers. By itself, revenue gives no indication of the ultimate *net income*.

Just as revenue must be contrasted with net income, so must it be vigorously contrasted with the *inflow of cash*. Revenue for the period is the amount of revenue "earned" during that period, whether you get paid for it in cash during the same period, during the preceding period, or in the following period. True, if our apparent revenue amounts initially to $100,000 and it later becomes clear that one or more of our customers will fail to pay us a total of $1,000 owed us, our revenue can properly be described in two fashions: (1) Our *gross* revenue is $100,000 and (2) our *net* revenue is $99,000. In other words, gross sales revenue for a given period is a summation of all sales for the period, whether for cash or on charge account, and *net* sales revenue is the gross minus any portion deemed to be uncollectible. (Gross sales minus "bad debts" equals net sales.)

Our discussion of revenue leads conveniently to the noting of a word commonly applied to accounting. When a sale is made, cash need not be collected on the spot in order to recognize (record) the revenue. We *accrue* revenue *when the sale is made or when the service is rendered,* and this is the revenue that is recognized (reported) in the income statement. The time of collection of cash proceeds from the sale, while by no means unimportant, has no direct bearing on the amount or the timing of the revenue. This is one facet of the *accrual concept;* because the concept is widely applied in business accounting, it is not unusual to hear an accountant speak of *accrual accounting.*

THE ACCRUAL CONCEPT

Accounting can be so performed that income is determined on either a *cash basis* or an *accrual basis.* Under the cash scheme, no income (revenue) is recognized in the accounts until it is received in the form of cash. (Note that a check is universally viewed as cash, unless doubt exists as to its worth.) And no expense is recognized in the accounts until cash payment has actually been made. The results of cash basis accounting range all the way from fairly logical to horrible.

Under accrual accounting, revenue is recognized in the period in which it is actually *earned,* that is, when the services are performed, the goods are delivered, etc. Whether the corresponding cash is collected before, within, or after the earning period has no bearing on the timing of the revenue recognition.

The aim of accrual accounting is twofold: (1) to record and report in any given period the revenues (e.g., from sales, rentals, interest, and royalties) *earned* during the period and (2) to report the expenses (of whatever kind) that properly are *to be matched* against the reported revenues. Thus, the overall effort is to reflect the earnings performance of the entity for the period. The amount of earnings for a period may have little or no relationship to the amount of net inflow or outflow of cash for that period. Generally accepted accounting principles mandate the use of accrual accounting for corporations that must report their financial statements to the public.

WHAT IS AN EXPENSE?

First, consider some clear-cut examples of true expenses. Perhaps the most obvious example is the amount paid for goods that are sold at retail. The long title for this particular expense is "merchandise cost of sales." Thus, buy something for $12, sell it for $20, and you have two amounts to be accounted for: first, sales revenue of $20; second, an expense of $12, which will be designated as Cost of Goods Sold. (Note that the goods, as long as they remain unsold on your shelves, are assets except to the extent that they suffer deterioration or obsolescence.) Modify the example a bit by assuming that the sale was made as the result of placing an ad in the newspaper for $5. We now have, as before, Sales Revenue of $20, Cost of Goods Sold of $12, and Advertising Expense, a new expense, $5.

Note the distinguishing characteristics of the so-called expenses in our example. In both cases we made a sacrifice of some value ($12 and $5); also, the sacrifices were made to produce revenue ($20). Furthermore, the two expenses are recognized in the period in which the corresponding revenues were produced.

Reflect on this situation for a moment. Accountants are called upon to produce income statements that are intended to show the amount of income earned in the period covered by the particular income statement. In short, net income is the amount of gain produced by the revenues of the period minus the expenses of the period. Expenses of a given period are a kind of cost— amounts given up to produce the revenues (and resultant net income) of the period. Thus, the amount expended to buy, or construct, a manufacturing plant and manufacturing equipment is *not an expense*. But as time passes and these assets are used for the production of goods that are sold for revenues, the plant and equipment depreciate. To the extent that such depreciation is ascribable to the manufacture of goods that are sold, it is an expense.

Now let's take a quick test. If we construct a building for our own use in manufacturing, spending $1,000,000, is this an expense? Not immediately. The million dollars is properly referred to as the "cost" of construction, or cost of buying a fixed asset. If the building has an estimated useful life of, say, 50 years, it may be reasonable to transfer one-fiftieth of the $1,000,000 each year to an expense classification (as depreciation). If we have an inventory of goods that we have manufactured at total cost of $1,000,000 and the goods are destroyed by fire, with no insurance, does this represent expense? No. Although we have had a "cost" in the amount of $1,000,000, it is not a revenue-producing cost, so it is not an expense—it is a *loss*. Similarly, other cases of outlays, sacrifices, etc., can be expenses if they are incurred to produce the revenues of the period, or they can be losses, or manufacturing costs, purchasing costs, and payments of accounts payable, depending on the circumstances in each case.

And so, given the amount of sales for a specific period, our task as accountants is to identify and report the kinds and amounts of expenses that were incurred to produce those revenues.

Expenses, then, in contrast with losses, are good things—they are beneficial in the sense that they create revenues. Needless to say, one does not incur expenses recklessly. They must be budgeted and carefully administered to the end that we maximize the difference between *total* revenues and *total* expenses—net income.

SOME OTHER OFFSETS TO REVENUE

Revenues are good; losses are bad; expenses are in between. You always strive to reduce expenses, but you can't prosper unless you incur them, sometimes on a grandiose scale. Another kind of business negative is the *revenue contra*, by which we mean anything that happens that *cancels* out revenue that we have recorded earlier. For a simple example, let's sell merchandise for $100 and, at the time of sale, record it as sales revenue (even though the customer charged it). Within the next week, however, any of the following three events occurs:

1. The customer brings the goods back and we agree to cancel the charge against him. (This is a sales return.)
2. The customer pays his bill in cash within 10 days and we allow him a discount of $2, so our net revenue becomes $98 rather than $100. (The $2 is known as a sales discount.)
3. The customer finds the product isn't quite what he wanted and proposes to return it, but we say, "Keep it and we'll deduct $10 from your bill." (The $10 is known as a sales allowance.)

All three of these cases constitute revenue offsets (contras). They are not expenses or losses but revenue corrections—we had originally recorded $100 of revenue in each case but later events required corrective reductions. On an income statement they are properly shown as subtractions from gross sales in order to depict net sales. Contras of these kinds arise because, at the time of a given sale transaction, we can only assume that the customer will pay in due course (even though we know from experience that a certain percentage of our clientele will, for one of the three reasons, fail to pay the amount initially billed).

WHAT ARE INCOME TAXES?

If there's anything that everyone of us has experienced, it's income taxes, and we'll skim over the subject here as lightly as possible (with a full chapter on the subject to come later). The question here is, are income taxes an expense, a loss, or a revenue contra, or do they have their own unique status? Most accountants would probably classify income taxes as expenses. (But how, by any stretch of the imagination, do they produce revenues?) Some accountants would classify income taxes as pure loss—but that would deny that government makes any contribution whatsoever to our well-being. Other accountants assert that the government is a sort of partner in every profit-making enterprise and that the income tax claimed by government is, thus, merely its share or division of the earnings. In some cases income taxes take on the appearance of revenue contra, as when, for example, we make sales of war material to the government and then the government claims a refund in the form of income taxes on the profit from the sales. Given all those views, it becomes quite a problem to choose any single one, so we are going to propose simply that income taxes be shown as a separately reported subtraction from the total revenues of the period. You will note that treatment in the illustrative income statement soon to follow.

INTEREST AND DIVIDENDS

Most accountants refer to interest as an expense, but interest is really a cost of borrowing money and surely in itself does not stimulate revenues as an expense should. In fact, the concept of interest cost is at least related to the concept of dividends. At one extreme, interest on first mortgage bonds accrues as a contractual liability, with dire consequences in case of default; at the opposite extreme, cash dividends on common stock may be skipped year after year with virtually not a whisper from the stockholders. However, between those extremes is a whole range of securities, all more or less hybrid, that require interest or dividend payments more or less regularly and that constitute a virtual spectrum of financial investment instruments. No one can successfully establish a clear boundary between true debt instruments and true ownership instruments, although we tend to regard the two, respectively, as bonds and stocks. Our conclusion is that all interest and all dividends should be treated as divisions of net income of the company, that the net income is an amount determined by subtracting expenses, losses, and taxes from the net revenues, and that interest and dividends are then properly displayed as sharers in that net income in order of their contractual rights. It will be noted in the illustrative income statement to follow that both interest expense and dividends on preferred stock are subtracted from the revenue total before income is determined. Although, as argued above, income may be said to result before the subtraction of one or both of the above items, the statement as presented is designed to emphasize the earnings of the common stockholder and is in a form that nowadays has considerable authoritative support.

INCOME STATEMENT ILLUSTRATED

There are very few rules to limit experimentation with income statement form, but only two basic forms are widely used for external reporting purposes. The first, and simplest, is usually called the *single-step form*. Highly

Figure 2.1   Single-step Form

ALBANY COMPANY
Comparative Income Statements,
Years Ended December 31

	20X4	20X5
Revenues:		
Sales (less returns & allowances)	$xx	$xx
Interest income	xx	xx
Total revenue	$xx	$xx
Costs & expenses:		
Cost of goods sold	$xx	$xx
Selling expenses	xx	xx
General & administrative expenses	xx	xx
Interest expense	xx	xx
Income before income taxes & extraordinary items	$xx	$xx
Income taxes	xx	xx
Income before extraordinary items	$xx	$xx
Extraordinary items (if any)	xx	xx
Net income	$xx	$xx
Earnings per common share:		
Income before extraordinary items	$xx	$xx
Extraordinary items (gain or loss)	xx	xx
Net income	$xx	$xx

condensed, the structure is more or less as shown in Figure 2.1. Alternatively, various subtotals may be shown with labels that are intended to identify them—a multiple-step statement, as shown in Figure 2.2.

COMMENTS ON ILLUSTRATIVE INCOME STATEMENT

1. The statement as shown is in comparative form; that is, two years (or periods) are presented side by side for purposes of comparison and analysis of change. This is quite customary in present-day reporting.

Figure 2.2   Multi-step Form

ALBANY COMPANY
Comparative Income Statements,
Year Ended December 31

	20X4	20X5
Revenues:		
Sales (less returns & allowances)	$xx	$xx
Less: cost of goods sold	xx	xx
Gross margin	$xx	$xx
Operating expenses:		
Selling expenses	xx	xx
General & administrative expenses	xx	xx
Total operating expenses	xx	xx
Income from operations	$xx	$xx
Interest income	xx	xx
Income before income taxes & extraordinary items	xx	xx
Income taxes	xx	xx
Income before extraordinary items	xx	xx
Extraordinary items (if any)	xx	xx
Net income	xx	xx
Earnings per common share:		
Income before extraordinary items	$xx	$xx
Extraordinary items (gain or loss)	xx	xx
Net income	$xx	$xx

2. Commonly the revenues are presented on two lines, viz., "net sales" and "other income."
3. The expenses are typically displayed on two or more lines, with "cost of goods sold" shown first and "selling and administrative expenses" next (subject to possible detailing either in the body of the statement or in a separate supporting schedule).
4. The expression "single-step form" refers to the fact that all the revenue deductions are added together and then deducted as a group from the revenues, so that an income balance is reached by a single subtraction. This is in contrast with "multiple-step" statements, in

which the various expenses are subtracted successively from the revenues, with a resulting sequence of intervening subbalances that may or may not have any worthwhile significance.

5. "Extraordinary items" are gains or losses that occur within a given period that are so unusual, and so unrelated to the regular operations of the enterprise, that their inclusion with the revenues or revenue deductions might seriously becloud the analyst's interpretation of the degree of success with which the enterprise was administered during the period under review. Accordingly, extraordinary items are entered as a separate element in the statement. Examples of items that have been cited as extraordinary are the sale or abandonment of a significant segment of the business, a major devaluation of a foreign currency, and the lump-sum write-off of goodwill as a result of unusual developments within the period. It follows that the more commonplace losses and gains (such as inventory write-downs and fluctuations in foreign currencies) are listed in the upper portion of the income statement, so that they do affect the amount labeled "income before extraordinary items."

6. It is fairly common practice to terminate the income statement at the point labeled "net income" and then present, as a separate schedule, a Statement of Retained Earnings. Such a presentation has the virtue of emphasizing the net income figures for the year in contrast with the retained earnings, which consist of the accumulated earnings of past years. A Statement of Retained Earnings is shown in Figure 2.3.

7. It now is generally accepted procedure to calculate and report at the foot of the income statement the earnings per share of common stock for the period. This is calculated by dividing net income by the weighted average of common shares outstanding during the period. Nowadays, with the invention of a number of hybrid types of stocks and bonds, as well as stock options and warrants, the determination

Figure 2.3   Statement of Retained Earnings

ALBANY COMPANY
Statement of Retained Earnings
for the Year Ended December 31, 20XX

Retained earnings 1/1/20XX	$xxx
Add: net income f/y/e 12/31/20XX	xxx
Subtotal	xxx
Less: dividends declared during 12/31/20XX	xxx
Retained earnings 12/31/20XX	$xxx

of earnings per share can become a complex problem in itself. In the illustration it is merely assumed that no complexities exist.

8. Occasionally within a given year there becomes apparent a gain or loss that would have been "picked up" (accountants' slang for "recognized" or "reported") in a prior year had sufficient information to determine its nature and amount then been available. When such an item does turn up and its amount is clearly significant, it should be reported as an adjustment of retained earnings rather than as an element in the determination of net income for the current period. Such items are rare, and the result is that retained earnings is, for all practical purposes, kept "clean"—that is, rarely is its beginning-of-the-year balance modified to reflect currently discovered corrections of prior-year earnings determinations.

TEST PROBLEM

REVENUE DATA

During the year 20XX, Tarrant Co. sold its products for a total of $5,627,483. Of that amount, $525,480 had not been collected in cash by the end of the year. During the year, the company collected $638,240 from sales made in earlier years. In addition to product sales, Tarrant earned $12,220 from dividends on stocks owned and $1,460 interest on bank deposits.

EXPENSE DATA

Assume that the company had no finished goods and no unfinished goods on hand at the beginning of the year. During the year, its manufacturing costs consisted of raw materials consumed, totaling $2,420,000; factory labor, $1,115,000; and other factory costs (factory overhead) of $1,247,000. At the end of the year, unfinished goods on hand (i.e., the work in process inventory) were valued at $384,000 and finished goods on hand cost $418,000. Selling expenses totaled $592,000, and general administrative expenses were $614,250 for the year. There were no interest expenses, and the company has no preferred stock outstanding. Income taxes were $154,000. During the year, the company suffered an uninsured flood loss of $125,000. Retained earnings at the beginning of the year, according to the accounting records, stood at $1,500,000. Cash dividends paid were $1 per share on 100,000 shares. The common stock outstanding during the year, averaged to reflect fluctuations in number and time outstanding, was 102,000 shares.

REQUIRED

Prepare (1) an income statement in a single-step format and (2) a statement of retained earnings based on the data given above; assume that the company employs accrual accounting. Enter the data below.

TEST PROBLEM SOLUTION SPACE

3

THE ACCOUNTING STRUCTURE

MANAGEMENT DECISIONS

As "boss," whether at the top, middle, or otherwise, you qualify for your title only because of the faith that one or more persons (including yourself) must have in your ability to make rational decisions. Bossing is essentially a combination of leadership and decision making or, if you prefer, leadership and the acceptance of responsibility. Some bosses are so ultracautious that they literally trust no one to make subdecisions or to assist them by supplying them with the right information for the exercise of their decision-making responsibilities. Those bosses finally get bogged down at their desks. Other bosses blithely delegate most of their decision making to their subordinates and concentrate on golf, racquetball, or martini formulas. The better bosses, and let's hope they constitute the majority, fit in between those two extremes.

All decisions, by definition, relate to the future—they invariably involve *judgments* as to the results of choice among alternative courses of action. When a decision situation arises, the good boss knows what kind of information is needed as a guide in applying *judgment* to the problem. Good bosses develop the supportive personnel necessary to be able to call for, and get, the relevant information in a hurry. They do not *develop* the information (with some exceptions); they *delegate* the job. But they should know what the information providers are doing with their time; they must understand what the information means *so that they can call for it as needed* rather than depend passively on their helpers to decide what they need. They will never allow their accountants to set up a private, impenetrable empire.

Accounting data are essential to a wide range of decisions, but the data that are stored by accountants are almost entirely the details of transactions, or events, that have occurred in the past. Well-trained accountants are capable of doing much more than perform the mere function of collecting and storing information for your use. They are also capable of "interpreting" the information for you, and, with the historical records plus current and probable future data, they should be of great help to you in your *planning activities*. Needless to say, planning covers a major portion of all executive activity, and we can merely mention it here.

However, the whole point of this section is to urge you, as an executive, to know what your accountants are doing so that you can call on them for information not only on a routine basis but, whenever necessary, on an emergency basis, and so that you can sensibly evaluate the information that they supply in response to your calls. To do so requires that you be able to speak the accountant's language. Perhaps that's the whole purpose of this book. Each chapter may involve getting you "over a hump," and we hope that you'll take the humps in stride. A major hump comes in the remainder of this chapter as we get down to the absolute elements of accounting, including the debit-and-credit lingo. We're going to review the elements of the typical accounting system—the forms, the journals, the ledgers, etc., and we probably will bore you.

BUSINESS FORMS

Basic to all accounting is something we all view as unpalatable—the red tape. This is the deadly job of making notations on *business forms*. If you have good internal accounting help, they have designed the forms that are needed. Business forms are the seeds that produce the valuable crops—the decision-supporting reports. Probably it's a good thing for executives to keep the form producers in the company constantly on the defensive. You must respect the concept of business forms, but don't allow the forms to spring up and flourish like weeds around you. If, as an executive, you find that basic business documents are routinely flowing across your desk, the chances are you're being put upon by somebody. Business forms are designed for *routine processing*. This means they should flow automatically to bookkeepers, computer operators, or other individuals who may (1) merely file (store) them, (2) process them and prepare a report to you of any "exceptional" items that call for action on your part, (3) summarize them in the form of a routine report (headlines only) for you as an executive, or (4) make accounting entries from them.

Business forms, in the accounting sense, are "source" documents; they are the raw materials of the formal accounting records. All the documents that record transactions or events that will affect your financial statements and supporting schedules flow to the accounting department. (Copies, of course, may go to other departments as needed.) And, most important, when computers are used for processing the accounting data, the forms must be designed to act as effective "input" media, or they may be omitted when the data are entered directly into the data processing equipment.

To record, in the formal accounting sense, means to *make an accounting entry* in a *journal* or in a *ledger.*

THE ACCOUNTING JOURNAL

Widespread computerization has, of course, greatly modified the physical trappings of accounting systems to the point where the traditional *journal*, as well as the various ledger forms, has virtually disappeared from the scene. However, the underlying need for some sort of journal/ledger structure has not been lessened, and the analysis of business transactions in the form of old-fashioned journal entries will be an important tool in the use of this book. In a later chapter we discuss computer software and how it can be used in businesses in a variety of ways.

When a transaction occurs, it must somehow be "recorded," usually as a whole, as an entry in some sort of business diary so that, at any future date, interested parties may refer back to the details of the transaction, in accounting form, when necessary. A given journal entry may be very simple, and the same entry, with varying dollar amounts, may be recorded many times daily; another journal entry may be very complex, as when a transaction involves changes in several financial aspects of the business. Actually, a complete journal entry always consists of two or more entries that are also to be recorded in the accounting ledger.

THE ACCOUNTING LEDGER

The journal, often referred to as a *book of original entry*, serves as a diary in which each transaction, or batch of similar transactions, is recorded intact. The next step is to take precisely the same transactions and record them over again in the ledgers, or *books of final entry*. The difference is that each piece of the entry recorded first in the journal is copied ("posted") in its own ledger account. So if a journal entry is composed of, say, five pieces, each of those five pieces will be posted to a separate ledger account. The journal is organized as a chronological record of transactions, as units, in the order of their occurrence; the ledger is organized into as many different pages (or "accounts") as are needed to accumulate the pieces posted (copied) from the journal but classified according to significant financial elements.

To illustrate. We borrow $1,000 from the bank. This is a transaction. It is recorded ("journalized") in the journal in technical form to show that two financial changes were caused by the bank loan: (1) The bank added $1,000 to our checking account, which is to say that our Cash in Bank increased by

$1,000, and (2) counterbalancing the $1,000 addition to our bank account is an addition of $1,000 to our liabilities, under the technical heading of Bank Loans Payable. In the journal the two effects are recorded as a matched pair—a whole transaction journalized as a unit. This is referred to as "dual entry bookkeeping," that is, each transaction must involve at least two different accounts. Next, the $1,000 increase of Cash in Bank is copied from the journal entry to a *ledger page* headed Cash in Bank and the $1,000 increase of Bank Loans Payable is copied (posted) to a ledger page (we set up a new sheet if we don't already have one) labeled Bank Loans Payable.

The *ledger*, then, consists of as many different sheets (accounts) as we feel we need to keep track of the many financial elements of the business. As a starter, let's assume that in our ledger we would, at least, have a separate account for each of the items to be listed in our balance sheet and our income statement. In fact, the ledger sheets (the ledger accounts) will be in loose-leaf form and will be filed in the same order as they appear in the financial statements. You see, the amounts shown in the financial statements are found by merely copying the balances of the ledger accounts into the arrangements chosen for the financial statements.

THE LEDGER ACCOUNT

It is quite common for companies to have their ledger pages printed according to their own prescription, but the fundamental structure remains the same. The classical account has two sides—left and right—separated by a vertical line, and the account is topped by a horizontal line on which the account's name (and an assigned account number) is written. We cannot afford to be concerned about bookkeeping details, so we'll ignore the various forms in which the account may be designed and stick to the fundamental shape, which is that of a T. Just visualize a page divided down the middle, representing the stem of the T, with a horizontal line about an inch from the top of the page, representing the crossbar of the T, on which the title (e.g., Cash in Bank) and the reference number (e.g., 101) are written (see Figure 3.1).

Figure 3.1   Skeleton Ledger Account

Cash in Bank		101	
Jan. 1, Bal.	1,242.50	Jan. 31	7,214.20
Jan. 31	6,857.28	Feb. 28	4,114.18
Feb. 28	7,142.86	Mar. 31	7,212.15
Mar. 31	4,125.19	Apr. 30	3,756.92
Apr. 30	5,147.31		
Bal. 2,217.49	24,515.14		22,297.45

Now, how do we use this gadget? You will need to memorize the formula, and then we'll use it throughout the book; when you get through, it should have become second nature to you.

Here's the plan. One side of each account will be used to record *increases* in the content of that account and the opposite side will be used for *decreases*. By using the fundamental accounting equation of Assets = Liabilities + Equity, it follows that increases to assets are to be recorded on the books and records as a left-side entry since assets are listed on the left side of the fundamental accounting equation. Similarly, decreases to asset accounts are recorded by use of right-side entries. Assets are also generally listed on the left side of the balance sheet. In accounting jargon, all left-hand entries are referred to as "debits," and all right-hand entries are referred to as "credits."

ASSET AND EXPENSE ACCOUNTS

In Figure 3.1 you see a T account for Cash in Bank to which a number of postings have been made. (We could call it a "skeleton ledger account" because it's stripped down to bare bones.) You should be able to read this account as follows: The company had a bank balance of $1,242.50 at the beginning of the year, January 1. Its deposits, posted as summary totals for each month (asset additions are shown on the left-hand side of an asset account), were $6,857.28 for January, $7,142.86 for February, $4,125.19 for March, and $5,147.31 for April. The accountant has informally "footed" this column in small pencil figures showing a total of $24,515.14 on the left-hand side. The withdrawals from the bank account, also shown in the form of monthly totals, are recorded on the right-hand side of the account. Again informally totaled, the withdrawals footing is $22,297.45 for the period, leaving a left-hand balance of $24,515.14 − $22,297.45, or $2,217.69. This should be the amount of cash in bank as of April 30, and it is the amount that would appear in the company's balance sheet dated April 30 were one to be prepared "as of" that date.

The other type of accounts that are increased by debits are expenses and dividends. Referring back to the fundamental accounting equation, and the balance sheet, it must be remembered that these two types of accounts have a negative impact on Equity, which is found on the right side of the equation. This is why these accounts are increased by use of a debit, or left-hand entry. In Figure 3.2 you see a T account for Miscellaneous Office Expenses. Like asset accounts, the T accounts for all expenses are "left-handed." There's one big difference, however. At the end of an accounting period the closing balance then existing in each asset account (after any corrections, updatings, or adjustments that may be required) is "carried forward" as the beginning balance of the next period. Note again the

Figure 3.2   Expense Account

Miscellaneous Office Expenses			
Jan. 12, 20X1	175.20	Dec. 31 (to close)	720.63
Mar. 26	214.18		
Sept. 19	129.20		
Dec. 7	202.05		

January 1 balance shown in Figure 3.1. This is the "opening" balance for the current year, which, of course, began as the final stroke of midnight closed out the preceding year; thus, the closing balance of one year (or other accounting period) becomes the opening balance of the adjoining year *when the cumulative amounts are actually carried forward from one period to the next.* But the expenses of one period pertain to that period only (if we've done a good job of accounting for our expenses).

Thus, we speak of the advertising expense, the depreciation expense, etc., of last year as compared with the advertising expense, etc., of this year. What this signifies is that each expense account *starts out each year with a zero balance.* The expense for one year is the expense for that year—it cannot at the same time be the expense for some other year. To repeat, all expense accounts have beginning-of-year (opening) balances of zero. During the year we make left-hand entries in them to keep track of each kind of expense as it builds up. Then at the end of the year we again empty the account (by simply making a right-hand entry in it sufficient to reduce its balance to zero) and we're ready to repeat the expense-recording process for the next period. These emptying-out entries are known as closing entries (more about the mechanics of closing entries follows later in this chapter). Now note in Figure 3.2 that a number of entries have been made to record Miscellaneous Office Expenses as they were incurred throughout the year, but there was no opening balance. Note also that we've made a closing (right-hand) entry equal to the sum of the left-hand entries and thus ended up with a zero balance—the account is swept clean in readiness for next year's "charges." The number of left-hand entries in Figure 3.2 in our case has no particular significance; only a few are needed to exemplify the accounting treatment of expenses.

To review, then, expenses and dividends (like assets) are recorded by entries on the left-hand side of each account involved; at the end of each accounting period (usually a year), a right-hand (closing) entry is made to reduce the account's balance to zero in readiness for the next period's entries to be made as a continuation of the same account. Note how the two sides of the expense account are footed and ruled to provide a clean start for the next year (see Figure 3.2).

EQUITY AND REVENUE ACCOUNTS

In order to use the terms *debit* and *credit* as accountants do, we must apply the rules just illustrated for assets, expenses, and dividends to the opposite side of the coin—that is, to the equity accounts and the revenue accounts, where they work exactly in reverse. To record asset increases, you make left-hand, or debit entries; but to record increases in liabilities, you make right-hand entries, or credit entries. That is perfectly logical because on the balance sheet, as you have seen, all the liabilities and equities are reported on the right-hand side. And, to wrap it all up, revenues are positive factors with respect to ownership accounts. That is, your sales revenue, your interest revenue, your dividend revenue, and your rent revenue all have the effect of increasing your ownership equity; so *revenue accounts* (the exact opposite of expense accounts in effect) also *are increased by right-hand entries (credits).*

Figure 3.3 shows an important liability account, Accounts Payable, and an important revenue account, Sales Revenue, with illustrative entries that bear out what has just been said. Note that Accounts Payable, a balance sheet account, has an opening and a closing balance (just like Cash in Bank), whereas Sales Revenue starts each year at zero, builds up as sales are made, and is "closed out" at the end of the year just as expense accounts are closed out.

You should now have no trouble interpreting the entries in the accounts shown in Figure 3.3. Accounts Payable shows six amounts on

Figure 3.3   Liability Account and Revenue Account

Accounts Payable			
Jan. 31	27,380	Jan. 1, Bal.	20,267
Feb. 28	36,120	Jan. 31	35,200
Mar. 31	39,170	Feb. 28	29,600
Mar. 31, Bal.	24,537	Mar. 31	42,140
	127,207		127,207
		Apr. 1, Bal.	24,537

Sales Revenue			
Mar. 31 (to close)	138,790	Jan. 31	43,010
		Feb. 28	39,640
		Mar. 31	56,140
	138,790		138,790

Figure 3.4   Rules for Accounts

Any Asset Account		Liability or Equity	
Increases	Decreases	Decreases	Increases
Any Expense Account		**Any Revenue Account**	
Increases	Decreases	Decreases	Increases

the right-hand side. To keep the illustration short, it has been assumed that the accounting period is three months rather than a year, so the right-hand items consist of the opening balance of $20,267 carried forward from December 31, plus a lump-sum addition at the end of each month. The left-hand side shows three lump-sum entries representing amounts of accounts payable paid off (decreases) and a figure that is the *balance* at the end of our assumed three-month accounting period. This figure makes the two sides equal; after footing and ruling both sides in fancy accounting style, the balancing figure is "brought down" on the right-hand side as the net amount owed at the start of the new period on April 1. Thus, the closing balance on March 31 becomes the opening balance on April 1.

The Sales Revenue account is easier to interpret. As in the case of expense accounts, there's never an opening balance in a revenue account at the start of a period; after entries are made on the right-hand side to record the revenue of each month, the whole amount is canceled out by a left-hand closing entry. To repeat, asset and equity accounts (balance sheet accounts) generally have opening and closing balances—amounts carried forward from one period to the next. Expense and revenue accounts have no opening or closing balances because they are swept clean at the end of each period by closing entries.

Figure 3.4 summarizes the rules that we have been examining.

THE PROCESS OF RECORDING COMPLETE TRANSACTIONS

Now for a very basic rule: *At all times the sum of all amounts accumulated by left-hand entries must be kept equal to the sum of all amounts accumulated by right-hand entries.* This is the secret of the balance sheet—this is why the total of the asset side always equals the total of the liabilities and equity side.

And now for a corollary rule: *Whenever any transaction is recorded, the accountant must make left-hand and right-hand entries that are equal in amount* (so that the basic rule is not violated).

Figure 3.5   Ledger Accounts

Cash in Bank		Capital Stock
(1) 100,000		(1) 100,000

Let's accustom ourselves to these rules by the process of making a few fundamental entries.

Assume (1) that a corporation is established by the issuance of common stock for cash in the amount of $100,000. To record this transaction (pretending that it is a single transaction), we must recognize the increase in the asset, Cash in Bank, by setting up a ledger account with that title and making a left-hand (increase) entry in the amount of $100,000. *And,* concurrently, we must record the creation of the owners' equity (they invested $100,000) by setting up a ledger account entitled Capital Stock and making a right-hand (increase) entry in it. Figure 3.5 shows the entire ledger of our new company after the first transaction has been recorded by equal left- and right-hand entries.

Could we prepare a balance sheet now by using the data in the ledger accounts? Certainly. The asset side would show a total of $100,000, consisting entirely of cash in bank, and the equities side would show a total of $100,000, consisting entirely of the owner's equity, capital stock.

Let's try another. Assume (2) that the company spends $40,000 of cash to purchase a building worth $30,000 on land worth $10,000. Here our balanced transaction is made up of left-hand entries of $30,000 to Building and $10,000 to Land offset by a right-hand entry of $40,000 to Cash in Bank. The accounts now stand as in Figure 3.6. Were we now to produce a balance sheet, it would show three assets totaling $100,000 and one equity with a balance of $100,000.

Figure 3.6   Amended Ledger Accounts

Cash in Bank		Capital Stock
(1) 100,000	(2) 40,000	(1) 100,000
Building		
(2) 30,000		
Land		
(2) 10,000		

Now try some more basic entries. Assume that the following transactions occur—starting with (3) to carry on our illustration:

3. The company borrows $10,000 by giving the bank an x percent, 60-day note payable (see entry 3 in Figure 3.7).
4. The company buys merchandise on account for $20,000 (see entry 4 in Figure 3.7).
5. The company sells merchandise on account for $30,000 (see entry 5 in Figure 3.7).

Figure 3.7   Transactions Added to Ledger Accounts

Cash in Bank				Capital Stock		
(1)	100,000	(2)	40,000		(1)	100,000
(3)	10,000	(6)	8,000			
	110,000		48,000			
✓ Bal.	62,000					

Building				Retained Earnings		
(2)	30,000			(8a)	8,000	(8c)	30,000
				(8b)	15,000		
					23,000		30,000
						✓ Bal. 7,000	

Land				Bank Loan Payable		
(2)	10,000				(3)	10,000

Merchandise				Accounts Payable		
(4)	20,000	(7)	15,000		(4)	20,000
	20,000					
✓ Bal.	5,000					

Accounts Receivable				Sales Revenue		
(5)	30,000			(8c)	30,000	(5)	30,000

Miscellaneous Operating Expenses				Cost of Goods Sold		
(6)	8,000	(8a)	8,000	(7)	15,000	(8b)	15,000

6. Cash is paid for miscellaneous operating expenses, $8,000 (see entry 6 in Figure 3.7).

7. A count (inventory) is made of the amount and cost of merchandise remaining on hand at the end of the period, which is found to be $5,000. This signifies that all the rest of the merchandise must have been transferred to customers in the sales transactions summarized in (5) above. In other words, the merchandise asset that cost $20,000 has been reduced to $5,000; that is, of the $20,000 of merchandise asset, $15,000 has been given up and constitutes an *expense* known as Merchandise Cost of Sales. (Many accountants call this Cost of Goods Sold.) So entry (7) consists of a right-hand entry of $15,000 in the Merchandise account and a left-hand entry to Cost of Goods Sold.

8. Now we make closing entries. To do so, as you will recall, we must reduce the balance of each expense account and each revenue account to zero by making offsetting (closing) entries on the "reducing" side of each account sufficient to reduce the balance to zero. Query: When we make a right-hand entry to Miscellaneous Operating Expense to close that account, where do we make our required, equal left-hand entry? Try Retained Earnings. Note that similar entries are made to close the other expense account, Merchandise Cost of Sales. And our only revenue account, Sales, is closed by a left-hand entry that is accompanied by a right-hand entry of the same amount to Retained Earnings. So, essentially, expenses end up on the left-hand (reducing) side of Retained Earnings and revenues end up on the right-hand side; and the expense and revenue accounts are left in a zero (closed) condition in readiness for the operations of the next accounting period.

THE GENERAL JOURNAL

It would appear that we're not getting first things first. Earlier it was said that entries should be recorded first in the journal, from which the items are posted to ledger accounts. That's true, but it's easier to depict the left and right sides of a ledger account; so we just skipped the journal for the time being. Now, in Figure 3.8 you'll find all the entries as they would appear in formal, chronological order in a simple journal form. Note that to symbolize debit, or left-side entries, we merely write the account title as far to the left as we can and put the corresponding dollar amount in the left-hand money column on the same line. Right-side, or credit, entries arc simply indented a half-inch or so, and their corresponding dollar

Figure 3.8   Simple Journal Form

The General Journal

Dates		LF	Left	Right
1	Cash in Bank	✓	100,000	
	Capital Stock	✓		100,000
	To launch the corporation, $100,000 of capital stock is issued at par for cash.	✓		
2	Building	✓	30,000	
	Land	✓	10,000	
	Cash in Bank	✓		40,000
	A building costing $30,000 on land, valued at $10,000, is purchased for cash.			
3	Cash in Bank	✓	10,000	
	Bank Loan Payable	✓		10,000
	Borrowed $ 10,000 from bank on x%, 60-day note.			
4	Merchandise Inventory	✓	20,000	
	Accounts Payable	✓		20,000
	Purchase of merchandise on account.			
5	Accounts Receivable	✓	30,000	
	Sales Revenue	✓		30,000
	Sales of merchandise on account.			
6	Cost of Goods Sold	✓	15,000	
	Merchandise Inventory	✓		15,000
	Cost of merchandise asset given up in sales recorded in (5) above.			
7	Miscellaneous Operating Expenses	✓	8,000	
	Cash in Bank	✓		8,000
8a	Retained Earnings	✓	8,000	
	Miscellaneous Operating Expenses	✓		8,000
	To close Miscellaneous Operating Expenses to Retained Earnings.			

(Continued)

Figure 3.8   Simple Journal Form (*Continued*)

	The General Journal			
8b	Retained Earnings		15,000	
	Merchandise Cost of Sales	✓		15,000
	To close Merchandise Cost of Sales.	✓		
8c	Sales Revenue		30,000	
	Retained Earnings	✓		30,000
	To close Sales Revenue.			

amounts are entered in the right-hand money column. Dates (in our case, transaction numbers) are inserted in a column on the left-hand edge, and a brief explanation is written after each journal entry. The complete journal appears in

COMMENTS ON FIGURES 3.7 AND 3.8

From the illustration that you have just traced through, you should now recognize that in the journal (which we should have prepared first as the book of original entry) each transaction (or summary of a group of similar transactions such as sales) is recorded as a unit so that you can see all aspects of it in one place. Next, each debit entry and each credit entry is posted to a ledger account that carries *precisely* the *same title* as is used in the journal entry. At the end of the accounting period, journal entries are made to close the revenue and expense accounts, so that their net effect is reflected in Retained Earnings. The revenue and expense accounts now have zero balances and are ready for similar entries in the next period; the balance sheet accounts are left open, so that their balances will carry forward into the next period. Note that the balances to be carried forward are singled out by the formal ruling and balancing procedure.

CLOSING ENTRIES REVISITED

Instead of closing each expense account and each revenue account directly to Retained Earnings, it is customary to close them first to a temporary summary account called Income Summary, or Profit and Loss; then the net balance of that account is closed to Retained Earnings. This keeps Retained

Figure 3.9 Closing Entries

8a	Income Summary (instead of Retained Earnings)	8,000	
	Miscellaneous Operating Expenses		8,000
	To close miscellaneous expenses to Income Summary.		
8b	Income Summary (instead of Retained Earnings)	15,000	
	Cost of Goods Sold		15,000
	To close cost of goods sold.		
8c	Sales Revenue	30,000	
	Income Summary (instead of Retained Earnings)		30,000
8d	Income Summary	7,000	
	Retained Earnings (finally, for net income only)		7,000
	To close Income Summary to Retained Earnings		

Earnings from becoming cluttered up with hundreds of entries. Closing entries performed this way are shown in Figure 3.9.

USE OF SUBSIDIARY LEDGERS

So far we have examined transactions through the accounting procedures that lead to your periodic financial statements and we've made debits and credits to *general ledger* accounts only. However, business constantly needs detailed information for reasons other than preparing periodic financial statements, such as its dealings with individual customers and creditors. Consider charge (credit) customers for a moment. If a business has significant numbers of such customers, what would happen if we made debits for every one of them to the same general ledger account when they bought goods or services from us, and made credits for every one of them to that same general ledger account when they paid us? Wouldn't that account become a genuine mess? How could we hope to tell later from that account how much each customer owed us? Which ones were entitled to discounts for early payment? Clearly we must find some alternative, and that is to use *subsidiary ledger* accounts.

Here's how: As customers buy goods and services from us, all of them are debited in total to a single Accounts Receivable account in the general ledger—called a *control* account (credits are made to Sales Revenue). We don't need to make an entry in the control accounts receivable account in the general ledger each time we make a sale. We can delay making the entry until the end of a month, for example, and then record it as a grand total, just so the account will be brought up to date for statement purposes. But let's systematically record each sale to a charge customer as a debit to that customer's *individual* subsidiary ledger account—we'll have one for each charge customer. And when the customer pays us, we'll credit that particular customer's subsidiary ledger account. These subsidiary ledger accounts look like, and are used like, the general ledger accounts we have been discussing.

Hence, at any time we should be able to go through each customer's subsidiary ledger account and find the complete story of each. However, if we're concerned only with our total (for financial statement purposes), we find it in our regular, general ledger control account for accounts receivable, which is posted up to date through monthly journal entries that record debits for all sales on account and credits for all payments received from charge customers.

If you've followed this, you will recognize that at the end of the month we could take an adding machine tape of the balances of all the customers' subsidiary accounts, and its total should agree with the balance of the general ledger control account for accounts receivable. Notice two things: First, most of the accounts in our general ledger are control accounts, each receiving aggregate rather than detailed debits and credits and being "supported" by subsidiary ledgers on which we keep track of details needed to operate the business efficiently and effectively, just as is done with accounts receivable (such as for accounts payable, raw materials, and individual jobs performed in a manufacturing firm, among many others). Second, subsidiary ledgers can take many forms, the T form we have discussed, or cards, or sheets of paper, to name but a few. Control and subsidiary accounts are used very extensively in cost accounting, as we shall see in later chapters.

THE TRIAL BALANCE

What should happen if we were now to make a list of all the general ledger account balances and, opposite each account, show the net balance of each as it now stands? Answer: We would have prepared a *trial balance,* and the total debits and total credits had better balance!

Fortunately, our illustration is a simple one and, because we made no mistakes, our trial balance does balance. See Figure 3.10. Note that we have listed all accounts, though some have no balances. Customarily, accounts with zero balances are not listed. However, a trial balance can be prepared any time that you want one; so let's see how ours would look had it been prepared *before* the closing entries (8a, b, c, and d) were made (see Figure 3.11).

Note that this trial balance shows no balance for Retained Earnings because (1) this is the first year of operation for our company and (2) the revenue and expense accounts have not yet been closed to Income Summary and to Retained Earnings.

Figure 3.10   Trial Balance After Closing

| | Balances | |
	Debit	Credit
Cash in bank	$ 62,000	
Building	30,000	
Land	10,000	
Merchandise	5,000	
Accounts receivable	30,000	
Accounts payable		$ 20,000
Bank loan payable		10,000
Capital stock		100,000
Retained earnings		7,000
Sales revenue		—
Merchandise cost of sales	—	
Miscellaneous operating expenses	—	
	$137,000	$137,000

Figure 3.11   Trial Balance Before Closing

	Debit	Credit
Cash in bank	$ 62,000	
Accounts receivable	30,000	
Merchandise inventory	5,000	
Land	10,000	
Building	30,000	
Accounts payable		$ 20,000
Bank loan		10,000
Capital stock		100,000
Retained earnings		—
Sales revenue		30,000
Merchandise cost of sales	15,000	
Miscellaneous operating expenses	8,000	
	$160,000	$160,000

Figure 3.12   An Income Statement Prepared from Trial Balance

<table>
<tr><td colspan="3" align="center">OUR COMPANY
Income Statement
for the Year Ended December 31, 20XX</td></tr>
<tr><td>Sales</td><td></td><td>$30,000</td></tr>
<tr><td>Expenses:</td><td></td><td></td></tr>
<tr><td>Cost of goods sold</td><td>$15,000</td><td></td></tr>
<tr><td>Miscellaneous operating expenses</td><td>8,000</td><td></td></tr>
<tr><td>Depreciation (omitted)</td><td>—</td><td></td></tr>
<tr><td>Interest on bank loan (omitted)</td><td>—</td><td></td></tr>
<tr><td>Income taxes (omitted)</td><td>—</td><td>23,000</td></tr>
<tr><td>Net income (to be closed to retained earnings)</td><td></td><td>$ 7,000</td></tr>
</table>

It is customary to prepare a trial balance at the end of each month (1) to reveal the existence of bookkeeping errors that would "throw the trial balance out of balance" and (2) to aid in preparation of monthly financial statements.

THE FINANCIAL STATEMENTS

Quite obviously, an income statement and a balance sheet can easily be prepared by copying the figures from Figure 3.11 (or from Figure 3.10) in the proper forms. Note, however, that we are for present purposes ignoring the fact that the building would have depreciated a bit during the year and we would owe some interest on the bank loan and some income taxes. The resulting income statement is shown as Figure 3.12 and the balance sheet as Figure 3.13.

CONCLUSION

Now you have had a glimpse at the traditional accounting financial statements and at all the traditional accounting routines except one. We have mentioned the need for making adjusting entries at the end of each accounting period; but the entries deserve more than a passing glance, so we'll examine them in the next chapter. *Adjusting entries* would be needed to recognize depreciation of the building and the end-of-period liability for income taxes. Those financial developments are nontransactional in nature, but must be recorded by the end of the accounting period in order to properly match revenues and expenses to the period in which they occurred.

Figure 3.13   A Balance Sheet Prepared from Trial Balance

OUR COMPANY
Balance Sheet,
December 31, 20XX

Assets			Equities		
Current:			Current liabilities:		
Cash in bank	$62,000		Accounts payable		$ 20,000
Accounts receivable	30,000		Bank loan		10,000
Merchandise	5,000				
Total current assets		$ 97,000	Total current liabilities		$ 30,000
Noncurrent:			Stockholder's equity:		
Land	$10,000		Capital stock	$100,000	
Building	30,000	40,000	Retained earnings	7,000	107,000
		$137,000			$137,000

For your exercise, a set of data and forms appear below for you to use in performing the accounting tasks described in this chapter. Formal solutions, as usual, are presented in Appendix A.

TEST PROBLEM

The problem that follows is designed to include only the barest essentials of the accounting cycle—a skeleton on which we can build, in logical sequence, to the end that we should be able to unravel the most perplexing of the problems of modern-day financial reporting and analysis. To solve this problem, you are asked merely to record a few basic transactions directly in the accompanying skeleton ledger accounts and to prepare a trial balance, statements, and closing entries in the forms provided. The assumed transaction data follow:

TRANSACTION DATA (MONTH OF JULY)

1. Empire Corp. is established and 10,000 shares of $10 par common stock are issued for cash, which is deposited directly in the bank.

2. A building is rented for $1,000 per month and July rent is paid. (Treat the rent as a miscellaneous expense.)
3. Store equipment is purchased for cash, $30,000.
4. Merchandise is purchased on account, $50,000.
5. Sales, all on account, total $60,000. The cost of the items sold was determined to be $35,000.
6. Miscellaneous expenses, all paid in cash, total $10,000.
7. The estimated useful life of the equipment is 20 years with no significant salvage value likely at the end of its life. Accordingly, the depreciation expense for July is determined to be one-twentieth of the cost divided by 12, or $1,500/12, or $125. (Treat as a miscellaneous expense.)
8. A trial balance is prepared.
9. An income statement is prepared.
10. A balance sheet is prepared.
11. Closing entries are made.

TEST PROBLEM SOLUTION SPACE

EMPIRE CORP.
Ledger

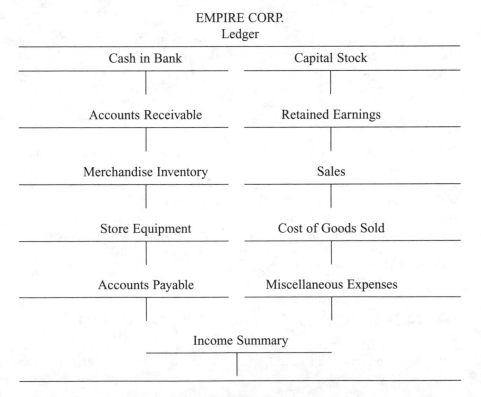

Cash in Bank	Capital Stock
Accounts Receivable	Retained Earnings
Merchandise Inventory	Sales
Store Equipment	Cost of Goods Sold
Accounts Payable	Miscellaneous Expenses
Income Summary	

(8) EMPIRE CORP.
Trial Balance (before closing)
July 31, 20XX

	Balances	
Account Title	Debit	Credit
	$	
		$

(9) EMPIRE CORP.
Income Statement
for July, 20XX

Sales		$
Expenses:		
Merchandise cost of sales	$	
Miscellaneous		
Net income		

(10) EMPIRE CORP.
Balance Sheet
As At July 31, 20XX

Assets		Equities	
Current:		Current liabilities:	
Cash in bank	$	Accounts payable	$
Accounts receivable		Total liabilities	$
		Stockholder's equity:	
Merchandise inventory		Capital stock	$
Total current assets		Retained earnings	
Store equipment		Total stockholder's equity	$
Total assets	$	Total liabilities &	$
		stockholder's equity	$

4

THE ACCOUNTING CYCLE

ELEMENTS OF THE ACCOUNTING CYCLE

No matter what kind of accounting system the individual business enterprise maintains, the so-called *cycle* (or sequence) of *accounting activities*
will be basically the same. The word "cycle" should not be defined too
precisely, however.

Although a specific "bit" of accounting data will typically flow
through the various stages of the cycle in consecutive order, such bits of
data are being introduced into the accounting system at all times throughout the period, and thus, within the business as a whole, several parts of the
cycle will be undergoing activity simultaneously.

In the order of their classical sequence, the stages of the accounting
cycle are:

1. *Underlying documents*. Transaction data are recorded (stored) in
   underlying documents or in computer storage files.
2. *Journalizing*. The transaction data on the underlying documents
   are sorted and entered in the *journal(s)* either individually or in
   batches as summarized lists.
3. *Posting*. The transaction data are "posted" from the journal(s) to the
   ledgers. In some cases individual journal items may be posted; in
   other cases, the journals are so designed that much of the journal
   data can be summed and posted in total to the ledger. (Much posting time is thereby saved, and accuracy is improved.)
4. *Trial balance*. A trial balance is prepared to test bookkeeping accuracy and to aid in preparation of the worksheet and statements.
   (Step 5 might well be labeled "Hunt for Errors," but we'll assume
   the trial balance did balance immediately.)

5. *Worksheet.* A worksheet may be prepared at the end of the period, before adjusting entries are made. The worksheet will be explained and illustrated later in this chapter.
6. *Adjusting entries.* The end-of-period adjusting entries are made. This means that they are (a) journalized and (b) posted to ledger accounts just as regular transaction entries are handled.
7. *Closing entries.* There's not much to be said about closing entries except that their purpose, at the end of an accounting period, is to sweep clean the income statement accounts (all revenue, expense, loss, tax, and interest accounts) to make them ready for the accumulation of similar information in the next period. The net result of the sweeping operation is entered in the Retained Earnings account as the net income for the year. (Here you can see why we must emphasize the need for care in the process of "matching" costs or expenses with revenues each period—to arrive at a sensible *net income* for the period.) The routine closing entry procedure was illustrated in Chapter 3.
8. *Financial statements.* After everything is shipshape, with all accounts adjusted up to date, with all liabilities determined, etc., financial statements are drafted. Fundamentally this operation involves no more than the copying of amounts, accumulated in the ledger accounts, into whatever forms the management elects to use in the structure of the income statement, the balance sheet, and the statement of cash flows (see Chapter 6).
9. *Independent audit.* When all the above steps have been taken, it may be appropriate (or mandatory) to engage a firm of CPAs to perform an "independent" audit. What this means in essence is that outside, professional auditors examine your financial statements and, to the extent deemed necessary, your accounting records, the supporting documents, and whatever else is needed, and express their opinion that your statements are prepared in accordance with generally accepted accounting principles. Over the years the CPA firms have expanded their activities to include tax return preparation, accounting systems design, budgeting, and a wide range of management consulting services.

WHAT IS MEANT BY THE ACCOUNTING PERIOD?

We generally think of the accounting period as a year—a 12-month passage of time—whether the year be a regular calendar year ending on December 31 or a so-called *fiscal year,* which closes at the end of whatever month suits the business. However, if 12 months is the formal accounting period, we must recognize that for the effective management of the business, as well as for effective disclosure of operations to absentee owners, financial reports are inevitably needed more frequently. Such reports are known as *interim statements*, and although the term is not too commonly used, we might refer to the time spanned by any report that covers less than a year as an interim period.

In the preceding section appears a list of the basic procedures that constitute a complete accounting cycle. From such a list it might be inferred that the only accounting activity within an accounting period is the accumulation of financial data on underlying documents followed by journalizing and posting of the data. However, depending on the size and needs of the organization, the accounting staff may devote a substantial amount of time to what is known as *internal auditing* and to the preparation of routine as well as special-purpose reports for the various levels of management. Essentially, internal auditing consists of systematically checking the data that flow into the accounting records to assure their accuracy. In many situations, it involves the continuous testing of the organizational controls that have been set up to prevent the commission of recording errors or thefts of cash or other valuable resources. The nature of routine and special-purpose reports for internal management will be discussed in Chapter 14.

Again, referring to the list of activities that constitute the formal accounting cycle, let it be noted that some of the steps can be omitted or abridged when we are dealing with an interim period. For example, closing entries will *not* be made at the end of each month or each calendar quarter; and adjusting entries (which are necessary for any interim period no matter how short) may be made on a worksheet, which is then used directly for the preparation of the interim financial statements.

The balance of this chapter is devoted mainly to the nature of adjusting entries and the use of the worksheet.

WHAT AND WHY ARE ADJUSTING ENTRIES?

If we do a good, thorough job of recording transactions as they occur, why should it ever be necessary to make adjusting entries at the end of the regular or interim period? The answer is that certain types of nontransactional events (those that "flow" continuously) cannot be kept up to date; and for certain types of "spot" transactions, when they are repetitive and individually relatively insignificant, it is more efficient to allow the data to accumulate and record them in periodic batches (that is, by periodic adjusting entries that, in effect, treat the stream of spot transactions as if they constituted a continuous flow). A true flow-type transaction, of course, is something such as depreciation or interest expense or interest revenue, all of which "flow" continuously.

By merely scanning the list of accounts that make up a typical trial balance, you'll readily understand the inevitability of adjusting entries. Now let's look at a few as samples.

Start with cash in bank. If we have carefully recorded every collection or other receipt of cash, every deposit in the bank, and every check that we've written, should any end-of-period adjustment ever be called for? The answer is yes. Banks have the habit of making service charges (which may depend on the number of checks, deposits, or other transactions handled in relation to the average balance maintained). Banks may make collections for you and report the collections via monthly statements. In short, any additions or reductions that the bank records with respect to your deposit account must be duplicated in your own accounting records, and the information for such "adjustments" may not be known to you until you receive the monthly bank statement.

Your company may hold, as temporary investments, marketable securities or other dividend- or interest-bearing investments as a means of obtaining some income on funds that are temporarily in excess of current operating needs. At the end of any accounting period, these investments must be reviewed to determine what interest and dividends may have been earned but have not yet been collected in the form of a spot-cash transaction. Adjusting entries are thus required to "accrue" interest and dividends receivable.

Accounts receivable are not always "good"—that is, almost every business is bound to have some deadbeats among its clientele. The recognition of so-called *bad debts* may be recorded on a spot basis (that is, whenever a specific account is determined to be uncollectible, it may be written off as a bad debt "expense"); or a periodic *blanket provision* may be made to reflect management's estimate of the portion of sales revenue that will never be collected. The latter procedure, which is in accordance with the generally accepted accounting principle of matching expenses with the same period that the revenue was generated, involves periodic adjustment to accrue the amount of bad debts estimated to have been accumulated within a given period. Typically this accrual adjustment is measured as a flat percentage of the total credit sales for the period, or is estimated based on an aging schedule of accounts receivable. The further past due a particular account receivable is, the more likely it will be uncollectible. Because this amount is unknown until the end of the period, an end-of-period adjustment is required.

Next, consider property, plant, and equipment. When an item is purchased, the event is, of course, recorded as an asset. However, with every subsequent period, this asset's usefulness is wearing out. Once again, in light of the generally accepted accounting principle of matching expenses to the same period(s) that revenues are being generated , there should be an accounting entry reflecting the "using up" or expensing of this asset.

The solution, of course, is to record an adjusting entry *at the end of the period* to reflect the expensing of this asset. This is done by making a debit entry to a Depreciation Expense account, and a credit entry to Accumulated Depreciation for the asset being depreciated. The Accumulated Depreciation account is known as a "contra asset" and is shown on the balance immediately beneath the asset being depreciated as a reduction.

The net value of the asset less accumulated depreciation is known as the asset's "carrying value", that is, the value of the asset being carried on the books. Why don't we make a credit entry to the asset directly? Because physically, the asset is still there, so we don't want it to disappear off the books and records until the asset is actually disposed of.

Almost every company pays in advance for various types of insurance. The moment the prepayment is made, the insurance begins to expire. We can't possibly record the expiration on a continuous basis, although we could make an accounting entry each day, or each week, or each month. Usually we settle for the once-a-month solution. That, again, illustrates the fact that *the real purpose of adjusting entries is to update all accounts that have been allowed to lag as a practical necessity.*

The examples given so far should suffice as a demonstration of the *need* for periodic adjusting entries. Next, let's go through an illustrative problem dealing with adjusting entries. At the same time, we'll introduce the accountants' worksheet.

PROBLEM DATA

Tuesday Co. uses the calendar year as its formal accounting period, and management has asked the accounting staff to provide an interim income statement and a statement of balance sheet at the end of each month. Accordingly, at the end of January the accounting staff prepares a trial balance of the accounts as they stand before any adjusting entries have been made. The trial balance is shown in Figure 4.1.

It is determined that adjusting entries must be made as follows for the reasons listed:

1. Bank service charges, in the amount of $72 for the month of January, are shown on the monthly bank statement which has just been received. The required adjusting entry must record a $72 reduction of Cash in Bank (this calls for a credit entry) and a recognition of $72 of expense which, for our purposes, we'll classify as administrative expense (a debit entry). The entry, in skeleton journal form, is:

    Administrative Expenses   72
       Cash in Bank   72

Figure 4.1   Account Balances

	Debit	Credit
Cash in bank	$ 5,000	
Marketable securities	20,000	
Accounts receivable	40,000	
Merchandise	60,000	
Prepaid insurance	3,000	
Land	8,000	
Equipment	60,000	
Buildings	80,000	
Allowance for depreciation		$ 30,000
Accounts payable		35,000
Notes payable		25,000
Capital stock		100,000
Retained earnings		21,000
Sales		85,000
Selling expenses	10,000	
Administrative expenses	10,000	
	$296,000	$296,000

2. The marketable securities consist entirely of government, industrial, and public utility bonds. The interest earned in January (on an accrual basis) is determined to total $130. The required adjusting entry, to show the receivable of $130 and the corresponding interest revenue, is:

| Interest Accrued Receivable | 130 | |
| Interest Revenue | | 130 |

Note that this entry depicts an increase in the asset Interest Accrued Receivable by a debit entry and an increase in the revenue account, Interest Revenue, by a credit entry.

3. This company's experience has shown that the bad debt rate has tended to be about 1 percent of credit sales. Since any uncollectible receivables that came into being during January would still be "on the books," an adjusting entry must be made to show that receivables totaling approximately 1 percent of sales for the month of

January are probably uncollectibles. The entry to record this adjustment is made as follows:

Uncollectible Accounts Expense   850
    Allowance for Uncollectible Accounts   850

The debit entry, to Uncollectible Accounts Expense, represents an
expense. Accounts receivable must also be reduced by $850, but
this is just an estimate; we don't yet know which specific accounts
are uncollectible. We perform an accounting trick: we make the
credit entry not to Accounts Receivable but to another contra-
asset, which is named Allowance for Uncollectible Accounts. You
should note that this is the practical equivalent of making a direct
reduction of the accounts receivable balance; but since the
accounts receivable are made up of accounts with, perhaps, hundreds of customers, we achieve the effect of a reduction by using
what all accountants call a contra account—Allowance for
Uncollectible Accounts. On the balance sheet, the account reads as
in Figure 4.2. By the procedure just demonstrated, we are able to
keep the (so far unidentified) uncollectible accounts receivable on
the books and, at the same time, match the probability that some
of those accounts receivable will be uncollectible to the same period
that the sale was made.

4. The $60,000 balance in the merchandise account consists of
$20,000 carried over from last year plus $40,000 purchased in
January. We have not attempted to record the merchandise cost of
sales accompanying each recorded sale. We now determine, either
by physical count or by estimate, that the cost of merchandise
remaining on hand on January 31 is $10,000. This means that
$50,000 has disappeared, we hope as the result of sales. Needless
to say, the $50,000 may also include disappearance by theft,
spoilage, and other forms of shrinkage. For the present we'll be
charitable and pretend the whole $50,000 represents cost of goods
sold. Then our required adjusting entry is to reduce the merchandise inventory (asset) account to $10,000 by a credit entry and

Figure 4.2

Current assets:		
Cash in bank		$ 4,928
Accounts receivable	$40,000	
Less: Allowance for uncollectible accounts	850	39,150

increase Cost of Goods Sold, an expense account, by a debit entry, as follows:

Cost of Goods Sold	50,000	
Merchandise Inventory		50,000

5. It is determined that the balance of Prepaid Insurance (often termed Unexpired Insurance) should be reduced by $100 to represent the amount that expired during January. A right-hand entry is made to reduce the asset, Prepaid Insurance, and a left-hand entry is made to increase our administrative expense, thus:

Insurance Expenses	100	
Prepaid Insurance		100

6. Equipment and buildings depreciate through use and with the passage of time. We'll look into this phenomenon later, but for the present let's assume that the depreciation for January totals $800. Now, rather than subtract the $800 directly from the numerous accounts that our company keeps for the various categories of equipment plus an account for the building, we again use the offset technique—the contra account—and make our right-hand entry to Allowance for Depreciation, and we split the debit entry (we'll assume it's a reasonable split) 80 percent to Selling Expenses and 20 percent to Administrative Expenses. Figure 4.3 is the entry in journal form.

7. Our sales clerks are paid weekly, and because January ended in the middle of a week, we must recognize "accrued wages payable" of $1,000, as follows:

Wages Expenses	1,000	
Wages Accrued Payable		1,000

You'll recognize the effects of this event—to increase Wages Expense by $1,000 and to increase a liability, Wages Accrued

Figure 4.3

Selling Expenses	640	
Administrative Expenses	160	
Allowance for Depreciation		800

To record equipment and building depreciation of $800, charging 80% to selling and 20% to administrative expenses.

Payable, by $1,000. Note again that the word *accrued* is used to indicate an interim recognition of a liability that is growing through time and is to be paid later.

8. Interest on our notes payable was paid on last December 31, but by the end of January we must recognize the accrual of (assume) $200 of fresh interest expense. The entry is:

Interest Expense	200	
Interest Accrued Payable		200

9. To round out our adjusting entries, we must recognize that we'll probably owe some income taxes. It's not easy to make a reliable estimate of the amount attributable to the first month of the year, but let's accept $2,500 as a reasonable guess. Our adjusting entry then is:

Income Tax Expense	2,500	
Income Tax Accrued Payable		2,500

Now if we can safely assume that there are no more adjusting entries to be made, we are ready to post entries 1 through 9 in our ledger accounts and prepare our monthly statements. But purely for educational purposes, let's now demonstrate the use of a worksheet as an instrument for the preparation of interim statements.

THE WORKSHEET

The accountant's worksheet is a most useful gadget, and it's something you are now well-equipped to handle. Here's the concept. We start with a sheet of columnar paper—one with a wide column at the left for the listing of our account titles followed by from a half-dozen to a dozen narrower money columns to the right. In the first pair of money columns, we list the amounts that make up our unadjusted trial balance as of any given date, placing those accounts with debit balances on the left-hand column and those with credit balances on the right-hand column. In the next pair of columns we make debit and credit entries (adjusting entries) to adjust the raw trial balance figures; then, we copy the trial balance figures, *as modified by the adjusting entries,* into the third pair of columns (which are headed Income Statement) and into the final pair (which are headed Balance Sheet). Whether a given item is copied in an income statement column or a balance sheet column depends simply on whether the item is to appear in the income statement or in the balance sheet. Thus, the adjusted amount for Cash in Bank would be carried to the debit (asset) column under the heading Balance Sheet, and the amount for Sales and for each class of expenses would be entered in the Income Statement columns. Then all that remains to be done is to copy the sorted amounts into your regular income statement and balance sheet formats, and there you have your financial statements all done.

Let's illustrate this procedure with the example in the preceding section on adjusting entries. Figure 4.4 is an eight-column worksheet in finished form. Note the trial balance in the first pair of columns, the adjusting entries in the second pair, the income statement amounts (as adjusted) in the third pair, and the balance sheet amounts (as adjusted) in the fourth pair.

THE WORKSHEET—COMMENTS

In order to be thoroughly familiar with worksheet procedure, you ought to follow through the details in Figure 4.4. For example, note that Cash in Bank, on the first line, had a balance of $5,000 but that, in adjusting entry (1), we made a credit entry of $72 to record the reduction caused by the bank's service charges. This same adjusting entry is shown in the credit adjusting entry column. Then, after all other adjusting entries have been entered on the worksheet, Cash in Bank, as adjusted by $72, is carried way over to the debit balance sheet column (because Cash in Bank is an asset). Exactly the same procedure was followed through the whole illustration.

Please note how the last two pairs of columns are "balanced." Obviously, if you carry the adjusted revenue balances to the credit (right) side of the income statement and carry the expenses to the debit side, the two sides won't be equal—you have to plug them to make them equal, and the amount of that plug is your net income (or loss). Also, if you carry the assets, the liabilities, the capital stock, and the retained earnings to the balance sheet columns, they won't have equal totals until you plug them for the net income (addition to retained earnings) for the period. You see, the retained earnings balance in the raw trial balance is the amount carried forward from December, and it is brought up to date as of the end of January only when you add January's net income to it.

FINANCIAL STATEMENTS

The financial statements for Tuesday Co. are prepared by copying the data in the last four columns of the worksheet into blank income statement and balance sheet forms. They appear as Figures 4.5 and 4.6. Please remember that financial statements do *not* have debit and credit columns. The different columns presented are only for presentation purposes.

Figure 4.4 Eight-column Worksheet

TUESDAY CO.
Eight-Column Worksheet.
as of January 31

	Trial balance		Adjusting entries		Income statement		Balance sheet	
	Debit	Credit	Debit	Credit	Debit	Credit	Debit	Credit
Cash in bank	5,000			(1) 72			4,928	
Marketable securities	20,000						20,000	
Interest accrued receivable			(2) 130				130	
Accounts receivable	40,000						40,000	
Allowance for bad debts				(3) 850				850
Merchandise	60,000			(4) 50,000			10,000	
Prepaid insurance	3,000			(5) 100			2,900	
Land	8,000						8,000	
Equipment	60,000						60,000	
Building	80,000						80,000	
Accumulated depreciation		30,000		(6) 800				30,800
Accounts payable		35,000						35,000
Notes payable		25,000						25,000
Interest accrued payable				(8) 200				200
Wages accrued payable				(7) 1,000				1,000

Account	Trial Balance	Adjustments Dr	Adjustments Cr	Income Statement Dr	Income Statement Cr	Balance Sheet Dr	Balance Sheet Cr
Income tax accrued payable			(9) 2,500				2,500
Capital stock	100,000						100,000
Retained earnings	21,000						21,000
Sales	85,000				85,000		
Interest revenue			(2) 130		130		
Bad debts		(3) 850		850			
Cost of goods sold		(4) 50,000		50,000			
Selling expenses	10,000	(6) 640; (7) 1,000		11,640			
Administrative expenses	10,000	(1) 72; (5) 100; (6) 160		10,332			
Interest expense		(8) 200		200			
Income taxes		(9) 2,500		2,500			
Net income				9,608			9,608
	296,000 296,000	55,652	55,652	85,130	85,130	225,958	225,958

Figure 4.5   Income Statement Prepared from the Worksheet

TUESDAY CO.
Income Statement,
January, 20XX

Sales		$85,000	
Interest revenue		130	$85,130
Expenses:			
Cost of goods sold	$50,000		
Selling	11,640		
Administrative	11,182	$72,822	
Interest		200	
Income taxes		2,500	75,522
Net income			$ 9,608

ARE INTERIM STATEMENTS DEPENDABLE?

The extent to which interim balance sheets and income statements are dependable is arguable. One thing is certain: They do have their weaknesses. Business executives, who should be making use of them, should certainly know enough about them to be aware of their weaknesses—in other words, not to make decisions on the basis of unreliable data, at least without knowing that minor, or even major, weaknesses exist.

It's too early in the game for us to explore the weaknesses of interim statements in detail, but if you're willing temporarily to take an opinion on faith, a couple of observations will be presented now and we'll examine the question of reliability more thoroughly later.

If we are going to divide the total lifetime of the enterprise into segments for financial reporting purposes, the most natural segment length would appear to be the year-whether or not December 31 is chosen as the annual cutoff date. However, statements prepared to report the results of operations even for a whole year (as well as balance sheets at year-ends) inevitably involve the exercise of judgment, the making of estimates, and some arbitrary decisions. To cut the year, in turn, into two, four, or even twelve segments for reporting purposes amplifies the level of uncertainty for a number of reasons, and it may well be contended that reports for periods shorter than a year should be prepared on a special-purpose basis only—that is, they should contain only data that pass the test of reliability. Data that do not pass the test should be clearly labeled as conjectural or speculative.

Figure 4.6   Balance Sheet Prepared from the Worksheet

TUESDAY CO.
Balance Sheet, January 31, 20XX

Assets

Current:		$ 4,928	
Cash in bank			
Marketable securities		20,000	
Interest accrued receivable		130	
Accounts receivable	$ 40,000		
Less: Allowance for uncollectible accounts	850	39,150	
Merchandise inventory		10,000	
Prepaid insurance		2,900	
Total current assets			$ 77,108
Property, Plant, and Equipment:			
Land		$ 8,000	
Equipment	$ 60,000		
Building	80,000		
	$140,000		
Less: Allowance for depreciation	30,800	109,200	
Total noncurrent assets			117,200
Total Assets			$194,308

Liabilities and Stockholders' Equity

Current liabilities:		
Accounts payable	$ 35,000	
Notes payable	25,000	
Interest accrued payable	200	
Wages accrued payable	1,000	
Income taxes accrued payable	2,500	
Total liabilities		$ 63,700
Stockholders' equity:		
Capital stock	$100,000	
Retained earnings	30,608	
Total stockholders' equity		130,608
Total liabilities & stockholders' equity		$194,308

INTERNAL CONTROL STRUCTURE

We have spent a significant amount of the preceding chapters discussing major aspects of the accounting system and the accounting cycle. We would be remiss if we didn't briefly discuss the *internal control structure*, which, briefly defined, is a combination of the attitudes, environmental factors, and accounting procedures and techniques utilized to ensure that the business objectives are attained in the most efficient and effective manner. The structure developed must depend on many things: use of computers versus manual processing of transactions; number of employees available to perform various functions; size of the business; nature of the business and its objectives; management's philosophy and operating style; and many others. Here we can only briefly present a few of the major factors involved.

There are two broad elements in the internal control structure: the control environment and control procedures. The control environment is extremely important, encompassing such things as developing an organizational structure that best leads to fulfilling the business objectives; assigning authority and responsibility for performing certain functions; having an adequate internal audit function; having a good system for hiring, training, and promoting employees; and providing proper monitoring and compliance with requirements imposed by external authorities, such as legislative and regulatory bodies. After this brief listing, however, we'll spend the balance of our time on *control procedures*, since these tie more directly into the accounting system.

Control procedures are utilized, first, to reduce the number of errors that are made in the accounting process and to find and correct those that are made and, second, to discourage those who might be inclined to defraud the business in some manner and to uncover fraud and embezzlement and those responsible when they do occur.

There are five major categories of control procedures:

1. *Proper authorization of transactions and activities.* Only certain individuals should have the authority to initiate certain transactions. These transactions should be well documented so that such individuals can be held accountable for their actions.
2. *Segregation of duties.* Different individuals should be assigned to the responsibilities of authorizing transactions, recording transactions, and maintaining custody of the related assets. For example, subsidiary ledgers make it possible for one individual to post to the general ledger and a different employee(s) to post to the subsidiary ledger, each acting as a check on the other. Or, the individual who deposits cash receipts in the bank *should not* make entries to the Cash in Bank account or reconcile the bank balance.
3. *Adequate documents and records.* Proper documentation allows the business reasonable assurance that all transactions have been recorded.

4. *Safeguards over assets.* For example, allowing only certain individuals to make cash disbursements, using a mechanical check protector, and appropriate physical segregation of assets.
5. *Independent checks on performance.* These include making timely periodic comparisons of book records with the physical assets represented by those records, such as inventories, securities, cash, and plant and equipment.

CONCLUSION

If you're still with us, you have now suffered through just about all of the mechanical details (call it bookkeeping if you wish) that we're going to deal with. No apologies are offered for the amount of bookkeeping that we have analyzed, because it will help us immeasurably in the discussion of the sequence of topics that follow. If you will apply your pencil to the summary test problem on the following pages and if you find that it presents no major difficulties, you should be all set to explore some of the more interesting aspects of accounting—particularly the ways in which accounting should be useful to you in your work.

TEST PROBLEM

The trial balance of Blitz Co. on December 31, before adjustments, is shown in the first two columns of the worksheet at the end of the chapter. Data on which end-of-year adjusting entries are to be based are as follows. (Assume that the company did not make interim adjusting entries in its formal records.)

1. Unrecorded bank service charges amount to $25.
2. The $100 balance in Allowance for Uncollectible Accounts is the amount remaining from last year's provision. The proper increment for this year is estimated to be 1 percent of total sales for the year.
3. The inventory of merchandise at year-end is determined to be $10,000.
4. Depreciation for the year is determined to total $4,000, of which 90 percent is selling expense and 10 percent is administrative.
5. Interest accrued payable on the bonds at the end of the year is $1,000.
6. Income taxes are to be accrued in the amount of $650.

REQUIRED

In the spaces provided, prepare a complete worksheet, an income statement, and a balance sheet.

TEST PROBLEM SOLUTION SPACE

BLITZ CO.
Worksheet
for the year Ended December 31, 20XX

	Trial balance		Adjusting entries		Income statement		Balance sheet	
	Debit	Credit	Debit	Credit	Debit	Credit	Debit	Credit
Cash in bank	2,500							
Accounts receivable	40,000							
Allowance for Uncollectible Accounts		100						
Merchandise Inventory	40,000							
Equipment	100,000							
Allowance for depreciation		35,000						
Accounts payable		20,000						
Interest accrued payable		25,000						
Income tax accrued payable								
Bonds payable								
Capital stock		50,000						
Retained earnings		13,400						
Sales		60,000						
Bad debts	10,000							
Cost of goods sold								
Selling expenses								
Administrative expenses	11,000							
Interest expense								
Income taxes								
Net income for year								
Totals	203,500	203,500						

BLITZ CO.
Income Statement
For The year Ended December 31, 20XX

Net sales	$	
Expenses:		
Cost of goods sold	$	
Selling		
Administrative		
Interest expense		
Income taxes		
Net income		$

BLITZ CO.
Balance Sheet
As At December 31, 20XX

Assets

Current:			
Cash in bank		$	
Accounts receivable	$		
Less: Allowance for uncollectible accounts			
Merchandise			
Total current assets			$
Noncurrent:			
Equipment		$	
Less: Allowance for depreciation			
Total assets			$ _____

Liabilities & Stockholder's Equity

Current liabilities:			
Accounts payable		$	
Interest accrued payable			
Income tax accrued payable		_____	
Total current liabilities			
Bonds payable			_____
Total liabilities			$

Stockholders' equity:

   Capital stock $

   Retained earnings

Total stockholder's equity $

Total liabilities & stockholder's equity $

5

C H A P T E R

WORKING CAPITAL

WHAT IS WORKING CAPITAL?

When accountants speak of working capital (or net working capital), they mean the *algebraic difference between the total of the current assets and the total of the current liabilities*. The term is used a great deal and, as a business executive, you should be quite familiar with it. However, it is a poor one because it simply doesn't convey its real meaning. *Capital* has several different meanings (e.g., the invested capital of the company and capital assets—the noncurrent assets), and to put the word *working* in front of *capital* doesn't seem to add much. But as the saying goes, we must see it "like it is," and that means "current assets minus current liabilities equals working capital."

To add to our difficulties, it is not unheard of for the banker, or other lender, to insist that you maintain a certain specified amount of working capital at all times. That not only leads to occasional arguments over what should be included in working capital but may also require you to be stingy with dividend payments to your stockholders and perhaps to accumulate more working capital than you can use economically.

Let's spend the next several paragraphs on simple illustrations of the more common transactions that affect our working capital. Just for practice in the use of accounting language and form, for each common working capital element we'll run through a few typical transactions. Part of the reason for this exercise will be to build up your familiarity with "debit" and "credit." Our aim in each case will be to list the more common transactions and show how they would be recorded in simple journal form.

CASH RECEIPTS TRANSACTIONS

Cash, a current asset, comes from many sources. The more common sources are depicted in the journal entries (with their explanations) that follow. Because the dollar amounts involved are of no importance to us at this point, in most cases, we'll just use x's in place of assumed figures.

(1)

Cash on Hand	xxx	
Capital Stock		xxx

To record the issue of capital stock when a corporation is formed. A debit (left-hand) entry is made in the Cash account as an asset increase, and a credit (right-hand) entry is made in the Capital Stock account as an equity increase.

(2)

Cash on Hand	xxx	
Bonds Payable		xxx

We borrow money by issuing bonds. Bonds Payable is a liability, and we must make a credit to record the increase. The debit to cash is obvious.

(3)

Cash in Bank	xxx	
Bank Loan (Notes Payable)		xxx

We borrow money from a bank. Our bank account (an asset) is increased (debit) and a current liability (Bank Loan Payable) is increased (by a credit).

(4)

Cash on Hand	xxx	
Sales Revenue		xxx

When we sell merchandise for cash, in addition to debiting cash we must record the increase in revenue by a credit.

(5)

Cash on Hand	xxx	
Accounts Receivable		xxx

This entry records the collection of cash from a customer who at an earlier time purchased merchandise from us "on account."

(6)

Cash on Hand	1,200	
Marketable Securities		1,000
Gain on Sale of Marketable Securities		200

We sell for $1,200 securities that cost us $1,000, and we realize a gain of $200 (which is shown as a credit because the gain constitutes an increase in the owner's equity).

(7)

Cash on Hand	800	
Loss on Sale of Marketable Securities	200	
Marketable Securities		1,000

We sell for $800 some securities that cost us $1,000, and we incur a loss of $200 (which is shown as a debit because the loss constitutes a decrease in the owner's equity).

(8)

Cash on Hand	3,000	
Allowance for Depreciation	6,000	
Retirement Loss	1,000	
Machinery		10,000

We sell for $3,000 machinery that some time ago cost us $10,000 but has been depreciated down to $4,000, and our apparent loss is the $1,000. Note that the accumulated depreciation over the years had been recorded in a contra account (as an offset to the machinery account); and when we dispose of the machinery, our contra account must be reduced along with the reduction of the machinery account. (We'll spend more time on this later.)

(9)

Cash in Bank	xxx	
Cash on Hand		xxx

To record a bank deposit.

CASH DISBURSEMENT TRANSACTIONS

Although statistical evidence of cash disbursement transactions is hard to find, it is likely that the bulk of all purchases of merchandise, raw materials, supplies, and services made by business firms are made on credit—that is, on account. As a matter of fact, when the company employs the so-called *voucher system* in formal fashion, even its cash purchases are recorded initially as if they were on account; this means that, at least theoretically, every cash disbursement is a payoff of an account payable. To illustrate, assume that our company buys $100 of merchandise for cash. The entry in journal form would be:

Merchandise	100	
Cash in Bank		100

But if the voucher system is in operation, this entry would be recorded in two steps, first as the assumed incurrence of an account payable when title to merchandise is received:

(1)

Merchandise	100	
Vouchers Payable		100

Second, the follow-up entry eliminates the account payable (voucher payable) by a debit, with a corresponding credit to Cash in Bank.

(2)

Vouchers Payable	100	
Cash in Bank		100

Two observations are pertinent at this point. First, good business practice dictates that *every* disbursement be made by check. This assures us of a formal record of the payment. Second, a voucher is *any document* that serves as evidence of a given transaction. Thus, if every check we issue is documented by an invoice (bill) or other piece of documentary evidence, we are likely to be in pretty good shape when the auditors come around to check up on our records. As documentary support of a cash disbursement, a voucher consists of one or more business forms detailing the transaction, and at some point, as a rule, some or all of the forms may bear signatures of vendors, officers of our company, or other parties. Such signatures constitute authorization for the issuance of a check. The use of the voucher system (with disbursements by check only) constitutes part of what is known as a system of *internal check and control*. We'll further develop this later.

To repeat. Under a strict voucher system, *since every payment is preceded by the setting up of a liability* (which may be a very temporary one) called *vouchers payable*, the only account that can be debited when we make a credit to Cash in Bank is Vouchers Payable.

In the absence of a voucher system, we will, of course, have credits to Cash in Bank accompanied by debits to whatever thing or service was acquired for cash. Thus, in addition to debits to Merchandise, we might make cash purchases of materials (debit Raw Materials), public utility services (debit Heat, Light, and Power), labor services (debit Labor Services), and so on. Also, we might have cash payments for dividends, interest, income taxes, or the payment of long-term debt. In each case Cash in Bank would be credited and the appropriate account (Dividends, Interest, Income Taxes, Bonds Payable) debited.

MARKETABLE SECURITIES

Only four transactions with respect to marketable securities are common. They are (1) purchase, (2) collection of interest and dividends, (3) resale at a gain or loss, and (4) end-of-period markdown to reflect loss of value. These may be illustrated in simple journal entries as follows (with assumed amounts):

(1)

Marketable Securities—Cost	12,000	
Vouchers Payable		12,000

We purchase nonspeculative, marketable securities to be paid for out of excess of cash currently on hand during a lull in business activity and to build up a fund for payment of income taxes at a later date.

(2)

Cash	600	
Interest Revenue		400
Dividends Revenue		200

To record receipt of interest and dividends earned on marketable securities.

(3)

Cash	9,300	
Marketable Securities—Cost		8,750
Gain on Sale of Marketable		550
Securities		

To record sale, for $9,300, of securities that cost $8,750.

(4)

Loss from Decline in Value of	400	
Marketable Securities		
Marketable Securities—Cost		400

Entry made at end of accounting period so balance sheet will show marketable securities at the lower of their cost or their current market value, per accounting convention of conservatism.

ACCOUNTS RECEIVABLE

Only three transactions commonly involve accounts receivable: (1) their origination at time of sale, (2) collection, and (3) charge-offs when found uncollectible. To illustrate each of these, observe the following:

(1)

Accounts Receivable	10,000	
Sales Revenue		10,000

To record our sales of merchandise for given dates, all subject to terms 2/10, n/30.

In the explanation to entry (1), note the terms, 2/10, n/30. This simply means that a 2 percent discount will be allowed if the bill is paid within 10 days and that in any case the whole bill is due within 30 days. Such terms vary. Thus, we could have 3/10, 2/30, n/60, which means the *face* of the bill is "net" if the customer waits more than 30 days but the net amount is 3 percent smaller if the bill is paid within 10 days and is 2 percent smaller if paid between 10 and 30 days from the date of the invoice (bill).

(2)

Cash	89,000	
Sale Discounts	1,000	
Accounts Receivable		90,000

To record collections from customers of invoices totaling $90,000 face, less discounts totaling $1,000.

With respect to the elements of entry (2), note that we have collected $1,000 less than the amount originally charged to the customers. Since the original charge was recorded by a debit to Accounts Receivable and a credit to Sales Revenue of $90,000, we must now reduce the recorded revenue by $1,000 because we are permitting the customers to pay off this debt *in full* by remitting only $89,000. In other words, when we sell goods or services with the understanding that the customer can take a cash discount if he pays, say, within 10 days, our initial recording of sales revenue (at gross) must be revised if we collect a smaller amount. We could simply debit Sales Revenue for the $1,000; but for purposes of keeping management informed on the amount of discounts the customers are actually taking, it may be better to make the debit to a contra account, Sales Discounts, which is treated as a subtraction from Sales in our income statement.

In Chapter 4, one of the end-of-period adjusting entries that was used for illustration showed how we recognize the probability that some accounts receivable will turn out to be uncollectible. To refresh your memory, the adjusting entry shown there was:

Uncollectible Accounts Expense	850	
Allowance for Uncollectible Accounts		850

As was explained, the "allowance" constitutes an estimated blanket offset to Accounts Receivable—a substitute for making a credit directly to Accounts Receivable—at a time when you are sure some of the receivables will not pay off but you don't yet know which ones. You can't make a direct credit to the receivables; therefore, you employ the bookkeeping trick of using a contra account.

Now let's assume that, after the lapse of a few weeks, we become certain that John Doe, who owes us $150, will never pay his bill. This means that $150 of the $850 is now identifiable with a specific account receivable, so we can transfer $150 from the blanket contra account to the credit side of Accounts Receivable. Our entry is:

Allowance for Uncollectible Accounts	150	
Accounts Receivable		150

The balance of the allowance account now stands at $700, which means that we expect to have additional write-offs of approximately $700 from sales made in the past period.

INVENTORIES

The routine transactions involving inventory items (such as merchandise, raw materials, work in process, and finished goods) consist of their acquisition (by purchase or by manufacture) and their consumption (by sale or by internal usage). Following are illustrative entries:

(1)

Merchandise Inventory	xxx
Accounts Payable	xxx

To record purchase of merchandise.

(2)

Raw Materials	xxx
Accounts Payable	xxx

To record purchase of raw materials.

(3)

Supplies	xxx
Accounts Payable	xxx

To record purchases of supplies.

(4)

Cost of Goods Sold	xxx
Merchandise Inventory	xxx

A physical inventory of goods remaining on hand is taken in order to determine the cost of goods that have been sold.

(5)

Work in Process	xxx
Raw Materials	xxx

To record cost of raw materials requisitioned for processing into finished goods.

(6)

Work in Process	xxx
Factory Labor	xxx

To transfer cost of factory labor into the account representing the cost of making finished goods.

(7)

Work in Process	xxx
Manufacturing Overhead	xxx

To transfer miscellaneous manufacturing costs into the account representing the cost of making finished goods.

(8)

Finished Goods   xxx
    Work in Process   xxx

To transfer from the work in process account to the finished goods account the cost of goods actually
    finished this period.

(9)

Cost of Goods Sold   xxx
    Finished Goods   xxx

To recognize the cost of finished goods that have been sold during the period.

PREPAYMENTS

To round out the accounts that make up the current asset sector of working
capital, we must mention various kinds of prepayments.

In general, prepayments (commonly called *prepaid expenses*) consist of amounts that have been paid in advance to suppliers of services.
The most common examples are prepaid insurance, prepaid rent, and prepaid property taxes. Under normal circumstances, only two common
transactions affect the prepayment accounts: (1) the payment made in
advance and (2) the amortization of the prepayment as it expires. To save
space and your time, the first of these will be illustrated in a single
bundle.

(1)

Prepaid Insurance   xxx
Prepaid Rent   xxx
Prepaid Property Taxes   xxx
    Cash in Bank   xxx

To record payments in advance for services to be received over various periods of time in the future.
    Entries made later to record the expiration of each of these follow.

(2)

Insurance Expense   xxx
    Prepaid Insurance   xxx

To record expiration of the portion of prepaid insurance allocable to past period.

(3)

Rent Expense   xxx
    Prepaid Rent   xxx

To record expiration of prepaid rent.

(4)

Property Tax Expense   xxx
    Prepaid Property Tax   xxx

To record expiration of prepaid property tax.

CURRENT LIABILITIES

The negative element in working capital is made up of all the current liabilities. Although the cash needed to pay the liabilities may not always be easy to find, the accounting entries for current liabilities present no significant difficulties. Examples are:

(1)

Merchandise   xxx
Raw Materials   xxx
Telephone Expenses   xxx
    Accounts Payable   xxx

To record amounts owed for purchases of merchandise, materials, and telephone services.

(2)

Accounts Payable   xxx
    Cash in Bank   xxx

To record payment of accounts payable.

(3)

Interest Expense   xxx
    Interest Payable   xxx

To record amount of interest payable as of end of period.

(4)

Labor Services   xxx
    Wages (Payroll) Payable   xxx

To record liability for unpaid wages as of end of accounting period.

(5)

Dividends   xxx
    Dividends Payable   xxx

To record the declaration of a dividend to be paid on (date).

Entries to record payment of each of the illustrated current liabilities are the same—simply debit the liability account (to show that you are reducing it) and credit Cash in Bank.

These examples do not by any means exhaust the possible kinds of current liabilities; however, you should have no trouble in applying the same pattern of entries to any other current liabilities that come to your attention.

WHAT CAN YOUR ACCOUNTANTS DO FOR YOU?

So far in this chapter we have really been doing nothing more than drill on the technique of depicting a transaction in journal entry form. By now you should begin to feel more or less at home with the notion of debit and credit.

Essentially, what we have done so far is study the procedure followed in recording *historical events*. This is the accountant's data-storage function, and by no means should it be sneered at. In order to know how much cash you have in the bank, you must keep some kind of record; in order to be able to send bills, you must keep accounting records of your customer's purchases and payments; in order to keep track of merchandise, raw materials, and other inventories, you need a record of your purchases; and you must either keep perpetual inventory records or take periodic physical inventories. All of this the accountant takes for granted, and it's done in the regular course of business.

On the other hand, your accounting staff should stand ready to supply you with special-purpose studies and reports whenever you need them, as well as with other reports of a more or less routine nature. We'll hope to tick off quite a number of such reports as we progress from chapter to chapter. They should give you a fairly good acquaintance with the things your accounting staff is capable of doing to assist you in the performance of your managerial functions; on the other hand, *you should never make the mistake of relying solely on accounting information when making a decision that should actually rest on information from additional sources as well. Such a mistake is altogether too common in business practice.*

Two examples of routine accounting schedules that commonly prove useful to management are the cash budget and the accounts receivable aging schedule. A brief section will now be devoted to each.

THE BUDGET

While this is by no means intended to be a book on corporation finance, it is inevitable that certain aspects of financial management will crop up as we progress from one aspect of accounting to another.

A budget stands midway between the accounting function and the financial management function in an enterprise. Usually you would expect the accountants to perform the actual task of *compiling* the budget. If, however, your company is large enough to have any job specialization whatsoever, the raw data that are to be fed into the budget must come from a variety of sources (including, for example, the treasurer, the sales manager, the production manager, and all others who are in a position to have a significant influence on financial affairs). Often the budgeting process is performed by a budget committee, which may begin its work 3 months or more before the start of the year for which the budget is being prepare.

Let there be no misunderstanding—*budgeting is absolutely essential to the welfare of the enterprise.* In case you don't share that enthusiasm for budgets, contemplate the following quotation from someone unknown: "Not to budget is not to plan." Do you believe in planning?

Budgets take various forms and are often prepared in segments prior to being brought together to form a "comprehensive" budget. One very important segment is the cash budget, which we'll now explain.

THE CASH BUDGET

The portion of the comprehensive budget that "plans" the *outflows, inflows,* and *balances* of cash as it stands at various points throughout the period is covered by the cash budget. Opinions vary as to the most satisfactory budget period, but in one I scheme, which perhaps is the most popular, fairly detailed plans for a full year are developed in advance and the budget schedule shows the flows and balances for each month. Visualize a 13-column schedule with a column for each of the 12 months and a thirteenth column for aggregates and planned end-of-year balance.

The generalized form of the budget schedule is the essence of simplicity. If we assume a year starting on January 1, the first figure in the first column should be the amount of cash held at the beginning of the year; this is the opening balance. For budgeting purposes the opening balance includes both cash on hand and cash in bank.

Following the opening balance, we list the various sources from which we plan to receive cash during the month of January and also list the anticipated amount from each source. Naturally, we next list the planned amounts to be disbursed during January. Needless to say, the formula Opening Balance + Receipts − Disbursements gives us a resulting end-of-month balance. This balance is, of course, automatically the start-of-month balance for February and the adding and subtracting process is repeated. So it goes throughout the 12-month period. The form of the cash budget is illustrated in Figure 5.1 for the first quarter of a year, with a total column appended.

Certainly an important reason for the *forward-looking* cash budget is to detect possible future cash stringencies and to make arrangements well

Figure 5.1   Cash Budget Form

PSEUDO CO.
Cash Budget, First Quarter, 20X1

	January	February	March	Summary
Cash balance, first of month	$ 5,000	$ 5,400	$10,165	$ 5,000
Cash receipts, routine:				
Collections on account	$28,000	$30,000	$27,000	$ 85,000
Cash sales	8,000	9,000	7,500	24,500
Miscellaneous	1,400	1,800	1,500	4,700
Total receipts	$37,400	$40,800	$36,000	$114,200
Total available (before financing)	$42,400	$46,200	$46,165	$119,200
Cash disbursements, routine:				
Payments for:				
Merchandise, materials,				
and supplies	$30,000	$20,000	$23,000	$ 73,000
Advertising	1,500	1,000	1,000	3,500
Utilities	300	350	350	1,000
Other outside services	1,200	1,200	1,200	3,600
Wages and salaries	6,000	6,000	6,000	18,000
Property taxes	—	—	2,000	2,000
Rent	500	500	500	1,500
Income taxes	—	—	3,500	3,500
Land purchase contract	1,000	1,000	1,000	3,000
Miscellaneous	1,500	950	550	3,000
Total disbursements	$42,000	$31,000	$39,100	$112,100
Minimum operating cash balance	5,000	5,000	5,000	—
Total cash requirement	$47,000	$36,000	$44,100	$ —
Anticipated cash excess or				
(deficiency)	$ (4,600)	$10,200	$ 2,065	$ —
Financing:				
Short-term bank loans	$ 5,000			$ 5,000
Loan repayments		$ (5,000)		(5,000)
Interest payments		(35)		(35)
Total financing	$ 5,000	$ (5,035)	$ —	$ (35)
Cash balance, end of month	$ 5,400	$10,165	$ 7,065	$ 7,065

ahead of time for coping with such shortcomings. Bankers insist on copies of up-to-date financial statements, which they will want to analyze carefully before agreeing to make a loan, but nothing is more useful than a detailed cash budget that shows the proposed loan, as a cash receipt within a given month, and then proceeds to show the repayment of the loan with interest, on schedule, among the disbursements of one or more later months. You will note that both a borrowing and a repaying transaction are illustrated in Figure 5.1, along with the routine cash flows, in and out, from collections as well as various types of payments. Note also that the schedule has a line for minimum operating cash balance. Such a balance may be formally decided upon by your company, and its introduction in the budget schedule works out well mechanically if it is added to the disbursements. (Money set aside or held as reserve is, in a rather farfetched sense, a sort of internal disbursement.) This treatment complicates the schedule a bit, but it soon becomes routine.

COMMENTS ON CASH BUDGET ILLUSTRATION

Note first that the amounts used in our budget illustration are purely hypothetical. In your own situation you must be supplied with acceptable predictions (plans) of sales for each month and a calculation of probable cash flow resulting from cash sales and collections from sales that are made on account. Past experience, the market outlook, and *plans for improvement* go into the preparation of the budgeted figures. Similar considerations govern the various classes of disbursements. Isn't it amazing the number of newly formed businesses that fail before they ever get off the ground? If everyone who contemplates setting up in business could somehow be required to prepare in detail a comprehensive budget for the first year or two, and in rough form for the first five years, what a lot of business failures would be avoided simply because they would not be started in the first place! Wouldn't you agree that, in general, a profitable business is an asset to society because it puts together raw materials and labor and management and converts them into something of *greater value* to society? An unprofitable (loss) enterprise is a detriment to society because it consumes materials and labor but its output is worth *less* than the materials and labor consumed! The loss enterprise, in effect, wastes valuable resources. All hail the budget as a means of avoiding losses by planning in advance.

One more word about cash. It's very poor business practice to have too much of it around for too long. Unused cash is nonproductive and, worst of all, it actually shrinks in value as that old bugaboo *inflation* eats its way into our economy. If the general price level goes up 9 percent in a year, it means that any cash that we've held throughout that year has lost approximately

9 percent of its power to buy goods and services. Also, claims to cash (accounts receivable) suffer the same shrinkage as does cash itself. So it's of real importance that we plan our cash flows in such a way as to minimize any cash balances in excess of current working capital needs. Obviously, the cash budget is a prime tool in accomplishing this aim.

CONTROL OF RECEIVABLES

As we progress in this book, we should be able to present new topics with lesser amounts of introductory explanation because you are accumulating a fundamental understanding of the rituals and concepts of accounting. You should soon need only to see a journal entry or an accounting report in order to understand it with minimal explanation.

Let's try this approach with another valuable accounting schedule, the widely used accounts receivable aging schedule. As in all cases, the scope, detail, etc., must be adapted to the size and complexity of your company, but whether your accounting system is operated strictly by pen and ink or is thoroughly computerized, an aging schedule is a great device for control of receivables.

The accounts receivable aging schedule lists the name of each customer and, in a series of columns after the name, shows (1) the total amount owed you and (2) a breakdown of that amount in terms of the length of time it has been owing. Space at the right-hand end of the schedule may be provided for comments, which may include references to communications with the customer, recommendations for actions to be taken, etc. In very abbreviated form such a schedule is shown in Figure 5.2.

COMMENTS ON AGING SCHEDULE

If the company is small enough for such attention, the aging schedule may be useful in providing management with details that lead to managerial (or legal) action with respect to individual customers. In all situations the column totals should prove useful in determining the quality of the accounts receivable total. What portion is in the older categories and at risk of becoming uncollectible? Are the proportions in the older, or more recent, categories changing for the better or for the worse? Should credit terms and credit pressure be modified? Is our present allowance for bad debts adequate? The schedule is commonly used to check out those questions by making estimates of the portion of each column total that is likely to be uncollectible. For example, we might derive the schedule shown in Figure 5.3 from the details shown in the aging schedule.

The aging schedule can be prepared as often as necessary to assist the credit or other manager to "keep on top" of the accounts receivable situation.

Figure 5.2   Accounts Receivable Aging Schedule

PSEUDO CO. CUSTOMER ACCOUNTS
Aging Schedule,
March 31, 20XX

Customer (or number)	Present balance	Under 31	31–60	61–90	91–180	181–360	Comment
A. A. Adams	$ 100	$ 100					
B. B. Black	50			$ 50			
C. A. Cream	70	30	$ 20	20			Paid in full on April 10
D. C. Duke	150					$ 150	Can't locate customer
Z. A. Zohn	220	220					
Totals	$58,120	$27,000	$16,700	$7,000	$5,400	$2,000	
Percentage of total	100%	47%	28%	12%	9%	4%	

Figure 5.3   Bad Debt Allowance Prepared from Aging Schedule

Test of Adequacy of Bad Debt Allowance
March 31, 20XX

Age group, days	Total	Estimated uncollectible, %	Estimates
1–30	$27,000	1	$ 270
31–60	16,700	3	500
61–90	7,000	5	350
91–180	5,400	10	540
180–1 year	2,000	50	1,000
Total	$58,100		$2,660
Present allowance			$1,600
Addition needed			$1,060

TEST PROBLEM

In the space provided for your solution, make simple journal entries to record the following transactions, all of which involve working capital items:

1. Sales of merchandise for $500 cash
2. Sales of merchandise for $600 on account
3. Collection of $196 from customers after allowing $4 of sales discount
4. Borrowing $5,000 from the bank by giving a 90-day, 8 percent note payable
5. Payment of the note in (4) at maturity
6. Sale, for $800 cash, of a machine which originally cost $2,000 and on which we have so far recorded (accrued) depreciation of $1,100
7. Provision for $500 of estimated bad debts
8. Write-off of an account receivable, $120
9. Recognition of end-of-year merchandise cost of goods sold based on opening inventory of $1,000, purchases of $10,000, and final inventory of $2,000
10. Recognition of insurance expiration of $300

TEST PROBLEM SOLUTION SPACE

Entry Number   Debits   Credits

(1)

(2)

(3)

(4)

(5)

(6)

(7)

(8)

(9)

(10)

6

STATEMENT OF CASH FLOWS

CASH RECEIPTS AND DISBURSEMENT STATEMENT

We might call the statement of cash flows "the club person's delight." Every club, society, and fraternity has a treasurer of sorts, and the financial report, be it presented monthly, quarterly, semiannually, or annually, consists of nothing more than a statement of cash receipts and disbursements. In this chapter we hope to start with a quick look at such a statement and then work upstairs to the technical details of such a statement.

Essentially, a statement of cash flows, not too surprisingly, consists of two offsetting lists: (1) the amounts of cash received (receipts), showing the sources in as much detail as is desired, and (2) the amounts disbursed, again in whatever detail is called for. The difference between list 1 and list 2 equals the net increase or decrease in cash during the period covered by the statement. Mechanically, if we show the opening (beginning-of-period) balance of cash at the top of the page and then enter the two lists, one below the other, so that their difference can be computed, the difference is shown as an addition to, or subtraction from, the opening balance to give us the final balance (as of the close of the period covered by the report). In the truest sense of the term, this describes a cash flow statement. By major types of events and transactions, it is designed to show what brought about the change in the cash balance during the period.

Without concerning ourselves with the amounts or the captions, we see the basic structure of a true cash flow statement in Figure 6.1.

Figure 6.1 Basic Structure of a Cash Flow Statement

JONES BIKE AND HIKE CLUB
Cash Flow Statement for the Summer of 20XX

Cash balance at beginning of season		$ 25.17
Cash receipts:		
Dues (see schedule 1* for details)	$175.50	
Picnic lunches sold	87.28	$262.78
Cash disbursements:		
Food (see schedule 2* for details)	$ 75.45	
Park rentals (see schedule 3* for details)	60.00	
Band-aid adhesive bandages	2.00	137.45
Net increase in cash		125.33
Cash balance at end of season (before banquet)†		$150.50

*These schedules are on file at your treasurer's house.
†The amount of $150.50 is now on deposit in the County Savings Bank.

Let's make a few observations by reference to the cash flow statement:

1. As far as the Jones Bike and Hike Club is concerned, the statement really serves two purposes: It gives a complete summary of the cash activities of the club for the season (prior to the banquet!). Anyone who really wants the complete details can visit the treasurer's house and examine the supporting schedules (or proofs). Also, because of the simplicity of the operations, the statement probably serves as an income statement (unless some dues are yet to be collected).
2. The form, or formula, of the funds flow statement could be used to depict the "flow" of any other balance sheet item. Thus, one might prepare an inventory flow schedule or a marketable securities flow schedule or an accounts receivable flow schedule; the possibilities are virtually limitless.

Now, let's take leave of the Bike and Hike Club and think again in terms of a modern business enterprise. Should the report to stockholders include a cash flow statement that shows every penny collected from every source and every penny spent for whatever purpose? Should the report also include flow statements for receivables, inventories, and all the other assets? In general, the answer is no. Such reports may, in truth, be of service to various levels of management, but to the inactive stockholder (and the general public) this kind of information could be overwhelming and of very limited use.

However, the accounting profession has concluded that cash flow information, by broad categories of inflows and outflows, is important to stockholders and creditors in making investing and lending decisions; therefore, a cash flow statement must be presented in the annual report as a major third statement, along with the balance sheet and income statement.

MAJOR SOURCES AND USES OF CASH

What are the major sources and uses of cash? Cash flows in and out of the entity are due to three major activities: investing, financing, and operating activities. Accordingly, the statement of cash flows will be divided among operating activities, investing activities, and financing activities. Once all of these changes are combined, the net increase or decrease due to these activities is added to (or deducted from) the opening balance to arrive at the cash balance at the end of the period (see Figure 6.11).

Investing activities normally are those concerned with changes in noncurrent assets. When you acquire land, buildings, machinery, or any other noncurrent asset, these are investing activities. Such assets are normally acquired by the use of cash (cash flows out) which has been borrowed on a long-term basis, generated by operations, or obtained through the issuance of common or preferred stock. If you dispose of such assets, cash often flows in. Such dispositions are part of investing activities, in a broad sense, but might better be called disinvestment activities. In any case, notice once again that cash is impacted, in the same direction and in the same amount, and therefore would be shown in the statement of cash flows.

Financing activities usually are those concerned with changes in long-term liabilities, preferred stock and common stock. When these securities are issued, normally cash flows in (cash is increased). On the other hand, cash is frequently used (cash is decreased) by a business when it buys back some of its bonds, for example, or preferred or common stock.

"FUNDS" PROVIDED BY OPERATIONS

Operating activities include all earnings-related activities of producing and selling goods and services to customers. For income statement proposes, all such activities are reflected on an accrual basis of accounting, as you learned in earlier chapters. Thus, net income is measured on an accrual basis of accounting.

In this chapter, we want to convert net income from an accrual to a cash basis in order to obtain *cash flow from operations*. In other words, we want to include all the cash inflows and outflows entering into the determination of net income, while excluding all those things affecting the determination of net income that do not affect cash.

Let's start by considering an easy illustration: Simple Company began operations on 1/1/1. Simple Company was indeed simple. All sales were for cash, and all expenses were immediately paid in cash. Simple Company operates in a no-tax economy and rents the building and equipment it needs on an operating lease basis. It sells all the inventory it buys. It obtained the cash for operations by issuing no-par common stock on 1/2/1 for $300,000. The company had no other transactions during year 1 other than operating transactions. Comparative balance sheets and the income statement for year 1 are shown in Figures 6.2 and 6.3.

Obviously, cash increased by $500,000 during the year, and so did working capital. What caused these increases? First, common stock was issued for $300,000 cash—a financing activity. Working capital also increased $300,000. Second, operations provided a net cash inflow of $200,000 since all sales of $1,000,000 were for cash, and all expenses of $800,000 were paid in cash. Note that net working capital also increased

Figure 6.2   Year 1 Comparative Balance Sheets

	SIMPLE COMPANY Comparative Balance Sheets	
	At 12/31/20X1	**At 12/31/20X0**
Current assets:		
Cash	$500,000	–0–
Noncurrent assets:	–0–	–0–
	$500,000	–0–
Current liabilities:	–0–	–0–
Noncurrent liabilities:	–0–	–0–
Stockholders' equity:		
Balance, January 1	–0–	–0–
Stock issued 1/2/1	$300,000	–0–
Retained Earnings	200,000	–0–
	$500,000	–0–

Figure 6.3

SIMPLE COMPANY	
Income Statement for the Year Ended 12/31/20X1	
Sales revenue	$1,000,000
Operating expenses	800,000
Net income	$ 200,000

$200,000. If we prepare both types of "funds" statements, they would be identical except for a few differences in terminology, as shown in Figure 6.4.

Now, let's make a slight, but important, change in the preceding illustration. Assume everything remains the same except that $75,000 of the sales were made on credit rather than for cash, and that the resulting accounts receivable had not been collected by 12/31/20XX. Comparative balance sheets and the income statement for year 1 would then be as shown in Figures 6.5 and 6.6.

Let's analyze the situation: During the year, the business had $1 million of sales on an accrual basis, but $925,000 ($1 million − $75,000) on a cash basis. During the year, cash increased $425,000: ($300,000 from the issuance of stock) and $125,000 (net income of $200,000 − $75,000 ending accounts receivable balance). In a word, you must convert net income from and accrual to a cash basis to obtain cash flow from operations. The statement of cash flows would now look as shown in Figure 6.7.

Figure 6.4

SIMPLE COMPANY	
Statement of Cash Flows	
for the Year Ended 12/31/X1	
Sources of cash:	
Operations	$200,000
Issuance of common stock	300,000
Total sources of cash	$500,000
Uses of cash:	
To increase cash balance	$500,000

Figure 6.5 Amended Comparative Balance Sheets

SIMPLE COMPANY
Comparative Balance Sheets

	At 12/31/20X1	At 12/31/20X0
Current assets:		
Cash	$425,000	–0–
Accounts receivable	75,000	–0–
Total current assets	$500,000	–0–
Noncurrent assets:	–0–	–0–
	$500,000	–0–
Current liabilities:	–0–	–0–
Noncurrent liabilities:	–0–	–0–
Stockholders' equity:		
Balance, January 1	–0–	–0–
Stock issued 1/2/1	$300,000	–0–
Retained earnings	200,000	–0–
	$500,000	–0–

Let's expand the illustration a bit more, by assuming the following:

Net income for 20X2:

Sales revenue	$1,500,000
Operating expenses	900,000 (includes depreciation expense of $100,000)
Net income	$ 600,000

All other operating expenses were paid in cash.

Accounts receivable:

12/31/1	$ 75,000
12/31/2	$ 125,000

Figure 6.6 Amended Income Statement

SIMPLE COMPANY
Income Statement for the Year Ended 12/31/2000

Sales revenue	$1,000,000
Operating expenses	800,000
Net income	$ 200,000

Figure 6.7

SIMPLE COMPANY
Statement of Cash Flows
for the Year Ended 12/31/20X1

Cash flows from operating activities:		
Net income	$200,000	
Deduct: Increase in accounts receivable balance	75,000	
Cash flow from operations		$125,000
Cash flows from financing activities:		
Issuance of common stock		300,000
Total cash flows		$425,000
Add: Beginning cash balance		–0–
Ending cash balance		$425,000

What would cash provided by operations be for the year 20X2? The $75,000 resulted from sales on account during 20X1, but which was collected in cash during 20X2. Therefore, net income on a cash basis for 20X2 is $75,000 higher than on an accrual basis, so the $75,000 must be added to the net income of $600,000. The $125,000 resulted from sales made on a credit basis during 20X2, but the cash will not be collected until 20X3. Consequently, net income on an accrual basis is $125,000 higher than on a cash basis, and therefore the $125,000 must be deducted from net income to arrive at cash flow from operations for 20X2. Since cash is not impacted by depreciation, $100,000 must be added to net income to determine cash provided by operations for 20X2. A summary of cash flows provided by operations follows in Figure 6.8.

Figure 6.8   Cash Flows Provided by Operations for 20X2

Cash Flow		
Net income		$600,000
Add: Depreciation	$ 100,000	
Deduct: Increase in accounts receivable	(50,000)	
		50,000
Cash flow from operations		$650,000

Of course, when expenses are converted from an accrual to a cash basis, the impact goes the opposite direction in terms of converting net income to cash flow from operations.

Assume the same facts as in the preceding illustration, but add the following balance sheet accounts:

Wages payable 12/31/20X1	$65,000
Wages payable 12/31/20X2	$85,000

When must the wages payable amount of $65,000 have come into existence? The answer is sometime during 20X1 when wages expense was increased (debited). When would the $65,000 have been paid? Answer: In early 20X2. Consequently, cash outflow for wages was $65000 higher in 20X2 than wages expense on an accrual basis. Keeping this in mind, it is easy to see that the $65,000 would have to be deducted from net income to convert to cash flow from operations.

The opposite is true, of course, for the ending of the year balance in wages payable of $85,000. The $85,000 was debited to wages expense and credited to wages payable sometime in 20X2, probably late in the year, and therefore impacted net income on an accrual basis in 20X2. However, the $85,000 will not be paid (no cash outflow) until 20X3; that is, it will not reduce net cash inflow from operations until 20X3. Therefore, wages expense is higher on an accrual basis than on a cash basis and would have to therefore be added to net income to convert to cash flow from operations.

Note, finally, that wages payable is a working capital item, so no additions or deductions to net income would be necessary to derive working capital provided by operations. The "funds" provided by operations section would now appear as shown in Figure 6.9.

The question remains: Which balance sheet account balances must be used to convert net income to cash flow from operations? Although there

Figure 6.9   Cash Flows Provided by Operations for 20XX × 2

Cash Flow		
Net income		$600,000
Add: Depreciation	$100,000	
Increase in wages payable	20,000	
Deduct: Increase in accounts receivable	(50,000)	
		70,000
Cash flow from operations		$670,000

are some exceptions, the answer is current assets [accounts receivable (net), inventories, and prepayments] and current liabilities (accounts payable, wages payable, interest payable, taxes payable, etc.).

You have probably noted a pattern in converting net income to cash flow from operations. You add the beginning balances in current asset

Figure 6.10   Year 3 Comparative Balance Sheets

COMPLEX CORPORATION
Comparative Balance Sheets

	At 12/31/3	At 12/31/2
Current assets		
Cash	$ 255,000	$765,000
Accounts receivable (net)	95,000	75,000
Merchandise inventory	96,000	150,000
Total current assets	$ 446,000	$990,000
Noncurrent assets		
Buildings (net of accumulated depreciation of $40,000)	$1,870,000	$ –0–
Machinery (net of accumulated depreciation of $50,000)	450,000	–0–
Total noncurrent assets	$2,320,000	$ –0–
	$2,766,000	$990,000
Current liabilities		
Accounts payable	$ 35,000	$ 50,000
Wages payable	45,000	40,000
Income taxes payable	50,000	–0–
Total current liabilities	$ 130,000	$ 90,000
Noncurrent liabilities		
Bonds payable	$ 620,000	–0–
Total liabilities	$ 750,000	$ 90,000
Stockholders' equity		
Common stock–no par	$1,100,000	$300,000
Retained earnings	916,000	600,000
Total stockholders' equity	$2,016,000	$900,000
	$2,766,000	$990,000

accounts and deduct the ending balances (or, if you prefer, add the decrease in current asset account balances, and deduct the increase). For current liabilities, the opposite is true—deduct the beginning balances and add the ending balances (or, again, if you prefer, deduct the decrease in current liability account balances, and add the increase). Lastly, should there be a sale of property, plant, and equipment at a gain or loss, the entire proceeds from the sale should be accounted for solely as an investing activity. However, the gain or loss component of the sale has an impact on net income. Therefore, the gain or loss must be removed from net income in the operating activity section of the cash flows statement (i.e., all gains must be subtracted from net income and all losses must be added to net income).

EXTENDED EXAMPLE

You are now ready for a somewhat more complex example: Assume Complex Corporation, during 20XX × 3, used some of the cash it had generated in past years, borrowed $620,000 on long-term bonds issued at par, issued additional no-par common stock for $800,000, and used most of the money to acquire buildings and machinery. Complex Corporation determined it was less expensive to do this than to continue to lease assets. All of these events took place on 1/1/3. Figures 6.10 and 6.11 are comparative

Figure 6.11   Year 3 Income Statement

COMPLEX CORPORATION		
Income Statement for the Year Ended 12/31/3		
Sales revenue		$1,700,000
Operating expenses:		
Cost of goods sold expense	$ 900,000	
Wages expense	250,000	
Insurance expense	20,000	
Depreciation expense	90,000	1,260,000
Operating Income		$ 440,000
Non-operating expense—interest		24,000
Income before taxes		$ 416,000
Tax expense		100,000
Net Income		$ 316,000

Figure 6.12   Year 3 Cash Flow Statement

COMPLEX CORPORATION
Statement of Cash Flows
for the Year Ended 12/31/X3

Cash flows from operating activities:		
Net income		$ 316,000
Add: Depreciation expense		
($40,000 + 50,000)	$ 90,000	
Increase in wages payable	5,000	
Increase in income taxes payable	50,000	
Decrease in merchandise inventory	54,000	199,000
Deduct: increase in accounts receivable (net)	$ 20,000	
Decrease in accounts payable	15,000	(35,000)
Cash provided by operations		$ 480,000
Cash flows from investing activities:		
Acquisition of buildings		
($40,000 + $1,870,000)	$(1,910,000)	
Acquisition of machinery		
($50,000 + $450,000)	(500,000)	
Cash used by investing activities		(2,410,000)
Cash flows from financing activities:		
Issuance of bonds	$ 620,000	
Issuance of common stock	800,000	
Cash flows provided by financing activities:		1,420,000
Net decrease in cash flows		(510,000)
Cash balance—12/31/2		765,000
Cash balance—12/31/3		$ 255,000

balance sheets and an income statement for year 3. Based on these data, the statement of cash flows would be as shown in Figure 6.12.

CERTAIN NONCASH ITEMS

One final note...the accounting profession feels there are certain events and transactions that could have such a material impact on the investing and lending activities of owners and creditors that their impacts should be reflected in the cash flow statement even though cash is not affected. These events and transactions encompass such things as exchanges of long-term assets, conversion of bonds payable to common stock, and the acquisition of noncurrent assets in direct exchange for bonds, preferred stock, or common stock issued. Obviously, these cannot be placed in the body of the cash flow statement, since cash is not impacted by them. Rather, they are reflected in footnote disclosure in the statement such as follows:

Conversion of bonds into common stock—$ 1,000,000
Exchange of buildings for land—$500,000
Acquisition of land in exchange for common stock—$750,000

TEST PROBLEM

The data in Figures 6.13 and 6.14 are from the accounting records of the Tipton Company, covering the calendar year 20X2. Some additional data about the Tipton Company include the following:

Cash dividends of $25,000 were paid in 20X2.
Plant was purchased in the amount of $50,000.
Land that cost $10,000 was sold for $15,000 cash.
Mortgage principal payments of $10,000 were made.
The increase in capital stock resulted from the issue of new shares for cash.

Figure 6.13 Year 2 Income Statement

Sales		$400,000
Gain on sale of land		5,000
Total income		405,000
Expenses		
Cost of goods sold	$220,000	
Selling and administrative	90,000	
Interest	4,000	
Taxes	23,000	
Net income		337,000
		$ 68,000

Figure 6.14   Year 2 Comparative Balance Sheets

	20XX × 1	20XX × 2
Cash	$ 20,000	$ 35,000
Accounts receivable (net)	25,000	20,000
Inventories	35,000	83,000
Total current assets	$ 80,000	$138,000
Equipment (after depreciation)	300,000	340,000
Land	20,000	10,000
Total assets	$400,000	$488,000
Liabilities & stockholders' equity		
Accounts payable	$ 25,000	$ 35,000
Wages payable	15,000	10,000
Total current liabilities	$ 40,000	$ 45,000
Mortgage payable	60,000	50,000
Capital stock	200,000	250,000
Retained earnings	100,000	143,000
Total liabilities &stockholders' equity	$400,000	$488,000

REQUIRED

Prepare a cash flow funds statement in accordance with Figure 6.12.

TEST PROBLEM SOLUTION SPACE

TIPTON COMPANY
Cash Flow Funds Statement
For The year Ended December 31, 20X2

7

INVENTORIES

WHAT ARE INVENTORIES?

The term *inventories*, like so many terms that we find in accounting, is widely used in ordinary conversation. It tends to refer to our "supply" of almost anything; thus, we might refer to our inventory of battleships or houses. Let's be more precise for accounting purposes; the best example of inventories is our stock of merchandise held for sale to customers, that is, our merchandise inventory (often referred to as our *stock in trade*). And if we're connected with a manufacturing company, the term embraces our raw materials, our semifinished goods (work in process, or "in progress"), and our finished goods. A dealer in marketable securities, such as stocks and bonds, would have a marketable securities inventory. Added to that, we generally allow the inclusion of various kinds of consumable supplies under the inventory heading. Supplies (not to be confused with *equipment*, which means more or less permanent assets) include auxiliary goods such as stationery, fuel, lumber, and repair parts. Technically, we should not include as inventories stores of lumber and building supplies that we may have purchased for use in the construction of our own buildings or manufacturing plant, because inventories are limited to the stocks of goods that qualify as current assets and are part of working capital. Public utility companies regularly err in their balance sheet presentation of construction materials and supplies by showing them as a current asset.

TYPICAL INVENTORY TRANSACTIONS

Without paying much attention to reasons or theory, let's now skim through a series of unrelated transactions represented in the form of simple journal entries. As in the series of journal entries presented in Chapter 5, no dollar amounts will be assumed in most cases because they would not be of significance to the illustrations.

(1)

Merchandise Inventory	1,000	
Accounts Payable		1,000

Purchase of merchandise at invoice price of $1,000, terms 2/10 eom.

The notation 2/10 eom means that if the account payable ($1,000) is paid within 10 days after the end of the month (eom), the buyer is granted a cash discount of 2 percent. Often you'll see terms such as 2/10, n/30 or 3/20, n/60. The first means that the bill is due in 30 days but the buyer can deduct 2 percent if he pays within 10 days from the date appearing on the invoice. The second is similar: 3 percent off if paid within 20 days; but if payment is delayed beyond 20 days, the face of the invoice becomes the net price. Thus, in the case of our $1,000 account payable, the net price is $980 until the tenth of the next month; after that, the net price becomes $1,000. When no discount is offered, the bill may merely bear the notation "terms net."

(2)

Accounts Payable	1,000	
Cash in Bank		980
Merchandise Discount		20

To record payment of account within 10 days after end of month to take advantage of cash discount.

How would you classify the account Merchandise Discount? Your logical conclusion should be that the credit constitutes a correction of the overstated $1,000 original debit to Merchandise. We recorded the purchase of merchandise at "gross," or $1,000. As things turned out, however, our cost of merchandise was only $980, so we could make a $20 credit directly to the merchandise account or (you guessed it) use a contra account to reflect the reduction in recorded cost. In the old days most accounting texts said, incorrectly, that a cash discount is a form of gain or revenue.

A better way to record the two transactions is to debit merchandise for the net amount initially and show accounts payable also at net. Surely under the terms of the purchase we owe only $980 until the tenth of the next month has passed. If you want to debate this point with your accountant, the proper "buzz words" are gross versus net. Barring some peculiar set of circumstances that make recording at net impractical, the net method is far superior, as the following entries show.

(1a)

Merchandise Inventory   980
   Accounts Payable   980

Purchase of merchandise at invoice price of $1,000 less 2% if paid by 10 eom.

(2a)

Accounts Payable   980
   Cash in Bank   980

Payment of invoice within discount period.

To add to your side of the argument, let's assume that payment of the bill is delayed until the discount period has expired. Then we must pay the entire $1,000, of which $20 is a penalty for waiting until the last minute. Under the net method, as the accounts will show, we now will pay off a debt that we recorded at $980 by giving up $1,000 for a loss of $20; let's label that loss Loss from Lapsed Discounts. The entry is:

(2b)

Accounts Payable   980
Loss from Lapsed Discounts   20
   Cash in Bank   1,000

Payment of invoice after expiration of the discount period.

Wouldn't you argue that the accounts should show discounts that have been lost through neglect rather than to emphasize, as the gross method does, the routine "taking" of cash discounts? Do you realize that with terms 2/10, n/30 the 2 percent amounts to an annual rate of 36 percent? (Payment 20 days earlier than necessary saves you 2 percent of the face of the bill. A 360-day year contains eighteen 20-day periods, and 18 times 2 percent is 36 percent.)

(3)

Accounts Payable   xxx
   Merchandise Returns and Allowances   xxx

To record returns of merchandise for credit and to record reductions in price (allowances) granted by the suppliers on goods found to be defective or not in accord with specifications.

(4)

Merchandise Inventory   xxx
   Accounts Payable   xxx

To record freight and transportation charges as an added cost of merchandise purchased.

(5)

Merchandise Inventory   27,000
Cost of Goods Sold   116,000
   Merchandise Inventory   143,000

To allocate cost of merchandise pool between goods left over (inventory) at the end of the period and the goods sold.

The amounts in (5) are determined by taking a physical inventory at the end of the period, finding its cost, and assigning the remainder of the total cost pool (opening inventory plus purchases) to Cost of Goods Sold. This is known as the physical, or periodic, inventory method. When we are dealing with items that are individually significant, we may use the continuous (or perpetual) inventory procedure. Then, each time that a sale is recorded, the corresponding cost of goods sold is recorded simultaneously.

(6)

| Supplies | xxx | |
| Accounts Payable | | xxx |

To record purchases of various kinds of supplies.

(7)

Selling Expenses	xxx	
Administrative Expenses	xxx	
Supplies		xxx

To record consumption of various kinds of supplies for various purposes as measured by amounts recorded on requisitions (underlying documents).

(8)

| Manufacturing Overhead | xxx | |
| Supplies | | xxx |

To record consumption of supplies by various factory departments, with the cost charged to Factory Overhead because it cannot be traced directly to units of product manufactured.

(9)

| Raw Materials | xxx | |
| Accounts Payable | | xxx |

Purchase of various kinds of raw materials for use in production in our factory.

(10)

| Work in Process | xxx | |
| Raw Materials | | xxx |

To record cost of raw materials used in production, as measured by amounts shown on requisitions issued and traceable directly to specific jobs in process.

(11)

Work in Process	xxx	
Payroll Payable		xxx
Manufacturing Overhead		xxx

To recognize direct labor and factory overhead costs chargeable to work in process.

(12)

Finished Goods	xxx	
Work in Process		xxx

To recognize cost of goods finished during the accounting period.

(13)

Cost of Goods Sold	xxx	
Finished Goods		xxx

To record the factory cost of goods sold during the period.

INVENTORY VALUATION

The values at which the inventories of merchandise, materials, work in process, finished goods, etc., are recorded have a dual significance in financial reporting. First, the amount shown in the balance sheet as a current asset is likely to be a significant working-capital component. Statement analysts may be expected to pay considerable attention to your working-capital position and special attention to the proportion of your current assets that consists of inventories. Thus, to the degree of choice that you have in reporting a valuation figure for your inventories, you will be in a position to influence the decisions of creditors and investors who look to your financial statements as a prime source of financial information. Second, and perhaps even more important, the accounting valuation that you place on your inventories directly affects the amount of net income for the period. Recall the following formula:

Inventory at start of period	xxx
Add: Cost of goods purchased (or manufactured)	xxx
Total goods available for sale	xxx
Less: Inventory at end of period	xxx
Cost of goods sold	xxx

Quite obviously, the amount shown as inventory at end of period directly affects the final amount, cost of goods sold. The greater the cost of goods sold, the less the net income. Or, to get right to the point, the greater the amount shown as ending inventory, the greater the net income, and the lower the ending inventory, the lower the net income.

The fact is that you do have substantial leeway in the valuation of your ending inventory, and the leeway is derived from the variety of choices available to you in your expressed assumption as to the manner in which the goods flow through your establishment. Let's examine the flow assumptions one by one, but first let's acknowledge one cardinal rule: Basic to all good accounting is the *rule of consistency*; we cannot shift back and forth from one flow assumption to another as suits our wishes or whims each year. This is a real handicap for those who want to manipulate the reported net income figures of their company.

SPECIFIC IDENTIFICATION METHOD

It is almost universally acknowledged that inventories should be reported at their cost (with due allowance for physical shrinkage, wear and tear, and shrinkage in value). If we acknowledge that cost is the appropriate target for inventory valuation, we may next ask, cost of what? The amount would seem to be the cost of the goods on hand. This is our inventory at any point in time. Many people overlook the fact that, carried to its logical conclusion, the expression "cost of the goods on hand" must mean the amount that we paid for the specific goods that remain unsold at the end of the period. Now, we may have bought several batches of certain items, and the prices that we paid per unit may have been different for each batch. Suppose at the end of the year we have on hand a few units from each batch. Because the units (though otherwise identical) cost different amounts, the identified cost concept requires that we inventory them at their respective costs. Thus, if we have on hand five units of material X and know that we paid $2 each for two of them, $3 each for two of them, and $4 for the fifth, our identified cost inventory of material X is $14.

Some people like to argue that it is perfectly ridiculous to list a series of identical items at different values. Yes, it would be ridiculous if our balance sheet was intended to show the current values of all our assets, but the balance sheet makes no such pretense. The general rule for nonmonetary assets is to record the assets at their cost. Under that view, the identified cost method is absolutely great except for one thing—it's usually not practical! Surely if you're a speculator in real estate, you can easily keep track of the cost of each lot, each house, or each farm that you buy, but it's just not feasible to identify the specific costs that attach to such things as specific gallons of gasoline, cubic feet of gas, pounds of flour, barrels of cement, or yards of cloth.

What do we do, then, when we want to apply the identified cost concept but find it totally impractical? Answer: We make a whopping big assumption as to the order in which the goods flow through our business and we "price" our inventory on the basis of our chosen flow assumption. Let's examine the popular assumptions.

FIRST-IN, FIRST-OUT

As a matter of physical fact, all goods, unless they are allowed to rot or rust in the storage bins, flow through the business in a first-in, first-out

(FIFO) procession. Of course, the flow is not perfect—some goods never become used or sold and are finally discarded or sold as scrap; some goods are slower moving than others. But the realistic assumption is that your raw materials, your supplies, your work in process, and your finished goods pass through your hands in an orderly FIFO parade. The oldest goods of a given category are constantly cleared from the shelves, and the inventory at any date may reliably be assumed to consist of the most recent purchases.

The FIFO assumption has no magic significance in itself; it is an assumption for the sake of convenience. It is a convenient way to simulate identified cost. Let's demonstrate the method by a simple example.

At the end of the year our company has 1,000 units of a particular item left over after starting with a beginning-of-year inventory of 800 and adding 9,000 that were purchased during the year. Clearly, a total of 8,800 have disappeared if we can now find only 1,000 of the 800 plus 9,000. If the 800 units on hand at the beginning of the year cost $1 each and we bought the 9,000 units in three batches of 3,000 each, costing $1.10, $1.20, and $1.40 per unit, what is the FIFO cost of the 1,000 in the final inventory? The answer is 1,000 at $1.40, the invoice price of the most recent purchase. The cost of goods sold is then assumed to be the difference between $1,400 (1,000 at $1.40) and the grand total cost ($11,900) of all units to be accounted for, or $10,500. The details may be displayed in schedule form as follows:

	Units	Per Unit	Total
Initial inventory	800	$1.00	$ 800
Purchase 1	3,000	1.10	3,300
Purchase 2	3,000	1.20	3,600
Purchase 3	3,000	1.40	4,200
Total to be accounted for			$11,900
Final inventory at FIFO	1,000	1.40	1,400
Cost of goods sold (or used)			$10,500

If it had been feasible to mark the cost on each unit as we purchased it, we could have totaled up the costs of the 1,000 left over at the end by examining each one and running an adding machine tape to get the total. But if we followed good housekeeping practice during the year, the likelihood is strong that almost all of the 1,000 remaining on hand at year-end came from purchase 3. And note this: If our assumption creates no significant error, we should employ it rather than go through the clerical process of marking and identifying each item as if it were an important individual.

WHAT ARE INVENTORY PROFITS AND HOLDING GAINS?

In a great many articles, the authors point out that net income is often affected significantly by the fact that the replacement costs and the selling prices of goods may rise (or fall) while the goods are being held in stock by the company. Such a development, so it is argued, creates holding gains or, as they are more commonly termed, inventory profits. The concept is more elusive than you might think. Let's dive into it with a mini-example.

Our company buys one unit of an item for $100, wholesale, when the retail price is $130. This specific item is not sold until later when the wholesale price has risen to $120 and, obediently, the retail price has gone to $156 (30 percent over cost). By traditional accounting, on a strict cost basis, our company would show a gross margin of $56 on the sale ($156 − $100) which, of course, would be offset in the determination of net income by various operating expenses and taxes. The point is that $20 of the gross margin (and a corresponding portion of the net income) could be attributed solely to the wholesale and retail price rises that occurred while we were "holding" the item. From this phenomenon have evolved three distinct schools of accounting thought. Let's take a look.

The Holding Gain School

One crowd says that holding gains are quite different from "trading" gains, which are the result of normal buy-and-sell transactions. (Trading gains are deemed to represent the fruits of managerial effectiveness—they are the real "operating" gains.) Our income statements should divide the gross margin into two parts: (1) holding gain and (2) trading gain. In our example, this school would report the gross margin as follows:

Sales	$156
Cost of goods sold, on replacement-cost basis	120
Gross trading margin	$ 36
Add: Given holding gain ($120 − $100)	20
Gross margin	$ 56

The Inventory Profits School

Another crowd says that inventory profits are illusory. To them the real cost of goods sold is not the identified (or FIFO) historical cost of the goods sold but, rather, the current, or near-current, replacement cost as measured by the amounts we have actually paid most recently for identical goods. To illustrate this notion, we must make an added assumption: that our company did buy a second item for $118 not long before it sold the first one. This group does not want to abandon the hallowed historical cost principle;

so as a substitute for the current $120 replacement cost employed by the holding gain school, cost of goods sold is calculated as being made up of the actual cost(s) of the goods most recently purchased. In other words, these folks would avoid the need for showing holding gain (which they consider to be a mirage) by making the highly artificial assumption that we didn't really sell the old $100 item—what we actually sold was the latest one we bought, the $118 item. This assumption is the reverse of FIFO and is known as LIFO (last-in, first-out). It really should be known as artificial LIFO because, actually, goods don't flow through a company in that cockeyed order. In our example, the anti-inventory profits (LIFO) school would report their gross margin as follows:

Sales	$156
Cost of goods sold, on LIFO basis	118
Gross margin	$ 38

The Identified Cost School

Now let's get back to basics. Most businesses are constantly buying, fabricating, and selling goods. Under the most common circumstances the stock of goods is maintained at minimum levels (to minimize costs of storage, protection, interest on investment, deterioration, and obsolescence); in other words, most enterprises are in business to trade, in the normal sense of the word, rather than to speculate on price increases. Fluctuations, up and down, in wholesale and retail prices are part of the economic environment, and there seems to be little reason for undertaking the complicated bookkeeping procedures that would be required to determine with any precision the amount of gross margin that is caused by holding gains. Nor would the reporting of such information often be of any real service to the statement analyst; on the other hand, it is totally wrong to deny that such gains have occurred and to repress their recognition (by use of LIFO). The identified cost group, then, would report as follows:

Sales	$156
Cost of goods sold, on FIFO basis	100
Gross margin	$ 56

Commentary

Now that you've had a glimpse at three interesting schools, perhaps you could be convinced that the third would be best *if those who use it would only adjust their historical dollar costs to reflect changes in the value of our measuring unit—the dollar.* Unfortunately, we must delay full explanation of the problem of our shaky dollar until later. Please, therefore, keep in mind the italicized words in the preceding sentence.

LAST-IN, FIRST-OUT

Although LIFO (Last-in, First-out) was touched upon in the preceding section, it's much too prominent in current usage to be dropped so quickly. The LIFO inventory valuation procedure is acceptable for income tax purposes and has widespread endorsement. We must at least scan the highlights of LIFO.

During periods of persistent inflation (which seems to be almost constant), our costs and selling prices tend to rise in parallel fashion. As was demonstrated in the preceding section in simplified form, use of the FIFO flow assumption, realistic as it may be, matches costs that may have been incurred days, weeks, or months ago against revenues from current sales— simply because, for each sale that is made, the accountant checks off against that sale the cost of the unit of inventory that has been on the shelves for the longest time. The result is a gross margin determination that includes the full amount of holding gain (or, as we'll see later, the illusory gain from deterioration of the purchasing power of our currency).

LIFO, on the other hand, artificially assumes that the oldest goods remain on the shelves (forever?). In fact, some refer to LIFO as FINO— first-in, never-out! If, for example, our company begins to use LIFO at a time when it has on hand 100 tons of steel that cost $500 per ton and if its ending inventory of steel for the next 20 or more years never goes below 100 tons, on its balance sheet for every one of those years the same 100 tons at $500 will be included in the inventory.

In its favor, it may be admitted that LIFO tends to suppress recognition of illusory gains from inflation. At best, however, it does so in a makeshift fashion, since prices of steel and other specific commodities do not move in concert with changes in the purchasing power of the dollar. Strongly in favor of LIFO is the possibility of stalling off payment of income tax on illusory gains, since LIFO is an allowable procedure for income tax purpose.

In very strong opposition to LIFO is the fact that the FINO inventory figures, which appear as current assets in the balance sheet, are farcical.

Let's look at one more example. Assume that a newly formed company makes the following purchases of a given item during its first year of existence:

Date	Quantity	Price per Unit	Amount
Jan. 1	1,000	$2.00	$ 2,000
Feb. 10	3,000	2.40	7,200
June 15	4,000	3.00	12,000
Nov. 5	3,500	3.50	12,250
Totals	11,500		$33,450

Assume also that sales of this item during the period, when price varied from $3.00 to $4.50 per unit, amounted to $40,000 and that on hand on

December 31 there remain 1,500 unsold units. First, let's see what our gross margin would be if we used FIFO.

Following is the FIFO schedule.

Sales		$40,000
Cost of goods sold:		
Purchases	$33,450	
Inventory, December 31 (1,500 @ $3.50)	5,250	28,200
Gross margin		$11,800

Next, the same schedule shows the gross margin if LIFO is employed.

Sales		$40,000
Cost of goods sold:		
Purchases	$33,450	
Inventory, December 31 (1,000 @ $2 + 500 @ $2.40)	3,200	30,250
Gross margin		$ 9,750

As you should recognize, the LIFO procedure shows $2,050 less gross margin. The difference is equal to the difference in the amount assigned to the 1,500 units of closing inventory. Under LIFO procedure the 1,500 units will constitute the beginning inventory for the following year at the same $3,200 valuation, and the same units and same value could, theoretically, remain in the financial statements for all time. FIFO procedure, on the other hand, tends to provide inventory costs that are continuously up to date.

DOLLAR VALUE LIFO

It does not seem appropriate here to explore the intricacies of so-called dollar value LIFO, but the rationale should be noted. For companies that handle standard materials or standard merchandise year after year, the LIFO procedure that we have just scanned is entirely feasible. However, many companies, especially retail stores, have more or less constant changes in the variety of goods handled. LIFO would be of little use to them, since they are persistently "selling out" their complete stock of items that are dropped from their line. In short, as originally conceived, a somewhat limited number of taxpayers could employ LIFO and all others were in a true sense being discriminated against. To remedy the discrimination, dollar value LIFO was invented. Essentially, dollar value LIFO treats a complex variety of materials or merchandise as a pool of dollars rather than as a quantity of physical units. By use of a series of price index numbers, goods on hand at the end of each year are valued at costs which are translated into earlier years, with an end result that simulates LIFO on a physical unit basis.

AVERAGE COST

To round out the discussion of inventory valuation procedures, it must be noted that some companies value their ending inventories on a moving average cost basis. This may mean that, for each class of materials or merchandise, the cost of the purchases for the year is added to the cost of the opening inventory and the sum is divided by the corresponding total number of units to obtain an average unit cost. This average unit cost is then applied to the number of units remaining on hand at year-end to determine the dollar valuation of the ending inventory. Where continuous (perpetual) inventory procedure is used, the average cost per unit may be changed whenever a new batch of a given item is purchased, and then the final inventory is priced at the average cost in effect at the year's end. Needless to say, the use of an average cost procedure is bound to result in a cost of goods sold figure (and a gross margin) that lies somewhere in between the corresponding amounts resulting from FIFO and LIFO.

COST OR MARKET, THE LOWER

Let's face it. Businessmen in general, and almost all accountants, are conservative in their financial affairs. An old-time guiding principle of accounting goes somewhat as follows: Recognize all losses, anticipate no gains. As translated, this means, "Write assets down and liabilities up, whenever any glimmer of doubt appears, but don't ever acknowledge any gain until it has been unquestionably realized in the form of cash (or claim-to-cash) proceeds." We could debate the doctrine of conservatism for hours, but that would be inappropriate here. Rather, as we pass from one area to another, we'll simply take note of the implications of conservatism as they are reflected in the current "generally accepted" practice.

As a prime example of accounting (and business) conservatism, it is generally assumed that inventories, unless valued at LIFO, must be valued at the lower of cost or market. The bulletin that prescribes the rules for determining the valuation is too technically complex for our detailed consideration. In simplified terms, however, the rule boils down to a requirement that if the goods on hand at the end of the period could be replaced (in customary quantities and through customary channels) at prices that are lower than those that were actually paid, the recorded costs of the goods on hand should be written down to their replacement costs (and a corresponding loss shown). The theory is that if your buying price for goods has dropped, it is likely that your resale price for the goods will drop also. Many comments (not all flattering) could be made about this rule, but one point stands out. If the replacement cost (market price) of goods has fallen, we must accrue a corresponding assumed loss; should the reverse occur—forget it! It should be added that income tax rules do not permit the use of cost or market if the taxpayer is "on LIFO."

INVENTORY TURNOVER

One of the relationships that financial analysts frequently use in appraising the financial quality of a firm is the ratio of the cost of goods on hand (inventory) to the cost of goods sold for an entire year. If, for example, the company now has on hand goods inventoried at $20,000 and the cost of all goods sold during the past year was $240,000, the ratio of 20 to 240 (1 to 12) indicates that the company's inventory approximates the needs for a month's sales. The relationship may be reported as a "30-day supply" (since accountants usually assume a 360-day year for ease in quoting such approximate relationships), or the term *turnover* may be used. In our example, the evidence indicates an inventory turnover rate of 12 times per year. Turnover is computed by dividing cost of goods sold for the year by the amount of inventory at year-end or, better, by the average of the initial and ending inventories (or even by the average of the inventory quantities at the ends of all 12 months). In general, of course, the higher the turnover rate the better.

If a company can operate successfully with a 10- or 20-day inventory, this means less funds tied up in merchandise and materials and, accordingly, lower costs. Needless to say, one important function of management is to seek and maintain optimum inventory levels. Overstocking means excessive interest costs, obsolescence, and high storage costs; understocking leads to loss of customers and loss of sales. The buzz word for understocking is "outages," and our current crop of management scientists delight in seeking to measure the cost of outages.

INVENTORY REPORTS FOR MANAGEMENT

If perpetual inventory records are kept or if inventory records are computerized, accountants should be able to keep management currently apprised of the firm's inventory position not only in terms of inventory totals but also in reports of significant over- or understock of specific items that are important to the welfare of the company. Quite a bit of research has been done by the operations research (OR) folks with respect to inventory management, including, for example, the development of formulas for determining the optimum quantity of goods to be purchased at a time.

GROSS PROFIT (OR GROSS MARGIN) METHOD OF INVENTORY ESTIMATION

There are certain times when it might be important to determine an approximation of inventory evaluation even though it might be highly impractical, if not impossible, to make an exact determination. One example of such a situation might occur if part or all of the inventory is destroyed by casualty or theft, leading to an insurance claim for the damaged inventory. Another example might occur if a determination needs to be made in order to prepare financial statements during the accounting period for purposes of obtaining a loan, or reporting interim financial statements in compliance with government mandate. One of the more common methods employed in making such an estimation is known as the gross profit method. This method relies on the determination of a reasonable "gross profit percentage", based on prior periods and any extenuating circumstances that might lead to an adjustment of historic gross profit percentages for this particular period. Once this percentage has been determined, the net sales for the period are determined based on the company's books and records to date. If we assume net sales for the period of $1,000,000 and a gross profit percentage of 40%, it then follows that the cost of goods sold would be the inverse percentage of the gross profit percentage, or 60%. Our books and records should also indicate the total amount of merchandise purchased during the period. Adding this figure to last period's ending inventory (found simply by perusing last period's financial statements) gives us the cost of goods available for sale. Obviously, the difference between the cost of goods sold and the cost of goods available for sale would be the cost of goods *not* sold, that is, the ending inventory amount.

EXAMPLE

Acme Inc.'s entire inventory was destroyed by hurricane on August 15, 20XX. Net sales for the current period were $1,000,000 and it has been determined that a reasonable estimation of gross profit for Acme was 40%. Multiplying the cost of goods sold percentage to the net sales figure yields an estimation of $600,000 for cost of goods sold. It has also been determined that merchandise purchases for the period were $400,000. Therefore, it follows that if last period's inventory was $300,000, then the total cost of goods available for sale was $700,000 ($400,000 purchased this period plus $300,000 left over from last period). If it is estimated that the cost of goods sold was $600,000, then the cost of goods *not* sold should be $100,000 ($700,000 available for sale − $600,000 actually sold).

TEST PROBLEM

On January 1 the raw materials inventory of a company, valued at FIFO cost, is $12,000; it consists of 20,000 pounds of material. The company buys 25,000 pounds at 80 cents per pound on January 10 (terms 2/10, n/30) and pays for them on January 19; the company buys 20,000 pounds at 90 cents per pound on January 20, under the same terms, and pays for them on January 31. All raw material purchases are recorded at net prices. Perpetual inventory records show a balance of 22,000 pounds of the material on hand on January 31.

REQUIRED

In simple journal form, record the purchases, the payments, and the usage during January with respect to the raw materials.

TEST PROBLEM SOLUTION SPACE

	Debit	Credit
January 10		
January 19		
January 20		
January 31		

8

PROPERTY, PLANT, AND EQUIPMENT AND DEPRECIATION

CLASSES OF NONCURRENT (LONG-TERM) ASSETS

In a very broad sense, accountants divide assets into two major groups: current and noncurrent. By tradition the noncurrent assets have come to be termed *long-term assets.*

In the noncurrent category, five principal subdivisions stand out. A corporation, a partnership, or a person, for that matter, may acquire the capital stock, bonds, notes receivable, or mortgages issued by other companies or persons, and the intent may be to hold the "securities" for a considerable period of time for their investment value—that is, for the interest and dividends or possible value growth that will be obtained. In contrast with purchases of marketable securities for the short-term employment of temporarily excessive cash funds, these securities are *long-term investments*, and they are properly classified as long-term assets in the balance sheet. Because we will be looking at these same securities from the standpoint of their issuers later, we will give them no special consideration in this chapter.

A second major category of long-term assets consists of all types of *natural resources*. Most commonly in this category we think of the land on which our buildings rest (site land), but this group also includes agricultural land, mining land, rights-of-way, etc. For most companies these assets present no major accounting problems, and we'll touch on them only lightly in this chapter.

The third category includes all types of *depreciable structures*, of which buildings constitute the principal subgroup. We'll concern ourselves with the questions of the valuation of structures when they're first acquired and as they age.

The fourth category consists of *machinery and equipment* of all types. As with structures, we'll be concerned with both the initial and the subsequent valuation of items in this group.

The fifth category is made up of all kinds of so-called *intangible assets*. It is very difficult to concoct a satisfactory accounting definition of intangibles because, for example, both accounts receivable and cash in bank are intangible but neither is included within the technical accounting category of intangibles. The best way out seems to be just to list the things that accountants usually classify as intangibles. They are goodwill, patents, trademarks, trade names, franchises, secret processes, and, possibly, leaseholds and long-term prepayments. You may think of others. In any case, we'll devote no more time to this category here but will take a closer look at goodwill at a later point in the book. Essentially, then, this chapter will be concerned with the initial and subsequent valuations of structures, machinery, and equipment, commonly referred to as "property, plant, and equipment."

INITIAL VALUATION OF PROPERTY, PLANT, AND EQUIPMENT

There tends to be very little disagreement as to the proper initial accounting for depreciable and nondepreciable fixed assets of all types. "Cost" has almost universal acceptance. (A few accountants believe that there may be numerous instances in which the buyer either clearly outwits the seller or is obviously outwitted and that accounting recognition should immediately be made of the implied gain or loss in the act of making the purchase. The vast majority of accountants rebel at that idea and prefer to let any "purchase gain" or "purchase loss" show up in the subsequent disposition of the asset.)

The determination of acquisition cost can be tricky sometimes. The easiest case, of course, is when we buy land, buildings, or equipment for cash (or by a down payment plus a mortgage or installment purchase contract). Be sure to include ("capitalize") all costs of acquisition up to the point at which the asset is *in place and ready for use*. Costs that should be capitalized include transportation, installation, and break-in, as well as basic construction costs when the company builds its own structures or equipment.

A more difficult determination of acquisition cost arises in the less common situation in which we issue capital stock to someone in exchange for an asset or a "basket of assets." In these days of intensive merger activity, it is not at all unusual for one company to acquire the "net assets" of another company by giving the other company an agreed-upon number of shares of capital stock. Two questions present themselves: (1) What actually is the *cost* to us of the assets that we acquire in this fashion (whether we get a basketful or a single asset)? (2) How do we allocate the total cost of the entire group of assets to the individual assets that make up the group? The usual (and apparently sound) accounting answers to these questions may be stated quite briefly. First, when capital stock is issued in the acquisition of assets, the assets should be recorded at the current market value of the capital stock that is being given and assign the same value to the assets that were acquired. If current market value of the stock is not ascertainable, an acceptable alternative is to value the assets acquired at their estimated *current market values* (with due allowance, of course, for their physical condition). The answer to the second question is that once the aggregate cost of a group (basket) of assets is known, the cost should be allocated to the component elements of the group in proportion to their respective market, or appraised, values.

The final acquisition deal for us to consider is the one in which we trade in an old asset on a new one—that is, a barter transaction in which, usually, we must give cash to boot. Here it is a great temptation to argue that the cost of the new asset is equal to the amount of cash (or future cash) we give plus the book value of the old asset traded in. Thus, if we trade an automobile that originally cost us $12,000, which we have depreciated down to a book value of $4,000, and if we give cash or notes payable to boot of $18,000, the cost of the new asset would be recorded at $22,000. That may be appropriate for income tax purposes, but it's poor accounting theory. Our real cost is the amount of cash paid ($18,000) plus the *current market value* (rather than our book value) of the asset traded in. If we assume the asset traded in had a current market value of $2,500, the correct cost of the new asset is $20,500. Many folks go astray in this same situation by being overly impressed by the list price of the new automobile. We all know that list prices are not to be taken very seriously. Thus, if the new car had a list price of $20,000, another wrong recording of the trade-in would be the following:

Loss on trade-in	2,000	
Automobile (new-at list price)	20,000	
Allowance for Depreciation (old)	8,000	
Cash in Bank		18,000
Automobile (old)		12,000

This concludes our discussion of the initial valuation of fixed assets. In every transaction, you are bound to encounter special circumstances that present difficulties. We have touched upon the major high points, and we hope that you'll be able to resolve the unique problems of each situation as they arise. Next we take a look at some of the alternatives with respect to asset valuation subsequent to acquisition.

HISTORICAL COST LESS DEPRECIATION

Accountants have strongly favored carrying property, plant and equipment on the books and on the financial statements at their historical dollar cost as adjusted for the amount of depreciation that has been recognized. In favor of this position is the ever-present affection that accountants have for "objectivity." They like to present figures that can be audited and confirmed. They also like to avoid estimates and appraisals as much as they can, because these tend to be "subjective" valuations subject to bias and manipulation which may be detrimental to the interests of investors and creditors. Further, they favor historical cost because, they say, profit is earned only as we make use of our assets and match (depreciate) their cost against the amounts (revenues) that we generate for their use. In other words, business profits are made through the current operations of the business, and not by the purchase of assets at a bargain or by the subsequent (assumed) increases in the values of the assets (most of which are no more than reflections of inflation). Many accountants who favor historical cost believe that cost should be restated in terms of the current value of the measuring unit—the dollar. We'll spend a whole chapter on this interesting subject later. Nothing has been so thoroughly neglected by accountants as the undeniable fact that our measuring unit has been changing in size by anywhere from 1 to over 20 percent each year (always shrinking) and that it is simply ridiculous to add together dollars of different vintages and treat them as if all of them had the same meaning.

REPLACEMENT COST

Practicing accountants have traditionally shown little enthusiasm for making formal recognition of appraised values for long-term assets in the accounts and financial statements. Admittedly, some knowledge of current values of the long-term assets of a business is important internally for purposes of getting adequate insurance coverage, and such information may be of considerable interest if property is the basis for rate regulation or is to be mortgaged in connection with a loan or bond issue. There are those (for example, the theoretical economists) who argue that the true income for any period is best defined as the difference between the amount of the net assets at the beginning and end of the period. (Net assets, to repeat, is the expression for the amount found by subtracting total liabilities from total assets—a difference frequently termed net worth.) The economists would, of course, require that the assets be recognized at their current values for their purposes in determining the net assets. Again we are faced with the question of recognizing holding gains as the fixed assets (which we intend never to sell) fluctuate in value. Many accountants have strongly resisted the notion that appraisal (versus historical cost) valuations be displayed even in the form of footnotes to the formal statements. Let's note some of their arguments against deviation from historical cost.

First, it would be quite costly to employ appraisers as often as once a year to supply us with their "educated" estimates of the current replacement costs of our properties.

Second, the basic definition of current value is most elusive: Does it mean replacement cost? Do we mean the *literal reproduction* of our existing buildings and machinery by using the same building materials, the same hand labor, the same building methods, etc? Or do we mean the cost of buying, in the present market, closely similar assets that will provide the same amount of service as the assets we are now using and with due allowance for the amount of depreciation that our assets have sustained to date? Or do we mean the amount for which we could sell the asset now? Needless to say, this question presents very major complexities.

Third, if we were to report the long-term assets in our balance sheet at their replacement values, would our investors have a significantly better basis for estimating the value of their company? Or does the *value of the company* depend more heavily on the effectiveness and excellence of the management?

Fourth, if we were to make the necessary adjustments for recognition of the change in the value of our monetary unit, wouldn't that pretty well solve the problem? It can be argued quite successfully that reproducible fixed assets never, or at least rarely, increase in true value, although their cost, restated in dollars of current purchasing power, is very much subject to change. In other words, true holding gains, even if we wanted to recognize them, are likely to be quite immaterial when allowance is first made for deterioration of the monetary unit.

Possibly a good compromise between historical and current costs would be to agree to recognize changed long-term asset values when and if it becomes perfectly obvious that some very substantial value changes have occurred—to the point at which the company should be asking itself if it might be better to dispose of certain assets in order to realize the big gains rather than continue to employ the assets in the business. It is quite probable that such value changes would almost never be called for except in rare cases when the company's land had undergone dramatic value increase. However, should a long-term asset lose a significant part of its revenue-generating potential before the projected end of its useful life, it might be necessary to reduce its carrying value (book value less accumulated depreciation). This process is known as *asset impairment*, and is an excellent example of the application of conservatism in financial reporting. Asset impairment analyses should be done on a periodic basis to determine whether the present value of future cash flows from the asset is less than the asset's carrying value. The reduction in carrying value would be reported as a loss on the income statement.

DEPRECIATION OF PROPERTY, PLANT, AND EQUIPMENT

Any formula for the computation of depreciation must make use of at least four factors: asset cost, useful life, probable terminal salvage, and timing of service extraction. It's sad, but true, that every one of those factors presents difficulties (in many cases absolute impossibility) of accurate measurement. Nevertheless, we must recognize depreciation. Because of the vast amount of uncertainty, a lot of different methods of measuring depreciation have been proposed, and it would seem quite important for any executive to have a nodding acquaintance with the more common procedures and to be on guard against being misled by the numerous false impressions that so many people have with respect to the accounting for depreciation.

WHAT IS DEPRECIATION?

Depreciation is the exhaustion of the useful service potential of an asset through the combined effects of utilization, wear and tear, aging, and obsolescence. The first three of those factors tend to cause the asset to deteriorate physically, and obsolescence means the loss of usefulness from all other causes. For example, the asset becomes obsolete because it is no longer large enough for our needs (our first computer), our competitors have acquired a more efficient machine and we must replace ours in order to match their reduced costs of production, or the output of our equipment has gone out of style. Depreciation does not include breakage or other casualty loss; these are losses rather than depreciation.

Accounting for depreciation consists of making accounting entries to recognize, with reasonable accuracy and in dollar amounts, the depreciation cost that should be assigned in each accounting period. Every depreciable asset has its *depreciable cost*, which means original cost minus the amount we expect to get for the asset when we retire it—the so-called salvage. If an asset costs $100 and we predict that we will use it for 4 years and then sell it secondhand for $20, the depreciable cost is $80 so far as we are concerned. So accounting depreciation boils down to this. Assuming use of historical cost of a given asset (or collection of assets), we must have a record of the cost, we must make an estimate (or assumption) as to the prospective terminal salvage (which, subtracted from the cost gives us the *depreciable cost*), we must make an estimate (or assumption) as to the useful life (i.e., how long the asset will be useful to *us*), and we must then determine the most *appropriate pattern* to be followed in the allocation of the depreciable cost to the individual accounting periods making up the useful life of the asset or collection of assets.

DEPRECIATION PATTERNS

Four general patterns are possible in the allocation of depreciable cost to the periods of useful life. One pattern assumes that each period realizes the same benefit from the asset and, accordingly, should bear the same depreciation charge. This pattern, logically enough, is termed straight-line depreciation. At the opposite extreme, one may predict that the utilization of the asset will vary in uneven fashion from year to year and that, instead of a *straight line*, we should contemplate use of a pattern of charges best depicted by a wavy line. This leaves only two other realistic choices. One is based on the assumption that most assets perform most effectively when new and that their effectiveness declines more or less continuously as they age, so that a decreasing line (to represent decreasing charges per period) may be appropriate. Lastly, in certain rare cases an increasing line may be chosen. From here on this chapter will be devoted to the respective merits and shortcomings of the various depreciation line assumptions.

STRAIGHT-LINE DEPRECIATION

The periodic straight-line depreciation accrual is determined by dividing the depreciable cost of the asset by the number of accounting periods contained in the estimated useful life of the asset. Depreciable cost, as defined earlier, is the total cost of the asset minus the expected net salvage. Gross salvage is the total amount that we hope to recover from the asset at the time of its final retirement and disposition; net salvage is gross salvage less any costs that are incurred in the process of obtaining the gross salvage. For example, in the razing of a structure we might plan to recover used bricks worth a total of $500 (gross salvage); but if the probable labor cost of razing the structure is $400, then the net salvage, to be used in the straight-line depreciation calculation, is only $100.

Straight-line is by far the most popular depreciation method used by American industry; oddly enough, such popularity is not really warranted. It has only two arguments going for it, and neither is laudable. First, it's the simplest method, and this may be true. To work a problem in straight-line depreciation would perhaps require education in arithmetic through the second grade in school, whereas the other popular methods might demand the higher mathematics covered in the third or fourth grade. Second, straight-line depreciation constitutes a compromise in a sea of uncertainty. We don't really know the useful life of an asset at time of acquisition and we don't know the pattern in which the asset's services will be extracted, so we make the unwarranted assumption that over the uncertain life the same amount of service will be extracted in each period.

On the other side, there are some fairly potent arguments against straight-line depreciation. First, assets typically perform most efficiently and productively when they are new; and if a given period receives the benefit of superior service, it should bear a correspondingly high depreciation charge. As the asset ages and performs less effectively, each period should receive a smaller depreciation charge. Certainly the straight-line pattern fails to match this performance picture. Compounding the inequity of straight-line depreciation charges is the typical pattern of repair and maintenance charges, which tend to increase perceptibly as the asset ages. So with straight-line depreciation we end up with increasing charges for decreasing services as time passes! A final argument against straight-line depreciation is a relative one. It is a less conservative method than certain others. It delays the expensing of the asset, and, if used for tax purposes, fails to capitalize on tax benefits that may possibly be derived from use of the accelerated depreciation methods allowed.

WAVY-LINE DEPRECIATION

A method of depreciation that results in a wavy line is commonly referred to as the *units of production method*. The formula is similar to straight-line except that the depreciable cost is divided not by the expected number of accounting periods in the asset's life, but by the total number of *units of output* that the asset is expected to render. Thus, in the case of a taxicab the depreciable cost might be divided by, say, 200,000 miles to obtain the estimated depreciation cost per mile. Then the total depreciated charge for a given accounting period would be found by multiplying the miles driven by the depreciation cost per mile. The production units method has considerable theoretical appeal. It is based on the sound premise that when you buy a depreciable fixed asset, you are acquiring a "bundle of services"; and it follows logically that, if the services are identical, one unit of depreciation occurs as each unit of service is detached from the bundle. For a useful analogy, think of the purchase for $100,000 of a mine that contains 100,000 tons of coal. As each ton of coal is extracted, the cost of the mine content remaining would naturally be expensed by $1. (The exhaustion of mines, oil and gas wells, etc., is called *depletion* rather than depreciation.) And so we find strong support for the units-of-production, wavy-line, method of booking depreciation *when the units of service output are identical and the total, original service-unit content can be ascertained within reasonable limits of accuracy.* The unfortunate fact is that industry has found relatively few situations in which those requirements can be met. It's virtually impossible to find a satisfactory definition of a service unit in the case of almost any structure, and it's even more difficult to make anything like a reliable estimate of the total number of service units that will be extracted from any piece of machinery. In short, the production units method has failed to gain widespread acceptance because of its apparent impracticability. In that respect it is similar to the specific identification method of valuing inventories, in which, as you will recall, accountants are prone to adopt flow assumptions that they believe satisfactorily *approximate* the realistic movement of goods. Something similar is done in the realm of depreciation when accountants adopt either a straight-line assumption or the decreasing-line assumption, which we are to examine next.

DECREASING-LINE DEPRECIATION

As we've noted repeatedly, most depreciable assets tend to turn out less and less service as they grow older. Such service deterioration may manifest itself in several ways. Some machines simply run slower and slower; some have more breakdowns and more downtime; most require more attention as they age—more maintenance and repair; and some get out of adjustment and cause more defective products as time passes. Few depreciable assets escape what we might term *service deterioration* as they age, and such deterioration shows up in different ways for different assets. Buildings used for offices, apartments, and other purposes lose their attractiveness as they cease to be "modern." In many ways, assets perform less satisfactorily as they get older; they may produce a reduced flow of services, or they may render an undiminished amount of service but at a higher operating cost, or the same physical service may have lower and lower market value. The old apartment house or the old motel, for example, provides just as much space for occupancy as when new, but the revenue (and net income) to the owner suffers because customers are attracted in fewer numbers and at reduced rents. This tendency, then, for a depreciable asset to render considerably more than half of its total service during the first half of its life strongly encourages the conclusion that the depreciation line, or curve, should have a downward slant. This is commonly known as *accelerated depreciation*.

There are two common plans for calculating the periodic depreciation charges under the accelerated concept. First is one that appears to be (and perhaps is) almost idiotic. It's called the *sum-of-years' digits* method. If an asset has a four-year life, you add the digits 1 through 4 (which equals 10) and your depreciation each year is found by applying a fraction, which consists of the numbers of years taken in reverse order over 10, to the depreciable cost of the asset. Assume that an asset costs $100 with an estimated life of four years and probably salvage of $10. Then the depreciation series for the four years would be: year 1, 4/10 of $90, or $36; year 2, 3/10 of $90, or $27; year 3, 2/10 of $90, or $18; year 4, 1/10 of $90, or $9, for a total of $90.

If you're unhappy with sum-of-years' digits, use the *declining-balance* method. In many cases, it allows you more depreciation earlier than is allowed under sum-of-years' digits. Again the calculation is easy: If an asset has a five-year life, the straight-line depreciation rate would be 20 percent each year applied to the initial cost of the asset minus its salvage. The (double) declining-balance method permits you to use *double the straight-line rate*, but the double rate is applied each year to the amount remaining in the asset account, and no salvage value is fed into the calculation. If we apply the declining-balance method to the $100 asset used in the preceding paragraph, the succession of depreciation charges will be: year 1, 40 percent of $100, or $40; year 2, 40 percent of ($100 − $40), or $24; year 3, 40 percent of ($60 − $24), or $14.40; year 4, 40 percent of ($36 − 14.40), or $8.64, for a total of $87.04. Note that under no circumstances should the total accumulated depreciation reduce the balance below its estimated salvage value of $10. The relative amounts recorded under the two plans are as follows (SYD = sum-of-years' digits plan; DB = declining-balance plan.)

Year	SYD	DB
1	$36.00	$40.00
2	27.00	24.00
3	18.00	14.40
4	9.00	8.64
Total depreciation	$90.00	$87.04

COMPOSITE AND GROUP DEPRECIATION

In spite of the availability of computerized depreciation accounting, common practice is to apply a single straight-line depreciation rate to all of a firm's assets or to subdivide the assets into related collections and apply an appropriate rate to each collection. Such procedure is known as *composite depreciation*, and the rates are supposed to be determined for each collection of assets by an averaging process.

Group depreciation is similar to composite depreciation except that, under group depreciation, the assets are classified into closely related groups in which, for example, each asset in a group has the same approximate useful life. The selected depreciation rate for the group then depends on the probable mortality of the component units within the group. Thus, one might apply group depreciation to all of the utility poles owned by a public utility company and, although the useful lives might range from 8 to 20 years, the average life used to determine the group rate would depend on the shape of the expected retirement curve for the poles.

One important characteristic of composite and group depreciation plans is that no loss or gain is recognized when a given member of the collection is retired. The reason is that the depreciation rate employed rests on the assumption that some of the assets will be retired sooner than average and some later than average—all to come out even in the long run.

TYPICAL DEPRECIATION ENTRIES

Some of the most common entries involving depreciation accounts are shown in the following illustrations:

(1)

Depreciation Expense	xxx	
Accumulated Depreciation		xxx

To record periodic depreciation by any method.

(2)

Accumulated Depreciation	900	
Cash	200	
Retirement Loss	400	
Machinery		1,500

To record sale of machinery in secondhand market for $200 when book value is $1,500 − $900, or $600, for a loss of $400.

(3)

Accumulated Depreciation	900	
Cash	800	
Machinery		1,500
Retirement Gain		200

To record the sale of machinery in secondhand market for $800 when book value is $600, for a gain of $200.

(4)

Accumulated Depreciation	1,300	
Cash	200	
Machinery		1,500

To record sale of machinery in secondhand market for $200 with no gain or loss recognized, since the machinery is being depreciated by composite plan.

(5)

Accumulated Depreciation	700	
Cash	800	
Machinery		1,500

To record sale of machinery in secondhand market for $800 with no gain or loss recognized, since the machinery is being depreciated by composite plan.

A CAVEAT

In spite of the arguments, pro and con, for using one method of depreciation for book purposes rather than another, many businesses generally, and most small business in particular, elect to use the same method for book purposes that they use on their tax return. This approach not only is simpler and less costly, eliminating the need to keep two sets of records for depreciation, it also avoids the major differences giving rise to an income tax allocation problem, as we discuss in that chapter.

CHANGE OF DEPRECIATION ESTIMATES

The amount of depreciation to be taken is based on two basic assumptions. First, the useful life of the asset must be estimated, and secondly, the asset's residual value, or salvage value, at the end of its useful life. Sometimes, during the course of the asset's depreciable life, it becomes apparent that one or both of these assumptions are incorrect. Perhaps technological innovation will materially curtail the asset's useful life and/or residual value, or unanticipated increased (or decreased) use of the asset may necessitate a change in the original estimate(s). Should such an event occur, the correct accounting treatment would *not* be to go back and restate depreciation for prior accounting periods, but rather to account for these new estimates on a prospective basis. This is done by first ascertaining the asset's *remaining* depreciable cost and applying the *new* remaining useful life and/or residual value. An example follows:

    X Co. purchased a piece of equipment two years ago for $50,000. Originally, it was estimated that the asset would have a 10-year useful life, and a $5,000 residual value. Straight line depreciation had been taken for the last two years. Now it has been determined that the equipment will not last more than five years with a residual value of $1,000. In order to calculate the new annual depreciation expense, the remaining depreciable cost must be determined. This is done by reducing the original cost of $50,000 by total accumulated depreciation to date. The original depreciable cost of $45,000 ($50,000 − $5,000 original residual value) was divided by 10 years to arrive at an annual depreciation expense of $4,500. Since the equipment was purchased two years ago, total depreciation already taken amounts to $9,000 ($4,500 × 2). Therefore, the *remaining* cost of the asset is $41,000 ($50,000 − $9,000). The next step is to reduce the remaining cost by the new estimated residual value in order to determine the remaining *depreciable cost*, and then dividing it by the remaining useful life of the asset. Since the new estimated residual value is $1,000, it follows that the remaining depreciable cost of the asset is $40,000 ($41,000 − $1,000). By dividing the $40,000 by the five-year remaining useful life, the new annual depreciation expense of $8,000 may be taken beginning with the period of change and for all following accounting periods.

DEPRECIATION FALLACIES

Some companies persist in using the term *reserve for depreciation* in their financial statements; many are now using *accumulated depreciation*. The former title is fast disappearing because of its misleading nature. When it is used, it leads many people to assume that the company always has reserved an amount of cash equal to the amount shown as the reserve for depreciation. That is totally foolish, but it is too common to be ignored. Should there be any misgivings in your own mind, just assume that in your balance sheet you show an allowance, or reserve, for depreciation in the amount of $100,000 and that you actually do have exactly $100,000 in the cash accounts—so they do match. What, now, is the entry to record the purchase of $100,000 worth of merchandise for cash? Obviously, it's a debit to Merchandise and a credit to Cash in Bank—with the allowance for depreciation completely undisturbed even though your cash has gone down to zero.

One of the more hideous fallacies related to depreciation is that depreciation in some way is capable of generating cash, or funds. Probably most nonaccountants (who give the matter any thought) have this misunderstanding. Cash flows in from the sale of merchandise and the collections from customers, whether you show $1 of depreciation or $100,000. The amount of depreciation recorded has absolutely no effect on the amount of cash inflow. True, depreciation is deductible for tax purposes with the result that fewer tax dollars are paid out as more depreciation is deducted, but this is not what the mistaken people have in mind. If depreciation produces funds, one should find at least a few dimes lying under her car at the end of each day at the office! Certainly, if a firm has an oversupply of cash, and poor management, it may hoard an amount of cash each year equal to the recorded depreciation, but the depreciation does not create the cash in any way.

A third fallacy, which actually stems from the one just mentioned, is that depreciation does, or must, provide for the replacement of an asset. That is simply impossible. Depreciation is nothing more or less than the spreading, or allocation, of the cost of an asset over the asset's useful life. If you want to "provide" for the *replacement of an asset*, you must set aside in a sinking fund, or in a portfolio of investments, cash that you collect from your customers. But that has nothing to do with depreciation. To illustrate the point, if you record depreciation of a given asset as $10,000 per year and at the same time want to dedicate some cash to the future replacement of that asset, you must make two separate and unrelated entries each year as follows:

(1)

Depreciation	10,000	
Accumulated Depreciation		10,000

To record depreciation.

(2)

Asset Replacement Fund		
(bank account)	10,000	
Cash in Bank		10,000

TEST PROBLEM

At the beginning of a year Our Company buys a machine for $10,000 cash. The estimated useful life is five years, and probable salvage is $1,500. At the beginning of the fourth year, the machine is sold for $3,000.

REQUIRED

In simple journal form record the depreciation for each of the 3 years and record the sale. Use the straight-line method, the sum-of-years' digits method, and the double declining-balance method.

TEST PROBLEM SOLUTION SPACE

	Debit	Credit

Straight-line procedure:

        Year 1

        Year 2

        Year 3

        Year 4

Sum-of-years' digits method:

        Year 1

        Year 2

        Year 3

        Year 4

Double declining-balance method:

Year 1

Year 2

Year 3

Year 4

9

CORPORATION ACCOUNTS

WHAT IS UNIQUE ABOUT CORPORATION ACCOUNTING?

The unique aspects of corporation accounting rest entirely upon one characteristic—the manner in which the enterprise raises its capital. Neither the sole proprietorship nor the partnership issues capital stock, but the corporation does. Neither the sole proprietorship nor the partnership employs a surplus (retained earnings) account, but the corporation does. The unincorporated enterprises do not issue bonds, as the corporation does if necessary. The financial statements of a partnership or proprietorship are usually not made available to the general public, whereas a corporation that is listed on one of the stock exchanges, or that otherwise has the requisite characteristics, must publish its financial statements regularly and may be required to submit to annual audit by independent public accountants.

In spite of the fact that the corporate form of organization has certain drawbacks, such as being subject to income taxation, lawsuits, etc., it dominates the American financial scene, which includes several million corporations ranging from corner grocery stores, to large farms, to giant conglomerates, to even larger nonconglomerates such as General Motors, ExxonMobil, and AT&T. The principal reasons for popularity of the corporate form include the facts that the owner's liability is limited to the amount of the individual's investment, ownership interests are readily transferable, and the value of one's investment (in the case of "listed" securities) is readily determinable on a day-by-day basis.

In recent years the managers of corporations have surely taken full advantage of the powers to issue securities of all shapes and sizes. Indeed, the tendency to invent special classes of securities has created some tough problems for the accountants and the financial analysts. In this chapter we'll look at the major types, but by no means can we exhaust the arsenal.

THE ISSUE OF CAPITAL STOCK WITH PAR VALUE

Much of the power of the corporation rests on the provisions of the charter and bylaws. The charter may provide for the issuance of shares of stock that do, or do not, have a par value. As a matter of fact, par value means very little aside from the fact that it sets a minimum issuing price for the shares. State corporation laws, almost without exception, stipulate that shares with a par value may not be issued at a discount; that is, they may not be issued for consideration that has a value less than the par value of the stock. Many companies establish what amounts to a nominal par value for their stock, which may be issued for many times the par value. In other cases the par value of the capital stock may start out at, say, $10 or $100 and then, as the result of several stock "splits," be repeatedly reduced. It may even become an almost inconsequential part of the overall stockholders' equity of the company.

When capital stock is issued at a price higher than its par value, the excess over par is typically recorded and reported as Capital Stock Premium, or as Paid-in Capital in Excess of Par, or simply as Capital Surplus. Use of the last title, because it contains the word *surplus*, has been strongly discouraged. For example, the Committee on Terminology of the American Institute of Certified Public Accountants, in its discussion of the undesirability of *surplus* as an accounting term, simply said, "The use of the term *capital surplus* (or, as it is sometimes called, *paid-in surplus*) gives rise to confusion." The committee went on to point out the obvious fact that the word *surplus* (like surplus fat) implies too much of something—something that the corporation plans, or should plan, to eliminate as soon as possible.

For an example of low-par stock as well as use of the term *capital surplus*, a well-known company in its consolidated balance sheet showed common stock with par value of $.50, totaling $1,212,000, and on the next line showed capital surplus of $234,150,000—more than 200 times the amount of the capital stock par. In these days when so much emphasis is being placed on the market value and trading volume, it is doubtful that many new corporate stock issues will carry the once familiar $100 par value designation.

Common stock is known as the *residual equity* of the corporation. This means that in the event that the corporation is dissolved, either voluntarily or involuntarily, the common stockholders get "what's left" (if anything) after the claims of all creditors and preferred stockholders (in that order) have been met as fully as possible. Preferred stockholders have priority over common stockholders with respect to the receipt of dividend payments as well as the restoration of stockholder investment upon distribution of corporate assets in dissolution. Additionally, the dividends on certain forms of preferred stock may "accumulate" from year to year if they remain unpaid. This type of preferred stock is commonly known as "cumulative preferred stock."

Entries to record the issue of common and preferred stock are the same. Assume, for example, that 100 shares of $10 par common stock are issued for $12 each, in cash. The entries are:

Cash in Bank	12,000	
Capital Stock (at par value)		10,000
Paid-in Capital in		2,000
Excess of Par Value		

THE ISSUE OF CAPITAL STOCK WITH NO PAR VALUE

No-par stock was invented in the hope of eliminating the confusion and opportunities for fraud that par-value stock appeared to create. It was thought that avoiding the expression *par value* would cause shareholders to view their shares as nothing more than evidence of fractional interests in the total common stock ownership of the corporation. Soon, however, it became common practice for a corporation's board of directors to establish a "stated value per share" for no-par shares and, as in the case of par-value stocks, amounts received in excess of the stated value were credited to Capital Surplus or to Paid-in Surplus. The practice is commonplace today, although the word *surplus* has nearly disappeared.

When no-par stock is issued for cash, the most logical entry is to debit Cash for the amount received and to credit Capital Stock—No Par *for the same amount.* If, however, there is an established stated value per share, it is almost unavoidable that only the stated-value portion of the proceeds of issue will be credited to the Capital Stock account and the excess will be credited to Paid-in Capital in Excess of Stated Value or a similar account.

THE ISSUE OF CAPITAL STOCK FOR PROPERTY

When capital stock is issued for cash, there is no question as to the dollar amounts involved, even though there may be some choice as to the accounts to be credited. However, when stock is issued in exchange for land, buildings, machinery, securities, or other forms of property, uncertainties can arise. One thing ought to be certain: When we issue stock for cash, we record the transaction for the amount of dollars that actually change hands, and few people would have the courage to argue that any different figure should be used. Therefore, when we issue stock for something other than cash, we should surely record the transaction, as accurately as we can, *at the cash value* of the thing received. Unfortunately, there is a school of thought that believes the absence of cash in the case of a stock issue gives license to pick a valuation of the thing received that may not bear even a remote relationship to its current value.

For the time being, let's be purists and at least attempt to record the noncash assets received in exchange for stock at the stock's current cash value, since the stock is the "currency' being used for the purchase. If, for example, we issue 10,000 shares of common stock with a fair market value of $2 per share, and a par value of $.50 per share for a tract of land worth $25,000, our entry should be:

Land	20,000	
Capital Stock Common		5,000
(at par value)		
Paid-in Capital in Excess of Par		15,000

Or if we issue 100,000 shares of no-par stock to the stockholders of another corporation in exchange for all the stock of that corporation that they hold, and if our stock has as aggregate market value of $2,500,000, our entry should be:

Investment in Common Stock	2,500,000	
of X Co.		
Capital Stock		2,500,000

Sometimes the current market value of the stock issued may not be readily ascertainable, whereas the current market value of the property received in exchange is known. Then there should be no objection to using the latter value in recording the acquisition of property.

TREASURY STOCK—WHAT, WHY, AND HOW?

Some time ago the *Wall Street Journal* devoted one of its splendid feature articles to the subject of "buying yourself," with the headline, "More Companies Find Their Shares Are Rewarding Investment." The first sentence of the article reads: "Keebler Co., a Chicago-based cookie and cracker maker, has found what it considers a hot investment for some extra cash it has on hand. The investment is called Keebler Co."

To "buy itself," a corporation merely places an order for some of its own outstanding shares in the stock market, much as any of us might purchase shares through our broker. When the corporation does acquire its own shares, they may be canceled and retired or they may be held in an inactive state in the corporate treasury (wherever that may be). Shares held in the treasury are aptly termed *treasury shares* or *treasury stock*.

Treasury shares have no voting rights and dividends cannot be paid on them, since such an act would constitute the farce of taking money out of your pocket, putting it right back in the same pocket, and claiming you had both paid a dividend and received some dividend revenue. Before Securities and Exchange Commission rules put an end to the charade, some companies were actually siphoning book dollars out of their "surplus" accounts to symbolize a dividend and were reflecting the very same dollars as "dividend income" in their income statements!

In describing what treasury stock is, we should also understand what it is not. The investments that your company makes and holds in the form of securities issued by other companies are, without a doubt, assets (either current or noncurrent); the "investments" your company makes in its own stock, contrary to the implications of the headline quoted earlier, are not investments—shares of treasury stock are not an asset.

Certain companies doggedly persist in displaying their treasury stock on the asset side of their balance sheets. But that is ridiculous (even when it appears that the shares are held primarily for distribution under executive bonus plans). How can a company own all its assets and also own, and treat as an asset, shares of stock that represent those same assets? Beginning students of accounting often protest that the shares of treasury stock may be readily salable and thus be a ready source of cash. The answer, of course, is that the possibility of obtaining cash is not in itself an asset; if it were, we should then also list as an asset any capital stock that is authorized by our charter but that we have not yet issued (unissued stock), and we should list the notes payable that we have paid off, because we could, perhaps, reissue them for cash on a moment's notice.

Among the more common reasons that corporation's repurchase their own shares are:

1. To reduce the total shares outstanding thereby hoping to increase the market price per share.
2. To reduce the total shares outstanding in order to increase the corporation's earnings per share (net income divided by outstanding shares).
3. To make fewer shares available on the market in the event of a hostile takeover bid by an outsider.
4. To distribute shares of stock as compensation to corporate employees without having to increase the share authorization with the state.

It is argued that it's fine to have some treasury stock around not only for employee bonuses but for possible use in accomplishing a merger with another company. An important amount of stock may be involved in a merger transaction, and in such a case use of treasury stock, rather than unissued stock, limits the total number of shares outstanding and tends to avoid the dilution of the amount of earnings per share of stock.

It goes without saying that some companies acquire treasury stock at bargain prices when they are confident that the market price at which the stock can be reissued is going to rise. The gain in cash resulting from successful accomplishment of that aim is not classed as taxable income.

The accounting entries to record the acquisition and reissue of treasury shares are simple. The most widely used procedure consists of recording the acquired stock at cost, regardless of the stock's par value. To illustrate, assume that our company buys 1,000 shares of its own $10 par common stock in the market for $25 per share. The entry is:

(1)

Treasury Stock	25,000	
Cash in Bank		25,000

To record purchase of 1,000 shares of our own stock at $25 per share, to be held in treasury as treasury stock.

To illustrate reissue of these shares, let's make three different assumptions, as follows: The shares are (a) reissued for cash at their purchase price of $25 per share, (b) reissued at $35, and (c) reissued at $15. The respective entries are:

(2a)

Cash in Bank	25,000	
Treasury Stock (at cost)		25,000

(2b)

Cash in Bank	35,000	
Treasury Stock (at cost)		25,000
Paid-in Capital—Treasury Stock		10,000

(2c)

Cash in Bank	15,000	
Retained Earnings	10,000	
Treasury Stock (at cost)		25,000

Note that no operating gain is recognized when treasury shares are reissued above cost; however, when they are reissued at less than cost, it is apparent that a loss of some sort has been incurred. If at the time of reissue at a loss there is a balance in the account shown in (2b) as Paid-in Capital—Treasury Stock, that account should be used rather than Retained Earnings. Lacking such a balance, Retained Earnings would appear to be the inevitable recipient of the reissue loss.

On the balance sheet, any treasury stock should be displayed as a subtraction (negative item) in the stockholder's equity section. There is general
agreement that the subtraction should be made from the total of the capital
stock and retained earnings as follows:

Stockholders' equity (section of balance sheet):	
Capital stock (with details shown)	$1,000,000
Retained earnings	375,000
	$1,375,000
Less: Treasury shares (1,000 at cost, $25)	25,000
Total Stockholder's Equity	$1,350,000

STOCK SPLITS—WHAT, WHY, AND HOW?

Stock-splitting surgery is usually performed when the management
believes that the stock would be more popular and have wider ownership if
the market price were brought to a lower level. To make the change, the
company may put in the hands of each existing stockholder two shares for
each share now held, or five shares for each four, or some other ratio that
increases the number of shares held, *without any additional investment* by
the stockholders and *without any reduction of the retained earnings* of the
corporation. Thus, if the current market price per share of the outstanding
stock is $100, a two-for-one split should cause the market price to decline
approximately to $50. The stockholder now owns twice as many shares but
realizes no income and is not liable for any income tax directly as the result
of the split.

A stock split has much in common with a stock dividend (which will
be examined in the next chapter), since each is likely to have the same effect
on the market price and neither is taxable. The only real difference is that in
the case of a stock dividend a certain amount of retained earnings disappear
from the balance sheet and become embedded in the Capital Stock account.

Generally, no accounting entry is made for a stock split, although a
memorandum entry should be made in the general journal to disclose the
change in par value per share and total shares outstanding. Assume that our
company has 100,000 shares of $5 par common stock outstanding. Because
the stock is selling for $120 per share, the company decides upon a four-for-
one split. A memorandum to reflect this action might be worded as follows:

On x/x/20XX, 400,000 shares of $1.25 par common shares were issued in
exchange for 100,000 shares of $5 par common shares in the form of a stock
split.

STOCK RIGHTS

The terms *rights*, *options*, and *warrants* tend to be used without distinction by persons speaking about securities. Although there may be no established legal basis for precise distinctions, for our purposes it seems best to attempt them and to take the terms up one at a time. In many jurisdictions, when a corporation undertakes to offer additional shares of a class of stock that is already outstanding, the existing holders of shares of that class must be given the opportunity to "preempt" the issue on a pro rata basis. That is, the existing holders have automatic, preemptive rights to buy the same fractions of the supplementary issue as they hold of the outstanding shares. Some states apparently require that preemptive rights go with any issue of stock; other states do not have such a requirement; and still others provide for waiver of the rights by a vote of the stockholders or by other appropriate action.

To illustrate, if a corporation has outstanding 100,000 shares of $10 par common with a current market value of $45 per share and it wishes to issue an additional 50,000 shares, it might offer the new shares to the holders of preemptive rights at a bargain price of any amount under $45, say, $39 per share. The offer would make the preemptive right attached to each old share worth $2, and the corporation would make provision for the rights to be separately traded on the market.

Because preemptive rights are embodied in the stock issue from its inception, the corporation makes no entry on its books when certificates evidencing ownership of rights are issued to present holders. After a month or so, the rights expire and the issue price of any leftover stock may be reset. In the meantime, shares issued at $39 plus two rights are recorded exactly as are straight cash issues. Assume that all the 50,000 shares are issued; then the entry is:

Cash	1,950,000	
Capital Stock Common (at par)		500,000
Paid-in Capital in Excess of Par		1,450,000

STOCK OPTIONS

An option also is a form of right, but commonly an option is acquired by some specific act or payment. Stockbrokers sell options that are known as *puts*, *calls*, and *straddles*, which respectively mean rights to sell, to buy, or to do either within a given period of time. They have no effect on the corporation's financial accounts, since they involve only deals among outsiders. On the other hand, during years with sky-high rates of personal income taxation and significantly lower tax rates on capital gains, corporations have made extensive use of stock option offers to present and potential executives of the corporation. In order to qualify for favorable tax treatment, a number of technical restrictions must be observed, but basically an executive stock option plan grants the executive the right (option) to purchase a specified number of shares of the company's common stock, at a set price, after specified intervals of continuous employment with the company. The expectation, of course, is that the market price of the stock will rise to a level that will make the purchase at the set price something of a bonanza for the officer. As history has shown, the bonanza is by no means guaranteed, and many option recipients have attached themselves to a company with exciting option grants only to see the stock tumble to so small a fraction of the initial value that the options become worthless. On the other hand, many corporate executives have realized spectacular gains through option programs—gains that far exceeded their basic salaries.

There is virtually no accounting for options of the type we are considering except to record receipt of cash and the issue of stock when an officer exercises his options. One might well theorize that the options are granted in lieu of a certain amount of cash salary (for the tax advantages), but most accountants have concluded that there is usually insufficient basis for determining a value for the options that are granted and that, accordingly, no entry is to be made on the corporate books until the shares of stock are actually sold to the executive.

With the recent significant reduction in the highest marginal tax rate for individuals and the virtual elimination of the difference between that rate and the capital gains rate, executive stock option plans have lost much of their appeal. Given Congress's penchant for altering the tax code, however, the rules could go back the other way, once again making stock option plans popular as a tax preference item.

STOCK WARRANTS

Warrants commonly are detachable rights that are originally attached to bonds or to preferred stock when issued. The warrants are exercised (or detached and sold) by detaching and turning them in, along with a specified amount of cash, for shares of common stock. In other words, when a share of preferred stock, or a bond, is issued with a warrant attached, the investor is actually buying two things—the preferred stock or bond *and* a warrant that entitles him, at specified dates in the future, to buy a share of common stock at a fixed price or a schedule of prices varying with time in the future.

Because the warrants are separable, accountants have ruled that, when the preferred stock or bond is issued, recognition must be given to the amount of the purchase price allocable to the attached warrant. Assume, thus, that our corporation issues 10,000 shares of $50 par preferred stock at $56 per share and that to each share is attached a warrant to buy one share of common stock at some future date at a specified price. Assume further that the market assigns a value of $3.50 to a warrant. In such case the entry for issue of the preferred stock and warrants is:

Cash in Bank	560,000	
Paid-in Capital—Common		35,000
Stock Warrants		
Capital Stock Preferred—$50 Par		500,000
Capital Stock Preferred—Premium		25,000

In the future, as each warrant is exercised, a debit of $3.50 is made to the warrant account, a debit is made to Cash for the contractual price, and a credit is made to the common stock accounts for the total.

In this day of exotic types of securities, we find some companies issuing warrants that are not attached to anything. Such a warrant is simply a right to purchase (option) a share of stock, sometime in the future, at a price that, we hope, will turn out to be a bargain. Warrants bear no interest, and no dividend is paid on them. If a corporation can issue them in exchange for income-producing assets, it would seem that the deal may be quite favorable from the corporation's point of view, unless the exercise price turns out to lead to excessive dilution of the value of the shares held by existing stockholders.

CONVERTIBLE PREFERRED STOCK

Somewhat akin to the various kinds of rights is the conversion privilege that attaches to convertible preferred stock. The essence can readily be explained by an example. Our corporation may issue shares of $100 par preferred stock with the understanding that for each $20 of par investors can convert their preferred stock into one share of common stock that now is selling for $16 per share. At first glance that doesn't look like much of a bargain; but if the conversion privilege extends over a period of many months or years, the chances may be excellent that the common will rise in value above $20 and make conversion profitable for investors.

Although, clearly, the conversion right that is embodied in the convertible preferred stock makes the preferred stock relatively more attractive, accountants have agreed that no attempt need be made to account for it separately, as is done with the detachable warrants described in the preceding section. In other words, when the convertible preferred stock is issued, the entries are the same as if no conversion privilege were present.

CALLABLE PREFERRED STOCK

Frequently, the issuing corporation would like to retain the option of recalling the preferred share issuance, should market conditions indicate that the stated dividend rate on the shares is too high, or the corporation has enough cash to unilaterally retire the issuance and avoid any future dividend payments. This feature is known as the corporation's right to "call' the preferred shares back from the shareholders. In order to preserve the marketability of the shares at issuance, the call price provided in the stock issuance is usually at a significant premium over the issue price.

COMMON STOCK EQUIVALENTS

In the preceding four sections we have been surveying not common stock itself, but some kinds of securities that have certain of the qualities of common stock as well as the potential for being exchanged for common stock. Stock rights, stock options, stock warrants, and convertible securities all benefit when the common stock for which they may be exchanged goes up in value; that is, these securities, or instruments, have the capacity to share in the speculative gyrations of the stock market. Rights, options, and warrants can be exchanged for common stock upon the payment of the required amounts of cash; convertibles can be exchanged for stock with no further cash payment. Each of these, then, represents a potential addition to the number of shares of common stock that a corporation already has outstanding. For purposes of determining earnings per share (EPS) on a more conservative basis, these potential additions to the number of common shares outstanding may have to be treated as if they were the actual equivalent of shares of common stock.

EARNINGS PER SHARE

Opinion No. 15 of the Accounting Principles Board, issued in May of 1969, has to do with setting equitable rules for computing, and reporting to investors, the amount that a corporation has earned per share (of common stock and equivalents) during the reporting period. This has been a difficult problem to solve. Little trouble exists in the case of the corporation with an elementary capital structure, that is, one with nothing but common stock and perhaps some old-fashioned bonds and preferred stock. In such a case, the EPS is determined simply by dividing net income for the accounting period by the common shares outstanding during the period. But if the company also has one or more of the so-called common stock equivalents in its bag, those equivalents may have to be translated into their equivalent number of common shares and added to the pure common total, which is then to be divided into the earnings available to common, with the resulting amount labeled EPS.

Even the elementary structure may call for some second-grade arithmetic. The earnings for the year should be divided by the weighted average number of shares outstanding during the year rather than by the simple number outstanding at the end of the year. If there has been a stock issuance, repurchase, split, or a stock dividend during the year, the average number of shares outstanding last year must be adjusted as if the shares had been split if a comparison is to be made between this year's EPS and last year's.

When the structure becomes more complex, we must be on the lookout for the potentially "dilutive" effects of stock options, rights, etc. Opinion No. 15 is nearly 30 pages long and makes tough reading. We cannot possibly present its content here faithfully; however, one paragraph from the summary opinion may serve to indicate the objective. Paragraph 15 is as follows:

> Corporations with capital structure other than those described in the preceding paragraph should present two types of earnings per share data (dual presentation) with equal prominence on the face of the income statement. The first presentation is based on the outstanding common shares and those securities that are in substance equivalent to common shares and have a dilutive effect. The second is a pro-forma presentation which reflects the dilution of earnings per share that would have occurred if all continent issuances of common stock that would individually reduce earnings per share had taken place at the beginning of the period (or time of issuance of the convertible security, etc., if later). For convenience in this Opinion, these two presentations are referred to as "primary earnings per share" and "fully diluted earnings per share," respectively, and would in certain circumstances discussed elsewhere in this Opinion be supplemented by other disclosures and other earnings per share data.

ORGANIZATION COSTS

Organization costs, commonly called organization expense by accountants, include the general costs of launching a business concern. This category consists of fees paid for legal services (such as the drafting of the corporate charter and bylaws), fees paid for accounting services, costs of issuing securities, printing, costs, etc.

Possibly because organization services are in the main invisible and do not clearly attach to any tangible asset, businessmen and their accountants seem to be anxious to get such costs written off as soon as possible. Actually, the cost of launching an enterprise may well deserve to be maintained as a significant asset for so long as the organization exists.

Tax rules allow the amortization of some of the organization cost items over a period of 60 months or more, but this permission does not apply to the costs of issuing securities, costs of transfer of assets to the corporation, or costs of reorganization.

TEST PROBLEM

The balance sheet of our corporation, at the end of a year, contains the following stock equity section:

Stockholders' equity:

Capital stock, 5%, $100 par preferred		$ 1,000,000
Capital stock common, no par,		
stated value $2, authorized		
2,000,000 shares, issued		
750,000 shares	$ 1,500,000	
Paid-in capital in excess of par value	8,500,000	
		10,000,000
Total Paid In Capital		11,000,000
Retained earnings		6,800,000
Total stockholder's equity		$17,800,000

During the next year the following transactions occur:

1. 250,000 shares of the unissued common stock are issued for cash at $45 per share.
2. A two-for-one common stock split is performed. This is accomplished by reducing the stated value to $1 per share and by distributing 1,000,000 unissued shares to the present shareholders.
3. A charter amendment is accomplished; it authorizes an additional 1,000,000 shares of no-par common (no entry required).
4. We acquire 100,000 shares of common stock for cash at $30 per share, to be held as treasury stock.
5. We sell 50,000 shares of treasury stock for cash at $35 per share.
6. We call in the preferred stock, in accordance with the written provisions of the issue, at a cash call price of $110.
7. We issue 10,000 shares of $100 par, 12 percent preferred stock. To each share is attached a warrant to purchase one share of no-par common for $42. The warrants will expire in five years. The market value of a warrant is estimated to be $4. The shares, with warrants attached, are issued for cash at $105.
8. Earnings retained during the year total $300,000 (no entry called for).

REQUIRED

Prepare journal entries to record the numbered transactions and, in the form provided, present the stockholders' equity section as it stands at the end of the year.

TEST PROBLEM SOLUTION SPACE

	Debit	Credit
(1)		

(2)

(3)

(4)

(5)

(6)

(7)

(8)

Stockholders' equity:
    Capital stock preferred, 6%, $100 par $
    Paid-in capital in excess of par
    Capital stock common, no par, stated
       value $1, authorized 3,000,000
       shares issued 2,000,000 shares $
    Paid-in capital in excess of
      stated value

    Capital stock common—warrants
    Total paid-in capital
Retained earnings

                                     $

    Less: Capital stock common in treasury
      at cost (50,000 shares)

10

DIVIDENDS AND RESERVES

WHAT IS A TRUE DIVIDEND?

If we were to prepare a catalog of business transactions and financial terms that are thoroughly misunderstood by laymen, *dividend* would appear high on the list.

Whereas a sole proprietorship and a partnership are made up of the individuals who contribute the capital, that is, the owners, this is emphatically not so in the case of a corporation. The corporation has legally constituted existence as an entity in its own right, quite separate from its owner-investors. The earnings of the sole proprietorship and of the partnership are legally earnings of the proprietors (sole proprietor or the partners), but the earnings of a corporation are legally earnings of the corporation; they do not become earnings of the investor-owners until a true dividend is declared by the board of directors. A true dividend is declared only when something is detached from the corporation and presented to the stockholders, and this transaction does not qualify as a true dividend to the extent of any reduction in the stockholders' paid-in capital accounts.

In short, a true dividend (in double-entry style) has two facets: (1) the stockholders are given something (usually cash, but it can be in the form of other valuable assets such as merchandise or even a "promise to pay" cash sometime in the future) and (2) the Retained Earnings account is correspondingly reduced.

Thanks to the accounting method of depicting transactions, the accounting entries to record the declaration and payment of the classical cash dividend are as follows:

December 15

Retained Earnings or	100,000	
Dividend Charges		
Dividends Payable		100,000

On December 15 the directors of our corporation meet and declare the regular quarterly cash dividend of $.25 per share on the 400,000 shares of $10 par common then outstanding; the dividend is payable on January 15 next, to those who are listed holders of shares (holders of record) on January 5.

January 15

| Dividends Payable | 100,000 | |
| Cash in Bank | | 100,000 |

To record payment of cash dividend declared on December 15.

Note the two effects of the dividend in this example. First, an asset, cash in bank, is reduced (and transferred to the stockholders); second, retained earnings is reduced by the same amount. Also, take particular note of the fact that the directors, at the moment on December 15 that they declare the $100,000 dividend, create a current liability.

In some cases a corporation may own shares of stock in another corporation and, for a variety of reasons, the directors will elect to distribute those shares, instead of cash, to the company's stockholders. The entries are the same except that, instead of Cash in Bank being credited on January 15, the credit is made to Investments or to Marketable Securities. This is a true property dividend.

On rare occasions, when it is short of cash but wishes to make a dividend distribution that the stockholders will be able to convert into cash, a corporation will mail promissory notes (scrip) to the stockholders for an amount of cash that is to be paid sometime later. Such a distribution qualifies as a true dividend, since the corporation establishes a legal liability to pay the stockholders. Entries for such a declaration and ultimate payment are:

December 15

| Retained Earnings | 100,000 | |
| Dividends Payable | | 100,000 |

To record declaration of dividend for which we will issue, on January 15, in the form of promises to pay, the cash sum of $.25 per share.

January 15

| Dividends Payable | 100,000 | |
| Dividend Scrip Payable | | 100,000 |

To record distribution of interest-bearing (or non-interest-bearing) scrip (notes payable) to stockholders (scrip to bear interest at 12% and to become due in 30 days).

February 14

Dividend Scrip Payable	100,000	
Interest Expense	1,000	
Cash in Bank		101,000

Cash payment of maturing scrip plus 12% interest for 30 days.

CORPORATE INVESTMENT IN AFFILIATED COMPANY

Although in the preceding section the corporation was characterized as a distinctly separate entity and, as a corollary, it was pointed out that earnings of a corporation are not concurrently or automatically earnings of the owners, the principle is routinely violated in modern accounting practice in one situation. That is when one corporation holds a majority interest (more than 50 percent) of the common stock of another corporation and the resources of the two affiliated corporations are not reported in combined form in a "consolidated" balance sheet. We'll look at the techniques of preparing consolidated statements later, but for the present let's assume that our dominant, or "parent" corporation elects not to prepare fully consolidated statements. When such a choice is acceptable, the parent will merely publish its "legal" balance sheet and will show, as a noncurrent asset, its investment in the affiliate (known as a subsidiary).

To report the investment at its cost, however, is held to be inappropriate under the circumstances mentioned. Rather, it is preferred practice to accrue, as an increase (or decrease) in the investment account, the parent company's share of the earnings of the subsidiary, even though the subsidiary has not paid them in the form of dividends. When the earnings are then received from the subsidiary in the form of true dividends, the investment account is literally converted into cash to the extent of the dividend received. Assume, for example, that our corporation does the following: (1) It buys 70 percent of the outstanding common stock of Subsidiary Corp. for $95,000; (2) at the end of the year Subsidiary reports earnings of $20,000 since the date of our company's investment; (3) lastly, next year Subsidiary pays a cash dividend of $15,000 and our corporation recognizes receipt of its 70 percent share. The entries on our corporation's books under the method that we have been considering are:

(1)

| Investment in Subsidiary Corp. | 95,000 | |
| Cash in Bank | | 95,000 |

Purchase of a 70% interest in the common stock of Subsidiary Corp. for cash.

(2)

Investment in Subsidiary Corp.	14,000	
Earnings of Subsidiary		14,000
Corp. (a revenue account)		

To accrue as income our 70% share of the $20,000 of earnings recorded by Subsidiary Corp. this year since the date of our acquisition of Subsidiary Corp. common stock.

(3)

| Cash in Bank | 10,500 | |
| Investment in Subsidiary Corp. | | 10,500 |

To record receipt of cash dividend from Subsidiary Corp. and to treat this as conversion of part of our investment into cash since our share of Subsidiary Corp. earnings has already been accrued in entry (2).

The reasoning in support of this violation of the entity convention is that (1) Subsidiary Corp. is in a field of activity so foreign to that which we are in that to consolidate the statements of the two companies might produce misleading results and (2) at the same time, the earnings strength of the affiliated companies may not be adequately disclosed unless the parent company's share of Subsidiary Corp. earnings is accrued on a current basis. This so-called equity procedure has become a generally accepted rule of accounting, even when ownership is less than 50 percent if the "investor" is able to exercise significant influence over affairs of the "investee."

LIQUIDATING "DIVIDENDS"

The term *dividend* is commonly applied to two classes of transactions to which it is not fully applicable. The first is the return of capital to the owners; the second, considered in the next section, is the stock dividend.

If we are to make good use of terms in accounting, we should be able to rely on the meaning intended by the user. Certainly most people who give it any thought at all think that someone who receives a dividend earns some revenue or income—a return on investment. Clearly, though, there is no income when the corporation is undergoing partial or total dissolution and the stockholder is merely having his investment returned to him—a return of investment.

Entries on the books of the corporation when a liquidating dividend is paid:

(1)

Paid-in Capital in Excess of Par	25,000	
Capital Stock—Par	75,000	
Cash in Bank		100,000

To record return of capital to stockholders, first by a reduction of "Excess of Par" to zero, thenby a debit to Capital Stock—Par for the balance of the payout.

Payments in liquidation, improperly termed liquidating dividends, occur when the affairs of a corporation are being wound up and also in extractive industries that make an investment in a single venture with no intention of continuing actively when that venture (e.g., a mine of limited extent) is terminated.

STOCK DIVIDENDS

To illustrate what are known, misleadingly, as stock "dividends," let's start with an assumed stock equity section for our corporation as follows:

Capital Stock, par $10, authorized 100,000 shares, issued and outstanding 60,000 shares	$ 600,000
Paid-in Capital in Excess of Par Value, common	120,000
Total Paid-in Capital	$ 720,000
Retained Earnings	1,000,000
Total Stockholder's Equity	$1,720,000

Now assume that our directors vote to "distribute" (what a poor word choice!) a 50 percent stock dividend. First, understand clearly that 50 percent means that we shall issue new shares in quantity equal to 50 percent of the number of shares now outstanding. (Many people think the 50 percent means we'll use up 50 percent of the retained earnings.) Second, with an issue in excess of 20 to 25 percent, the amount to be recorded should be par value (in this case $10 per share). If the issue is less than 20 to 25 percent, as we'll note next, we encounter certain restrictions. The entry to record this fifty per cent stock dividend would be:

At Declaration Date

Stock Dividends (Retained Earnings)	300,000	
Common Stock Distributable (at par value)		300,000

To record the declaration of a 50% stock dividend on common stock.

At Distribution Date

Common Stock Distributable	360,000	
Capital Stock (at par value 30,000 shares × $10)		300,000
Paid-in Capital in Excess of Par Value		60,000

To record issuance of a 50% stock dividend, or 30,000 shares, capitalized at $10 per share.

If you analyze the above entry, you will recognize clearly that a stock dividend is in no sense of the word a true dividend. The corporation gives up absolutely nothing; the stockholders, individually and as a group, receive absolutely nothing but an additional piece of paper to represent exactly the same fractional ownership that they each held before the event. For example, if you owned 3,000 shares before the stock dividend, you would own 5 percent of the corporation (3,000/60,000 shares). After the stock dividend was distributed, you would own 4,500 shares, but the total common stock issued and outstanding would have increased to 90,000 shares. Your fractional interest in the corporation would thus remain at 5 percent. There are, however, two effects of stock dividends that may in some cases be quite significant. First, some retained earnings is wiped out as such and is established in a frozen state in the legal capital accounts. Since this eliminates the retained earnings (in our case $300,000) as a possible future basis for dividend appropriation, perhaps some of the stockholders may be worse off as the result of the so-called dividend. Second, the earnings per share and the market value of the stock, should drop, since we now have 90,000 rather than 60,000 shares representing exactly the same net assets. This second effect could improve the marketability of the stock because the price per share should drop about one-third.

In recent years it has become quite popular for certain "growth" companies to issue stock dividends of less than 10 percent; in fact, some companies started the practice of declaring "regular" stock dividends, even on a quarterly basis, of 2 percent or some similar amount. Undoubtedly the stockholders have believed that they are actually getting paid dividends of 2 percent per quarter while the corporation, at the same time, is enabled to retain its cash resources for expansion! These companies typically pay no cash dividend until they have attained their desired size (if ever). In some other companies, minor stock dividends are issued in order to accomplish a minor increase in cash dividend payout without having to change the traditional cash dividend per share. Thus, instead of increasing the cash dividend from $1 to $1.02 per share, the company presents each holder with two new shares of stock for each 100 held and continues to pay $1 per share.

It appears that the use of minor stock dividends may have been subject to abuse in view of the average stockholder's total ignorance of its significance. The trouble is that the market price of stock upon distribution of a 2 percent stock dividend should go down proportionately, but investor psychology (or ignorance) is such that the price is just about as likely to remain unchanged or even to rise. So in order to put a damper on the excessive use of such "distributions" (and, believe it or not, brokers, financial writers, and other experts even use the word "payout" for a stock dividend), the New York Stock Exchange, among others, has established the requirement (for the companies subject to their influence) that, when a stock dividend is under 20 to 25 percent, the corporation must capitalize an amount equal to the current market value per share. That, of course, can make a great difference in the amount of retained earnings that is frozen by the stock dividend action. Consider, for example, a corporation with a common stock par of $1.50 per share and a current market value of $75 per share. The entry on date of distribution would be as follows (assuming 100,000 shares of common stock was outstanding prior to the declaration of the stock dividend and a 10 percent stock dividend):

Common Stock Distributable	750,000	
Common Stock (10,000 shares		15,000
@ par value of $1.50)		
Paid-in Capital in Excess of		735,000
Par Value, Common		

A final word on stock dividends. Truly, a stock dividend (particularly if it ranges above 25 percent in size) amounts to nothing more than a stock split with one added feature—the capitalization of retained earnings.

WHAT DO ACCOUNTANTS MEAN BY "RESERVES"?

One dictionary lists seven meanings for *reserve* used as a noun; of these, the one that addresses itself to financial matters says a reserve is "money or its equivalent kept in hand or set apart usually to meet liabilities." The first of the seven definitions leans in a similar direction, stating that a reserve is "something stored for future use." That is not what accountants have in mind.

For many decades accountants have made liberal use of *reserve*, and for a comparable period of time the uninitiated reader has been totally confused. The upshot of all this is that now accountants have all but eliminated the confusing word from their vocabulary. In the next three sections we'll become acquainted with three different ways in which "reserve" formerly was used and will see what obedient accountants are now using in its place.

CONTRA ACCOUNTS USED TO BE CALLED RESERVES

As the annual reports from the companies whose stock you hold come rolling in, examine the balance sheets to see if any show a reserve for depreciation or a reserve for uncollectibles. A reserve for depreciation is an expression, a measure, of the amount by which depreciation has been recognized in the accounts with respect to the related assets. In other words, a reserve for depreciation is a subtraction from depreciable assets; it's a representation of services that have been removed from the asset's original bundle. Far from being anything that has been set aside, a reserve for depreciation is, figuratively, a hole in an asset.

Numerous times in this book we have mentioned contra accounts— accounts that are used as negatives or as offsets to other accounts. That is precisely what every reserve for depreciation is—a contra account. So also is the reserve for uncollectibles or bad debts.

SOME LIABILITIES USED TO BE CALLED RESERVES

One still occasionally sees such titles as Reserve for Federal Income Taxes and Reserve for Product Warranties in present-day position statements. Why? What do they mean?

In these cases the word *reserve* is probably used solely because the dollar amount involved is an estimate, an approximation. The accounts are, clearly, liabilities. The first signifies that we owe "some" income taxes, but the final definite amount due for this year has not yet been established. Also, we undoubtedly have some outstanding customer claims under our warranty agreements, but the sum of those claims is, at best, an educated guess. Does the fact that the amount of a liability is uncertain justify dodging a true liability title? Obviously not. Let's be candid. Correctly, the two titles should be changed to Estimated Liability for Federal Income Taxes and Estimated Liability under Warranty Agreements.

Another situation in which the confusing terminology has been used is in the case of accrued pension obligations. Here we have a tangled skein of accounting preferences and theories and a variety of uncertain actuarial calculations sufficient to render the result quite speculative, but there is no justification for dodging the estimated liability label through use of the term *reserve*.

In short, when you're tempted, because of the uncertainties of the situation, to call a liability a reserve, don't.

RETAINED EARNINGS MAY BE RESERVED

In the good ol' days many of us chose to use the word *reserve* to designate reservations of retained earnings. It's a bit hard to determine just what is accomplished by such reservations, but in order to attain the ultimate in shunning a misleading term, let's even restrict it here.

A couple of examples of retained earnings reservations may be worth mentioning. First, the corporation laws of many of our states specify that, if a corporation holds any treasury stock, the retained earnings of that corporation, in an amount equal to the cost of the treasury stock, must be reserved; that is, this amount of retained earnings stands unavailable for dividend charges so long as the treasury stock remains on hand. Some companies make no entries in the Retained Earnings account and merely state, parenthetically in their balance sheets, that so many dollars of retained earnings are restricted because of treasury stock holdings; other companies make explicit entries, somewhat as follows:

Retained Earnings   xxx
   Retained Earnings Reserved   xxx
     for Treasury Stock

To record reservation of retained earnings in amount equal to the cost of stock now held in treasury.

Note that such an entry reserves retained earnings, but it still avoids the outright use of a reserve; there is no Reserve for Treasury Stock.

In summary, with respect to reserves in general, we may conclude that the title Reserve is a dead one. Don't use it at all under any conditions. If you have an account that nobody can explain, don't resort to the old dodge of calling it a reserve; get rid of it some way and stick to accounts that are clearly understood.

DEFERRED CREDITS WHEN IN DOUBT

Accountants need a convenient receptacle or two into which they can deposit (dump or hide?) certain debits and credits that they don't clearly understand. One of the modern favorite dumping sites is under the caption Deferred Credits. But let's back up a minute.

When you were introduced to the statement of financial condition, the balance sheet, you were quite willing to accept the proposition that the formal financial structure of any business enterprise consists of two coequal quantums—the aggregate of assets expressed as a dollar total and the aggregate of liabilities and equities expressed as a dollar total, with the latter in turn made up of amounts due to creditors and the residual, or amount assigned to the owners. To cut through the verbiage, let's just say that one side of the financial coin consists of all the assets of the enterprise and the opposite side shows the allocation of the very same total as between amounts owed to outsiders and the amount left over, known as the owner's equity. "Assets" equal "liabilities and equities."

Then what in the devil are deferred credits? They always appear on the equities side of the balance sheet, but do they then represent claims other than those of outsiders and insiders? Perhaps there's life on Mars after all!

Here are some typical deferred credits. The *Friday Monthly Post* collects subscriptions, running from one to three years in advance, totaling $100,000. Its accountant makes the following entry:

(1)

| Cash in Bank | 100,000 | |
| Deferred Subscription Income | | 100,000 |

To record collections from subscriptions during month of June.

How do You Like that Entry?

Well, the debit title is OK and we must assume the dollar amounts are correct (although most of us are suspicious of "round" numbers), but the accountant stumbles badly in coining the credit title. Now, in exchange for the $100,000 cash received, the company is obligated to deliver 12 monthly copies per year to each subscriber. As each monthly batch of magazines is sent out, the company "earns" one-twelfth of the amount it has collected on each annual subscription. So, as deliveries are made, the accountant will make the following entry:

(2)

| Deferred Subscription Income | xxx | |
| Subscription Revenue | | xxx |

To recognize revenue earned by delivery of magazines against subscriptions collected in advance.

Quite obviously the $100,000 collected and recorded in entry (1) is not yet revenue, but it becomes revenue as deliveries are made. Thus, the accountant reasons, the $100,000 initially is "deferred" revenue (surely not "income"). But then the accountant flunks the course by failing to recognize that, when trusting people have put a wad of money in your hands in the expectation of receiving future services, you have a simple, old-fashioned liability.

Most so-called deferred credits will turn out to be liabilities if properly analyzed. Think, for example, of advance collections of insurance premiums, club dues, telephone service charges, and a host of similar transactions.

Remember that the equity side of the balance sheet reflects where the assets came from, who made them available. Equities are the sources of the resources (assets) of the firm.

A few deferred credits, on the other hand, are actually contra-assets. One large factoring company, in buying notes receivable from automobile dealers, recorded the purchase transaction essentially as follows. (The inserted percentage figures merely signify amounts.)

Notes Receivable—Face	100%	
Cash in Bank		92%
Deferred Discount Revenue		8%

In this situation the finance company will collect 100 percent (plus interest) from the customer at maturity; and since the company paid only 92 percent face for the notes taken over, the balancing 8 percent becomes a gain, or revenue, from the factoring operation. But is there no better place than a Deferred Credits section of the balance sheet in which to report the unearned discount? Of course there is. The company paid 92 percent for this batch of notes because at the time the notes have a value of 92 percent of face. The proper conclusion, then, is to show the discount of 8 percent as a contra (subtraction) from the notes receivable on the balance sheet.

CUMULATIVE PREFERRED STOCK

As you recall from the prior chapter, preferred stock carries two primary advantages or "preferences" over common shares. One of these preferences is the right to receive dividends before the common shareholders. However, as we have learned earlier in this chapter, the board of directors of a corporation is never obligated to declare a dividend, not even to the preferred shareholders. Moreover, if the corporation does not have retained earnings it would not be possible to declare in dividends to preferred shareholders. In order to ensure that preferred shareholders do not lose their dividend preference for any one year, some corporations will issue "cumulative" preferred stock. If the stock is cumulative preferred stock, any undeclared preferred dividends will accumulate from year to year, and the corporation must pay the entire accumulated amount to the preferred shareholders before the common shareholders get a dime of dividends. Dividends that carry over are known as "dividends in arrears." An example follows:

Corporation X has 20,000 shares of $100 par value 5 percent cumulative preferred stock outstanding. The annual dividend that preferred shareholders can expect to receive would be $100,000 ($100 × 5%, or $5 per share). If the board of directors do not declare a dividend during 20X7, then there would be $100,000 of "dividends in arrears" in 2008. In other words, the preferred shareholders must receive the $100,000 dividend in arrears *and* the $100,000 dividend for 20X8 before common shareholders may collect a dividend. Should the board declare total dividends of less than $200,000 for 20X8, the difference would be dividends in arrears for 20X9.

Dividends in arrears are not presented as a liability on the corporate balance sheet, since the corporation has no obligation to pay any dividend before the board of directors declare one. However, it should disclose the amount of dividends in arrears as a footnote to the financial statement. For example, Corporation X above might provide the following disclosure in its 20X7 financial statements:

On December 31, 20X7 the corporation was in arrears by $100,000 ($5 per share) on dividends to its preferred shareholders. The company must pay all dividends in arrears to its preferred shareholders in addition to its current year dividend before paying any dividend to its common shareholders.

TEST PROBLEM

At its meeting on March 15, the directors of Our Company declare a 10 percent stock dividend that is distributed on April 15. Also at the meeting the directors ask the accountant to establish two retained earnings reserves of $100,000 each: a reserve for possible fire losses and a reserve for general contingencies. At the date of the directors' meeting, the stockholders' equity section of the position statement stands as shown below. At the time of the stock distribution, the current market value is $25 per share.

Stockholders' equity:	
Capital stock common, par $5	$1,000,000
Paid-in capital in excess of par	500,000
Total paid-in capital	$1,500,000
Retained earnings	750,000
Total stockholder's equity	$2,250,000

REQUIRED

Give journal entries to record the reservations of retained earnings and the issuance of the dividend shares.

TEST PROBLEM SOLUTION SPACE

	Debit	Credit
March 15		

April 15

11

LONG-TERM DEBT

WHY GO INTO DEBT?

Debt is often viewed as undesirable. We worry about the size of the national debt and fret over the balance of our credit card balances. But, actually, if one really makes a science of it, isn't it possible for debt to be a thoroughly useful, profitable instrument of financial management?

One can readily think of at least four solid reasons for going into debt. First, it is unbelievable that an enterprise of any size would pay cash on the spot for everything it buys; in fact, it would be virtually impossible to avoid getting in debt on a day-to-day basis with the employees of the company. Debt, particularly the short-term variety, is a great *convenience*.

Wages are paid at weekly intervals; vendors' invoices are accumulated and paid monthly. But that is true primarily of interest-free short-term debt. Why does a company incur long-term debt?

Very often long-term debt is incurred to provide the company with more working capital. So often we find that when the business is growing— just as everything seems to be going well—we're short of cash. What has happened is that we've increased our sales and, at the same time, we've gone into the lending business ourselves by allowing our customers to buy on credit. Also, with the growth of business we must carry more inventories (which earn no interest!). If we're running a family-owned corporation, we refuse to raise money by selling stock to outsiders, so we must either get long-term bank loans or issue bonds. In other words, long-term debt becomes a *necessity*. Even if our company is not closely held, we may not wish to increase the amount of common stock outstanding because market conditions are unfavorable.

Perhaps the most popular reason for long-term debt financing is covered by the word *leverage*. This is the more modern term for what used to be called *trading on the equity*, and all it means is that you borrow somebody's money at an interest rate that is lower than the rate that you can earn on that money. If, for example, you can borrow a million dollars for a year at 12 percent and can employ the million dollars so that it produces a return of 14 percent, you should be a net gainer (before taxes) of 2 percent. That is the strategy used by many corporations to enhance the earnings rate on the common stock equity. Thus, if our company has assets of $2,000,000 that earn 14 percent and if half of our funds have come from a 12 percent bond issue, the earnings of our stockholders will amount to 14 percent on the $1,000,000 that they invested plus 2 percent leverage gain on the bond money, for a total of 16 percent.

One should not overdo a good thing, however. If, for instance, the financial structure of the company were made up of 10 percent equity ($200,000 of capital stock) and 90 percent debt ($1,800,000 of 12 percent bonds), the return on common stock would skyrocket to 14 percent of $200,000 (or $28,000) plus 2 percent of $1,800,000 (or $36,000) for a total of $64,000 divided by $200,000, or 32 percent. This would be known as a "thin" equity position. The net income before interest charges would be 14 percent of $2,000,000, or $280,000, which covers the $216,000 interest requirement, but the pretax $64,000 margin of coverage is not sufficient to assure the bondholders of being paid during hard times. In other words, the thinner the equity, the more risky the situation, and the determination of how far to go with leverage requires exercise of managerial intelligence.

The final reason for the popularity of long-term debt is that interest charges are legitimate tax deductions. Thus, with a corporate tax rate of approximately 50 percent, the net cost of the interest payments is only half of the gross cost. That is, for every $1 of interest paid out, $50 of income tax is saved (provided, of course, that we are operating at a profit). This fact alone accounts for a great deal of the long-term debt. Some banks, for example, issue bonds (debentures) on which they must pay 12 percent interest and invest the funds in tax-exempt municipal bonds on which they earn only 7 percent. Since the 12 percent interest has a net cost of about half that much and the 7 percent is nontaxable, the bank earns a net of approximately 1 percent on the borrowed funds.

Long-term debt takes many different forms, although the principles are basically the same. Since this is a book on accounting rather than corporation finance, let's take a look at some of the debt forms and examine them by the method of *accounting analysis*, that is, by reducing them to journal entry form.

INSTALLMENT PURCHASES

It seems quite unlikely that there is anybody old enough to read this material who hasn't at some time participated in an installment purchase. Because of the risk of running afoul of legal technicalities, let's not attempt to define our terms too precisely. Typically, when you buy something under an installment contract, you make periodic (monthly) payments of equal amount that apply first to accumulated interest and then to the principal of your debt.

We can't afford much space on any of these forms of debt, so let's go directly to an example and journalize enough of it to be sure it is fully understood.

Our company buys a machine at a price of $12,000 under an installment contract that calls for a down payment of $2,000 and quarterly payments of $500, including interest at 15 percent per annum. The machine is delivered and the contract signed on September 1.

The entries through the first three payments are as follows:

September 1, 20X1

Machinery	12,000	
Cash in Bank		2,000
Installment Contract Payable		10,000
(Explanation of terms)		

December 1, 20X1

Interest Expense	375	
Installment Contract Payable	125	
Cash in Bank		500

Payment of first quarterly installment of $500, of which $375 pays the interest up to date on $10,000 for 3 months, leaving $125 applicable to the debt itself.

The interest portion of the above payment is calculated by using the equation of principal ($10,000) multiplied by the interest rate (15/100, or 15%) multiplied by the amount of time (3 months, or 3/12).

December 31, 20X1

Interest Expense	123	
Interest Accrued Payable		123

To accrue unpaid interest, for purposes of end-of-year financial statements, at 15% on balance of debt ($9,875) for one month ($123.44 rounded to nearest dollar).

March 1, 20X2

Interest Accrued Payable	123	
Interest Expense	247	
Installment Contract Payable	130	
Cash in Bank		500

Payment of interest accrued on December 31, and interest for January and February, and balance of $130 on debt.

June 1, 20X2

Interest Expense	365	
Installment Contract Payable	135	
Cash in Bank		500

Payment of interest for 3 months on contract balance of $9,745 and payment of $135 on debt.

There's no point in continuing the journal entries through final payment. Needless to say, the debt would finally be paid off through the installments that include a bit less interest expense each quarter as the principal of the debt diminishes. The final payment would undoubtedly be some odd figure necessary to pay a very small amount of interest and the balance of the debt. Incidentally, you will occasionally hear someone say that when you are paying off a debt in installments, you are "amortizing" it.

LEASES AND SALE-AND-LEASEBACK TRANSACTIONS

We all know that to lease something is the equivalent of renting something—except that a lease implies the signing of a contract to pay the agreed-upon periodic rental for a minimum number of periods, usually a year or more. From the accounting standpoint the recording of the performance of such contracts would be easy were it not that the lawyers and others have figured out ways to complicate matters. In the absence of complications, our periodic entry is merely to debit Rent Expense and credit Cash in Bank for the contractual amount. This is known as an "operating lease."

Actually, there are only two complications of importance. First, if the lease is noncancelable, it has some of the earmarks of a long-term debt; in fact, if we add certain other features, it becomes almost impossible to determine whether you are dealing with a lease or the transaction is in actuality an installment purchase.

Some accountants (a minority) argue that any noncancelable lease, because it is a promise to pay a periodic series of fixed amounts, is nothing less than a debt from the start. They want you to show the sum of the payments to be made in the future as a long-term liability and to show the same amount on the other side of the balance sheet as an asset. Note one important qualification: We aren't merely to use the sum of the future payments; rather, we find the *discounted, present value* of those payments and show it on both sides of the balance sheet. These accountants argue that you have a fixed obligation and a valuable right of occupancy that can be disclosed effectively only if they are entered in the balance sheet. At the risk of oversimplification, let's attack this position by asserting that, although you may have an obligation to pay the series of rents, you have no true liability for any one of them until you have received the service (the occupancy for one month, etc.). You are dealing with an "executory" contract, which essentially means you have agreed to buy a series of services one at a time; and in spite of your inflexible agreement, you don't actually owe for any one of the services until it is delivered to you. Conclusion: Treat the lease exactly as you would a common rental, but be sure to *disclose* any significant terms of the lease in a footnote to your statements.

Now, there are certain features that may be written into a lease that can make us believe the lease is actually an installment purchase. For instance, if the agreement includes an option to buy the item at much less than its fair value at the end of the lease, doesn't that imply pretty clearly that you will effectively purchase the asset during the initial term of the lease? This is known as a "bargain purchase option." Or if the lease term is equal to at least 75 percent of the estimated economic life of the leased property, doesn't that also imply that you actually are *paying for the asset* during the initial term on the lease? The guiding rule nowadays is that we must interpret an agreement as an installment purchase, rather than as a lease, if either of those conditions is present. This is known as a "capital lease."

An interesting complication appears when a company, by prior agreement, (1) buys or constructs a building or other asset, (2) sells the asset to another company (a subsidiary?), and (3) immediately leases the asset back. This is a sale and leaseback. The point of the whole thing is that whether the sale was made at a profit or at a loss, it is generally assumed that such gain or loss is part of the *sale-and-leaseback* plan and is really just a fiction because the parties to the contract are not likely to have an arm's-length relationship. This brings us to the conclusion that the gain or loss should not be recognized as such in the year of the sale but should be prorated over the life of the lease. Thus, if a lease calls for rental payments of $12,000 per year for 20 years and if the lessee (occupant) built the asset for $100,000 and sold it to the lessor for $120,000, then the $20,000 of gain would be recognized at the rate of $1,000 per year, which, in effect, produces a net rental cost of $11,000 per year. In journal form the entries to depict this deal are:

(1)

Building	100,000	
Cash, etc.		100,000

To record cost of constructing (or buying) a building.

(2)

Cash	120,000	
Building		100,000
Deferred Gain on Sale of Building		20,000

To record sale of building to subsidiary.

(3)

| Rent Expense | 12,000 | |
| Cash | | 12,000 |

Rent payment for first year.

This assumes that the lease back is accounted for as an operating lease.

(4)

| Deferred Gain on Sale of Building | 1,000 | |
| Rent Expense | | 1,000 |

Portion of gain recognized in first year.

For a final subtopic on leases, note that some companies practice what has come to be known as *off balance-sheet financing*. The major (parent) company establishes a satellite corporation (a subsidiary) and owns all its stock in exchange for cash or other assets. The subsidiary issues bonds or other debt and constructs or buys an asset that, by prearrangement, it will lease to the parent corporation. The subsidiary pledges the lease proceeds as security for the bonds or other form of debt so that, in a sense, the parent company is really the guarantor of the subsidiary's debt. By following this procedure, the parent has use of the asset, but the debt incurred to buy the asset does not show on the parent's position statement—*unless the parent prepares a consolidated position statement.* The fact is that the preparation of a consolidated statement is called for under these circumstances. (We'll look at the subject of consolidations later, but for the present, we will merely assume that a consolidated statement is essentially one that combines the statements of two or more affiliated companies.)

LONG-TERM NOTES

Possibly the most common form of long-term (more than one year) debt consists of borrowing from banks, insurance companies, pension funds, and other institutional sources on the basis of a promissory note with a specified maturity date. A well-known variation of this is the so-called *line of credit* with a bank, whereby the borrower is extended the right to draw funds at will, up to an agreed-upon maximum, and to repay them at will. Under the line-of-credit plan the borrower will be charged a modest rate of interest on the unused portion of the available funds.

One cost-producing feature of borrowing from banks is the common requirement that if a company borrows, say, $100,000 at a stipulated interest rate, no more than $80,000 will actually be withdrawn; in other words, a "compensating balance" equal to a stated fraction of the loan must be left unused even though interest is paid on it. A typical fraction is 20 percent.

Accounting for long-term borrowing via promissory note presents no special problems. The interest costs of the loan should, of course, be recognized on an accrual basis.

MORTGAGE LOANS

A mortgage loan, commonly referred to as a *mortgage payable*, consists simply of a long-term note that is backed by a legal instrument known as a mortgage on real or personal property. When the security is personal property, the mortgage is called a *chattel mortgage*. Essentially, the mortgage itself is a document that lists the provisions of the loan and what will happen in the event of default. If the borrower does fail to comply with the mortgage provisions, title to the property is transferred to the lender. However, the defaulting party may be entitled to recover the property (the so-called *equity in redemption* provision) if the repayment is made within a year. (See your lawyer for further information on this subject.) Mortgage notes are customarily paid off in regular monthly installments including interest.

MORTGAGE AND DEBENTURE BONDS

A bond is, again, a form of note payable with a definite maturity date except when callable "by lot." A *debenture bond* provides no collateral security; that is, the general credit of the company constitutes the security. A mortgage bond is backed by a mortgage on some or all of the real estate of the company.

Bonds commonly are issued in $1,000 denominations and are quoted in the bond market at prices that fluctuate with changes in the financial condition of the company and with changes in the bond market. The bond market responds continuously to fluctuations in market rates of interest. For example, if we issue a series of 14 percent, 20-year bonds at par (i.e., in a 14 percent market) and later the prime interest rate (a mythical interest rate that big New York banks charge their "prime" customers for loans) rises to 16 percent, then our 14 percent bonds will be attractive only if they can be bought at a discount. To explain further, a 14 percent bond is a $1,000 bond that pays $70 of cash interest each 6 months, for a total of $140, or 14 percent, per year. Because the amount of cash interest cannot conveniently be varied from year to year as the market rate of interest fluctuates, the value of the bond itself fluctuates, with the result that a buyer will pay for the bond an amount above par (premium) or below par (discount), which will result in his earning whatever rate is necessary, provided he holds the bond until it matures.

Let's issue some bonds at par, some at a premium, and some at a discount. For an example, assume that our company issues $100,000 in 14 percent, 20-year, first-mortgage bonds (1) at par, (2) at a premium that will produce a true yield rate of 12 percent, and (3) at a discount that will produce a true yield rate of 16 percent. For each alternative the entries on our books through the first two years are as shown below. Assume in each case that we issue the bonds on January 1 and that interest is paid through the use of coupons.

(1) Issue at Par
January 1, 20X1

Cash	100,000	
Bonds Payable		100,000

To record issue at par.

July 1, 20X1

Bond Interest Expense	7,000	
Cash		7,000

To record payment of first interest coupons (14% for 6 months).

December 31, 20X1

Bond Interest Expense	7,000	
Bond Interest Payable		7,000

To accrue interest from date of latest payment to end of year.

January 1, 20X2

Bond Interest Payable	7,000	
Cash in Bank		7,000

Payment of second interest coupons.

July 1, 20X2

Bond Interest Expense	7,000	
Cash in Bank		7,000

Payment of third interest coupons.

December 31, 20X2

Bond Interest Expense	7,000	
Bond Interest Payable		7,000

Accrual of interest for fourth 6-month period.

At maturity, we merely debit Bonds Payable and credit Cash in Bank for repayment of the $100,000 borrowed initially.

(2) Issue at a Premium
January 1, 20X1

Cash	115,046	
Bonds Payable		100,000
Bonds Payable—Premium		15,046

To record issue of 14%, 20-year bonds at a price (premium), which will provide a true earning rate of 12% to holder to maturity.

July 1, 20X1

Bond Interest Expense	7,000	
Cash in Bank		7,000

Payment of first interest coupons.

Bonds Payable—Premium	376	
Bond Interest Expense		376

To amortize one-fortieth of the initial bond premium as a reduction, or offset, to our interest expense, since we will repay only par to the lender at maturity.

December 31, 20X1

Bond Interest Expense	7,000	
Bond Interest Payable		7,000

Accrual of interest to year-end.

Bonds Payable—Premium	376	
Bond Interest Expense		376

Same as entry on July 1.

January 1, 20X2

Bond Interest Payable	7,000	
Cash in Bank		7,000

Payment of second coupons.

July 1, 20X2

Bond Interest Expense	7,000	
Cash in Bank		7,000

Payment of coupon 3.

Bonds Payable—Premium	376	
Bond Interest Expense		376

Amortization of one-fortieth of initial premium.

December 31, 20X2

Bonds Payable—Premium	376	
Bond Interest Expense	6,624	
Bond Interest Payable		7,000

Same as December 31, 20X1, with entries combined.

The logic of the entries for the bond issued at a premium should be clear to you. Because the bonds pay an excessively high cash interest, the lenders are willing to pay us a premium of $15,046 that they will never get back, and the result is that they effectively earn only 12 percent rather than the "nominal" 14 percent. We, in turn, spread the $15,046 evenly over the life of the bond as a sort of gain, but, more accurately, as an offset to our cash interest cost.

(3) Issue at a Discount

January 1, 20X1

Cash	88,075	
Bonds Payable—Discount	11,925	
Bonds Payable		100,000

To record issue of 14% bonds at discount of $11,925, which will provide lender with a true earning rate of 16% if held to maturity when the full $100,000 is repaid.

July 1, 20X1

Bond Interest Expense	7,000	
Cash in Bank		7,000

Payment of coupon 1.

Bond Interest Expense	298	
Bonds Payable—Discount		298

To accumulate one-fortieth of the original discount as an addition to interest expenses, because at maturity lender must be paid amount borrowed ($88,075) plus the discount ($11,925) for a total of $100,000.

December 31, 20X1

Bond Interest Expense	7,000	
Bond Interest Accrued Payable		7,000

To accrue coupon 2.

Bond Interest Expense	298	
Bonds Payable—Discount		298

To accumulate one-fortieth of the discount to be paid at maturity.

January 1, 20X2

Bond Interest Accrued Payable	7,000	
Cash in Bank		7,000

Payment of coupon 2.

July 31, 20X2

Bond Interest Expense	7,000	
Cash in Bank		7,000

Payment of coupon 3.

Bond Interest Expense	298	
Bonds Payable—Discount		298

To accumulate one-fortieth of the discount.

December 31, 20X2

Bond Interest Expense	7,298	
Bond Interest Accrued Payable		7,000
Bonds Payable—Discount		298

To accrue coupon 4 and accumulate one-fortieth of the discount. (This again illustrates use of a combined journal entry.)

At the end of the second year, since we have recorded the bond issue and interest expense under three different assumptions, the bonds would be displayed in the balance sheet as a long-term liability in the following manner:

(1) Par:		(2) Premium:		(3) Discount:	
Bonds		Bonds		Bonds	
payable—		payable—		payable—	
par	$100,000	par	$100,000	par	$100,000
				Less:	
		Bonds		Bonds	
		payable		payable—	
		premium	13,542	discount	10,733
			$113,542		$ 89,267

A couple of more comments should be made concerning bonds issued at odd prices. First, bond discount is a contra account. It measures the difference between the maturity value (par) and the present book value (initially, the amount borrowed) of the bonds. Some old-time accountants still believe bond discount is prepaid interest, a logical impossibility, and they insist on showing it as an asset. Second, bond premium is an "adjunct" to bonds payable—to show the effective amount of debt at any given time, it must be added to the face amount of the bonds. Some old-fashioned accountants classify bond premium as a deferred credit—a monstrosity.

Finally, we could use the true interest rate (also known as the yield rate or the effective rate) in recording the interest expense each period and our results would be more accurate. Instead, we have used the simpler straight-line procedure. Using the prior example (2) where the bond was issued at a premium, the following journal entries would be made if the effective interest method was used:

January 1, 20X1

Same entry as the straight-line method.

July 1, 20X1

The amortization of the bond premium at each payment date will now be equal to the difference between the cash paid at each interest payment date ($100,000 × 14% × 1/2 = $7,000) and the bond's carrying value multiplied by the real, or effective interest rate. For July 1, 20X1, this would be $115,046 × 12% × 1/2 = $6,903. The difference ($7,000 − $6,903 = $97 rounded) would be the decrease to Bond Interest Expense and the amortization of the Bond Premium, as follows:

Bond Interest Expense	7,000	
Cash in Bank		7,000
Bonds Payable—Premium	97	
Bond Interest Expense		97

The amount of the Bond Premium amortization will then increase with each succeeding amortization period. For instance, the entry on December 31, 20X1 would be:

Bond Interest Expense	7,000	
Cash in Bank		7,000
Bonds Payable—Premium	103	
Cash in Bank		103

($7,000 less the carrying value after the prior amortization period $115,046 − $97 = $114,949 × 12% × 1/2 = $6,897).

SALE OF BONDS BETWEEN INTEREST PAYMENT DATES

In our previous examples it was assumed that bonds were issued on their interest payment date. However, in real life bonds are frequently issued between interest payment dates. Because of the administrative hardship it would impose for issuing corporation's to calculate the exact number of days between issuance and the first interest payment date for each bond purchase made, a full six months of interest will be paid to bondholders regardless of the actual issue date. In order to ensure that the bondholders are not compensated for the period of time that they did not hold the bond, the corporation will charge "accrued interest" for the time period starting with the interest payment date *before* issuance until the issuance date.

For example, suppose Romulus Corp. sold $300,000 of 10 percent, 10-year bonds at par on May 1, 2007. The interest payment dates are on January 1 and July 1. The entry to record the sale of the bonds would be:

May 1, 20XX		
Cash	310,000	
Bond Interest Expense		10,000
Bonds Payable		300,000

To record the issuance of $300,000 10%, 10-year bond on May 1, 20XX.

The extra $10,000 charge was calculated simply by multiplying the $300,000 principal amount by the rate of 10 percent, and then multiplying that result by the amount of months from the last interest payment date (January 1) until the issue date (May 1), or 4 months divided by the months in a year, or 4/12.

The entry on the first interest payment date would be:

July 1, 20XX

Bond Interest Expense	15,000	
Cash		15,000

To record the 6 months interest paid on the interest payment date ($300,000 × 10% × 1/2).

The net balance of the interest expense on July 1 is a debit of $5,000, representing interest paid for the period that the bondholders actually held the bond (May 1 to July1).

CONVERTIBLE BONDS

When the market rate of interest for debenture bonds issued by a company with our credit standing is around 15 percent and our common stock is being traded in the market at around 35 percent, we elect to issue 20-year *convertible* bonds with a 12 percent coupon and the proviso that the buyers can trade the bonds in for common stock at the exchange ratio of one share of common for each $40 of bond principal. The bonds can be "called" by us, after five years, at 105 per 100. (Bonds are always quoted at so much per 100 of par.)

Needless to say, people will not pay us par for 12 percent bonds if the market says we must pay 15 percent, but they might pay us par for 12 percent bonds if the bonds also carry the privilege of being converted into our common stock whenever the bondholders want to. In other words, we can get by with a significantly lower interest payment until the price of our stock rises to the point at which the bondholder would gain by exercising the option to convert. All this assumes, of course, that the market has real hope of a surge in the market value of our common stock.

From the investor point of view, a convertible bond has a certain attraction. The investors stand able to "get a piece of the action" if the value of our stock rises above 40; on the other hand, should the value of our stock tumble, they will not lose heavily because the market value of their bonds will fall only to the point at which the effective yield is approximately 15 percent. The convertible bond thus has an unlimited ceiling in value and, at the same time, a floor that limits the size of the possible loss.

Entries to record the issue of convertible bonds are made exactly like those to issue regular bonds. If and when some or all of the bonds are converted into common stock, there are two acceptable methods of recording the conversion. One is known as the book value method. This method assigns the difference between the bond's book value and the stock's par value to paid-in capital in excess of par value. The second method is called the market value method. Under this method the stock issuance is recorded at fair market value and a gain or loss is recorded upon the conversion. The form of the entry under both alternatives is as follows (assuming the bonds were issued at par and the stock's market value was $45 per share):

Book Value Method

Bonds Payable—Par	1,000	
Capital Stock—Common—		250
Par Value $10		
Paid-in Capital in Excess of		750
Par Value		

To record conversion of bond into 25 shares of common stock on the basis of 1 share for each $40 of bond.

Market Value Method

Bonds Payable—Par	1,000	
Loss on Conversion of Bond	125	
to Common Stock		
Capital Stock—Common—		250
Par Value $10		
Paid-in Capital in Excess of		875
Par Value		

($45 market value less $10 par value $\times$ 25 shares)

It has been estimated that about one-third of the bond issues in recent years have been convertibles.

BONDS WITH WARRANTS ATTACHED

In some cases a company may issue bonds that carry warrants that can be detached and turned in for common stock at a specified price. To illustrate, assume that we issue a series of 12 percent bonds, each with a warrant with a fair market value of $5 each. It has been widely argued that we are really issuing two securities rather than one; we're issuing a bond plus a warrant. If we issue the package at par, since part of the proceeds are attributable to the warrant, the bond itself is actually being issued at a discount. The question then is: What is the value of the bond without the warrant? To illustrate, assume that the bond provisions are as just described and that the bonds are valued at 99 without the warrants (ex-warrants). The entry to record this bond-and-warrant issue for $1,000 will then be:

Cash	995	
Bonds Payable—Discount	10	
Bonds Payable—Par		1,000
Common Stock Warrant Outstanding		5

To record 20-year, 12% bond issued with warrant.

This way the initial carrying value of the Bond Payable would be $990 (99% of the face value). The common stock warrants should be shown in the stockholders' equity section of the company's balance sheet.

TEST PROBLEM

Our Company issues $100,000 in $1,000 par, 20-year, 13 percent debenture bonds with warrants attached that provide for purchase of one share of our $10 par common stock at $5 per share. Each bond carries 10 warrants. Interest is paid semiannually. Without warrants, our bonds would have to carry 15 percent interest coupons to be salable at par, so the bond portion of the package is determined to amount to $87,406. The bonds and warrants are sold to a bank for $97,000.

REQUIRED

Journal entries (1) to issue the package, (2) to pay interest at the end of the first 6 months, and (3) to record exercise (conversion) of all the warrants into common stock. Assume the use of the book value method.

TEST PROBLEM SOLUTION SPACE

Debit   Credit

(1)

To record issue of 100 par $1,000 bonds, each with 10 warrants to buy one share of $10 par common stock for $5.

(2)

To record payment of coupon 1.

(3)

To record issue of 1,000 shares of common stock at $5 cash plus one warrant per share.

12

BASIC COST ACCOUNTING

WHAT IS COST ACCOUNTING?

Actually, cost accounting is not a separate area of accounting; but because it employs a few technical words and procedures of its own, we often think of cost accountants as somewhat separate from the so-called *financial accountants.*

The cost accountants specialize in finding the "cost" of products that we make, or the "cost" of operating a department within the manufacturing area of the company. In more recent years the talents of the cost accountants have been applied more and more to finding the costs of nonmanufacturing departments as well. For example, cost accountants now do a lot more cost accounting in banks and insurance companies, where there is no product output in the physical sense, and they also work in the areas of selling and administrative expenses as well as in the manufacturing area.

WHAT ARE THE PURPOSES OF COST ACCOUNTING?

There are three well-recognized purposes of cost accounting. The first, which is routine, is to help in the process of *determining the income* of any given accounting period. That consists primarily of determining the manufacturing costs and the amounts assignable to end-of-period inventories so that we can compute the cost of goods sold. When the company makes a variety of products, the determination of the manufacturing costs of each kind of product and the cost of goods sold for each class of product is no simple task.

167

A second and tremendously important responsibility of cost accounting (and, again, a routine one) is to assist in *cost minimization*. By this, of course, we mean minimizing cost while still accomplishing the production and sales objectives of the company each period. The cost accounting devices that are specifically aimed at cost minimization are such things as standard costs, flexible budgets, and responsibility accounting. We'll look into them later.

The third major contribution of cost accounting is to assist management in *making decisions* when costs are a factor (aren't they always?). Most of these are ad hoc decisions—decisions that call for special studies and intelligent selection of cost factors relevant to the decision.

In the present chapter we'll concentrate mostly on the first purpose—the routine job of income determination. We're concerned here about assigning costs to departments, reassigning the costs of service departments to producing departments, and then applying those costs to the product output so that we can determine the cost of goods sold and its complement, the cost of goods remaining in inventory. This whole chapter will be devoted to what is usually called "historical" or "actual" cost accounting in contrast with "standard" cost accounting, which we'll investigate later.

JOB-ORDER VERSUS PROCESS COST ACCOUNTING

Although the distinction is not always clearly defined, it is customary to recognize two general kinds of "actual cost" accounting. One is known universally as *job-order* cost accounting and the other as *process* cost accounting. "Job order" means that the company makes things that are, usually, designed specially to a customer's order. A good example would be the construction of houses, each of which is designed by an architect to comply with the wishes of the buyer. Here each job is a separate project and one would, of course, keep a separate cost account for each. There are many examples of job-order manufacture, although, obviously, they are not mass-production industries. On the other hand, an individual "job" may call for production of any number of identical products. The key feature of job-order cost accounting, then, is that we must keep a cost sheet for each job (a subsidiary record) and be sure to record on each cost sheet all the costs we incur that are chargeable to that job.

Process cost accounting is applied in situations in which one or more products are being manufactured on a more or less continuous schedule. Here, rather than find the cost of each unit separately, we accumulate our costs for a period of time (often for a month) and then divide the total cost for the period by the number of product units to get an average unit cost. In job-order situations the product is usually made to order and is not held in storage for future sale; in process situations we commonly manufacture finished goods that are stored for future sale.

Needless to say, many manufacturing situations represent a mixture of job-order and process activity, and hybrid accounting techniques are then applied to determine costs of manufacture, inventories, and costs of goods sold. In general, when there is room for choice, the simpler costing procedure seems to be in process cost accounting; when a choice exists, one should probably lean toward process rather than job-order cost accounting procedures.

In the sections that follow, we'll try to describe and illustrate the "actual" cost procedures in accounting for raw materials, direct labor, and, finally, manufacturing overhead under job-order and process cost conditions.

USE OF SUBSIDIARY LEDGERS

In job-order cost accounting, raw materials are charged to a raw materials account in our general ledger as they are purchased. Because a manufacturing company may use a great number of raw material items, it is necessary to do some extremely detailed accounting in order to keep track of the raw materials purchased, used, and remaining in inventory at a given point in time. Suppose we consume 3,000 different raw material items—could we ever record them in a single ledger account and hope to tell later from that account how much we've bought of each? Used of each? And have left over of each? Clearly not, so we must use subsidiary ledger accounts, as described in Chapter 3.

Let's systematically record *each* purchase of raw material on a card form (with a separate card for each kind of stuff we buy), and let's make entries on those cards the moment we receive and accept a batch of raw material. Therefore, if we stock 3,000 different kinds of raw materials, we'll have 3,000 such cards, and we'll call them our *subsidiary ledger* for raw materials (computerized, of course).

Each of the subsidiary ledger cards needs three columns: one to show debits for purchases, the second to show credits for materials issued as authorized by our requisition system, and the third to show our "running balance" of the item. Hence, at any time we should be able to go through our raw materials subsidiary ledger cards and find the complete story of each kind of material that we use. And, remember, when we need our total for financial statement purposes, we find it in our regular, general ledger control account.

JOB-ORDER COST ACCOUNTING

Accounting for Raw Materials

When raw materials are purchased (have been received, examined, and found to be acceptable), the quantities and dollar amounts of each kind are immediately posted in the received (debit) columns of the raw materials subledger accounts. As each entry is made on a subledger card, the third (balance) column is also updated to show the revised quantity on hand and dollar balance. The entries are the same whether we are operating under a process or a job-order cost accounting system. The technical accounting can be depicted in the following journal entry:

Raw Materials—Control (end of month only)   xxx
(also to subsidiary ledger cards in detail as each purchase is made)

Accounts Payable—Control (end of month only)   xxx
(also to subsidiary ledger accounts in detail as each purchase is made)

To record purchases of raw materials during a given month.

An employee is allowed to draw raw materials from the storeroom upon presenting a "requisition," which has been signed by someone in authority and identifies the job or department to be charged. As currently as feasible, the quantity of each raw material shown on each requisition is "priced" and entered in the issued (credit) column of the appropriate subsidiary ledger card. Pricing is done by looking at the appropriate subsidiary ledger card to see what the particular raw material cost per unit is. (This cost may be determined on an average-cost basis or on a first in, first out [FIFO] basis.) Regardless of whether we are using job-order or process costing, the credit entries to withdraw raw materials from stores are the same. At the end of the month the requisitions are totaled and one aggregate credit entry is made to the general ledger control account.

Under job-order cost circumstances, raw materials are requisitioned for application to specific jobs. The monthly summary debits for materials used will go to a control account called Work in Process, which controls a very important subsidiary ledger consisting of a cost sheet for each job that we are working on. Thus, a requisition for raw material gives rise to immediate credits to raw material subledger accounts and immediate debits to the cost sheets representing the various jobs; at the end of the month a summary entry is made (for total of all raw materials requisitions) crediting Raw Materials and debiting Work in Process for materials directly applied to the job, and manufacturing overhead for indirect materials used (see subsequent discussion on manufacturing overhead). An example of a direct raw material would be the paper used in the production of this book.

An example of an indirect material would be the glue used to bind the book. In journal form such an entry is as follows:

Work in Process—Control   xxx
    (for direct materials at the end of month)
    (also to subsidiary job cost sheets in detail as materials are requisitioned)

Manufacturing Overhead   xxx
    (for indirect materials at the end of the month)

    Raw Materials—Control (end of month)   xxx
    (detail to subledger cards currently)

To record raw materials usage for month.

Needless to say, the great volume of repetitive entries makes accounting for raw materials inventories and usage a prime candidate for computerization.

Accounting for Direct Labor Cost

Direct labor is labor cost that can (conveniently) be traced to a specific job and can readily be added to the cost of a specific job. The term is particularly appropriate in the case of job-order costing to distinguish direct labor from indirect labor that cannot be attached to a specific job but has to be prorated over all jobs that benefit from it. Indirect labor costs (i.e., factory maintenance personnel) would be another instance of a manufacturing overhead cost.

In this section we're concerned only with direct or productive labor. The whole trick here is to keep track of how much time each productive worker devotes to each job or task and feed the information to payroll clerks, who translate the time into money terms and then feed it on to the cost clerks, who copy the amounts onto the affected job cost sheets or process cost sheets. The secret here is time keeping via time clocks or time-keepers and code numbers for the jobs being worked on and for processing operations, all inscribed on time tickets. The fact is that so many variations in mechanics are possible that what is said here is intended only to convey the underlying aim of direct labor costing, which is to trace as much of your labor cost as feasible to the things that are produced by it so that your job cost sheets or process cost sheets will accumulate accurately, within tolerance limits, the "actual" raw materials and direct labor costs.

In journal entry form the direct labor costs, under a job cost system, are recorded as depicted in the following journal entry:

Work in Process (end of month only)   xxx
(Also to subsidiary job cost sheets in detail currently from direct labor time
    tickets)

    Wages Payable (or Payroll)   xxx

To record direct labor payroll for month.

First, let's consider the simpler situation—process costing. What we seek to do, when we use "actual" costs, is find the overhead costs of operating each service department and each producing department. We might refer to this step as our primary overhead.

Manufacturing Overhead Cost Accounting

It would complicate things beyond belief even to try to apply each manufacturing overhead cost separately to the various jobs produced under job-order conditions. Remember that we keep a separate job cost sheet for each job and that the direct raw materials and direct labor costs of each job are currently recorded on the cost sheets as the work progresses. But this can't be done with manufacturing overhead for three major reasons. First, by definition, manufacturing costs are the costs that simply cannot be traced directly to individual jobs; second, even if they could be so traced, we probably wouldn't make the effort because there are so many different items of overhead that the clerical cost would be exorbitant; and third, the overhead cost (unlike direct labor and direct materials) that happens to be incurred at the same time that specific jobs are being worked on is by no means likely to be the amount that is assignable to those jobs.

To get to the point: Under "actual" cost accounting (1) we estimate what the actual total manufacturing overhead will be for the coming year, (2) we estimate what our total direct labor hours, or total machine hours, will be during the coming year, (3) we then divide the estimated hours into the estimated overhead total to get an overhead rate per hour, and (4) as a given job progresses, we keep track of the hours spent on it and charge that job with the actual hours times the overhead rate. Thus is manufacturing overhead charged to jobs in a job-order system. Let's analyze this procedure.

The overhead rate is based on an estimate of total manufacturing overhead and total hours (of machine use or of direct labor) for the entire coming year, because use of a year's average overhead per hour makes so much more sense than it would to charge a given job (or group of jobs) with the overhead costs that just happened to occur while they were being worked on. An obvious case in point would be maintenance costs. It is quite typical that important maintenance programs are scheduled for times when plant activity is at its lightest, and it would be totally inequitable to charge such cost to the few jobs that happened to be "in the works" at the time. Some factory costs do, of course, increase and decrease along with fluctuations in production activity (these we call variable overhead), but many occur simply with the passage of time (these tend to be the fixed overhead costs such as manager's and supervisor's salaries, property taxes, and depreciation). In short, the most equitable solution to finding an overhead rate appears to be to use the estimated total for the coming year divided by the estimated hours.

An important refinement of our discussion of overhead rates is the development of a separate overhead rate for each production department. Many companies use what we have just been describing—a single plant-wide rate. However, there's no doubt that improved accuracy results when a job is charged with high overhead during its stay in a high-overhead department and low overhead while it's in a low-overhead department. The development of departmental rates requires, first, estimating the overhead costs for all departments, including service departments, then allocating the estimated service department costs to the producing departments, and, finally, dividing each producing department total by its estimated labor or machine hours or whatever other application base may be used.

Now let's follow through hypothetical manufacturing overhead entries and assume use of departmental rates.

(1)

Recording Actual Manufacturing Overhead During the Period
(e.g., utilities, factory rent, depreciation, etc.)

Manufacturing Overhead—Control	xx	
Credits to various accounts		xx
(Accounts Payable, Accumulated Depreciation, etc.)		

To record actual manufacturing overhead costs in general ledger control account.

(2)

Recording the Applied Manufacturing Overhead to the Various Jobs

Work in Process	xx

(Also to subsidiary job cost sheets in detail as jobs are finished; charges are based on hours worked on each job in each department multiplied by the overhead rate in each department.)

Manufacturing Overhead—Control	xx

To charge Work in Process and the individual jobs with overhead, at departmental hourly rates, as determined at the beginning of the year, and to credit the actual overhead accounts for the same amounts.

Obviously, the amount applied to Work in Process during the accounting period (entry 2) will not be the same exact amount as was actually incurred (entry 1). Therefore, the manufacturing overhead account will have either been overapplied (if a credit balance at the end of the period) or underapplied (if a debit balance at the end of the period). In most cases, the over- or underapplied amount will be closed to the cost of goods sold account.

PROCESS COST ACCOUNTING

Equivalent Units

In process cost systems manufacturing costs are accumulated on a department by department basis. In order to allocate the proper amount to each department, equivalent units of production must be calculated. Equivalent units are the units that would have been produced if the department was completing units one by one instead of mass producing the units in stages. In other words, 10,000 units 50% completed would be the equivalent of 5,000 completed units. Total department costs for the period must then be allocated between those units transferred to the next department for further processing (or to finished goods inventory) and the costs for units that have not yet been completed as at the end of the period (ending in Work in Process inventory for that department).

Companies using the process cost system issue departmental production reports that summarize the various component costs (direct materials, direct labor, and manufacturing overhead) incurred by the department during the accounting period.

Preparing a Departmental Production Report

Let us assume that Clink Corp. uses three different processes in manufacturing its product. The initial step in preparing a production report for Department 1 is to account for the physical flow of units. If 2,000 units were on hand at the beginning of the period and another 12,000 units were put into the production during the period and 3,000 units were left in the department at the end of the period, the beginning of the production report would read as follows:

Units to Account For

Work in Process, beginning	2,000	Units completed & transferred during the period	11,000
Units started during the period	12,000	Units remaining at the end of the period	3,000
Total units to be accounted for	14,000		14,000

In step 2 the total cost of production within the department for the period must be determined. This is done by adding total costs incurred by the department during the period to the costs previously allocated to the units in the beginning Work in Process inventory. In our example, raw material cost transferred in was $3,400 and direct labor and overhead used during the period was $5,000.

In step 3 the Equivalent Units of Production will be determined. This is done by taking the total units left over in the ending inventory and multiplying those units by their percentage of completion during the period. In this example, 11,000 units were transferred on to the next process, so it can be assumed that 11,000 units were 100% complete. If our analysis determined that only one-half of the materials were used on the leftover units, and only 40 percent of the direct labor and overhead were applied, equivalent units would be as follows:

	Total	Materials	Direct Labor & Overhead
Units completed and transferred to Dept. 21	11,000	11,000	11,000
Units Ending Work in Process Inventory	3,000	1,500	1,200
Total Equivalent Units of Production	14,000	12,500	12,200

In step 4, the cost of equivalent units must be determined. This is done by dividing the total costs (step 2) by equivalent units (step 3). In our example, materials cost per equivalent unit would be $3,400/$12,500 = 27.2 cents. Direct Labor and Overhead costs (known together as conversion costs) would be $5,000/$12,200 = 41 cents. Therefore, the unit cost to be allocated between the units to be transferred out and the units to be leftover is 68.2 cents (27.2 + 41). Accordingly:

Total costs transferred out equal 11,000 units $\times$ 68.2 cents =	$7,502
Total costs in Ending Inventory =	
Materials—1,500 units $\times$ 27.2 cents = $408	
Conversion Costs—1,200 units $\times$ .41 = 492	900
Total Cost of Production for the Period	$8,402

Managers use cost information provided by the departmental production report in many ways, such as analyzing whether material, labor, and manufacturing overhead costs are consistent with prior projections. Companies using process costing systems manufacture products on a continuous basis.

Completion of the Cost Flow Analysis

As the goods are completed, the transfer of the goods from the work in process stage to the finished goods stage is recorded by crediting the Work in Process account and debiting another inventory account known as "Finished Goods Inventory." This inventory account is analogous to the Merchandise Inventory account of a company that purchases already made goods for resale. Upon the sale of any item in the Finished Goods Inventory, Cost of Goods Sold would be debited and the Finished Goods Inventory would be credited for the cost of the particular item sold.

Internal Cost Statements

The reports that cost accountants prepare for management use are, of course, designed according to the ground rules of each situation. Two major reports tend to be widely used—the statement of costs of goods manufactured (and sold) and schedules of departmental overhead costs. In addition, there are unlimited varieties of reports on departmental labor and raw material usage. Following are pro forma examples of the two major reports:

OUR COMPANY
Cost of Goods Manufactured and Sold
Year Ended December 31, 20XX

Materials used:		
Materials Inventory, January 1	xxx	
Purchases	xxx	
	xxx	
Materials Inventory December 31	xxx	xxx
Direct labor		xxx
Manufacturing overhead:		
(List actual items and amounts)—actual	xxx	
Less: Amount not applied ("unapplied")	xxx	
Manufacturing overhead applied to production		xxx
Total manufacturing costs		$xxx
Add: Work in process on January 1		xxx
		$xxx
Less: Work unfinished on December 31		xxx
Cost of goods manufactured		$xxx
Add: Finished goods on hand on January 1		xxx
		$xxx
Less: Finished goods on inventory December 31		xxx
Cost of goods sold (see income statement)		$xxx

TEST PROBLEM

Shown below are a number of spaces for making journal entries to record the flow of costs through a departmentalized job-order system. For each journal entry the explanation is given, but the accounts and amounts to be debited and credited have not been entered. On the basis of each explanation, it's up to you to fill in the debit and credit entries. Then prepare a statement of cost of goods manufactured. As usual, a solution is given in Appendix A.

TEST PROBLEM SOLUTION SPACE

	Debit	Credit

(1)

Record purchase of $100,000 of direct raw materials on account and indicate subledger record.

(2)

Record $97,000 of direct raw materials requisitions for materials going into work in process. Show subledger entries also.

(3)

Record $364,000 of direct labor and wages payable going to work in process. (Note for later use: $174,000 of direct labor was performed in Production 1 and $190,000 in Production 2.)

(4)

Record $643,000 of overhead to Factory Overhead Control, charging $127,000 of this to Service 1; $94,000 to Service 2; $236,000 to Production 1; and $186,000 to Production 2. Make your credit to Various Accounts.

(5)

Transfer $127,000 from Service 1 as follows: to Service 2, $34,000; to Production 1, 863,000; to Production 2, 830,000. Make general ledger debit and credit to Factory Overhead for total.

(6)

Transfer balance in Service 2 ($ 128,000) to Production 1, $64,000, and Production 2, $64,000. Both debit and credit Factory Overhead—Control for $128,000.

(7)

Charge Work in Process $614,000, and indicate posting to subledger job cost sheets, for overhead applied in Production 1 at the rate of 200% of direct labor in Production 1, which was $174,000, and at the rate of 140% of direct labor in Production 2, which was $190,000.

(8)

Cost of goods finished as shown on job cost sheets was $960,000.

(9)

Close unapplied overhead remaining in Production 1 and Production 2 to Cost of Goods Sold.

OUR COMPANY
Statement of Cost of Goods Manufactured
Year Ended December 31, 20X1

Raw materials used		$
Direct labor		
Manufacturing overhead—actual	$	
Less: Unapplied overhead		
Total cost of manufacturing	$	
Add: Work in process, January 1		$ 100,000
Less: Work in process, December 31		
Cost of goods manufactured		$

C H A P T E R

13

COST STANDARDS

WHAT'S A STANDARD?

Now that we've spent an entire chapter exploring "actual" cost accounting, we're about to examine the proposition that actual cost accounting isn't as actual as it seems to be. Paradoxically, standard cost accounting is really more actual than actual cost accounting is.

Perhaps we can go directly to the point. Cost accounting focuses on finding the *cost* of an activity or a thing, such as a product. Certainly we'd like to avoid wild guesses and get as near to the *actual* cost of the activity or thing as we can (without wasting money in the effort). Now, standard cost accounting holds that when we set out to make or do something involving cost outlays, we may be less efficient than we should be; and if we're below par in efficiency, we are wasting time, money, or both. Under standard cost philosophy we assert that the *costs* of inefficiencies should be separated from the costs of the activity or thing we're working on. Actual cost accounting makes no real attempt to separate out those wastes, and they become incorporated indistinguishably as part of the actual cost of the product or activity. Under standard cost accounting the *actual cost* of a product can include *only the costs that are applied effectively* and all excesses are *costs of waste* rather than costs of product. Such excesses are called *variances*, and almost the whole aim of standard cost accounting is to sort out, to detect, variances (wastes) and report them to management *immediately* for remedial action. So "actual" costs are not actual costs, standard costs are actual costs!

Now, what's a standard? It is a scientific (engineered) *predetermination of what something should cost.* If you know in advance what something should cost, then that serves as the model, or standard, against which you compare your actual outlays; and your differences (materials, labor, overhead) are accounted for not as *cost* of the thing, but as variances (usually wastes). In short, under standard cost accounting, the total incurred costs are separated into two categories: the costs that are effectively incurred (the standard costs) and the costs that are wastefully incurred (the variances).

ILLUSTRATION OF STANDARDS—STANDARD COST PER UNIT

Because you're interested in concepts rather than bookkeeping complexities, we'll deal with a relatively simple situation. Assume that our company makes just one product and that all the work is done in a one-room, one-department plant. A committee of company personnel, including our cost accountant, our production manager, our engineer, our purchasing agent, and any other persons who can make a contribution, is set up to "figure" a standard cost per unit of our regular product. Here's what they finally develop:

OUR PRODUCT
Standard Cost per Unit

Raw material, 50 pounds of material A @ $1	$ 50.00
Direct labor, 10 hours @ 810	100.00
Manufacturing overhead, 10 hours @ $15	150.00
Total standard cost of one unit	$300.00

We'll refer to these figures repeatedly in the discussion that follows.

RAW MATERIALS STANDARDS

The standard cost specifications for our product allow us to consume 50 pounds of material A, no more and no less. The 50-pound quantity should be based on extremely careful analysis of all factors. First, the 50 pounds should be based on that *quality* of raw material that we'll buy. We might buy a cheaper material, but that would perhaps cause us to waste more and thus need to use more; use of a poorer quality of material might lead to more labor and more manufacturing overhead cost. Therefore, our engineers pick the raw material of quality that they believe will minimize our costs, and they determine how much (the standard quantities) we should use in producing one unit (or one batch) of our product.

The standard quantity of raw material to be used does not contemplate complete avoidance of scrap, but it does contemplate an allowance for scrap that aligns with other aspects of the work. You can't saw a board in two without producing some sawdust; you can't cut shoes out of a hide without some leftover, worthless clippings, and so on. But the important point is that the 50 pounds in our illustration should be "tight" enough to exclude needless (waste) scrap yet "loose" enough to allow our labor and machinery to work efficiently.

Thus, our engineers finally conclude that we should allow a standard quantity of 50 pounds of raw material per unit even though the final product may weigh only 45 pounds, since the standard must include a scrap allowance if called for under the circumstances.

In the meantime our purchasing expert has been making a thorough study of the market for our raw material (and has kept the engineer posted so his computation can incorporate purchase-price alternatives). For the quality selected, the price varies somewhat in relation to the quantity ordered. After taking into consideration the costs of storage, it is concluded that the price of $1 per unit is optimal and a *standard price* of $1 is agreed upon.

Needless to say, all prices fluctuate and a standard may soon become out of date. However, it is necessary to compromise here. We want our standard costs to be current, but to change them with every fluctuation in market price would be expensive and would actually sacrifice one major advantage of standard costs—the avoidance of varying prices for the same things as they flow through the factory. So it appears that most companies, even though they may avow that they employ current standards, do not adjust their standard prices more than once a year.

RAW MATERIALS ACCOUNTING—STANDARD COSTS

The big objective of standard cost accounting is cost minimization or cost control. Everybody realizes that the longer a leak goes untended the greater the loss. The rewards of a standard cost system are realized in proportion to the quality of the job of setting the standards and the speed with which variances from standard are reported to those in a position to stop the leaks. In many situations variances in materials and direct labor costs are reported daily. Contrast that with old-fashioned actual cost systems, which claim victory if their relatively unhelpful reports reach management sooner than the second week after the end of each month.

To speed the disclosure of materials variances and, equally important, to relate the variances insofar as possible to the persons responsible for them, the favored practice is to recognize *variances in purchase prices* at the point of receipt of the materials and *variances in quantities* consumed at the point of requisitioning or as soon thereafter as possible. In other words, materials variances fall into two general types—price and quantity. Price variance on a purchase of materials is the amount paid above or below the standard price. It is recognized at the point of receipt as follows:

(1)

Raw Materials (at standard)	35,000	
Materials Price Variance	3,500	
Accounts Payable		38,500

To debit Raw Materials at the standard price of $1 per pound for the actual purchase of 35,000 pounds of material A and credit Accounts Payable for the actual purchase quantity at the actual cost of $1.10 per pound and to charge the variance of $.10 per actual pound to Materials Price Variance. This cleanses the price variances out of the recorded materials costs.

A debit to the Materials Price Variance account indicates an unfavorable variance, since the actual price exceeded the budgeted (standard) price.

Note in entry 1 that material A will be inventoried at its standard price of $1; it will be carried through the accounts to its ultimate disposition as part of cost of goods sold at the same $1 price. If all purchases of material A throughout the year also are recorded at $1, this eliminates any need to use first in, first out or average-cost schemes for pricing the requisitions; $1 is the standard price on all requisitions. This saves bookkeeping.

At the end of the year, whatever amount has been accumulated in the Materials Price Variance account may be closed out to our Income Summary account as an expense for the year or, if the amount is significant, a proportionate part of the variance may be added to the standard cost inventory for balance sheet purposes. Actually, materials price variances, whether on the debit or credit side, are not really losses and gains; they theoretically attach to the materials that have gone on out or have remained in the ending inventory.

The cost of raw materials used is, of course, two-dimensional—quantity × price. If we cleanse the materials for all price variances as we buy them and put them in the storeroom, the price dimension has been translated from actual to standard. This means that we need only look for quantity variances, the other dimension, as the materials are drawn from stores and pass on to work in process, finished goods, and, finally, cost of goods sold. Techniques for finding quantity variances on a "realtime" basis (i.e., as they occur) must be worked out by accountants and production personnel within each particular set of conditions. For our purposes of understanding the basics, let's assume that in our one-cylinder plant we requisition, at the beginning of each day, enough material A for the planned production of our product for that day. Pretend we set out to produce 1,000 units today. We might issue a requisition for 50,000 pounds of material A, which is the standard quantity for 1,000 units. But let's not let our standard cost system overpower our production system. We know, actually, that we'll produce somewhat more or, maybe, somewhat less, than 1,000 units; also, we've set our material quantity standard fairly tight, so we'll likely have a quantity variance of, say,

5 percent. Let's be on the safe side, to avoid running out of material a half hour before quitting time, and requisition an extra 10,000 pounds. (We can always return the stuff to stores at the end of the day if necessary.)

Now we go to work and turn out as many of our product as we comfortably can, and we end up making 1,040 units during the day. We then find we have 4,000 pounds of unused material A, which we dutifully cart back to stores and get credit for (possibly an adjustment or correction on the original requisition). We're now ready to make an entry for the day's usage of raw materials, as follows:

(2)

Work in Process (standard quantity	52,000	
used × standard price per pound)		
Materials Quantity Variances	4,000	
Raw Materials (actual quantity		56,000
used × standard price per pound)		

To record consumption today of 56,000 pounds of material A used at a standard price of $1 per pound for production of 1,040 units of our product at 50 pounds per unit, or 52,000 pounds standard quantity for variance of 4,000 pounds at $1.

Once again, the debit to the Variance account indicates that it is unfavorable, due to the fact that more raw materials had to be used than was budgeted.

It is, of course, unlikely in practice that a journal entry would be made each day; but a simple three-column register could be used to keep track of the three elements of the entry, one line for each day, and at the end of the month one grand entry could be made for the totals. In the meantime, the daily output and daily variances would be reported to the appropriate persons.

Regretfully, we cannot explore the myriad of production situations under which materials quantity variations may be accounted for—this is what thick cost accounting textbooks are for. However, it should be appropriate for you to inquire about the accounting recognition of such variances in your company and learn how the variances are analyzed once they're disclosed. For example, in a multidepartment situation with more than one kind of material, the quantity variances may be broken down by departments (to "lay the blame"), by causes, and by kinds of material as well. Such data can be systematically produced in endless detail by computer, with resulting enhancement of managerial control.

DIRECT LABOR ACCOUNTING—
STANDARD COSTS

Some of the same concepts that we have outlined in the section on raw materials apply equally to direct labor. Again, let's stick to basics.

Direct labor cost, like raw materials cost, is two-dimensional. We are again concerned with quantity (hours) and price (wages). The major difference is that we can't stock up on labor hours in our storeroom as we can materials, so we don't issue requisitions.

Assume continuation of our example in which, today, we produce 1,040 units with standard labor content of 10 hours each and standard wage rate of $10 per hour. This means our standard labor cost for today is 1,040 × 10 × $10, or $104,000. Actually, however, we used 10,730 hours of labor and the employee's earnings were $109,075. Right away you recognize that we missed our target by $109,075 minus $104,000, or $5,075. How do we analyze this "gross" variance into its quantity and price components?

First, let's find the wage rate variance. For working 10,730 hours the employees earned $109,075. Is $109,075 more or less than the standard wage total for 10,730 hours? Merely multiply 10,730 by $10 and compare. We find 10,730 times $10 is $107,300, which shows that we are paying a wage rate variance of $109,075 minus $107,300, or $1,775.

Second, do we have a quantity variance? The answer is yes, and in the case of labor it's usually called an efficiency variance. Having cleansed all labor hours for the wage variance, we merely find the differences between actual and standard hours and multiply by the standard wage rate of $10. Thus, our labor efficiency variance is 10,730 actual hours minus 1,040 × 10 = 10,400 standard hours, or 330 hours, which at $10 per hour gives an efficiency variance of $3,300. Added together, the efficiency variance of $3,300 and the wage variance of $1,775 equals our gross labor variance of $5,075 for the day.

In journal entry form, the recognition of gross labor liability, standard cost, and variances for the day is recorded as follows:

(3)

Work in Process	104,000	
(standard rate × standard hours)		
Labor Rate Variance	1,775	
(actual hours × difference in rate)		
Labor Efficiency Variance	3,300	
(standard rate × difference in hours)		
Wages Payable (actual rate × actual hours)		109,075

Both variances were unfavorable since the actual hours (10,730) exceeded the budgeted hours (10,400) and the actual wage rate ($10.16) exceeded the budgeted rate ($10).

Again, the techniques for determining the standard labor time (with scientific time-study methods), the standard wage (which can be an average wage for each type of labor in each department), and the real-time efficiency variances must be developed by experts within your particular environment and cannot be elaborated upon here. It can only be added that in competitive industry it makes real sense to have a standard cost system for all aspects of manufacturing costs in order to operate profitably in an atmosphere of thin profit margins.

MANUFACTURING OVERHEAD ACCOUNTING—STANDARD COSTS

One of the better inventions in cost accounting in recent years is the flexible overhead budget. Sure, we take liberties with all budgets and the budgets become flexible in a certain sense, but this one works on an entirely different principle. What happens so sensibly under a flexible overhead budget is that at the end of each month (or other period) you determine what your output and manufacturing overhead costs have been for that month and then determine what your manufacturing overhead should have been for the production of that actual output.

For the moment let's assume that your manufacturing overhead is completely variable and that your scientific analysis of costs shows your overhead, at optimum level, to be $1 per standard direct labor hour. Then if your output for the month just ended was such as to justify 2,000 direct labor hours, your overhead cost should have been $2,000. In other words, the flexible budget doesn't tell you how much you should allow for overhead cost for the coming month in a given department; rather, it works entirely by hindsight. When the month is ended, you count your actual output, compute allowable overhead at that level, and compare allowable with actual.

Actually, as you well know, some overhead costs are quite variable, some are quite sticky, and some fall in between. So a flexible budget for a department is a list of all the overhead costs that department will incur and, in a series of columns representing various levels of activity for a month, the dollar amount of each overhead item at each activity level. The activity level can be designated as percentages of capacity, or direct labor or machine hours, units of output, or any other sensible measure of departmental activity. Commonly, the activity levels are within the normal operating range and at intervals of 10 percent, which means that if you operate at, say, 86 percent of capacity, you'll have to estimate the dollar allowance for each overhead cost because it falls between your 80 percent and 90 percent column. A highly condensed example of a flexible budget is shown in Figure 13.1.

Let's utilize the budget in Figure 13.1 as a continuation of the example of Our Company. Assume that the actual amount debited to Manufacturing Overhead this month turns out to be $170,000, made up of nonvariable expenses of $60,000 and variable expenses of $110,000. How do we evaluate these figures?

Figure 13.1   Flexible Overhead Budget for One Month

	Capacity					
Expenses	**50**	**60**	**70**	**80**	**90**	**100**
Variable (list them)	$ 60,000	$ 72,000	$ 84,000	$ 96,000	$108,000	$120,000
Nonvariable (list them)	60,000	60,000	60,000	60,000	60,000	60,000
Totals	$120,000	$132,000	$144,000	$156,000	$168,000	$180,000
Direct labor hours	6,000	7,200	8,400	9,600	10,800	12,000
Standard overhead rate per direct labor hour (180,000/12,000)						$ 15.00

First, is the $170,000 total more or less than the amount justifiable by our actual activity for the month? To answer, we use hindsight to develop a budget. We note in the Figure 13.1 budget that the variable expenses regularly are scheduled at $10 per direct labor hour while the nonvariable expenses remain stable at a total of $60,000. We worked 10,730 direct labor hours, but we should have worked only 10,400 (which is the number of units produced—1,040 times the standard number of direct labor hours per unit). Should we expect our variable overhead actually to fluctuate with the allowed standard labor hours or with the actual direct labor hours? It would seem that one must acknowledge it as good performance if the production workers keep the variable overhead costs down to $10 per actual labor hour, because they could hardly be expected to avoid variable overhead costs that result from all labor hours, including those in excess of standard labor hours. So our overhead budget for 10,730 direct labor hours is $60,000 of nonvariable plus variable equal to $10 × 10,730 actual direct labor hours, or $167,300. The difference between the budget of $167,300 and the actual variable overhead of $170,000 is $2,700, which we label our spending variance.

Let's examine the overhead variance further. If we turned out 1,040 units of product and have a standard overhead cost of $150 per unit, our standard overhead cost for the month is clearly $150 × 1,040, or $156,000, while our actual total was assumed to be $170,000. It would appear that we have a gross variance of $14,000. We have identified $2,700 as so-called spending variance. Can we pinpoint the remaining $11,300 of gross variance? Yes.

We worked 10,730 direct labor hours to produce what we should have attained with 10,400 hours, and in our budget we have allowed $15 per actual hour. So if we wasted 330 hours, we can ascribe $4,950 of overhead cost to inefficiency. We do, in fact, always calculate an overhead efficiency variance as the number of hours wasted (330) times the standard overhead rate ($15).

So now we have accounted for $2,700 plus $4,950, or $7,650 of our $14,000 gross variance. Where is the remaining $6,350? The answer is so-called idle capacity variance. This variance deals with nonvariable costs only, and it is easy to compute. We worked 10,730 hours as compared with 100% capacity of 12,000—the plant was idle for 1,270 hours this month. Our cost of being ready to work (our plant, or nonvariable, costs) is exactly $5 per hour at capacity ($60,000 divided by 12,000 hours), and 1,270 wasted hours at $5 each equals our $6,350 of idle capacity variance.

The calculation of these overhead variances is summarized in Figure 13.2. It should be noted that many companies use partial standard costs and do not fully analyze their gross overhead variances.

Each of these three overhead variances was unfavorable. The spending variance was unfavorable due to the fact that the budgeted variable cost per hour was less than actual. The efficiency variance was unfavorable

Figure 13.2   Schedule of Overhead Variances

Spending variance:			
Actual total overhead for month		$170,000	
Budget for 10,730 direct labor hours:			
Variable (10,730 × $10 standard rate)	$107,300		
Fixed	60,000	167,300	$ 2,700
Efficiency variance:			
Actual labor hours at standard rate			
(10,730 × $15)		$160,950	
Standard labor hours at standard rate			
(10,400 × $15)		156,000	4,950
Idle Capacity variance:			
Hours of unused (idle) capacity			
(12,000 − 10,730) = 1,270 hrs. @ $5			6,350
Gross overhead variance			
($170,000 − $150 × 1,040)			$14,000

because actual labor hours used exceeded the budgeted amount, and the idle capacity variance was unfavorable due to the fact that the company could have used the plant longer than it actually did.

STANDARD COST APPLICATIONS

The concept of standard costs can be applied in almost any spending situation, including administrative and selling departments. Of course, the setting of standards is likely to be most accurate when you are making only one simple product on a mass output basis and have loads of experience to rely on. Standards can always be set, no matter how great the uncertainty, but the greater the uncertainty, the more careful you must be in your interpretation of the resulting variances. Quite obviously, an inaccurate standard produces variances that are equally inaccurate, and management must simply adjust its reactions to the existing condition. When standards can be set with great accuracy, small variances have much more meaning than they have with standards that are based on rough estimates.

It follows that the bookkeeping for standard costs is a small part of the battle. The most important job is to analyze the variances as to their causes and to take remedial action before the leaks have become costly. The inventive construction of a standard cost system of accounting provides, insofar as possible, for the automatic assignment of *variance responsibilities* to departments and even to individuals within departments.

TEST PROBLEM

The problem that follows is quite similar to the one used for illustrative purposes in this chapter. You are given the standard cost specifications of a hypothetical product and a series of transactions, from which you will trace the flow of costs through a standard cost system in journal entry form.

The standard cost specifications for the product, which is always manufactured in batches of 100 units, are as follows:

Standard Cost per Batch

Raw materials, 5,000 square feet @ $2	$ 10,000
Direct labor, 300 hours @ $12	3,600
Manufacturing overhead 300 (labor) hours @ $20	6,000
Standard cost, 100 units (one batch)	$ 19,600

The standard overhead rate was determined on the basis of budgeted overhead costs at capacity of 8,000 direct labor hours for a month, as follows:

Variable costs, 8,000 hours @ $12	$ 96,000
Nonvariable costs	64,000
Total at capacity, 8,000 hours @ $20	$160,000

REQUIRED

In the spaces that follow, make journal entries to record the information already shown in the explanation to each entry. Assume these to be summary entries for one month.

TEST PROBLEM SOLUTION SPACE

	Debit	Credit

(1)

To record purchase of 120,000 square feet of raw material at $2.04 per square foot. Raw material price variances are recorded at point of purchase and the materials are put in inventory at standard.

(2)

To record requisitions for 102,000 square feet of raw material used to produce 20 batches of finished product. (Make a debit, at standard cost, directly to Finished Goods.)

(3)

Finished Goods
Labor Wage Variance
Labor Efficiency Variance
    Wages Payable

To record $75,640 of wages payable for 6,100 hours of direct labor in the production of 20 batches. (Again, make a debit directly to Finished Goods for the standard cost of 20 batches.)

(4)

Manufacturing Overhead
    Various Accounts

To record all kinds of manufacturing overhead costs incurred during the month, $140,000, made up of variable costs of $76,000 and nonvariable costs of $64,000.

(5)

Finished Goods
Overhead—Spending Variance
Overhead—Efficiency Variance
Overhead—Idle Plant Variance
    Manufacturing Overhead

To charge Finished Goods with standard overhead cost of goods finished and to allocate the gross variance to three variance accounts.

14

INTERNAL MANAGEMENT ACCOUNTING

THE CONCEPT OF MANAGEMENT ACCOUNTING

Nobody is quite sure where accounting, in its narrowest sense, leaves off and where management, in the active sense, begins. First, we ought to agree that any accounting that is not helpful in some way should be scrapped. In all of its phases, "useful" accounting is useful to some sort of management, whether it be the officers and subofficers of the company, the investors and potential investors, the creditors and potential creditors, or one or more government agencies. Each of these users of accounting data manages its relationships with the enterprise, in part at least, on the basis of accounting reports—all of which thereby qualify as management-serving.

For the purposes of this chapter we are limiting management to insiders only—the whole spectrum of persons on the corporate organization chart who have responsibilities for reaching decisions that will influence costs and revenues or be influenced by them. And we'll define as management accounting the accumulation, classification, storage, reporting, and interpreting of cost and revenue data to provide management with the optimum amount of useful information to help in the formulation of decisions.

Certain management accounting procedures are continuous in nature. The accounting documents and ledger accounts are so organized that the data are accumulated and reported continuously without any special call for help by the management who will receive the information. We'll consider these very briefly under the headings of responsibility accounting, standard costing, and direct costing.

RESPONSIBILITY ACCOUNTING

In recent years a lot of fuss has been made over a very obvious, prosaic idea. The idea is this: Some costs are beyond a person's control, so let's not charge them to that person. If you agree with that proposition, you will next agree with the converse, that in making cost allocations we should examine each one, determine *who was responsible for it*, and then charge the cost against that person's department. *It is probable that almost every cost incurred by an enterprise can be traced to someone as the responsible party.* In general, operating costs are recurring, so it follows that a fixed pattern of cost assignments usually will be established—at least with respect to most costs.

An important accompaniment to "responsibility" cost assignments is a structure of departmental budgets, preferably flexible budgets, so that at the end of each quarter, or each month, the actual costs charged against each department can be viewed in comparison with the amount budgeted for the attained level of activity.

As a postscript to the definition of responsibility accounting, it must be added that the responsibility basis should be the guiding factor in the primary spreading of expenses. In many situations the expenses of service departments can, secondarily, be transferred to the producing departments on a responsibility basis. However, that will not always be true, and some costs may then remain in service departments. They also must be assigned to producing departments on a "best judgment" basis in order to complete the job of costing the goods manufactured in the producing departments; but such "judgmental" allocations, since they are beyond the control of the producing departments, should be excluded from any reckoning of the performance efficiencies of the producing departments.

The concept of responsibility accounting also works very well in the effort to control your selling and administrative expenses. What is needed is an organization chart clearly defining departmental responsibilities and identifying the responsible department heads so that one or more ledger accounts can be set up for each and the expenses can then be assigned and the departmental efficiencies evaluated. A budget may, again, be developed for each department; however, since it is quite difficult to measure performance when there is no objective unit of output, the budget may simply be a forecast, planned expense allowance for each month in advance.

STANDARD COSTING

Because Chapter 13 was devoted to it, standard costing is mentioned here only to have it prominently included among the internal management accounting devices.

As may not have been made fully evident, the management value in standard costing is found in the reporting and analysis of variances. The process reflects the principle of exceptions, one of the old, well-worn principles of managerial control. The principle holds that we report to busy management only the exceptions (variances from standard). If everything is "nominal," as the astronauts say, no report is necessary. Why flood the boss with "bed sheets" full of figures that merely show that nothing untoward has happened? A corollary is that, in any report to management, it may be possible for the accountant to underline or otherwise emphasize each item or figure that calls for action. The idea is to keep those reports condensed and put details in supporting schedules.

In standard cost accounting it is possible to devise an infinite number of variance accounts. For example, you could have a separate materials price variance account and a separate quantity variance account for each kind of material, and you could then subdivide each into departmental accounts. Probably that would be absurd in almost any situation, but the point is that the variances are worth recognizing and reporting only *if they're actionable*. In other words, it doesn't do much good to report month after month a variance that simply cannot be rectified.

DIRECT COSTING

The last of the routine management accounting processes that we'll examine is direct costing. As in the case of standard costing and responsibility accounting, the ledger account system may be so structured that the routine accounting is conducted on a continuous rather than an ad hoc basis.

"Direct costing" is a misnomer. We have always reserved the term direct cost to identify a cost that can be traced directly (without apportionment) to some end product. What accountants now mean when they speak of direct costing is that in accounting for manufacturing costs they will feed into the inventory accounts (which are current assets) only *costs that vary with the amount produced*. The fixed (nonvariable) costs, because they will be incurred whether we produce anything or not, will be charged off against income in the period in which they are incurred. The fixed costs, under this scheme of things, are often referred to as *period* costs for that reason.

Direct costing is great for one important reason: If it is practiced, it means that the company has studied the behavior patterns of its various kinds of costs and is in a position to deal intelligently with them. As has been noted several times, costs may vary with the level of production or with some other activity measure, or they may remain relatively nonvariable. In between the costs that are completely variable and those that are completely fixed lie the behavior patterns of all other costs. Some rise, in a curved fashion, slower or faster than the activity measure to which they are related; they are commonly termed semivariable costs. Others rise in stair-step fashion as activity increases; they are commonly termed *semifixed costs*. Knowledge of cost behavior is of critical importance to the preparation of budgets, whether flexible or not, and it is also critical in the fashioning of some of the decisions we are about to discuss.

On the other hand, direct costing doesn't appear to fare well theoretically in the preparation of periodic financial statements. In other words, the very basic direct cost notion that the fixed costs are period costs is hard to defend. In short, in compiling the costs of goods manufactured, is it reasonable to assert that the manufacturing process causes no depreciation, no property taxes, no insurance, and no supervisory costs? To take an extreme example, assume that for a given year a company, for whatever reason, chooses to refrain from all selling activity and devote its full resources to the making and stockpiling of goods for sale in future periods. Would it make sense to suggest that the company has operated all year at a loss equal to its nonvariable manufacturing costs? Are those costs actually losses rather than costs of manufacturing? You should reject direct costing for annual statement purposes (it has not received the blessing of the income tax folks as of this date) and stick to its opposite form, which is universally known as *absorption* or *full absorption costing*.

DIFFERENTIAL COSTS AND RELATED DECISIONS

Most of the remainder of this chapter will be devoted to cost aspects of decisions that may need to be faced from time to time in an ad hoc fashion—decisions that are not based on routine cost accumulation and reporting but rather call for selective cost groupings. In other words, we're now concerned with what is so often referred to as the need for different costs for different purposes.

The term *differential costs* has gained much prominence in recent years, and it will probably become increasingly recognized as a cost concept to be reckoned with.

Differential cost means the total addition to costs caused by any addition to output. It's that simple. If your total costs that would be incurred in a given period by producing, say, 20,000 units would be $100,000 and your total if you were to produce 25,000 would be $115,000, then the differential output is 5,000 units, the corresponding differential cost is $15,000, and the unit differential cost for that particular set of assumptions is $3. Thus, differential cost is the added cost of doing something extra. The concept has numerous decision-making applications, but it should be applied with caution. Let's consider a few examples.

Our Company in a given year produced and sold 100,000 units of its product. Total manufacturing costs were $1,000,000 (for an average unit cost of $10); total selling and administrative costs were $300,000. Our plant capacity for a year is 150,000 units, and we learn that next year the federal government will be in the market for 50,000 units, on which we are invited to bid. We immediately make a cost behavior study and determine that 30 percent of all our costs ($1,300,000) are nonvariable and the remainder are, for all practical purposes, variable. From this we conclude that our differential (you may prefer to call it incremental) cost of making and selling 50,000 incremental, or differential, units to the government would be 50 percent of the variable costs we incurred at the 100,000-unit level, or 50 percent of 70 percent of $1,300,000, which is $455,000, or $9.10 per unit (as compared with an average total cost of $13 per unit at the 100,000-unit level). Knowing this differential cost puts management in a position to increase total profits by supplying the 50,000 units to the government at any price above $9.10 (assuming, of course, that we can continue to sell the 100,000 through regular channels and at regular prices). In other words, the unit cost with which management should primarily be concerned in this case is the unit differential cost. It should always be borne in mind, in working from a differential cost base, that to seek volume increases by cutting prices invites price cuts by one's competitors, so the differential cost approach to pricing must be applied with great care.

Another interesting application of differential costs exists when a company, say the one we have just been considering, has made sales only for cash or has followed an ultraconservative policy in making credit sales. Assume that we produce 100,000 units as before and sell all of them for cash at $15 each for a before-tax profit of $200,000. Query: What percentage of bad debts could we afford if we were to allow customers to charge their purchases, assuming we continue to sell 100,000 for cash and, as the result of permitting credit sales, believe we can sell an additional 50,000 units? The answer lies in a differential cost calculation. If we produce and sell 50,000 more units, our total differential cost, as in the earlier example, will be $455,000; and this is the net amount we must receive to break even on the additional sales. The gross dollar amount of the additional sales will be 50,000 × $15, or $750,000, which indicates that we could incur bad debts of $750,000 − $455,000, or $295,000, and not be worse off. Our incremental bad debt loss could be as high as $295,000 divided by $750,000, or more than 39 percent! Needless to say, the temptation to begin selling on credit might be great under those circumstances; and similar calculations to test the wisdom of more generous extension of credit, when credit is already being granted on a limited basis, may encourage policy changes. Extreme care should most certainly be used in calculating the differential costs (and don't overlook increases in bookkeeping costs for accounts receivable) and the probable effects of any such policy changes.

In our next topic, the make-or-buy decision, we'll consider another possible differential cost situation.

SHOULD WE MAKE IT OR BUY IT?

A great many articles have been published on the subject of "make or buy," and we surely cannot treat it exhaustively here. We're now concerned with questions such as these: Should we start making this particular part which up to now we have been buying ready-made from an outsider? Should we set up a garage for maintenance of our trucks and service cars, or should we continue to have the maintenance done outside? We're paying out a lot of money for printing and duplicating services; shouldn't we set up our own shop? We've been buying our tools and dies from specialty shops that seem to be making a good profit; why don't we make our own tools, dies, jigs, and fixtures? And a much more far-reaching make-or-buy type of question: Should we continue to sell through wholesalers; should we deal directly with retailers; or should we even set up our own retail outlets?

Underlying every make-or-buy survey is the belief, or maybe only the suspicion, that "our supplier is getting fat off us" and "we could just as well be making that profit ourselves."

Certainly a most fundamental question in approaching any make-or-buy decision is this: Which will be the more economical policy for us? And a most critical aspect of any economy study, of course, is the matter of costs.

In make-or-buy analysis, the adage "use different costs for different purposes" seems to be most relevant. The fact that so many articles appear on the subject suggests a condition of uncertainty, which is no doubt the case. For our purposes, two somewhat opposing schools of thought will be presented.

The first school recommends the differential cost approach to make-or-buy. To illustrate it, let's assume we have been buying part X for $90 each and we feel that our earnings might be improved if we produced the thing ourselves. We call on our cost accountant to estimate our costs if we were to make part X. He presents the following condensed schedule:

PART X
Estimated Production Costs
(per 100 units)

Materials (including costs of ordering, receiving, storing, etc.)		$ 1,142
Direct labor (details in supporting schedule)		3,260
Variable overhead (at 120% of direct labor)	$3,912	
Fixed overhead	2,608	6,520
Estimated total cost of 100 units		$10,922

It takes but a moment to make a superficial, differential cost analysis of these data. Our total cost per 100 units is $10,922, which is higher than the total cost ($100 \times \$90 = \$9,000$) of buying them; but our total cost includes $2,608 of fixed costs, which are excluded in determining differential cost (i.e., the costs that would be incremental to our present total were we to make rather than buy). We determine our differential cost to be total cost of $10,922 minus fixed costs of $2,608, or $8,314, and this "clearly indicates a potential saving (earnings increase) of $9,000 minus $8,314, or $686, on every 100-unit batch of part X." Let's get busy and make those parts!

It is possible that many differential cost analyses go no farther than that, and it is equally possible that many of the decisions are faulty. Let's look at the full cost approach to the same question.

In general, the full cost approach to make-or-buy rests on the contention that fixed costs are a fact of life. The only basis for excluding them in make-or-buy decisions is that you clearly have excess, unused capacity. That is, you must feel that not only your plant assets but also your supervisor and managerial personnel are not fully occupied and, even more important, that in the foreseeable future the plant and managerial personnel will continue to be inadequately occupied unless you take on such activities as the manufacture of your own component parts. Stated differently, the only reason for excluding fixed costs is that you are clearly incurring them and they're going to waste and you see little or no prospect that you can step the volume of your regular activities up enough to soak up the reserve energies and reserve capacity of your personnel and plant.

The great risk of taking on the manufacture of something you've been buying—that is, doing so on the basis that you can exclude fixed costs from your tally of costs to make—is that new fixed costs will "creep" into the picture. The creep effect is most likely to occur if you take on a sideline manufacturing or service operation and later increase your mainline activities. Then you won't have enough plant and personnel capacity to go around and the fixed costs will creep in. And you're likely to find that it's much more of a problem to disengage from an old activity than it is to add a new one.

The conclusion to be reached from the full cost approach to make-or-buy is that one should not take on (except, perhaps, temporarily to fill in short-term dips in activity) sideline activities unless the supplier's price exceeds your total costs plus the rate of profit that you make on your mainline activity.

Needless to say, a make-or-buy decision, even though it relies heavily on cost analyses, must also take other noncost matters into consideration. For example, we might decide to make part X simply because that is the only way we can assure ourselves of a steady supply and good quality. On the other hand, it might be politically expedient to farm out as much as we can in order to maintain good public relations.

Thus, the make-or-buy question is not a simple one even in what may appear to be a simple situation. In general, one might very well lean in the "buy" direction and insist that any decision to "make" be rigorously documented.

DECISIONS TO ACQUIRE PLANT ASSETS

How often is a new structure, a new unit of machinery, or other capital asset purchased or constructed on the recommendation of a wise old production manager with no objective analysis of the need and no concrete assurance that the capital outlay is a wise one? Admittedly some plant additions are made simply because they're unavoidable; they may even be required by legal action, as in the case of antipollution equipment. In many instances, however, financial management, equipped with relevant information, should be in a position to endorse or veto a capital outlay on the basis of logical analysis. The present custom is to refer to such analysis and planning of fixed asset acquisitions as capital budgeting.

Capital budgeting is not a precise tool; its employment does not assure the avoidance of mistakes, since estimates of future cash flows form a major portion of the analysis; but the chances are overwhelming that employment of systematic capital budgeting will reduce the number and cost of mistakes significantly.

Basically, the two major aspects of capital budgeting are (1) the ranking of capital outlay requests in the order of their probable value to the firm and (2) the determination of which outlays show promise of being worth making.

Underlying all capital budgeting techniques is our old friend "net cash flow." Here's a quick review. If we invest $100 in a depreciable asset that will produce cash savings, or cash proceeds, of $50 per year, the gross cash flow is $50 annually. The net cash flow is the $50 minus any and all cash expenditures needed to produce the gross inflow. Let's assume cash outflows will amount to $10 per year; then the net cash flow is $40 per year. Note specifically that depreciation does not enter into this calculation. The $40 net flow hopefully will provide for "recovery" of depreciation, and any excess will be profit.

Three principal forms of analysis are applied in capital budgeting. The first of these is the so-called *payback period*, which is strictly a "no-go" check. What it does is rule that a particular capital asset shall not be acquired unless its payback period is less than a prescribed number of years. If, for example, we insist that every capital asset we buy must have a payback period no longer than four years, we aren't using the procedure to determine what assets should be acquired; we're merely ruling against all acquisitions that do not meet the payback schedule. The example in the

preceding paragraph, with an annual cash flow estimated at $40, has a
2½-year payback period, so it would meet a 4-year test readily. However,
a payback period of under four years does not in itself constitute justification for the purchase of any asset. Quite obviously, if other things were
equal, we might turn down a proposed 2½-year payback asset if we were
short of funds and had alternative outlays with payback periods shorter
than 2½ years. Again, a rule-of-thumb payback requirement is strictly a
no-go tool—it rules that we shall not acquire an asset with a payback
period of greater length, but it gives little help in choosing which assets
with shorter payback periods should be chosen. In fact, it is doubtful that
the payback method really has much to commend it for any part of the
capital budgeting decision, because it overlooks so much that is of far
greater importance. Nevertheless, the payback device is a popular one, and
it should be well understood by executives.

Each of the two remaining tools depends on the use of compound
interest arithmetic, and the two are closely related.

The great objection to the payback method is that it pays absolutely
no attention to the "tail of the dog." Let's assume that we drill two wells, A
and B, and both produce enough water, oil, or gas to pay back our full
drilling cost in exactly four years. Are the wells of equal value? Certainly
not if well A goes dry at the end of four years and well B continues to produce. In other words, the tail period (after payback is complete) is an important element in any capital budgeting decision. Of course, like most aspects
of capital budgeting, the tail period will probably be a matter of estimate,
but it certainly wouldn't make sense to choose well A, because of its four-
year payback, if it appeared probable that well B would pay back in
five years and would then continue to flow for another five years.

Hence, we need some device for evaluating two factors at the same
time—the size of the flow and the persistence of the flow. It should be
added that the timing of peaks and valleys in the flow is also a matter of
concern, although it is very difficult to predict with any assurance of
reliability.

One method of evaluating both size and duration of flow is to reduce
the estimated future net cash flow to a single present-value figure. This is the
present-value method. To employ it with respect to a proposed acquisition
requires estimating (1) the periodic net cash flow and (2) the number of periods that the flow will last. For practical purposes it will probably be acceptable to assume that the flow is the same every year, although a more
sophisticated (more certain?) prognostication may be employed. Also, finding the present value of something means that you "discount" the thing at an
acceptable interest rate. When the estimates have been made and the net cash
flow has been discounted to a single present-value figure, that amount must
be larger than your proposed commitment (i.e., worth more than the amount
you are proposing to commit in the fixed-asset investment).

To illustrate the present-value procedure, assume you are contemplating investment of $100,000 in an asset that you believe will produce net cash flow of $30,000 per year throughout a five-year life. All that needs to be done is to refer to compound-interest tables to find the present value of the flow at your required rate per annum (say 12 percent) and then compare it with the $100,000 initial investment. The effect of the discounting operation is to put the series of periodic payments on effectively the same time base (namely, the date of the initial investment) as the initial investment. The present value of $1 per period for five periods, discounted at 12 percent per period, is approximately $3.61. The present value of $30,000 per period, discounted at 12 percent, is 30,000 times $3.61, or $108,300. The fact that the present value of the cash flow annuity exceeds the amount of the proposed investment indicates that the return on investment exceeds 12%, and gives us a green light for this outlay, provided that it meets whatever other tests need to be considered.

A third test, which is something of a complement to the second, seeks to determine what rate of return is represented in the estimates we have made. In other words, if our $100,000 investment will return $30,000 of net cash flow each year for five years, how good an investment is that in terms of rate of return? The solution again calls for use of compound interest tables. Now we are to determine what interest rate our asset earns per year over the assumed five-year period based on the known $100,000 and the anticipated $30,000 of annual cash flow. Obviously, the answer is not simply 30 percent (30,000/100,000), since the basic $100,000 is presumed to depreciate down to zero during its five-year life span. The answer, again, is determined by use of compound-interest tables somewhat as follows:

1. $100,000 is the present value of $30,000 per period for five annual periods at the unknown interest (discount) rate.
2. If (1) is true, then $100,000/30,000, or $3.33, is the present value of $1 per period for five annual periods at the same, unknown earning rate.
3. Compound-interest tables (the present value of $1 per period for n periods) show for each assumed interest rate the present value of $1 for a number of assumed periods ranging from one up to 50 or more. Since we know that we are dealing with five periods, we merely look in the various columns, at the amount shown for five periods, and find the one nearest our $3.33. The interest rate appearing at the top of the column is, then, approximately the sought-after rate—close enough for practical purposes.
4. Since compound-interest tables may not include high enough interest rates to include our required answer, a satisfactory treatment is to deal with, say, one-half of the annual $30,000 by assuming that $15,000 is

earned semiannually. Thus, $100,000/15,000 = $6.667, which represents the present value of $1 per period for 10 periods at the unknown rate. In line 10 in the 7 percent column the amount is 7.024, which falls between the amounts shown for 8 percent and 10 percent. This indicates that our rate of return is a bit over 8 percent per half year, or around 17 percent per year, compounded semiannually.

To summarize this very abbreviated discussion of capital budgeting, any proposed capital addition may well be subjected to the three tests outlined in this section: (1) determination of the payback period, (2) determination of the estimated cash flow per period throughout the asset's life and comparison of the present value of the cash flow, discounted at our required interest rate, with the expected amount of the investment, and (3) determination of the actual rate of return that is implied in the cash flow that we have predicted. If the proposed investment meets all three of those tests and does it as well as, or better than, any competing opportunities to invest the funds, it should be safe to proceed with the investment.

MISCELLANEOUS TOPICS

It is clearly impossible to outline, let alone describe exhaustively, all the devices that accountants and other quantitative information men have invented. Today's buzz words include MIS (management information systems), which is a very interesting computer-oriented story in itself. Also, the mathematicians have worked up many interesting business applications under the label "operations research." They include linear programming, Monte Carlo method, Bayesian analysis, simulation, PERT (program evaluation and review technique), economic order theory, and waiting line models. Much of this is in its infancy, although the third generation of computers seems to be stimulating the aging process to a point where reliability is greatly enhanced.

TEST PROBLEM

Here's a short one on capital budgeting. Our Company is considering purchase of a machine with a 10-year life that should reduce annual labor costs by $10,000. Operating costs of the machine, excluding depreciation, will be about $3,000 per year. List price of the machine is $41,000. Should we buy it? We require a maximum payback period of six years, and our minimum rate of return is 10 percent. Added information: The present value of an annuity of $1 for 10 periods at 10 percent is 6.144.

TEST PROBLEM SOLUTION SPACE

Computation of payback period:

Computation of present value of machine at 10 percent discount:

15

FEDERAL INCOME TAX CONCEPTS

E veryone can appreciate the tremendous importance of the federal income tax. Some entities find the tax to be one of the largest single expenses of doing business. As significant as it is, we must recognize that it is but one segment of a total tax structure that includes other federal taxes, such as excise, employment, gift, and estate taxes, as well as state and local income, property, and sales taxes. This chapter deals only with the federal income tax.

The tax applies both to individuals and to corporations. Although the two applications are often thought of as separate taxes and are shown separately in government statistics, both are incorporated in the same Internal Revenue Code (IRC) and in most respects are surprisingly similar. We will focus primarily on corporations, but we will also mention some aspects of the individual tax, primarily as that tax impacts on corporate employees (including executive-owners).

A chapter of this nature must be prefaced with an important caveat. In these few pages we cannot pretend to cover the many details that are essential to understanding the application of the tax law to specific situations. This discussion is intended to make you aware of some of the basic concepts in order that you can (1) recognize many of the important tax opportunities and pitfalls, (2) intelligently discuss the tax ramifications with your tax advisers, and (3) efficiently extend your tax study into some of the comprehensive tax volumes.

It is important to be aware that the tax is all-encompassing and that Congress has broad latitude in levying it. The constitutional authority derives from the Sixteenth Amendment, which grants Congress the "power to lay and collect taxes on incomes, from whatever source derived." In defining "gross income," Congress incorporated wording directly from the Sixteenth Amendment but at the same time reserved to itself the right to determine specifically what shall be taxed. The IRC (or Code) states that "Except as otherwise provided in this subtitle, gross income means all income from whatever source derived ..." Thus, it is clear that Congress could base the tax on total income, with no income exempted and with no deductions allowed. However, since the initiation of the income tax in 1913, Congress has chosen to levy the tax on its version of "net" income and to exempt certain types of income from tax and make certain expenses deductible. In essence, that leads to the two most fundamental of all tax concepts: All income is taxable unless some authority to the contrary can be found, and nothing is deductible unless some authority so indicates.

Another set of broad concepts surrounds the doctrine of "business purpose." On several occasions the courts have held that the Internal Revenue Service (IRS) may not substitute its judgment for the judgment of management or the taxpayer with regard to a transaction or other business activity, provided that some valid business purpose (other than simply reducing taxes) underlies that judgment. However, in the absence of a valid business purpose, the government has very broad authority to ignore "sham transactions," to reallocate income among related parties, to look through the "form to the substance" of a transaction, and to collapse two or more "steps" in a series of transactions to arrive at the actual substance of the action.

TAXPAYERS AND TAX RETURNS

There are three basic types of income taxpayers: individuals, corporations, and fiduciaries. The fiduciary of each trust or estate files a Form 1041 and pays a tax on the income not distributed to the beneficiaries. However, this chapter will deal only with individuals and corporations. It is important to recognize the similarity in tax treatment of the two. Both are taxed according to the same IRC, and most sections of that code apply to all types of taxpayers. Figures 15.1 and 15.2 show the route from total income to the final balance due and illustrates where the tax treatments are common and where they diverge. However, even within each of these major categories there are subgroups that are subject to different rules and, in some cases, different tax rates.

Individuals

All individuals file a Form 1040, an abbreviated Form 1040A, or Form 1040EZ. The tax on Form 1040 or Form 1040A is computed according to four different rate schedules:

- Single
- Married individuals filing jointly

Figure 15.1   Individual Income Tax Formula

Total income

− Exclusions

= Gross income

− Deductions for adjusted gross income

(Self-employed business expenses,

Net capital loss up to $3,000

Payments to retirement plans

Alimony

Moving expense

Self-employed health insurance premiums

½ Self-employment tax

Student loan interest)

= Adjusted gross income

− Itemized deductions (discussed later)

− Personal & dependency exemptions

= Taxable income

× Tax rates

= Total tax

− Credits

= Tax liability

− Prepayments

= Balance Due (Overpayment)

- Married individuals filing separate returns
- Heads of households

Form 1040EZ can only be used by taxpayers filing as single or married filing jointly with no dependents. Currently (for the tax year 2006), such taxpayers must have taxable income of less than $50,000 and no other income than wages and up to $1,500 of interest income. No deductions may be taken on Form 1040EZ other than the standard deduction. The only credit allowed is for withholding tax taken by the taxpayer's employer. Form 1040A may be used by taxpayers of any filing status with any number of dependents. However, their sources of income are limited

Figure 15.2   Corporate Tax Formula

	Total income
−	Exclusions
=	Gross income
−	Business expenses
	70%, 80%, or 100% of dividends received
	Deduction
	Amortization of organization costs
	Net operating loss
	Charitable contributions (limited to 10% of taxable income)
=	Taxable income
×	Tax rates
=	Total tax
−	Credits
=	Tax liability
−	Prepayments
	Balance Due (Overpayment)

to wages, interest, dividends, pension and annuity income, and unemployment compensation. IRA deductions may be taken, but no itemized deductions. Taxpayer may also claim credits for withholding, child care, and earned income.

For many years there was only one tax table for individuals, but a major inequity arose between married couples in community property states and those in common law states. A married couple with one income of $40,000 was taxed in community property states, such as California and Texas, as though the $40,000 were two separate $20,000 incomes. By use of graduated tables, the combined tax on two $20,000 incomes is less than the tax on one $40,000 income.

In response to the difference in treatment, several states were in the process of shifting to community property laws when Congress agreed that the federal income tax law should not force such a major change on the states. To obviate the need for the change, the "joint return" was introduced; on it, the income, deductions, and credits of both spouses were combined. When the joint return was first adopted, the combined incomes paid exactly doubled the tax an unmarried person owed on one-half the income.

Several years later Congress recognized that an unmarried head of household (typically a single parent with dependent children living at home) has many of the same expenses and responsibilities as a married couple. The result was the third rate schedule, in which the tax was approximately halfway between the joint return tax and the separate return tax on the same income.

When the three rate schedules were in place, unmarried taxpayers complained that they were being taxed unfairly. Thus, after many years Congress reduced the rates, somewhat, for unmarried taxpayers. However, Congress did not want to encourage married taxpayers to file separate returns, so it left the old unmarried rates in place solely for married persons filing separate returns. Thus, today the tax break vis-à-vis married and unmarried individuals no longer applies for two-earner couples and may be reversed for those earning above average income. For instance, a married couple each of whom earns $100,000 will generally pay more tax on their $200,000 joint return than will two unmarried individuals who earn $100,000 each. There has been much publicity on this so-called "marriage tax." In recent years, Congress has taken action to minimize this unfair tax on married couples.

In lieu of the ordinary tax rate schedules, Congress implemented an alternative tax rate system in 1969. Originally, this alternative tax rate system (known as the Alternative Minimum Tax, or AMT) was designed to ensure that high-income taxpayers paid their fair share by disallowing some of the aforementioned tax deductions, allowing an AMT exemption, and then taxing the excess "alternative taxable income" at a flat rate, which was originally considerably lower than the higher ordinary tax rates. If this alternative calculation yielded a higher tax liability the taxpayer had to add the excess to his ordinary tax liability.

Today, ordinary tax rates are much lower than ordinary tax rates in 1969. Unfortunately, alternative minimum tax rates are not. The consequence, as you might have imagined, is that many more individuals are currently affected by the AMT, most of whom belong to the upper middle class. Ironically, most of the mega-wealthy individuals who were supposed to come under the AMT actually manage to avoid it! It has been estimated that if nothing is done to remedy the situation, as much as 25 percent of individual tax returns could soon be subject to this additional tax. Although you hear a lot of rhetoric in Washington about the unfairness of the current system, little, if anything, is currently being done about it.

Partnerships

A partnership is treated as a group of individual taxpayers, and not as a separate taxpaying entity. As a convenience for both the government and the partners, the partnership files a Form 1065 to report the operating income and deductions of the entity and then separately states amounts allocated to each partner for such items as capital gains and losses, interest income, and charitable contributions from net partnership income from operations. This is because each of the "separately stated" items may be treated differently on each partner's individual income tax return. For instance, each individual may only deduct capital losses *in excess of capital gains of $3,000 per year*.

Whether or not a partnership capital loss can be currently deducted will be determined by each individual partner's other capital transactions during the year. The partnership will report each partner's allocable share of income and deductions in a separate schedule known as a K-1. The partners then report the allocated amounts on their respective individual tax returns (Form 1040). Thus, partnership income or loss flows through to the partners and is taxed (or deducted) only at the individual level.

Corporations

The tax law follows the concept of a corporation as a separate legal entity distinct from its shareholders. Thus, the corporation files a Form 1120 or 1120-A (short form) and pays a tax at the corporate level, and the same income is taxable again to the shareholders when distributed as dividends. Dividends are not deductible by the distributing corporation. This separation of the taxable entities can be both a disadvantage and an advantage. Much has been written about the "double taxation" of corporate income. Special provisions discussed elsewhere in this chapter allow substantial relief (70 to 100 percent) when dividends are paid to another corporation. Dividends paid to individuals, while still subject to double taxation, will be taxed at a reduced rate if they are categorized as "qualified dividends." Generally dividends received from publicly held, domestic corporations will qualify. If the individual taxpayer's marginal tax rate (the rate at which the last dollar of taxable income would be paid) is more than 15 percent, the tax rate on the qualified dividend would be 15 percent. If the taxpayer's marginal tax rate is 15 percent or less, the qualified dividend rate would be 5 percent. For tax years 2008–2009 this 5 percent rate is to be reduced *to zero percent*! These reduced rates are currently set to expire in 2010.

Tax planning opportunities can arise from the separateness of the entities. It is possible for a shareholder to also be an employee of the corporation. In that case, salary payments are deductible by the corporation and taxable to the employee (as long as the payments are reasonable in relation to the amount of services performed by the shareholder), and various fringe benefits can be deductible even though they are not taxable to the employee-stockholder. Many closely held corporations manage to pay out substantially all of their income in salaries plus fringes. Of course, if the shareholders of a closely held corporation are in a higher tax bracket, it might be advisable to leave some taxable income in the corporation. In this way, the corporate taxable income will be taxed at a lower rate than if it was taxed to the shareholder as additional compensation.

For instance, the first $50,000 of corporate taxable income is taxed at a rate of 15 percent. If the shareholder's marginal tax rate was already 35 percent (the maximum rate), then by leaving it in the corporation the income would be taxed at less than half the shareholder's tax rate. The shareholder can then receive the money as compensation in a subsequent year, when his or her individual tax rate is lower. It should be noted that the IRS has rather broad authority to disallow a portion of an "unreasonable salary" and treat it as a dividend—taxable to the recipient but not deductible to the payor. Although it is possible for professional individuals or partnerships (accountants, attorneys, doctors, etc.) to incorporate as "professional corporations," each dollar of corporate taxable income is taxed at the top corporate rate, currently 35 percent. For that reason, it would be wise for professional associations to consider becoming an S corporation or a limited liability partnership. The tax consequences of these two business entities will now be discussed.

S Corporations

The sharp contrast in the tax treatment of corporations and partnerships quite logically meant that the tax law became one of the most critical factors in determining the form of business organization selected for many small businesses. Congress recognized that and enacted Subchapter S, which allows qualified closely held corporations to elect not to pay the federal income tax. The corporation files a Form 1120S, but the shareholders report their allocated shares of income or loss on their individual returns (1040s) in much the same manner as partners in a partnership (see prior discussion). Thus, Subchapter S offers a "flow-through" characteristic similar to that of a partnership, including the categorization of separately stated items on each shareholder's Form K-1. However, it also contains many limitations and restrictions that differ in several respects from those of a partnership.

Where the tax consequences differ, partnership tax rules generally provide a more taxpayer-friendly result. For example, in certain circumstances, capital gains will be taxed at the corporate level rather than passed through to the shareholders if the property's appreciation occurred before it had elected to be taxed as an S corporation (the Built-In Gains Tax). Partners may also be allowed to currently deduct losses that S shareholder's may not be able to deduct due to the fact that an individual may only deduct losses to the extent of their "basis" in the business. Partnership debts provide each of the partners with additional basis, since they bear personal liability for partnership debts. S shareholders do not receive additional basis for S corporation debts, since corporate shareholders are not personally liable for corporate debts.

In order to qualify as an S corporation, several criteria must be met:

1. There can be no more than 100 shareholders. Family members may be aggregated as one shareholder for this purpose (e.g., spouses, parents, children).
2. There can be no corporate or partnership shareholders.
3. There can be no nonresident alien shareholders, since the shareholder must be a U.S. taxpayer.
4. The corporation must be a U.S. corporation.
5. The corporation must only issue one class of stock. However, the corporation can distinguish between voting and nonvoting shares.

Limited Liability Companies and Limited Liability Partnerships

In recent years the limited liability company (LLC) and limited liability partnership (LLP) have emerged as popular forms of business entities. These forms of business combine the non-tax advantage of limited liability for its owners together with the tax consequences of an unincorporated entity. Treasury Department regulations currently allow LLCs to be taxed *either* as a corporation or as an unincorporated entity. What this means is if the LLC has at least two owners, it may be taxed as a partnership. Should the entity only have one owner, then it may be taxed as if the sole owner is a sole proprietor. The unincorporated alternative will be presumed unless the LLC files a written election to be taxed as a corporation. An LLP will automatically be taxed as a partnership, since by definition it would have multiple owners and all of the legal characteristics of a partnership except for limited liability for the acts of other partners, or those being supervised by other partners.

Multiple Corporations

Through a myriad of highly technical provisions, a group of related corporations is allowed to file a consolidated tax return if a timely election is made by the group. This is conceptually similar to the accounting consolidated income statement and provides for the elimination of intercompany transactions. Also, losses of some members of the group can offset incomes of other members. Affiliated corporations, for tax purposes, include the parent-subsidiary relationship (where one corporation owns at least 80% of the voting shares *and* total shares of another corporation).

Special Corporate Taxes

There are two provisions in the tax law that penalize closely held corporations if they do not distribute sufficient earnings to their shareholders. The personal holding company (PHC) has sometimes been referred to as an incorporated investment portfolio. In greatly oversimplified terms, a PHC is a corporation (1) in which over 50 percent control (direct or indirect) is held by five or fewer shareholders and (2) which receives at least 60 percent of its income from various passive sources such as interest, dividends, royalties, and rents. In addition to the regular tax, a PHC is subject to a separate tax on its undistributed income. The tax rate through 2010 will be 15 percent, which coincides with the maximum rate of taxation on qualified dividends to individual shareholders (see above discussion). This tax does not apply to S corporations.

Corporations other than personal holding companies are subject to an additional 15 percent tax (through 2010) known as the accumulated earnings tax. This tax is based on the current year's undistributed income, which is unnecessarily retained in the corporation for the purpose of avoiding the tax on dividends at the shareholder level. Income retained for expansion of the operations and for reasonable working capital needs is not subject to this tax. There is a presumed "reasonable" accumulation of $250,000 of earnings for most corporations that would not be subject to this additional tax. However, if the corporation were a personal service corporation engaged in the fields of health, law, accounting, architecture, engineering, actuarial science, performing arts, or consulting, the presumed reasonable accumulation would be reduced to $150,000. Like the personal holding company tax outlined above, this tax does not apply to S corporations.

Both taxes apply only to income after taxes, and both can be avoided by dividend distributions during the year or within 2½ months after the year ends.

With the significant drop in 1986 in the highest marginal tax rates of individuals below the highest rates for corporations, these so-called "penalty" taxes have lost much of their significance. The problem now is not how to retain earnings in a corporation and avoid taxes, but how to distribute them through salary, rental, and other payments and avoid double taxation.

ACCOUNTING PERIODS AND METHODS

Some of the basic tax concepts, some tax planning opportunities, and some interesting interrelationships with general corporate accounting are embodied in the areas of accounting periods and methods.

Tax Year

A new regular corporation may elect almost any tax year that is desired. Partnerships, S corporations, and personal service corporations have certain restrictions in this regard in order to coordinate the tax year of the business with that of the principal owners.

The tax law recognizes the calendar year, the fiscal year, and a 52-53-week year. The calendar year is assumed if no alternative is elected and is required if the taxpayer does not maintain an adequate set of accounting records. A fiscal year may end with any month, but it must end on the last day of the month. Many businesses prefer to account on the basis of 13 four-week periods. These are more standard and more comparable than 12 months of varying lengths. The tax law accommodates this preference by what is known as a 52- 53-week year, which ends near the end of any month selected. Through the automatic action of the calendar, four or five years of exactly 52 weeks are followed by a 53-week year in which the thirteenth period has five weeks rather than four weeks. This is necessary in order for the end of the year to remain near the end of the same month and not move ever earlier in the year.

It is possible to change to a different tax year, although most changes require the approval of the IRS. Such a change will create a short period between the old and the new, and usually the income for the short period must be annualized for tax reporting purposes. A short period that is the first or last period for a taxpayer need not be annualized.

Cash Method

The tax law recognizes three distinct methods of accounting: the cash method, the accrual method, and a hybrid method. The cash method generally reports all income received in cash minus all expenses paid in cash. There are certain exceptions, most of which are intended to avoid either intentional or unintentional distortions of income. Capital expenditures must be capitalized and deducted over a period of years through depreciation or amortization. Income must be reported if it is "constructively received" even though cash is not actually received. A constructive receipt occurs when the income is unequivocally available to the taxpayer even though not actually in the taxpayer's possession; for example, interest credited to a savings account is income when credited, not when withdrawn in the form of cash. Also, to avoid distortion, the cash method is generally not allowed if inventories are significant in the calculation of income. However, businesses with inventories are permitted to use the cash method if the average annual gross receipts for the past three years do not exceed $1 million.

Most individuals, including most professionals and many other service businesses, report on the cash method even if they keep their own records on the accrual basis. This allows for some tax planning such as the timing of deductible expenditures and the delay or advancement of the billing-collecting cycle. Regular corporations are only allowed to use the cash method if average annual gross receipts for the prior three years do not exceed $5 million.

Accrual Method

With a few important exceptions, the tax version of the accrual method is essentially consistent with normal accrual accounting. The tax law embodies a concept that is known as the "wherewithal to pay taxes." In essence it provides that income should be taxed when the taxpaying capability exists even though the income is accrued during some other period. In some instances it is mandatory; in others it is optional. Income received in advance is taxable when received. If five years of rent income is received in advance, all of it is taxable even though four years of it will be deferred for general accounting purposes. Two important exceptions are worth noting. Accrual basis taxpayers may defer recognizing income related to the advance payments for inventory if the taxpayer's accounting method for the sale is the same for tax and financial accounting purposes. Accrual taxpayers may also defer payments received for future services to the year following the year in which payment was received. Revenue related to future years must be reported in the year following the year of receipt even if the payments relate to several future years. This exception does not apply to rent, insurance premiums, interest, or warranty contracts.

Tax accrual accounting can also differ from financial accounting in the area of estimated expenses. For most expenses other than depreciation, the tax authorities will normally demand that a definite liability must exist and that its amount must be reasonably certain. Thus, estimated warranty or repair expenses, or estimated bad debts that are accrued for book purposes will probably not be deductible until actually paid. Within the accrual method there are several instances in which the taxpayer may elect to treat things differently for tax purposes and book purposes. For example, different depreciation methods and different methods of accounting for bad debts are allowed.

Whenever the tax treatment and financial reporting differ only as to the timing of an income or deduction (e.g., rent received in advance, depreciation), the consequence is a troublesome accounting problem often referred to as "tax allocation." The tax effect should be reflected in the income statement when the income or expense is so reflected, even though the same item will be reported for tax purposes in a different period.

Hybrid Method

The cash method is not allowed if inventories are significant in the income calculation. In its place, primarily for the benefit of small businesses, is a hybrid of cash and accrual methods whereby sales and cost of goods sold are reflected on the accrual basis but the operating expenses may be reported on the cash basis.

Change of Accounting Method

A taxpayer must secure approval from the IRS to change the general accounting method, such as cash to accrual. In most instances permission also must be secured in order to change a specific accounting method such as methods of depreciation or inventory accounting. That is so even when sound accounting would dictate that the change is a substantial improvement.

INCOME

Inclusions

The constitutional authority to tax "all incomes from whatever source derived" is extremely broad, yet it has certain basic limitations. The overall assumption is that any economic benefit received by the taxpayer will be subject to income taxation unless specifically excluded elsewhere in the IRC. "Income" is not a precise term, and the Constitution does not define it. Economists, lawyers, accountants, and the tax authorities have somewhat different views as to what should be included. All seem to agree, at least conceptually, that "income" must be distinguished from "return of capital," which is not taxable under an "income tax." Through the years, Congress and the courts have refined the concepts of income, and it is helpful to understand "realization," "recognition," and the "fruit-and-tree doctrine." The tree is the asset that produces the income (the fruit). One may not assign the income "growing" from the asset, thus avoiding the income tax consequences from such growth, without also assigning the tree. For example, one could not avoid income taxes by assigning his or her right to receive interest from a certificate of deposit (CD), while still retaining ownership of the CD itself. Additionally, mere increases in an asset's value usually do not result in the recognition of income for tax purposes. For objectivity in valuation, the income tax will not be levied until the increase in value has been verified through sale to an outside party. Thus, an increase in value of land, shares of stock, or other assets is not recognized until the asset is sold, and the taxpayer has the "wherewithal to pay" the income tax on the asset's appreciation in value.

However, it is neither reasonable nor correct to assume that income is recognized only when received in cash. Even cash basis taxpayers must recognize income whether received in cash or in property. Thus, shares of stock issued to the promoter who formed the corporation constitute taxable compensation income. A bonus paid to a corporate executive in shares of stock may be compensation income. In certain "qualified" stock option or stock plans, Congress has intentionally deemed that such income may be deferred. Income received in property is measured by the fair market value. Thus, a cash basis taxpayer does not avoid income by "bartering" services for property or property for property. (That seems to be widely misunderstood or simply ignored by participants in the so-called "informal or underground economy.") In exchanges of property, the value will normally be established by whichever side of the transaction is more readily measured. Whether such a transaction results in income or return of capital depends on the relationship of the value received to the cost or adjusted basis of the asset given up.

However, there are certain provisions in the law specifically deferring gains and losses from such noncash transactions, discussed later in this chapter.

Exclusions

Congress has moderated its authority to tax "all income from whatever source derived" by mandating that a few types of income will be fully exempt from federal income tax, others will be partially exempt, and the tax on some types of income will be deferred. The more significant items that are fully exempt and not reported on the annual federal income tax returns are:

- State and local bond interest
- Life insurance proceeds
- Gifts
- Inheritances
- Disability benefits (if taxpayer paid the premiums on the policy)
- Scholarships and fellowships
- Certain fringe benefits such as life insurance, health insurance, and employee discounts

The common application of the tax law to both individuals and corporations can be seen in the list of exclusions; these items are described in the IRC without reference to the type of taxpayer. Some of the items obviously apply only to individuals because of the nature of the income, but they are not differentiated by the tax code. Thus, interest on state and local bonds is exempt whether received by a corporation, a trust, or an individual. Similarly, life insurance proceeds are exempt whether received upon the death of a spouse or the death of the corporate president.

A couple of types of income are only partially nontaxable:

1. Dividends received by one corporation from another corporation; 70 or 80 percent of the dividend received may be deducted (100 percent in the case of affiliated corporations).
2. A certain amount of gain on the sale of a principal residence by an individual. If the individuals file as married filing jointly, and have used the home as their principal residence for two of the last five

years, they can exclude up to $500,000 of their gain. For all others, they may exclude up to $250,000 of gain as long as they meet the ownership and use tests described above.

The present value of money plus the impact of inflation can make the deferral of tax highly advantageous. Some of the situations in which the tax is deferred are:

1. Exchange of property for a controlling interest in corporate stock or a partnership interest.
2. Exchanges of certain "like kind" business assets
3. Certain types of installment sales
4. Deferred compensation contracts
5. Employer contributions (and in some circumstances employee contributions) to qualified pension plans
6. Contributions to individual retirement plans

The first two items will be discussed further in the section on property transactions.

DEDUCTIONS

As indicated earlier, Congress presumably could base the income tax on total income with no deductions allowed. However, substantial deductions have always been and are likely to continue to be allowed.

1. Business expenses. Both corporations and individuals are allowed, in general, to deduct expenses related to one's trade or business.
2. Rental expenses.
3. Individuals are allowed to itemize and deduct only a few personal expenses which further certain objectives:
   a. To encourage certain socially desirable activities:
      - Charitable contributions
      - Home ownership (property taxes and mortgage interest are deductible)
   b. To alleviate serious hardship:
      - Casualty losses
      - Medical expenses in excess of a substantial de minimis
   c. Expenses related to production of income, preservation of property, or tax compliance that are not deductible under the business expense category mentioned above.
   d. An individual has the option to deduct a flat amount in lieu of all itemized deductions.

Literally thousands of items may be deductible under these broad classifications. The IRC describes dozens of deductions in great detail (e.g., interest, taxes, depreciation, contributions, losses), but it also has several broad generic deduction sections such as "all the ordinary and necessary expenses paid or incurred during the taxable year in carrying on any trade or business."

However, there are several general concepts in the tax law that transcend all the deduction sections and identify types of expenditures that are not deductible even though they may appear to meet all the criteria of one or more specific deductions.

1. Capital expenditures are not deductible. Thus, otherwise deductible items (e.g., employee wages) must be capitalized (i.e., treated as additions to assets rather than as expenses) if the employee spends time constructing a new building.
2. Expenses related to the production of tax-exempt income are not deductible. Business insurance premiums paid are a normal expense, but premiums on officer life insurance with the corporation as beneficiary are not deductible. Interest on loans the proceeds of which are used to purchase or carry tax-exempt bonds is not deductible.
3. Related party transactions. A loss on a sale to a related party is not deductible, but the loss may be used by the purchaser to offset gain on a subsequent sale. Interest or other expense paid by an accrual basis taxpayer to a related party who reports on the cash method is not deductible unless actually paid within 2½ months after the close of the year. "Related parties" include such entities as corporation and a controlling stockholder, or a partner and partnership, as well as family relationships.
4. Illegal expenses and expenditures contrary to public policy are not deductible. Thus, bribes and fines are not deductible. Some fines—such as those on overweight trucks—are often considered an ordinary cost of doing business, but they still are not deductible. It is interesting to note that although an illegal expense is disallowed, many expenses of an illegal business may well be allowed. This produces an interesting dichotomy between an "illegal expense of a legal business" (nondeductible) and a "legal expense of an illegal business" (deductible). Income from an illegal business is taxable, and the legitimate type of expense of producing that income would be deductible. Gambling may be illegal under local law, but it is not illegal under federal law. Thus, ordinary wages, rent, and utility bills are deductible. If, in order to stay in the gambling business, bribes are paid to local police or other officials, they are illegal expenditures and are not deductible.
5. Activities not entered into for profit. Normally, business profits are taxable and business losses are deductible—either from other

forms of income or from profits of other years. However, income-producing activities such as some hobbies and the rental of vacation homes can be so structured that they produce losses every year or nearly every year. In such a situation, one may deduct only enough expenses to offset the income. A net loss is not deductible.

6. "Ordinary, necessary, reasonable." Several deduction sections in the Code include one or more of those adjectives. As a practical matter, a disallowance on the ground that an expense violates any of the criteria is rare and arises only in related party situations. The courts have decreed that the IRS is not to substitute its judgment for that of the taxpayer or of corporate management in deciding whether or not an item is ordinary, necessary, and reasonable.

PROPERTY TRANSACTIONS

Some of the most important and more complex income tax rules relate to the acquisition, use, and disposal of property. Congress, for many years, has utilized the tax law to stimulate or dampen the economy or to encourage investments in specified types of property.

Depreciation and Amortization

Probably no single area has ever created more controversy between taxpayers and tax authorities than depreciation. The tax law has always recognized that the taxpayer should be allowed to recover the cost of assets used for the production of income. However, tax as well as accounting has required that the cost of long-lived assets should be recoverable over their useful lives. This well-accepted concept has led to numerous controversies on three points: which expenditures should be capitalized, the useful life, and how rapidly the cost should be written off over the useful life.

Although the accounting notion of depreciation has been fundamental in the tax law, Congress has also used the cost write-off as one of its tools in attempting to bring about certain economic consequences. For example, a straight-line, five-year (more specifically, 60-month) amortization was allowed on "emergency facilities" during World Wars I and II. Subsequently it was allowed for investments in "grain storage facilities" when there was a serious shortage of grain elevators. More recently, the 60-month amortization has been allowed for specified types of expenditures incurred during the specified periods; they include expenditures for railroad rolling stock, on-the-job training facilities, child-care facilities, rehabilitation of certain historic structures, rehabilitation of low-income rental housing, and certain pollution control devices.

"Depreciation" for tax purposes differs markedly from the accounting concept, and perhaps it should be thought of as a capital cost recovery allowance rather than as depreciation.

An overview of the current provisions can be provided by a summary of the rules that apply to most tangible property, new or used.

1. Methods. For property acquired after 1986, taxpayers must use the Modified Accelerated Cost Recovery System (MACRS). MACRS rules classify property based on class life (5-year, 7-year, 27.5-year, etc., property) for purposes of determining the applicable depreciation method, and the applicable recovery period. As long as a taxpayer uses the property class life, the decision will not be contested.
2. Salvage value. To alleviate another area of controversy, the law has specified that salvage value can be ignored in making the depreciation computation.
3. Section 179 expense. This is a special first-year allowance that is of benefit primarily to small business, although it is available to all taxpayers, subject to certain limitations. It allows for an immediate write-off of up to $108,000 in 2006 (adjusted upwards each year for inflation) for expenditures related to tangible personal business property, with any remaining balance eligible for MACRS depreciation.
4. Recapture of depreciation. In general, any gain recognized upon the disposal of equipment must be reported as ordinary income up to the amount of any depreciation deducted after 1961, even if the transaction is one that otherwise would justify capital gain treatment. For all practical purposes this means that any gain on the sale or exchange of equipment will be ordinary income except in the relatively rare instance when the item is sold for a price that exceeds its original cost. For real property, depreciation recapture generally will only apply to the excess depreciation deducted over straight-line depreciation. For this reason, depreciation recapture will not apply to real estate placed in service after 1986 since only straight-line depreciation could be taken for tax purposes.

Disposition of Property

The treatment of gains and losses upon the sale or exchange of property is affected by both the nature of the asset and the type of the transaction. The rules in this area are numerous and complex. This brief discussion can cover only the more general situations, and it is important that it be used only as a base for further study or as an entree for consultation with a tax specialist. There are basically three steps in analyzing a property transaction: realization, recognition, and characterization.

First, the realization of the actual amount of gain or loss follows a format similar to that of general accounting. The proceeds from the sale (after selling expenses) are compared to the "adjusted basis," which is similar in concept to the accounting net book value: cost (or other basis) plus capital additions minus depreciation and other capital recoveries. The tax "basis" of property, similarly to financial accounting, is usually cost, assuming the asset is purchased. When the asset is acquired other than by purchase, as by gift, inheritance, or any transaction in which gain or loss is postponed, the tax basis is subject to many complex rules. Generally, property acquired by inheritance has a basis equal to its fair market value on the date of the decedent's death, while appreciated property acquired by a lifetime gift has a basis equal to the basis of the donor. Gifted property that had declined in value since its purchase will have a basis to the donee equal to the lower of its adjusted basis to the donor or its fair market value on the date of the gift.

The second step in considering property transactions is to learn how much of the determined gain or loss will be recognized for tax purposes in the current year. Generally, gains and losses are recognized except in a few very important situations such as:

1. A loss on the sale or exchange of a personal use asset (e.g., personal residence, jewelry, household furnishings, etc.) is not recognized.
2. A loss on a sale to a related party is not recognized.
3. A significant amount of gain on a personal residence is not recognized in certain circumstances (see prior discussion in this chapter).
4. There are some transactions on which some or all of the gain or loss is not recognized but is deferred:
   a. On contribution of property to a business entity (e.g., corporation or partnership) solely in exchange for ownership rights in the company. For transfers made to a corporation, the owner(s) making the transfer must, in the aggregate, have 80 percent control of both voting shares and total shares of the corporation immediately following the transfer.
   b. Gain is not recognized on an involuntary conversion if the insurance or other proceeds are reinvested in a similar asset. Loss is recognized, and gain is recognized to the extent of any nonreinvestment proceeds.
   c. On exchanges of certain types of business assets for similar assets (a "like kind" exchange), loss is not recognized (i.e., is postponed) and gain is recognized only to the extent that cash or other "boot" is received. Note that this must be an exchange. The sale of a business asset accompanied by a purchase of a replacement asset does not qualify for deferral of gain or loss, unless strict guidelines are followed preventing the "seller" from the use of the proceeds and providing for a timely identification

(within 45 days after sale) and repurchase (before the earlier of 180 days after sale or due date of the return for the year of sale) of like kind property.

d. A loss on the sale of stocks or bonds is deferred if identical securities are acquired within 30 days before or after the loss transaction—the so-called "wash sale."

The third and final step, characterization, requires that all recognized gains and losses be classified as capital or ordinary. Inasmuch as long-term capital gains presently receive preferential treatment for all taxpayers, it is normally to those taxpayers' advantage to have ordinary losses and capital gains, since the excess of net long-term capital gains over net short-term capital losses are taxed at a maximum of 15 percent, while ordinary losses are deductible without limitation. However, once a transaction is consummated, the taxpayer has no choice; the tax rules dictate whether it is capital or ordinary. The taxpayer does have considerable planning opportunities in determining the form and the timing of the transactions, but it is essential that this planning take place in advance.

The tax law defines capital gain and loss quite narrowly, but it then allows capital treatment of other transactions in certain circumstances. A capital gain or loss arises only from the sale or exchange of a "capital asset," which is defined as all property except:

- Inventory or property held for resale in the ordinary course of business
- Real or depreciable property used in a trade or normal business
- Accounts or notes receivable
- Copyrights, compositions, letters, or memoranda created by or for the taxpayer
- A few other relatively unimportant items

It is evident that the definition excludes nearly all business assets except those held for investment. Thus, true capital gains or losses arise primarily from the sale or exchange of investment assets (e.g., stocks and bonds) or personal assets (e.g., personal residence). However, losses from the sale or exchange of personal use property are not deductible at all (see prior discussion).

A separate section of the Code grants capital treatment to a group of noncapital transactions, but only if gains exceed losses for the entire group. If losses exceed gains, then every transaction is treated as an ordinary gain or loss. Thus, the timing of any one transaction has the potential to convert the entire group from capital to ordinary, or vice versa. The group includes all recognized gains and losses from the following transactions, but only for assets held more than one year:

- Sale or exchange of real or depreciable business assets (excluding ordinary income from the recapture of depreciation)

- Condemnation (government right of eminent domain) of business property or of capital assets
- Casualties (fire, flood, etc.) of business property or of capital assets, but only if gains from all such casualties exceed losses from all such casualties

All capital gains and losses and all items to be treated as though they were capital gains and losses are assembled and sorted into two categories: (1) short-term (items held one year or less) and (2) long-term (items held more than one year). The net gain or loss is computed for each of the two categories. The two net figures are then combined to produce either a "net capital loss" or a "net capital gain."

To this point, everything on acquisition, use, and disposition of property, including realization, recognition, and characterization, has applied in essentially the same fashion to both corporations and individuals. The treatment of the final net capital gain or net capital loss differs dramatically for individuals and corporations.

Net Capital Gain

If the comparison of the net short-term and net long-term figures results in a net capital gain, it is then necessary to look back at the two preceding figures to find if there is an "excess of net long-term capital gain (NLTCG) over net short-term capital loss (NSTCL)." It is the "excess," if any, that is given beneficial tax treatment. For individual taxpayers the benefit is a reduced tax rate on excess long-term capital gains. For most taxpayers the reduced rate is 15 percent. However, if your ordinary marginal (highest) tax rate is 15 percent or less, then the tax rate on your excess long-term capital gain is only 5 percent (0 percent for tax years 2008 and 2009)! These reduced rate provisions are currently scheduled to expire in 2010. Here are some examples:

NSTCG	10,000		
		NCG $7,000	No excess; $7,000 is taxed as ordinary income.
NLTCL	(3,000)		
NSTCL	(4,000)		
		NCG $9,000	Excess is $9,000 and is treated as described above
NLTCG	13,000		
NSTCG	5,000		
		NCG $16,000	Excess is $11,000 (NSTCL is zero).
NLTCG	11,000		

Corporations are not allowed any tax rate advantage for net long-term capital gains.

Net Capital Loss

Corporations get no current deduction for net capital loss, but the loss can be carried back up to three years, and forward up to 20 years to offset capital gains in those years. The carryover item is considered a short-term loss, regardless of the nature of the original loss transactions.

Individuals can deduct up to $3,000 from their ordinary income for net capital loss. In computing the deduction, the portion of the net capital loss that arose from the short-term transactions is used first. Individuals may carry all unused losses forward in the original short- or long-term category indefinitely until they have been consumed.

CREDITS AGAINST TAX

Unlike a deduction, a credit reduces one's tax liability dollar-for-dollar and provides the same amount of tax savings regardless of the taxpayer's marginal tax bracket. On the other hand, tax deductions merely reduce taxable income so that the tax benefit is only equal to the deduction amount multiplied by the taxpayer's marginal tax rate. Therefore, if you were in the highest tax bracket, a $100 deduction would only return a $35 tax benefit (less if you are subject to the AMT). If you were in the 15 percent marginal tax bracket, that same deduction would only provide a $15 benefit. However, a $100 tax credit provides a $100 tax benefit, regardless of one's tax bracket.

Several credits are available to both corporations and individuals or only to individuals, including credits for children, dependent care, taxes paid to a foreign country, and earnings for low-income individuals.

RATE STRUCTURE

One of the basic tenets of the U.S. income tax law has always been that the burden should be shared on the basis of "ability to pay." Thus, individuals have been taxed on a progressive rate basis; taxpayers with higher incomes have paid a higher rate of tax. Sometimes it is assumed that each additional dollar of income will pay more tax than the preceding dollar. Some interpret a "progressive" rate schedule to mean that not only does the tax increase as incomes go up, but the rates on all taxable income increase.

It can be argued that the "ability to pay" concept is relevant only to individuals. A corporation as an artificial entity really has no "ability to pay" per se. Any tax paid by a corporation is ultimately borne by people (e.g., stockholders, employees, customers) through lower dividends, lower wages, or higher prices. Economists have attempted for years, and unsuccessfully, to measure the true "incidence" of the corporate tax, that is, how much is passed on to each group. The ultimate burden is shifted to someone, and it is not possible for it to be passed on to individuals in proportion to their ability to pay. Nevertheless, the corporate tax tables reflect considerable progression.

The "marginal rate" is the percentage of tax that will be paid on the next dollar of income. This is the rate that is relevant in most tax-planning decisions. Earlier discussions have included several features of the tax law that modify the rate progressions, sometimes rather substantially. For example, the marginal federal tax rate on state and local bond interest is zero, whether the interest is received by an individual or a corporation.

Alternative Minimum Tax (Both Individuals and Corporations)

Congress, especially in recent years, has frequently used the tax law to motivate taxpayers to make certain investments or to influence economic behavior in some other way. When the taxpayer reacts as Congress wishes, some type of preferential tax treatment is granted. As Congress increased such preferences, it became apparent that some taxpayers—including some with very high incomes—were able to avail themselves of tax preferences sufficient to eliminate all tax liability. Congress decided the preferences were still needed but that no one should use them to avoid tax entirely. Therefore, Congress identified certain of the tax preferences and ruled that at least a minimum tax should be paid thereon. The more common preference items relate to depletion in excess of the adjusted basis of the interest, intangible drilling costs, depreciation in excess of the straight-line amount, and, for individuals, certain itemized deductions such as state and local income taxes, real estate taxes, and miscellaneous itemized deductions, among others.

TAX SHELTERS

In recent years, much has been written about "tax shelters," but with no real agreement on definitions and with a great deal of myth and misinformation. Some define shelters very broadly to include anything that allows any income to be free of income tax. That view of shelters would encompass such provisions as the personal exemption, IRAs, 401(k)'s, and the exemption of state and local bond interest, all of which are available to taxpayers at all levels of income.

A narrower, and more common, view of tax shelters relates to the various investment vehicles structured to take advantage of various benefits in the tax law that allow taxpayers to offset ordinary income from other sources. Certain basic features of tax shelters are fairly common:

- Maximum tax deductions are allowed in the first year or two.
- Income is deferred until later years
- The income is realized as long-term capital gain when possible.
- The entity is usually a partnership (often a limited partnership) in order that the benefit of the deductions can flow through to the owners immediately.

It was not unusual for investors to receive tax deductions of 60 to 80 percent of their investments in the first year and 100 percent in the first two or three years. In certain circumstances it is still possible to deduct substantially more than the total investment, although an "at-risk" rule was adopted to stop some of the more flagrant abuses. Typically, the shelter partnership uses substantial borrowed capital and thereby can generate deductions far in excess of the partners' investments. Under present rules each limited partner is allowed to deduct losses only to the extent of the actual investment, the amount for which the partner is at risk. When it has been determined that the loss is deductible under the at-risk rules, then the passive activity loss rules are then applied.

A passive activity is any activity that involves the conduct of a trade or business in which the taxpayer does not materially participate. Thus, a passive activity is not determined by the nature of the activity per se—any type of activity can be passive—but, rather, by the degree of participation in the activity by the taxpayer.

The basic rule is that losses from a passive activity are only deductible against income from a passive activity. You cannot, for example, deduct a passive loss against earned income (wages, self-employment), or portfolio income (interest, dividends, etc). Unused passive losses are not lost, however, but are suspended (carried over) until they can be offset by passive income in a future tax year, until the entire activity is disposed of in a fully taxable transaction, or until the taxpayer dies. As you can visualize, it might be years before a passive loss could be deductible, thereby postponing the reduction of taxes that have to be paid. This is a disincentive for investing in such activities.

There are several areas of concern or potential problems to be aware of:

- First, and foremost, a tax shelter should be examined on its merits as an investment, not merely as a means of tax savings.

- Income is usually deferred several years.
- The investor may not be able to sell out easily.
- Just as early deductions may exceed cash outflow, later taxable income may exceed cash inflow.
- There may be substantial gain or income on termination of the shelter with little or no cash received at that time with which to pay tax.

A partial deduction (up to $25,000) against nonpassive income may be allowed for certain taxpayers for rental real estate losses if the taxpayer "actively participated" in the rental activity, and taxpayer's adjusted gross income (AGI) was under $150,000 without the loss. The requirements for active participation are somewhat less onerous than the "material participation" required to have the activity declared nonpassive or active.

SUMMARY

Corporations and individuals are subject to the federal income tax as described in the IRC, which contains thousands of pages of complex and specific rules. Although most basic tax concepts and many of the rules relating to income, exclusions, deductions, and credits apply to both types of taxpayers, there are some important distinctions. Through proper economic and business planning, taxpayers often have an opportunity to reduce their tax liability. It is legal and ethical to structure one's affairs in such a way as to minimize taxes so long as one complies with the law. In these few pages we have examined the basic structure of the tax law and looked at some of the areas in which tax-planning opportunities are available.

TEST PROBLEMS

1. It is conventional income tax wisdom to "gift cash, sell property that has gone down in value, and hold property that has gone up in value until your death." Why?
2. From time to time, bills have been introduced into Congress to grant tax relief for college expenses. Some have proposed a "deduction" of, say, $1,000; others have proposed a "credit" of, say, $300. (a) Contrast a tax deduction and a tax credit. (b) What is the principal argument in favor of each action?

3. We need to replace a piece of business equipment that cost $40,000 six years ago. Depreciation of $28,000 has been deducted during the six years. The manufacturer will sell us the new item we need for $50,000 cash or will allow us to trade in the old unit and pay a cash difference of $21,000. Alternatively, we can sell the old unit to a paving contractor in a neighboring city for $29,000. Thus, our net cash outlay will be $21,000 either way. (a) Discuss the tax considerations involved. (b) How would the tax considerations change if depreciation deducted in the past six years had been $7,000 rather than $28,000 and all other facts were unchanged? (c) If the market for used earthmoving equipment were very tight and we were able to sell our old unit for $43,000, describe the tax consequences. (Assume the $28,000 depreciation example.)

16

PERSONAL COMPUTERS AND SOFTWARE

I n today's world of ever-developing technology there is an abundance of personal computer manufacturers and software developers for their products. The choices put before us can seem quite overwhelming and cause great angst when trying to chose the best configured P.C. and software that will make our lives easier. The machines and software that they run range from the very simple single home office user to the enormous networks used by Fortune 500 companies.

Given today's fast-flowing information and general work environment, computers and the software they run are essential. The cost-benefit question goes beyond whether or not "do I purchase a computer or stick with the manual ledger system?" The question should be which computer configuration and software will best suit the company's needs for the money you will be spending. It is extremely important to understand the software you are using. It is important to know its limitations or you might be sorry you chose it. Even worse, you might be sorry you recommended it to one of your clients. If you do not have a complete understanding of a product you recommend, it will be difficult to explain why it cannot provide what the end user needs. Clients will lose confidence in you and your ability to provide them with the answers they come to you for.

Whether you are a long-time sole practitioner or just starting out, your computer should be capable of running, at a minimum, word-processing, spreadsheet, accounting software (general ledger and tax), communication software, data back-up utility, and desk top publishing. This is where the inexperienced computer geek might want to seek the help of a professional.

The amount of memory some of these programs utilize can be enormous, thus causing your machine to run at a slower pace than desired. The professional should easily be able to assess the amount of memory and disk storage space needed for you.

The cost of a reliable computer today pales next to the time they broke onto the scene. A work station with most of the software you need, can cost as little as $800 (excluding a laser printer). This will most likely exclude the cost of your general ledger and tax preparation software. I do not recommend having a computer constructed at the local computer shop. While it is not all that difficult to build a computer, not all the separate parts making up the whole machine are compatible. Major computer manufacturers have sophisticated diagnostic and quality controls. Before a new machine leaves the assembly line, the manufacturer will more than likely know a component is going to cause problems. This comes from personal experience discussions with colleagues. It is wise to form a solid relationship with a competent computer consultant. Although these machines enable our professional lives to run more efficiently, they can have off days and not perform as desired. Your machines should be checked periodically. You want to make sure you remain virus free and that your data are backed up regularly. The computer consultant should make sure you have reliable antivirus software installed and that a back-up of your data is done regularly. These steps are, for the most part, automated, but it is recommended that the consultant periodically check that everything is running as it should. The money is worth spending. The increased productivity will quickly offset the additional cost of the extra software and the computer consultant's time.

Depending on the software you will be using, the power of information will be at your fingertips ready to promote marketing campaigns to new and/or existing clients. When entering client information into your database, be as detailed as possible. Many data software packages will let you sort data in countless ways. This is invaluable when sending out mass-marketing letters via the U.S. post office or e-mail. The power of this information will help you better serve your clients. You will have the ability to make better tax and financial planning decisions. You can even use the information for mailing out birthday cards. Even when providing exemplary service, a little bit of goodwill can go a long way.

Record retention has been incumbent on professionals for some time. Whether you are an accountant, financial representative, or attorney, the physical space needed to fulfill our requirements is enormous. Many professionals who work in the field outside of their offices will tell you how difficult and sometimes costly it is to move work papers from one locale to another. This is where the laptop, portable document files (pdf), and Internet connection can be your best friend.

Permanent files are now being scanned into computer hard drives and are accessible at the touch of a button. Prior period work papers are stored in a similar fashion. The time and transportation costs of these documents can now be virtually eliminated. You can give clients secure and immediate access to documents such as tax returns, wills, trust documents, interesting articles, etc. This ability will save your company in phone time, photocopying, and postage. All this eventually translates to value added for your clients. The time saved can now be allocated to developing more business and using otherwise wasted resources to better serve your existing client base.

Travel can devour what could otherwise be a productive use of time. The ability to e-mail a client draft documents for client discussion over the phone can save countless hours in what turn out to be duplicative meetings. Busy clients appreciate this ability as well, since their time is just as precious as yours. The advent of computers and the Internet does not obviate the need for personal meetings with clients. There is truth to the saying "out of sight out of mind." If accountants do not meet with their clients regularly, clients will feel ignored and not important. This can lead to hard feelings and worse the loss of a client. However, delivering a final document in person rather than making two or more trips or mailings to discuss its finalization is much more sensible. Clients do not like paying for a professional's travel time. Nor do professionals enjoy losing the opportunity to perhaps provide valuable service to an existing or prospective client.

If the idea of using a computer intimidates you or if you are fearful of exploring further the ways it can simplify your work, don't be. There are many introductory and intermediate lessons available. They can be taken live or right on your P.C. via the Internet. Web-based seminars are becoming increasingly popular and often afford the professional time flexibility. It is important to be able to balance your personal and professional responsibilities while taking these informative seminars.

Whether you are self-employed or work for a medium or large firm, the desire to work remotely from a home office has become increasingly popular. You may have a particular day of the week you choose to work at home or you just need to be home for personal reasons. The creation of tools such as virtual personal networks (VPNs) has made accessing files in a secure and efficient manor as easy as turning on your computer. These systems create a direct portal into your company's database so retrieving client files are fast and easy. This is something that should be set up by an experienced information technology expert. Remember, you will be pulling information from your main database and working remotely. This can leave your system vulnerable to uninvited guests if not properly secure. The potential for data corruption or becoming a victim of cyberterrorism must always be considered.

Working remotely saves at many levels. Transportation costs are greatly reduced as is lost production in travel time. The unseen savings such as less auto emissions and overall fuel consumption provides for a cleaner environment.

In summary, the computer is an extremely useful tool for financial professionals, especially accountants. When choosing a system, ask your colleagues and professional groups about their decisions and observe what others are using. This will help your confidence in making an educated choice. Become educated about what is out there. You do not have to be an expert, but you should be familiar with the different products. Do not rush into things. It is sometimes shorter to take longer. However, you need to take the initiative and take advantage of what technology has to offer. Technology is forever changing, and service providers as well as clients are more in synch with each other than ever before. Professionals and the clients they serve are forming a level playing field in the world of data exchange.

ACKNOWLEDGMENT

The author gratefully acknowledges the contribution of Frank Bove, CPA, to this chapter. Mr. Bove is a partner at the New York City accounting firm of Dinowitz & Bove, LLP, and a Certified Quickbooks Pro Advisor.

17

CONSOLIDATED STATEMENTS

WHAT IS A CONSOLIDATED STATEMENT?

Basically a consolidated balance sheet, or income statement, is one in which we have combined the financial data of two or more affiliated companies in accordance with certain rules of the game.

But why in the world should we combine the data of two or more companies? Answer: Under appropriate circumstances a combined (consolidated) statement of two or more companies conveys financial information better than if our financial report presented the statements of each company separately.

For example, if our company, in addition to its cash, inventories, machinery, buildings, etc., owns as a long-term investment all of the outstanding capital stock of another company, we could present our company's own (legal) balance sheet and it would show, among the noncurrent assets, its investment in the other company. That investment would probably be shown at cost, as noncurrent assets are customarily shown. Then, for us to analyze the financial position of our company, we would need to "look behind" the investment; that is, we would also want to see the current balance sheet of the other company, particularly if the cost of our company's investment in the other company constituted a significant element among our company's assets.

The task of examining our company's legal balance sheet and also the legal statement of the other company might be relatively easy. Because our company owns 100 percent of the stock of the other company (i.e., we own the whole works), we would probably add together, mentally or on paper, the cash of our company and that of the other (subsidiary) company to determine our overall cash position. We would also add together the assets of each other category and then add together the liabilities. In other words, ownership of stock in our company at the same time effectively constitutes ownership in the other (subsidiary) company. Now, if the officers and directors of our company, through our company's ownership of all the stock of the other company, can control all the affairs of the other company, just as if that company were a mere branch of our company, why don't we save the readers a lot of bother and combine the statements for them? That's just what we do; only instead of calling the result a combined statement, we call it a *consolidated statement.*

You should now be ready for a definition. A consolidated balance sheet is one that presents the assets, liabilities, and owners' equities of two or more affiliated companies in a single balance sheet as if the affiliated companies were a single legal entity. Let's face it. We're not really dealing with a single legal entity, we're dealing with two or more entities. So please observe now, and remember, that every consolidated statement contains an element of fiction: The statements are drawn up as if they represented a single entity even though they truly consolidate the data of a parent company and its subsidiary companies.

Once again, let's remember that a balance sheet lists (1) the assets owned by the corporate entity, (2) the liabilities owed to outsiders by the corporate entity, and (3) the (residual) equity, or net worth, of the company.

WHY ISN'T A CONSOLIDATED STATEMENT A COMBINED STATEMENT?

To prepare a simple, combined balance sheet for two or more companies would involve nothing more than listing all the cash, all the receivables, and all the "everything else," but then you would not have a consolidated statement. So please hold on tight as we travel through the next sentences. If we present the separate, legal balance sheets of two companies, we'll show *all* the assets and all the liabilities of each. If we consolidate the two, any debts that one owes to the other will be canceled out (for consolidation purposes only) because when the two are hypothetically brought together *as a single entity,* such debts cease to be owed to or by outsiders.

The key to the preparation of consolidated statements lies in recognizing the need for eliminating mirror items. By *mirror items* we mean items that, figuratively, bridge the space between two separate but affiliated corporations. If you consolidate their statements, you eliminate the space between them and, in so doing, eliminate the bridges. Such a bridge, or pair of mirror items, is the $100 debt that the other company owes our company. On our legal balance sheet it shows as a $100 account receivable, while on their legal balance sheet it shows as a $100 account payable. If, then, we consolidate and make up a single balance sheet, the $100 item is eliminated because it becomes, for this purpose only, strictly an internal debt (within the family). Thus, in the case of your own company, when an employee signs out a tool from the toolroom, he owes something to the toolroom and the toolroom has a claim against him, but since this liability-receivable relationship is all intramural, it would not show up on your balance sheet.

A consolidated statement is in a true sense a fiction. It brings together what would otherwise be the separate, legal statements of two or more affiliated companies, and, in so doing, it shaves off all mirrored items so as to avoid duplication.

CONSOLIDATION BUZZ WORDS

The accountant's vocabulary includes a bunch of words that relate primarily to consolidated statement matters. A preview of them will save our stopping for definitions when we look into the actual process of making consolidated statements. Here are some, but certainly not all, of the buzz words. The definitions are loosely presented, since few formal definitions exist.

Affiliates

Companies are said to be affiliated when they have more or less permanent relationships, usually through stock ownership. For our purposes, when Company A owns an influential portion of the total voting stock of Company B, we will refer to A and B as affiliated companies, or simply as affiliates.

Parent Company

When one affiliate owns a "controlling interest" in the stock of another company (also an affiliate), the owner company is the parent company. Technically, to be a parent company requires more than 50 percent ownership interest in the affiliate's stock, but this requirement is subject to relaxation when the owner company, as a practical matter, controls the affairs of the other company.

Subsidiary Company

The affiliate whose stock is owned by a parent company is the subsidiary company. It is, of course, possible for Company A to exercise overwhelming influence over Company B while holding less than 50 percent of B stock, and consolidated statements may be required in that case.

Majority Interest

A majority interest refers to the stockholding of the parent company; it must be more than 50 percent of the stock that the subsidiary has outstanding.

Minority Interest

A minority interest refers to shares of subsidiary stock held by persons, corporations, etc., other than the parent corporation. Thus, if the parent holds a 51 percent majority interest, the minority shareholder, or shareholders altogether, hold the remaining 49 percent, which could be held by any number of minority stockholders from one to many.

Controlling Interest

If a corporation (or a person) owns more than 50 percent of the outstanding voting (usually common) stock of another corporation, it has considerable power to control the decisions of that corporation, including the determination of who shall be its officers and directors and the determination of dividend declarations. In fact, when ownership of the balance of the voting stock is widely scattered, such decision control can be exercised through holdings of much less than 50 percent of the total shares. On the other hand, serious obstacles to the exercise of such control sometimes exist, as when the company the majority of the stock of which is owned is located in a foreign country that is sustaining internal upheaval such as severe economic crisis or armed revolt.

In short, a controlling interest exists only when supported in fact by exercisable power to control the subsidiary company. The presumption is that when control exists in both the technical (over 50 percent) and effective sense, the financial statements are to be consolidated. When control exists in the practical sense but with holdings under 50 percent, traditionally a substitute concept is employed to depict the fact of control. That concept is referred to as the "equity" method of recording investments in another company. It consists of accruing, as an addition to the reported amount of the investment, the investor company's percentage share of the earnings or losses of the investee company with corresponding credit or debit to a revenue account, which might be labeled "Equity in Earnings of Affiliated Company." As a rule, the allowed minimum holding in instances such as this is 20 percent of the outstanding voting stock of the investee company.

However, the Securities and Exchange Commission (SEC) has suggested that consolidation may be appropriate where control exists without majority (over 50%) ownership of controlling shares. The Financial Accounting Standards Board (FASB) has expressed that control exists, without majority ownership, if any of the following situations exist:

1. The parent company has the right to appoint or elect a majority of the members of the governing board of directors. This might occur, for example, as the result of a voting trust, the controlled corporation's bylaws, or certificate of incorporation.
2. The parent company may elect a majority of the governing board through a large noncontrolling (i.e., less than 50 percent) voting interest. This may be done by trust, agreement, or the entity's certificate of incorporation or bylaws. This type of interest is present if it can be expected that it is to cast at least one-half of the votes actually cast to elect the governing board, not the total outstanding shares entitled to vote. If another group also holds a significant interest (deemed to be more than one-third the size of the parent company's interest).
3. The parent has the ability to elect a majority of the members of the governing board of an entity through the ownership of securities that can be exercised or converted to obtain sufficient shares of voting common stock.
4. The parent has the unilateral ability to assume the role of general partner in a limited partnership through the present ownership of convertible securities that are currently exercisable.

Intercompany Items

These are the mirror items referred to earlier. The major examples are:

1. Parent makes a loan (advance) of $100,000 to Subsidiary. On Parent's books the loan is a receivable; on Subsidiary's books (and on Subsidiary's legal statement) the same loan is a liability. As a group, these cases are referred to as intercompany debt. They show as debit items on lenders' books and credit (liability) items on borrowers' books. Both disappear upon consolidation.
2. Parent owns 51 percent of Subsidiary common stock. On Parent's legal statement this stock is shown as a single figure labeled Investment in Subsidiary. On Subsidiary's legal statement this stock doesn't show separately but is included as part of the total stock outstanding. (Let's refresh our memories here. Each corporation, even though an affiliate, remains a separate legal entity, and its "legal" statement is its own balance sheet or income statement, not a consolidated one. A consolidated statement combines the legal statements of two or more affiliated companies.)

3. Parent sells merchandise to Subsidiary. On their respective legal statements the sales by Parent are shown in their entirety, as are the purchases by Subsidiary. In effecting a consolidated statement, with the companies' statements combined, these intercompany sales and purchases fade out since, as a family, the transactions are the same as if they were mere movements of goods from one department to another within a single enterprise.
4. When one affiliate sells something to a subsidiary at a profit, the price (cost) of the thing to be recorded on the buyer's books is higher than it was on the seller's books. This markup is reflected (a) in a higher price (cost) on the buyer's books and (b) in retained earnings on the seller's books. Thus, "intercompany profits," so long as the marked-up item remains in the family, constitutes an intercompany item. There are numerous other forms of intercompany items, but these should suffice for your understanding of their nature.

ELIMINATION ENTRIES

So-called elimination entries must be made for all intercompany items. Thank goodness they all fit neatly into our basic debit-credit structure. Let's introduce them by an example. In the preceding section, the example given for what was there listed as group 1 items had Parent lending $100,000 cash to Subsidiary. You know that on Parent's books making the loan would be recorded by the following entry:

(1)

Loans Receivable to Subsidiary	100,000	
Cash in Bank		100,000

To record loan of $100,000 to our affiliate, Subsidiary Co.

On the books of Subsidiary, the receipt of the cash from Parent would be recorded as follows:

(2)

Cash	100,000	
Loans Payable from Parent		100,000

To record receipt of cash advance from our affiliate, Parent Co.

In these entries you should clearly recognize the intercompany items (Loans Receivable to Subsidiary and Loans Payable from Parent). Now, when the position statements of Parent and Subsidiary are to be consolidated, we must first make the following eliminating entry. (Later, we'll note that the eliminating entries are made only on the worksheet—not on actual books.)

(3)

Loans Payable from Parent	100,000	
Loans Receivable to Subsidiary		100,000

To eliminate intercompany items resulting from advance from Parent to Subsidiary.

The second group of intercompany items listed in the preceding section consisted of intercompany stockholdings; Parent owns more than 50 percent of the outstanding voting stock of Subsidiary. Assume that Parent had bought 90 percent of Subsidiary common stock from the present stockholders of Subsidiary for $1,170,000 cash, at a time when the stockholders' equity section of Subsidiary's legal position statement stood as follows:

SUBSIDIARY CO.
Stockholders' Equity, December 31, 20XX

Capital stock, common, $10 par	$1,000,000
Retained earnings	300,000
	$1,300,000

The entry to record this acquisition on Parent's books is:

(4)

Investment in Subsidiary Stock	1,170,000	
Cash in Bank		1,170,0000

To record purchase of 90% of Subsidiary common stock for cash.

What entry would be made on Subsidiary's books? Of course, there would be none. Subsidiary's stock outstanding merely changed hands, and there is no direct effect on Subsidiary's assets or equities. However, the mirror item is already on Subsidiary's books in the form of existing stockholders' equity, and we'll again have to do some eliminating in the process of consolidating. Here's the way it's done:

(5)

Capital Stock Common, $10 par (90%)	900,000	
Retained Earnings (90%)	270,000	
Investment in Subsidiary Stock		1,170,000

To eliminate intercompany 90% stock ownership as of date of acquisition.

Entry 5 needs more clarification. When Parent bought up 90 percent of the outstanding stock of Subsidiary, it acquired 90 percent of the Subsidiary stockholders' equity. In a sense, 90 percent of the $1,300,000 stock equity (or $1,170,000) is now "owed" to Parent (and Parent has a sort of claim of the same amount against Subsidiary). This intercompany item is made up of 90 percent of the stock and 90 percent of the retained earnings (at date of the stock purchase by Parent—at "acquisition" date). Before we proceed to the next group, note that the $1,170,000 cost of shares assumed in our example exactly matched 90 percent of the stock equity as it stood on the books of Subsidiary. Such perfect matching will rarely occur in real life, and we'll run into problems of accounting for the disparities. Entries shown later will demonstrate the handling of these cases.

The third group of intercompany items consists of intercompany sales of merchandise. Assume that Parent, during a given year, makes cash sales totaling $500,000 to Subsidiary. The entries on both sets of books are:

(6)

On Parent's Books

Cash	500,000	
Sales		500,000

(7)

On Subsidiary's Books

Purchases	500,000	
Cash in Bank		500,000

The intercompany, or duplicating, items in entries 6 and 7 are Sales and Purchases. The obvious eliminating entries for purposes of consolidation are:

(8)

Sales	500,000	
Purchases		500,000

The fourth group of intercompany items includes the "unrealized profit" (the markup) on assets, of whatever kind, sold by one affiliate to another and remaining in the hands of the purchaser affiliate as of the date of our consolidated statement. Please bear in mind that the profit is truly realized so far as the selling and buying entities are concerned, but when the balance sheets (and income statements) of the affiliates are consolidated, the profit lodged in any assets is strictly "in house" profit and must be treated as unrealized. If we didn't eliminate it, the profit would make room for some first-class shenanigans. For instance, Parent could buy a ping-pong ball for $.25 and sell it to Subsidiary (on account) for $1; without elimination entries, the consolidated position statement would show the ball at "cost" of $1 and would include a $.75 gain in the Retained Earnings account of Parent. For real fun, bounce the ping-pong ball back and forth between Parent and Subsidiary, with each buying it at one price and immediately reselling it at a higher price to the other. We might end up with the world's first million-dollar ping-pong ball!

Now, for an illustration, refer again to entries 6 and 7, where Parent sold merchandise to Subsidiary for $500,000. We then made an elimination entry 8 to cancel the mirrored sales/purchases of $500,000. Next assume that Subsidiary has resold 80 percent of these goods to outsiders before the end of the accounting period. Subsidiary's position statement will still include 20 percent of the $500,000, or $100,000 unsold, priced at the intercompany sales price. Now assume that the goods include a markup by Parent of 40 percent of selling price. Clearly, then, the goods remaining on Subsidiary's shelves had a cost to the family of only $60,000, and $40,000 of unrealized profit must be eliminated by the following entry:

(9)

| Retained Earnings (Parent) | 40,000 | |
| Inventories (Subsidiary) | | 40,000 |

To eliminate the $40,000 of unrealized profit in Subsidiary inventory.

You might wonder why we don't also eliminate the intercompany profit on the remaining $400,000 of sales from Parent to Subsidiary. The answer is that, to the degree that Subsidiary resells goods bought from Parent, Subsidiary's expenses (cost of goods sold) will be inflated by an amount that matches the profit we allowed Parent to claim. That is, Subsidiary resold $400,000 of the goods that had been marked up by $160,000, so Subsidiary's cost of goods sold is inflated by that amount, which exactly offsets the $160,000 profit that we allowed Parent to claim when we eliminated only $40,000 of the $200,000 gain that Parent booked from the sales. We'll do some further tinkering with this subject in illustrating consolidated income statements.

WHERE ARE ELIMINATION ENTRIES RECORDED?

By now you must be wondering how it is possible to record a journal entry in which a debit is made to an account on one entity's books and the related credit is made to an account on another entity's books. For instance, in entry 8 we debited Sales to eliminate intercompany sales from Parent's financial data and we credited Purchases for the same amount to eliminate the mirrored item from Subsidiary's financial data—all to match the data ready for consolidation. (We might insert here that a consolidated statement can properly be called a combined statement of the financial data of affiliated entities after the effects of intercompany transactions have been eliminated.)

The answer to our pending question is that the elimination journal entries are not made in any set of books. The legal accounting records of Parent and the legal accounting records of Subsidiary are not touched in the consolidation process. Each entity may, if desirable, issue its legal financial statements. The entries are entirely hypothetical and need not actually be written down anywhere just so long as you see to it that you do eliminate all the intercompany items before you combine the statements.

In actual practice the preparation of consolidated statements is usually done on a multicolumn worksheet. What you do is list the legal balance sheet data of Parent in the first pair of columns; list the data of Subsidiary in the next pair of columns; make all necessary debit and credit elimination entries in the third pair of columns; and then combine (consolidate) what's left. If your company has one or more subsidiaries, you might ask the accountant in charge of preparing consolidated statements to show you the consolidated working papers and explain them to you.

Because in this book we're concerned with the understanding rather than the mechanics of accounting, in our consolidation examples, coming up next, we will not utilize worksheets. Instead, we will employ a journal entry procedure because it is more flexible and useful for our particular purposes.

CONSOLIDATION OF BALANCE SHEETS AT ACQUISITION DATE

Assume that Parent Co. buys 80 percent of the outstanding common stock of Subsidiary Co. on January 1, 20XX, for $120,000 and that the legal balance sheet data of the two companies, in condensed form, stand as follows on that date just after Parent Co. buys the stock in Figure 17.1.

If we wish to prepare a consolidated balance sheet immediately after the stock acquisition, what elimination entries must we make before we

Figure   17.1

	Parent Co.	Subsidiary Co.
Assets		
Current	$100,000	$ 50,000
Investment in S Co. (cost)	120,000	—
Plant (net)	80,000	100,000
	$300,000	$150,000
Liabilities & Stockholders' Equity		
Current liabilities	$ 40,000	$ 20,000
Capital stock	150,000	100,000
Retained earnings	110,000	30,000
	$300,000	$150,000

combine the data? For the sake of simplicity, assume that the two compa-nies have had no dealings with each other. Then the only elimination items are the investment account on Parent's books and 80 percent of the stock-holders' equity on Subsidiary's books. The needed elimination entry (with one item temporarily omitted) is:

(10)

Capital Stock-Subsidiary (80%)	100,000	
Retained Earnings (at date of acquisition)—Subsidiary (80%)	30,000	
Balance	16,000	
Investment in Subsidiary		120,000
Minority Interest (20% 3 Capital Stock + Retained Earnings)		26,000

To eliminate intercompany investment and corresponding capital stock and "purchased" retained earnings.

What do we do about the $16,000 tentatively labeled "balance"? The tradi-tional answer is that it must represent a mix of two things: (1) unrecognized appreciation (or inflation) assignable to the various assets owned by Subsidiary and (2) goodwill. The accepted rule is to replace the balance with debits to Subsidiary asset accounts, insofar as such write-ups are justified, and charge only any leftover balance to consolidated goodwill. So if we assume that Subsidiary's current assets are up to date but that the plant has a current appraised value of $110,000, we replace "balance" by a debit to Plant of $10,000 and to Goodwill of $6,000 and revise the entry as follows:

(10a)

Capital Stock—Subsidiary	100,000	
Retained Earnings—Subsidiary	30,000	
Plant	10,000	
Goodwill	6,000	
Investment in Subsidiary		120,000
Minority Interest		26,000

Preparation of a consolidated balance sheet now requires only that we com-bine the original data, as modified by our "eliminating" entry. Our consol-idated statement (with helpful notations) becomes as shown in Figure 17.2.

CONSOLIDATED BALANCE SHEET SOMETIME LATER

Ten years have passed since Parent acquired its 80 percent interest in Subsidiary, and we are now expected to prepare the annual consolidated

Figure 17.2   Consolidated Balance Sheet, January 1, 20X1

PARENT CO. AND SUBSIDIARY CO.
Consolidated Balance Sheet,
January 1, 20X1

Assets		Liabilities & Stockholders' Equity		
Current (sum)	$150,000	Current liabilities (sum)		$ 60,000
Plant (sum plus $10,000)	190,000	Minority interest (20% of Subsidiary equity)		26,000
Goodwill (new item)	6,000	Stockholders' equity:		
		Capital stock	$150,000	
		Retained earnings	110,000	260,000
	$346,000			$346,000

balance sheet. The statement data at this moment stand as follows in the books of the two affiliates:

	Parent Co.	Subsidiary Co.
	Assets	
Current	$150,000	$ 75,000
Investment in S Co. (cost)	120,000	—
Plant (net)	120,000	150,000
	$390,000	$225,000
	Liabilities and Stockholders' Equity	
Current liabilities	$ 60,000	$ 30,000
Capital stock	150,000	100,000
Retained earnings	180,000	95,000
	$390,000	$225,000

Assume that (1) Parent now owes Subsidiary $10,000, (2) the current assets of Parent include merchandise inventory purchased from Subsidiary on which Subsidiary recorded profit of $5,000, (3) the plant adjustment in entry 9a must be reduced to reflect depreciation of $8,000, and (4) the goodwill adjustment in entry 9a must be reduced to reflect amortization of $1,500. As before, our first step is to prepare the necessary elimination (and adjusting) entries. They are:

(11)

Capital Stock	100,000
Retained Earnings (80% of amount	30,000
at acquisition, as before)	

Plant	10,000	
Goodwill	6,000	
Investment in Subsidiary		120,000
Minority Interest		26,000

To eliminate intercompany investment, corresponding capital stock, and "purchased" retained earnings and to recognize the $16,000 amount paid in excess of book value as an adjustment of Plant and Goodwill of Subsidiary.

(12)

Retained Earnings (Parent)	9,500	
Plant		8,000
Goodwill		1,500

To charge off against consolidated retained earnings the amounts indicated as accumulated depreciation and amortization, respectively, of plant and goodwill adjustments made at date of acquisition.

(13)

| Current Liabilities | 10,000 | |
| Current Assets | | 10,000 |

To eliminate intercompany debt.

(14)

| Retained Earnings (Subsidiary) | 5,000 | |
| Current Assets | | 5,000 |

To eliminate unrealized Subsidiary profits from inventories of Parent.

Our final "elimination" entry is not actually an elimination. Rather, it consists of splitting the retained earnings of Subsidiary between the minority and the parent company majority interests. We have already reduced Subsidiary's retained earnings by $5,000 in entry 13, leaving a balance of $90,000. Of this, 20 percent belongs to the minority and the rest (less the $24,000 "purchased" at acquisition date) goes to consolidated retained earnings. This may all be put in journal entry form as follows:

(15)

Retained Earnings (Subsidiary)		
(95,000 − 5,000 in entry 13)	90,000	
Minority Interest*		12,000
Investment Account (already entered in 9a)		30,000
Consolidated Retained Earnings		48,000

To allocate retained earnings of Subsidiary between minority and consolidated (majority) interests.

*20% of Retained Earnings debit less 20% of Investment Account credit.

We are now ready to combine the leftovers in a consolidated balance sheet, which is shown as Figure 17.3.

Figure 17.3   Consolidated Balance Sheet, 10 Years Later

PARENT CO. AND SUBSIDIARY CO.
Consolidated Balance Sheet, 10 Years Later

Assets			Liabilities & Stockholders' Equity		
Current (sum minus $10,000 and $5,000)		$210,000	Current liabilities (sum less $10,000)		$ 80,000
Plant (sum plus $10,000 less $8,000)		272,000	Minority interest (20% of $195,000 less $5,000)		38,000
Goodwill ($6,000 less $1,500)		4,500	Stockholder's equity Capital Stock	$150,000	
			Retained earnings ($180,000 minus $9,500, plus $48,000)	218,500	368,500
Total		$486,500	Total		$486,500

CONSOLIDATION OF INCOME STATEMENTS

To illustrate the preparation of a consolidated income statement, assume the following income statement data for the tenth year of affiliation:

	Parent Co.	Subsidiary Co.
Sales	$200,000	$100,000
Cost of goods sold	$120,000	$ 60,000
Other expenses and taxes	60,000	30,000
	$180,000	$ 90,000
Net income	$ 20,000	$ 10,000

Assume as before that Parent owns 80 percent of the outstanding common stock of Subsidiary, that $90,000 of the sales of Subsidiary were shipments to Parent, and that by year-end Parent had resold $40,000 of those goods to outsiders (leaving $50,000 in Parent's end-of-year inventory). The requirement is to prepare a consolidated income statement. For this purpose assume that all goods sold by Subsidiary Co. provide the same rate of profit.

There are several ways in which this problem and other problems like it can be handled, and each has its supporters. No doubt all would agree that we should eliminate the $90,000 of sales shown on Subsidiary's books as going to Parent. From here on practices differ, but we'll follow through with only one plan and assume that you will discuss it and its alternatives with your accountants if the matter is of interest to you.

If, as the assumption states, the profit margin is the same on all of Subsidiary's sales, then total profit on sales to Parent this year was 90 percent of $10,000, or $9,000. This profit, as we've noted before, represents within-the-family markup, and we should trace its impacts on the legal statements and eliminate them in a logical manner. The tip-off is the statement that Parent has resold $40,000 of the goods to outsiders. This means that $4,000 of the $9,000 profits has been carried into the Parent cost-of-goods-sold account, and the remainder, $5,000, must still be lodged in Parent's inventory. Next, if we eliminate part ($90,000) of Subsidiary's sales, don't we then have to eliminate the same proportion (nine-tenths) of Subsidiary's cost of goods sold? Yes. And if the other expenses of Subsidiary were proportionately related to the sales made to Parent, the same share (nine-tenths) of them will also be eliminated. Now we have all the necessary elements of our elimination entry, which comes out as follows:

(16)

Sales (of Subsidiary, 90%)	90,000	
Cost of Goods Sold (of Subsidiary, 90%)		54,000
Other Expenses and Taxes (of Subsidiary, 90%)		27,000
Cost of Goods Sold (of Parent, 4/9 of $9,000)		4,000
Merchandise Inventory (of Parent, 5/9 of $9,000)		5,000

To eliminate intercompany sales and related expenses, as well as related profit.

The resulting consolidated income statement may now be prepared. It is shown as Figure 17.4, with informal notations added for purposes of clarification.

CONSOLIDATED STATEMENTS—CONCLUSION

We have only scratched the surface of the world of consolidated statements. The mere mention of consolidated statement problems to anyone who is about to take CPA exams will usually bring on a cold sweat. The student has practiced doing consolidations of horrendous complexity and fully expects the worst. CPA examiners delight in setting problems involving a flock of, rather than only two, affiliates or problems involving subsidiaries and sub-subsidiaries. Sometimes when only a couple of affiliates are involved, each owns some of the capital stock of the other (mutual holdings),

Figure 17.4   Consolidated Income Statement, Tenth Year of Affiliation

PARENT CO. AND SUBSIDIARY CO.
Consolidated Income Statement, Tenth Year of Affiliation

Sales (sum minus $90,000 eliminated)		$210,000
Expenses:		
Cost of goods sold (sum minus $54,000 and $4,000)	$122,000	
Other expenses and taxes (sum minus $27,000)	63,000	185,000
Total net income (sum less $5,000 unrealized)		$ 25,000
Minority interest (20% of $10,000 less $5,000 unrealized)		1,000
Consolidated net income		$ 24,000
Proof of consolidated net income:		
Earnings of Parent		$ 20,000
Parent's share of Subsidiary earnings (80% of $10,000 less $5,000)		4,000
		$ 24,000

ownership interests may change in mid-year, bonds are issued at a discount by one affiliate and are purchased in the open market at a different price by another affiliate, etc.

One nice thing about the consolidation problems of a given company is that, once consolidated statements have successfully been prepared, their repetitive preparation in future years, or months, becomes pure routine.

All we've attempted to accomplish here, of course, is to present an outline of some of the typical problems along with one pattern of solution. From this point on you should be able to think along with your accountants in terms of consolidated data as well as the data of the individual affiliates.

TEST PROBLEM

On January 1, 20XX, Our Company acquires 90 percent of the outstanding common stock of Their Company for $82,000 cash. On this date the position statement data of the two companies (condensed) stand as follows after the stock purchase:

	Our Company	Their Company
Current assets	$ 50,000	$ 30,000
Investment in Their Company (at cost)	82,000	
Plant assets (net)	118,000	70,000
	$250,000	$100,000
Current liabilities	$ 20,000	$ 20,000
Capital stock	180,000	50,000
Retained earnings	50,000	30,000
	$250,000	$100,000

REQUIRED

1. Assume that there have been no intercompany transactions and that the payment in excess of book value represents goodwill. Prepare elimination entries and a consolidated position statement as of January 1, 20XX.
2. Next, assume that each company earns $20,000 during 20XX, and that at year end Their Company owes Our Company $5,000. Assume also that $500 of consolidated goodwill must be amortized. The position statements at the end of 20XX contain the following:

	Our Company	Their Company
Current assets	$ 83,800	$ 41,000
Investment in Their Company (at cost)	82,000	
Plant assets (net)	115,000	67,000
	$280,800	$108,000
Current liabilities	$ 20,000	$ 20,000
Capital stock	180,000	50,000
Retained earnings	80,800	38,000
	$280,800	$108,000

Prepare elimination entries and a consolidated position statement as of the end of 20XX.

TEST PROBLEM SOLUTION SPACE

(1) Elimination entries on January 1, 20XX:

	Debit	Credit
Capital Stock		
Retained Earnings		
Goodwill		
Investment in Their Company		

OUR COMPANY AND THEIR COMPANY
Consolidated Balance Sheet
January 1, 20XX

Assets		Liabilities & Stockholder's Equity	
Current	$	Current liabilities	$
Plant		Minority interest	
Goodwill		Stockholders' equity:	
		Capital stock	$
		Retained earnings	

(2) Elimination entry on December 31, 20XX:

	Debit	Credit

(1)

	Debit	Credit
Capital Stock		
Retained Earnings		
Goodwill		
Investment in Their Company		

(2)

	Debit	Credit
Retained Earnings		
Goodwill		

(3)

	Debit	Credit
Current Liabilities		
Current Assets		

OUR COMPANY AND THEIR COMPANY
Consolidated Balance Sheet
December 31, 20XX

Assets		Liabilities & Stockholder's Equity	
Current	$	Current liabilities	$
Plant		Minority interest	
Goodwill		Stockholders' equity:	
		Capital stock	$
		Retained earnings	

18

INCOME TAX ALLOCATION

WHY BOTHER?

It's a tough enough job just to determine how much income tax your company owes at the end of any year—why complicate things by attempting to "allocate" your taxes to periods other than the ones in which they become due?

This question has led to countless arguments among accountants and nonaccountants, and it has, in general, helped to keep the profession of accounting from becoming deadly dull.

The answer to the question "why bother?" can be reduced to a brief statement that will require elaboration, but here it is: The determination of periodic enterprise income rests upon the process of matching costs with revenues on a logical basis. Such matching is virtually synonymous with *accrual basis*, rather than *cash basis*, accounting. Income tax allocation is synonymous with accrual accounting; nonallocation is synonymous with cash basis accounting. Therefore, we must allocate. To summarize, the question is: Why isn't the income tax that we actually have to pay the amount of income tax that we should show as our current income tax expense in our income statement? The answer is that the income tax burden must be matched (accrued) with the items of revenue and expense that generate it. To treat the tax as an expense in a given year only because we pay it, or owe it, makes no sense at all.

WHAT CONDITIONS MAKE INTERPERIOD ALLOCATION NECESSARY?

We would have almost no tax allocation problems at all if the rules for measuring taxable income were made to conform to the generally accepted principles of accounting or if the principles governing accounting were made to conform to the tax rules. Either change, however, is only a creature of the dream world. The tax folks are too anxious to get their hands on the taxpayers' hard cash to allow them full exercise of sound accounting principles; at the same time, the taxpayers would be most reluctant to give up certain tax-deferring opportunities that do not fit well into their accounting records and reports. So tax allocation is needed when either the revenues or the expenses that we record in our books and financial statements differ from the amounts that we report (honestly) on our tax return. It should be added that we're not concerned with accounting or reporting errors, nor are we concerned with possible tax evasion. The differences are almost entirely the result of timing. Thus, a particular $10,000 may be recognized as revenue in our books in one year and may be shown on our tax return as revenue in either an earlier or a later year, and the same may be true of certain expense outlays. For purposes of completeness, we'll divide this part of the discussion into four segments, as follows:

1. Cases in which *revenues* show up in our books and financial statements *before* they are subject to tax (i.e., before they are reported on our tax returns). An example would be accounts receivable for a cash basis taxpayer.
2. Cases in which *expenses* show up in our books and financial statements *before* they are used as tax deductions (i.e., before they are reported on our tax returns). An example would be accounts payable for a cash basis taxpayer.
3. Cases in which *revenues* show up in our books and financial statements *after* they have been taxed (i.e., after they have been reported on our tax returns). An example would be prepaid income for performance not yet rendered.
4. Cases in which *expenses* show up in our books and financial statements *after* they have been used as tax deductions (i.e., after they have been reported on our tax returns). An example would be a prepaid expense.

GENERAL PRINCIPLES OF INTERPERIOD ALLOCATION

The all-encompassing principle of tax allocation requires that we employ the accrual method (not the cash method) of recognizing income taxes as an expense. Corollaries, or subprinciples to this general principle, with more detail added, may be phrased as follows:

1. If income is recorded in the books and financial statements before it has been subjected to income tax, we must accrue an appropriate

amount of tax in order to avoid overstatement of income. This is done by debiting Income Tax expense and crediting Income Tax payable for the difference.

2. If taxes are paid on "income" before being properly recognized in the books and financial statements, the tax charges, from the standpoint of our books, have actually been "prepaid" and should be so shown in our financial statements pending recognition of the income. Therefore a Prepaid Tax expense account should be created against the cash payment.

REVENUE RECOGNIZED BEFORE IT IS TAXED

The weight of accounting opinion nowadays favors comprehensive use of accrual accounting; more specifically, it favors the recognition of sales revenue at the time a sale is made, even though it may be an installment sale, so long as collection of the sales price is reasonably assured. On the other hand, the government allows the cash basis of accounting for certain types of installment sales in determining *taxable* income (subject, of course, to meeting technical tax rules). The installment method of accounting is presently allowed for tax purposes only for reporting gains from *nondealer* sales of property other than inventory. In other words, sales of real or personal property in the ordinary course of a taxpayer's trade or business may no longer be reported on the cash basis. However, it is still a good example for income tax allocation problems, so let's assume the property sold qualifies for following the installment sales method for tax purposes. What this means is that on an installment gain you are able to defer the actual payout of tax money beyond the point of sale by taking advantage of the tax provision that says your income may be taxable in proportion to the fraction of the sales price that you actually collect each year.

Let's take a fairly clear-cut example. Assume that we sell for $20,000 an asset that cost $5,000, and assume that the buyer pays 10 percent down (and no more during the year of sale). Our entry at the time of sale, using accrual accounting, is:

(1)

Installment Account Receivable	18,000	
Cash	2,000	
Asset—Cost		5,000
Gain on Sale of Asset		15,000

Assume that the tax rate on this kind of gain is 25 percent; however, since we've collected only 10 percent of the selling price, only 10 percent of the gain is taxed this year, for a total tax of $375. When we recognize this tax liability, our entry is:

(2)

Income Tax Expense	375	
($15,000 sale × 10% received × 25% tax rate)		
Income Tax Payable (or Cash)		375

Now the question is, would it be "fair" reporting to show this portion of our income statement as follows?

Gross gain on sale of asset	$15,000
Less: Tax on collected portion	375
Net income from sale of asset	$14,625

Quite obviously this is a misleading presentation, because we have claimed the entire gross gain in this accounting period but have charged against it only the "cash" portion of the income tax that presumably will have to be paid. This situation clearly calls for a tax allocation (accrual) entry to charge against the gain recognized this period the tax that will become payable on the total gain. The obvious solution is to accrue the 25 percent tax on the remaining 90 percent of the gain in the year of sale. Such an entry is made as follows:

(3)

Income Tax Expense	3,375	
Deferred Tax Liability		3,375

To accrue 25% tax on $13,500 ($15,000 × 90%) of installment gain recognized in the accounts but subject to tax only in the future as cash installments are collected.

With entry 3 on the books, the income statement will now show the following:

Gross gain on sale of asset	$15,000
Less: Income tax expense (including $3,375	
deferred on installment basis)	3,750
Net income	$11,250

Alternatively, entries (2) and (3) could be combined into the following compound entry:

Income Tax Expense	3,750	
Income Tax Payable		375
Deferred Tax Liability		3,375

This discussion is necessarily abbreviated. Its aim, however, is to introduce you to the concept of tax allocation. Upon further reading, and discussion with your accountants, you will find that the tax allocation entry requires a credit to a "deferred tax liability" account. The conclusion would appear logical since whenever revenue that will at some time be taxed is recognized in the accounts as earned before the period in which it actually becomes subjected to tax, a charge should be made to the tax expense account to accrue the future tax so that the current period's statement will not be distorted. The related credit, therefore, is an accrued liability.

Other cases in which revenue may be booked before it is taxed occur in connection with accounting for long-term construction contracts, in the technical handling of leaseholds on the books of the lessor, and in connection with current earnings of foreign subsidiaries under certain circumstances.

EXPENSES RECOGNIZED BEFORE THEY BECOME TAX DEDUCTIONS

The Internal Revenue decision makers have steadfastly refused to allow businesses to deduct expenses of a conjectural or strictly estimated nature, such as estimated future inventory losses and estimated outlays for product warranties, but generally accepted accounting principles provide that the accrual of such expenses is thoroughly logical and necessary on a timely basis in order to avoid overstatements of income. What this boils down to is that such expenses are shown on the income statement as reductions of earnings, but income taxes, in fact, are not correspondingly saved. Again the question: Do we show on our income statement only the income taxes we actually pay (or owe), or do we allocate the taxes to make them match up with the revenues and expenses that we have booked, knowing that the differences are almost entirely matters of timing and will eventually wash out? The answer, again, would appear to be that when we pay a tax in one year that really should be matched against the income of the next, or later, period, we should hold the tax charge in abeyance until its proper time for appearance in the income statement. This is done by treating the tax as being "prepaid" or, as the practitioners prefer to call it, "deferred."

For an example, assume that Our Company accrues $100,000 of product warranty expense in the year in which the sales of these products are recorded as revenues, and assume also that our income tax rate is 30 percent. The company had $500,000 of taxable income for the year. The warranty entry and the tax entries are:

(1)

| Product Warranty Expense | 100,000 | |
| Accrued Liability for Product Warranty | | 100,000 |

To accrue as warranty expense and liability the percentage of sales that has been found by experience to be reasonable.

(2)

Income Tax Expense	120,000	
($500,000 − $100,000 × 30%)		
Deferred Tax Asset ($100,000 × 30%)		30,000
Income Tax Payable		150,000

Other examples of expenses booked before they become tax deductible could easily be cited. However, the conclusion would appear to be sound that under circumstances in which expenses are recognized in the books before they are deductible, the tax payment made as the result of such nondeductibility should be set up as a prepayment or deferred charge to be transferred to tax expense as the accrued expenses materialize in the form of actual outlays.

REVENUE TAXED BEFORE IT IS RECOGNIZED

Apparently under many circumstances the government assesses income taxes on collections of cash that a business firm may make in advance of rendering a service. Thus, rents collected in advance, dues in advance, subscriptions in advance, payments for correspondence lessons in advance, etc., may be taxable in the period of receipt (i.e., on a cash basis) rather than in the period when the services are rendered, and the revenue is recognized in accordance with sound accounting principles.

Needless to say, the accountant resists showing advance cash collections as revenue. The entry to record these takes the following general form:

(1)

Cash	xxx	
Unearned Income (a liability account)		xxx

As the services are rendered, whether in later periods or the current one, the earning (realization) of revenues is recorded as follows. (Assume that we're dealing with rents collected in advance.)

(2)

Unearned Income	xxx	
Rent Revenue		xxx

If entry 1 occurs in one year and entry 2 in the second, then the income tax will be payable in year 1 on revenue that is not recognized until year 2.

Fortunately, again, we can resort to the accrual methods of accounting. To do so, the tax that we pay in year 1 (on the revenues to be earned in year 2) is debited to a prepaid (or deferred) tax account; like any other prepayment, it is treated as an asset to be written off as it is used up. In the second year, when the rent revenue is recognized, the amount in the prepaid tax account is transferred to the tax expense account so that it will become matched with the rent revenue in the second year's income statement.

The general conclusion, thus, for all cases in which income taxes must be paid prematurely on cash advances from customers or clients is to hold the tax in a prepaid expense (or deferred charge) account as an asset to be written off in the period or periods in which the services are rendered to the customers and the advances are transferred from liability to revenue accounts.

EXPENSES AS TAX DEDUCTIONS BEFORE THEY ARE RECOGNIZED

This final category of interperiod tax allocation cases has created much more controversy than the others. The circumstances are these: We own a depreciable asset that has an assumed five-year life. On our books we use the straight-line depreciation method, whereas we use the accelerated cost recovery system (ACRS) or modified accelerated cost recovery system (MACRS) (depending on when the property was placed into service) method for tax purposes. The result is that our tax deduction for depreciation during the first two years is greater than our book depreciation and during the final two years it is less. (In the third year the two are identical.) Over the full five years, the depreciation totals are, of course, alike. The timing, however, differs as between book and tax depreciation. The respective annual depreciation charges are shown in Figure 18.1 for an asset assumed to have cost $900.

If we assume that our company has net revenue (after deducting everything except depreciation and tax) of $300 per year and an effective

Figure 18.1   Book and Tax Depreciation

Year	Book (straight-line)	Tax (ACRS)	Differences
1	$180	$300	$+120
2	180	240	+60
3	180	180	—
4	180	120	−60
5	180	60	−120
Total	$900	$900	$ —

Figure 18.2 Our Company's Tax Liabilities

Year	Revenue before depreciation	Tax depreciation	Taxable income	25% tax
1	$ 300	$300	—	—
2	300	240	$ 60	$ 15
3	300	180	120	30
4	300	120	180	45
5	300	60	240	60
Total	$1,500	$900	$600	$150

tax rate of 25 percent, its actual income tax liabilities for the five-year period will be as shown in Figure 18.2.

Were our company to present its income statements without allocation of taxes, it would, of course, show a relatively high net income in the first two years and a relatively low net income in the final two years. The customary buzz words for a presentation of this sort are "flow through"; that is, we ignore the inconsistent relationships between the taxes we pay, as compared with the revenues and expenses that we record, and merely let the cash tax consequences flow through. In Figure 18.3 are shown the income statement data for the five years on a flow-through basis.

Surely anybody making an analysis of Our Company's progress as reflected in its net income trend would be quite pessimistic because of the

Figure 18.3 Comparative Income Statements on Flow-through Basis

OUR COMPANY
Comparative Income Statements on Flow-through Basis

	Years					
	1	2	3	4	5	All
Net revenue (before depreciation and tax)	$300	$300	$300	$300	$300	$1,500
Depreciation per books	180	180	180	180	180	900
Net before tax	$120	$120	$120	$120	$120	$ 600
Tax (actual)	—	15	30	45	60	150
Net income	$120	$105	$ 90	$ 75	$ 60	$ 450

persistent decline. That is exactly what is wrong with flow through; again, it consists of an unfortunate mix of accrual accounting for all data except taxes, which are naively recognized on a cash basis. One of the more popular inequities that regulatory commissions throughout the country have imposed on our public utility companies has been to require the companies (1) to use one of the rapid depreciation methods for tax purposes, (2) to use straight-line depreciation in their books, and (3) to use the flow-through scheme for determining income subject to regulation. The early effects of such requirements are, of course, an apparently inflated amount of earnings, which the commissions then proceed to chisel down with no promise of compensatory adjustment as the tide reverses itself in later years.

Next, let's apply tax allocation techniques to these same data. In year 1, $300 of the asset's cost was written off as a tax deduction (leaving only $600 for future write-offs in the next four years). On the other hand, only $180 of cost was written off in the accounting records. If we present a flow-through income statement (as in Figure 18.3), do we properly disclose the fact that in this first year we have, in a sense, borrowed some $120 of depreciation deductions from our future? Does it put the reader on notice that our remarkably low tax bill was achieved at the expense of higher tax bills in the future? Wouldn't it be more honest to accrue an appropriate amount of income tax charge against the $120 of apparent earnings, on the ground that because we are using up $300 of depreciation deduction now we'll be obligated to pay commensurately more taxes in future years? All those questions would appear to point in the direction of tax allocation. Stated most simply, our cash tax has, indeed, been delayed (deferred), but it has not been evaded or avoided; our tax burden should be accrued on the basis of our pretax book income. In the present instance the tax charge has been only temporarily reduced, and the amount of this temporary reduction is found by multiplying our tax rate (25 percent) by the amount of extra depreciation taken for tax purposes ($120). We should accrue against this year's earnings 25 percent of $120, or $30, as deferred income tax. The entry is:

(1)

Income Tax Expense	30	
Deferred Tax Liability		30

In year 2 the amount deferred is 25 percent of $60 (which is tax depreciation of $240 minus book depreciation of $180), or $15. In year 3 no allocation entry is needed. Then, in the final two years the situation turns around. The difference between tax depreciation and book depreciation becomes negative, so our allocation entries are the reverse of those made in the first two years, or as follows:

	Year 4 (2)	
Income Tax Expense	30	
Deferred Tax Liability	15	
Income Tax Payable		45

	Year 5 (3)	
Income Tax Expense	30	
Deferred Tax Liability	30	
Income Tax Payable		60

If tax allocation entries are recorded in the fashion illustrated, the income statements for the five years should produce the same amount of net income each year, since all other things were unchanged. In Figure 18.4 the income statements are presented again with the effects of the tax allocation entries clearly disclosed (as they should be).

There are those who believe that the same allocation results could be obtained more logically if the amounts of additional tax accrued in the first two years and the tax reductions of the last two years were treated instead as adjustments of the straight-line depreciation accruals. The theory is that, in

Figure 18.4   Comparative Income Statements on Full Accrual Basis

OUR COMPANY
Comparative Income Statements (on full accrual basis)

	Years					
	1	**2**	**3**	**4**	**5**	**All**
Net revenue (before depreciation and tax)	$300	$300	$300	$300	$300	$1,500
Depreciation, straight-line ($900/5)	180	180	180	180	180	900
Net revenue before tax	$120	$120	$120	$120	$120	$ 600
Income tax:						
Cash	$ 0	$ 15	$ 30	$ 45	$ 60	$ 150
Accrual	30	15	0	(15)	(30)	0
	$ 30	$ 30	$ 30	$ 30	$ 30	$ 150
Net Income	$ 90	$ 90	$ 90	$ 90	$ 90	$ 450

consuming $300 worth of tax depreciation in the first year, we "sapped" the asset of some of its future cash flow power and this should be reflected as additional depreciation. Were this plan adopted, our income statements would show as tax expense the amounts actually owed each year, and the periodic depreciation would be the $180 of straight-line charge increased by $30 and $15, respectively, in the first two years and decreased by $15 and $30, respectively, in the last two years; net income would be the same—$90 for each year.

We have gone through the alternatives to gain a better understanding of the issues involved; remember, however, that the flow-through method is not allowed for purposes of presenting external financial statements.

TAX ALLOCATION AND PERMANENT DIFFERENCES

So far we have looked at tax allocation procedures when differences between the books and the tax returns are only differences in timing; in other words, the cumulative difference eventually reduces to zero for all practical purposes. There are some situations, however, in which certain items of income or expense recorded in the books are never to be included in the income tax determination. Some examples would include interest income on municipal bonds, expenditures for fines and penalties, and life insurance proceeds. Quite obviously, here we have no problem of allocation; no allocation entries are to be made because the two (books and tax returns) never catch up with each other. That is the case with all permanent differences. However, pretax financial income must be adjusted by these permanent differences when computing income tax expense for the period.

ARGUMENTS AGAINST TAX ALLOCATION

Some persons feel that no tax allocation entry should be made in the case of depreciation differences because the company could, by continually expanding at a uniform or accelerating rate, permanently delay part of its tax payments. Flow through, so they argue, is then the only proper course. Accountants have strongly rejected that view; they point out that it would be much like arguing that a growing company should treat its current liabilities as part of retained earnings because the total is never likely to be reduced below a certain level.

TAX ALLOCATION WITHIN A PERIOD

Even within a single year taxes may require allocation. That happens in the relatively unusual cases when income determination items are shown partly in one part of a statement and partly in another. If, for example, your income statement reports an extraordinary gain, the gain will be shown at the bottom of the statement. Quite logically, the gain should carry with it its full share of operating expenses and income taxes; so just as income may be shown in two different places in the income statement, taxes also may be split.

Also, on rare occasions we may make charges or credits directly to Retained Earnings to record corrections of earnings carried forward from prior years. To the degree that such entries enter into the income tax determination, a portion of the tax (sometimes a negative portion) should be allocated to them. One obvious result of such allocations is that the tax remaining in the income statement approximates the amount chargeable against the income reported therein (by excluding the amount attributable to the entry in retained earnings).

TEST PROBLEMS

For the following four problems, assume that the items listed are the only tax allocation item:

1. Assume that our tax rate is 30 percent. If Our Company uses the accrual method to record installment sales, with a resulting net income (before taxes) of $100,000, and we use the cash (installment) method for tax purposes, with a resulting taxable income of $40,000, we should make the following tax allocation entry:

   Debit

       Credit

2. If we accrue product warranty expenses of $100,000 that are not allowable tax deductions until we actually incur the expenses, and our net income after deducting income tax expense is $500,000, we should make the following tax allocation entry:

   Debit

       Credit

3. If we collect $100,000 in rents and earn only $60,000 of that amount this year, we should make the following tax allocation entry at year-end:

   Debit

       Credit

4. If we record total straight-line depreciation of $100,000, while reporting $250,000 for tax purposes, we should make the following entry:

   Debit

       Credit

19

BUSINESS COMBINATIONS: MERGERS, ACQUISITIONS, AND CONSOLIDATIONS

HOW BUSINESS COMBINATIONS ARE ACHIEVED

Nothing has created more interest, for those who enjoy a good fight, than the battle during recent years among accountants and financiers, low and high, over the manner in which we should account for various types of business combinations. It has been said repeatedly that many mergers simply would not be carried out if the companies were not permitted to account for them the way they want to. This is sad! In any case, let's apply accounting analysis to the major patterns of combinations so we can see what the argument was all about.

Prior to Financial Accounting Standards Board (FASB) Statement No. 141 in 2001, there were two methods available to record the acquisition of a company, known as purchase and pooling. The more usual method was the purchase method. Under this method, all assets and liabilities were recorded at their estimated fair market values. If the purchase price exceeded these values, the excess was debited to the intangible asset goodwill. This asset, which was amortized over a 40-year period prior to the issuance of FASB No. 142 in 2001, now is no longer amortized. Instead the asset may be written down due to its subsequent impairment. The other acceptable method was known as the pooling method. Under this method, all assets and liabilities are recorded at existing book values, therefore eliminating the recording of goodwill.

Purchase and pooling were never intended to be a matter of choice. The pooling method was only intended to be available for a merger of two corporations of equal value. Accordingly, generally accepted accounting principles used to provide that pooling transactions had to meet certain criteria, including the fact that 90% of the target corporation's common stock be received in exchange for the acquiring corporation's common stock. Because the pooling method was perceived by the acquiring corporation to be advantageous to the purchase method, many business combinations were arranged so that they would fit within the pooling criteria. Some of these perceived advantages are:

1. The combined corporation's net income would be higher than under the purchase method due to the fact that depreciable assets (and the depreciation expense related thereto) would not be increased to fair value.
2. The combined entity's retained earnings would increase immediately, which made prior periods look more profitable.
3. The acquiring corporation's net income would be increased by the entire year's net income of the target even if the acquisition took place on the last day of the accounting year.

Also recall that prior to 2001, under the purchase method, goodwill had to be expensed over a 40-year period, thereby further reducing net income for the acquiring entity. Because of these advantages and the subsequent manipulation of business combinations to fit all business combinations within the pooling method criteria, the pooling method of accounting for a business acquisition was eliminated in July 2001.

VALUATION USING THE PURCHASE METHOD

All assets acquired and liabilities assumed are to be recorded at their current fair market value. If an active market exists for the item, then quotes of fair value should be used. If there is no active market for the item, qualified independent appraisals, discounted cash flow analysis, and similar types of valuation methods may be used. As far as liabilities are concerned, short-term (current) liabilities generally have a current fair value equal to their book value. Long-term liabilities may have fair values different from current book value should the face amount of the interest rate not fluctuate with current market conditions. Should the purchase price paid by the acquiring company exceed the sum of net fair market values, the difference must be debited to the intangible asset, goodwill.

The process of allocating valuation among the various assets purchased should start with the determination of tangible assets purchased (e.g., inventory, equipment, furniture and fixtures, etc). The next step would be to locate any "identifiable" intangible assets, such as trademarks, patents, covenants not to compete, etc. Only if the purchase price should exceed all of these fair market values (net of liabilities) should goodwill be recorded. Once recorded, goodwill is no longer amortized, although it should be subsequently evaluated, and if found to be impaired, expensed down to its fair value.

THE PHYSIOLOGY OF AN ACQUISITION UNDER THE PURCHASE METHOD

The management of A Co. has an excess of working capital and wants to employ it by acquiring the business (the net assets) of B Co. There are several ways in which it can do so. For purposes of discussion we'll assume that the balance sheet data of the two companies stand, at the moment of decision, as shown in Figure 19.1.

For our first variation, assume that A Co. bargains directly with B Co. and the two agree that A Co. is to pay B Co. cash, in the amount of

Figure 19.1   Balance Sheet Data at Time of Acquisition

	A Co.	B Co.
Assets		
Current	$ 700,000	$100,000
Plant	500,000	500,000
Total	$1,200,000	$600,000
Liabilities & Stockholders' Equity		
Current liabilities	$ 100,000	$ 50,000
Bonds payable	400,000	—
Capital stock, par $1	500,000	450,000
Retained earnings	200,000	100,000
Total	$1,200,000	$600,000

$650,000, for the net assets of B Co. (which consist of the asset total of $600,000 minus the liability total of $50,000).

On the books of A Co. we can delay the difficult part of the acquisition entry a few minutes by making the following initial entry:

(1)

Investment in Net Assets of B Co.—Cost	650,000	
Cash in Bank		650,000

To record purchase of B Co. net assets, with book value of $550,000, for $650,000 cash.

We could now leave B Co. to its own devices if we wanted to, since it will have no subsequent effect on A Co. Just for the sake of this excursion, though, let's assume that B Co., now flooded with cash and nothing else, elects to dissolve. The entries, including the sellout, are:

(1a)

Cash	650,000	
Current Liabilities	50,000	
Current Assets		100,000
Plant		500,000
Gain on Sale of Net Assets		100,000
(or Retained Earnings)		

To record sale of all net assets to A Co. for cash.

(2a)

Capital Stock	450,000	
Retained Earnings (with	200,000	
$100,000 added)		
Cash in Bank		650,000

To record distribution of cash to stockholders in liquidation.

In the meantime, A Co. must face the problem of recognizing on its books and statements the net assets acquired from B Co. The easy way out would be simply to debit the various asset accounts for the same amounts at which they were carried on the books of B Co., credit liability accounts also for the amounts formerly owed by B Co., and then credit the investment account with the amount of its $650,000 balance and make a "plug" entry to goodwill to make the entry balance. Such an entry would appear as follows:

(2)

Current Assets (in detail)	100,000	
Plant (in detail)	500,000	
Goodwill (plug to balance)	100,000	

Current Liabilities (in detail)		50,000
Investment in Net Assets of B Co.—Cost		650,000

To replace investment account with accounts for specific assets and liabilities acquired from B Co., at B Co. book values, and to charge Goodwill for the amount paid ($100,000) in excess of the book value of the net assets.

Needless to point out, entry 2 balances because we made it balance with the goodwill plug, but the entry makes no sense whatsoever. There is not the slightest reason (other than indolence or stupidity) for continuing the book values of B Co. on the books of A Co. following their purchase for cash. It would make equal sense, if you were to buy your neighbor's car for $2,000, for you to record it on your books at $3,500 with an allowance for depreciation of $2,000 (a net of $1,500) and charge the $500 difference (2,000 × 1,500) to goodwill simply because the neighbor had originally paid $3,500 for the car and had, to date, recorded $2,000 of depreciation.

The point is that we should, at least initially, record assets at cost. When we buy a basket of assets (cum liabilities) for $650,000, it should mean that we have appraised the lot and can allocate the purchase price to them on a reasonable basis, including, perhaps, a lump sum for goodwill (which is often simply debited with the amount that is left over).

For a more sensible solution, assume that the current assets are found to be worth approximately their B Co. book values, the plant assets are appraised at $530,000, and goodwill is valued at $70,000. Now the entry to clear the investment account becomes:

(2)

Current Assets (in detail)	100,000	
Plant (in detail)	530,000	
Goodwill	70,000	
Current Liabilities (in detail)		50,000
Investment in Net Assets of B Co.—Cost		650,000

To replace the investment account with specific asset and liability accounts at their current values.

For another variation, assume that A Co. issues bonds payable to B Co. for $650,000 instead of paying cash. The acquisition and investment-clearing entries (assuming the same values as before) then become:

(1)

Investment in Net Assets. of B Co.	650,000	
Bonds Payable		650,000

(2)

Current Assets	100,000	
Plant	530,000	
Goodwill	70,000	
Current Liabilities		50,000
Investment in Net Assets of B Co.		650,000

The same end results can be obtained if the acquisition is made through the purchase of the outstanding capital stock of B Co. and the company is then liquidated. Alternatively, B Co., after purchase, can be "kept alive" as a subsidiary, and the combining of assets and liabilities then is accomplished only in consolidated statements. The first entry, in either case, records purchase of the capital stock. Assume that a total of $650,000 cash (or it could be in bonds) is paid. The purchase entry is:

(1)

Investment in B Co. Common Stock	650,000	
Cash in Bank		650,000

To record purchase of 100% of B Co. common for $650,000.

(2)

Current Assets	100,000	
Plant	530,000	
Goodwill	70,000	
Current Liabilities		50,000
Investment in B Co. Common Stock		650,000

To record dissolution of B Co.

IMPACT OF ACQUISITION TRANSACTION ON INCOME

The accounting for a business combination by the "acquisition" route may have a very drastic effect on net income. Prior to acquisition, B Co. might be reporting annual earnings of, say, $60,000 per year, or a rate of return of 10 percent on total assets; however, this amount is based on book values at historical cost. If, as we assumed, the price paid for the assets places them at a total valuation of $700,000, the rate of return drops to $60,000 divided by $700,000, or 8.6 percent, as the result of increasing the "rate base." But that is not all. If the depreciable asset valuations are stepped up and the useful lives are assumed to be unchanged, then the periodic depreciation charges are increased and this causes the net income to decline by the amount of the depreciation increase less the related reduction in income taxes. Furthermore, and this could be the real hitch, we came up with goodwill in the amount of $70,000. Accounting logic requires that this asset be amortized over a reasonable (10- to 40-year) period. In our example, 10-year amortization of the $70,000 of goodwill would reduce the net income by $7,000 per year (with no income tax relief). Thus, from a 10 percent return before acquisition, the purchased business might provide less than 8 percent on the basis of revised asset valuations, depreciation, and amortization. For that reason, businessmen and a lot of accountants have argued stoutly for the continued privilege of recording business combinations by what is known as the pooling-of-interests, or pooling, method whenever certain prerequisites are met. However, this currently is not an option for reasons discussed earlier.

REQUIRED DISCLOSURE UNDER THE PURCHASE METHOD

For the period in which a purchase occurs, a schedule disclosing the fair values of assets purchased must be included in the financial statement footnotes. Additionally the following information must also be included within the financial statement footnotes:

1. The name of the company acquired.
2. The percentage of voting shares acquired.
3. The reasons for the acquisition and the determination of goodwill.
4. What part of the financial period of the acquiring company are the results of the acquired company included.
5. Full disclosure of any options, commitments, or contingent payment agreements contained within the acquisition agreement.
6. Whether and to what extent any research and development costs were acquired and expensed during the period.
7. Full disclosure if any portion of the purchase price was not yet determined with the reason why such determination had not yet been finalized. Any subsequent allocation adjustments must be disclosed.

During the acquisition period, there must also be

1. Footnote disclosure as to the results of operations as if the purchase was made as of the first day of the acquisition period, as well as

2. The operating results for the immediately prior period if comparative financial statements are issued.

The footnote disclosure must include revenue, income before extraordinary items and cumulative effect of accounting changes, net income, and earnings per share. The footnote would also include the impact of values assigned to the various accounts in the acquisition.

TEST PROBLEM

The condensed balance sheet data of Our Company and Your Company stand as follows:

	Our Company	Your Company
Assets		
Current	$ 100,000	$ 80,000
Noncurrent	400,000	320,000
	$ 500,000	$ 400,000
Liabilities & Stockholders' Equity		
Current liabilities	$ 50,000	$ 40,000
Capital stock, par $10	300,000	200,000
Retained earnings	150,000	160,000
	$ 500,000	$ 400,000

The current market value of the common stock of Our Company is $40 per share, and of Your Company is $19 per share. Management of Our Company believes that the stockholders of Your Company would be willing (a) to exchange all their common stock in the ratio of two shares for one share of Our Company (which is better than the market ratio) or (b) to exchange all their common for 12 percent, 20-year, convertible debenture bonds of Our Company on the basis of a $1,000 par bond for each 50 shares of stock. The debentures would be convertible into Our Company common at the rate of 22 shares for each bond, and the bonds would not be subject to call until after 10 years. The bonds would probably have a market value of par. Assume that the current assets of Your Company are worth approximately the amount of their book value, the plant is appraised at $350,000, and acquisition costs to Our Company would be $50,000.

REQUIRED

Assume, first, that the combination is effected by the offer described in (a).

1. Prepare a journal entry to record, on the books of Our Company, the issue of 1,000 shares of common stock in exchange for the 2,000 outstanding shares of Your Company.
2. Next, prepare a journal entry to record the dissolution of Your Company. Assume that method (b) is followed.
3. Prepare an entry to record the initial investment.
4. Then prepare an entry to record the dissolution of Your Company. Assume that the bonds are worth par.

TEST PROBLEM SOLUTION SPACE

	Debit	Credit

(1)

Investment in Your Company Common Stock
    Capital Stock, Par $10
    Paid-in Capital in Excess of Par Value
    Cash

To record exchange of 1,000 shares of Our Company common for 2,000 shares of Your Company common.

(2)

Current Assets
Noncurrent Assets
Goodwill (to balance — cost)
    Current Liabilities
    Investment in Your Company Common Stock

(3)

Investment in Your Company Common Stock
    Convertible Bonds Payable
    Cash

To record purchase of Your Company common in exchange for our 12% convertible bonds with par and market value of $400,000.

(4)

Current Assets (appraised)
Noncurrent Assets (appraised)
Goodwill (to balance—cost)
  Current Liabilities (per books)
  Investment in Your Company Common Stock

To record dissolution of Your Company and recognition of assets at current value, including goodwill.

CHAPTER
20

ACCOUNTING FOR FOREIGN OPERATIONS

OUR FOREIGN RELATIONS

Financial involvement in foreign countries has the capability of generating interesting, even exciting, accounting ramifications. At the outset it may be worthwhile to review, briefly, some of the various forms that such involvement can take. They may range from relatively simple purchases of raw materials from abroad to complex multinational situations encompassing foreign branches and subsidiaries around the world.

ACCOUNTS RECEIVABLE

For the least complicated cases, assume that we, located in the United States, advertise our products for shipment to Canadian customers at prices quoted in Canadian dollars and that our terms of sale stipulate that payment is due in Canadian dollars 30 days from date of our invoice. Under those circumstances we would record accounts receivable, as usual, in U.S. dollars. The amounts, however, would have to be in harmony with the specified Canadian dollar amounts, which would be translated into their U.S. dollar equivalents as of the dates of sale. The U.S.-Canadian dollar relationship is a variable one; and when we receive the customer remittance in a check drawn on a Canadian bank, we are likely to end up with an amount of U.S. dollars that differs from our original debit to Accounts Receivable. Differences of that sort are known as "exchange gains and losses," and they are properly treated as elements in our current income determination.

In addition to the exchange gains and losses realized at the time of collection, there is also implied (or accrued) gain or loss in the accounts receivable that have not been collected and remain on the books at the end of the accounting period.

ACCOUNTS PAYABLE

If we make purchases from foreign suppliers and are obligated to remit specified amounts of foreign funds, the U.S. dollar equivalents of our accounts payable are subject to fluctuation in the same manner as the accounts receivable. If we receive invoices priced in Canadian dollars and we elect to delay payment in accordance with the suppliers' terms, we must translate the stated prices into U.S. equivalents at the time of our recognizing them as accounts payable. The amounts of U.S. dollars ultimately expended to make the required Canadian dollar remittances, perhaps 30 to 60 days later, are likely to vary (often significantly) from those recorded at the dates of purchases. Also, the amounts remaining unpaid at the end of an accounting period will usually require adjustment to reflect accrued translation differences. Such adjustments, at time of remittance or at time of financial statement preparation, are, again, exchange gains or losses and should be interpreted as an element in our current income determination. Note that our discussion so far has been related to current "monetary assets" (accounts receivable) and current "monetary liabilities." Note also that when we hold receivables denominated in Canadian dollars, we have an exchange gain when the Canadian dollar "gains" (i.e., goes from 90 to 91 U.S. cents) but an exchange loss on any Canadian-denominated payables.

FOREIGN BRANCHES

In order to maintain continuity, a U.S. corporation may establish "branch" sales offices in one or more foreign countries. Sooner or later it may broaden the scope of the branch's activities to include not only sales but also warehousing, the assembly of components shipped from the United States, and, ultimately, the manufacture of parts or complete products designed either for overseas consumption or for shipment back to the United States. Such foreign operations may be continued in the form of unincorporated branches.

Branch accounting has its interesting aspects, and they are amplified when the branches are maintained in foreign countries. The connecting link between the foreign branch and the "home office," insofar as the accounting is concerned, is likely to be one or more pairs of "reciprocal" accounts. On the books of the home office an account may be labeled Due from Branch, and its counterpart at the foreign branch would naturally be labeled, in the opposite sense, Due to Home Office. Then, as long as the respective sets of accounting records are accurately maintained and are up to date, the debit balance shown as Due from Branch should be a mirror match of the credit balance, on branch books, shown as Due to Home Office. There is one complication: the ever-varying difference in the monetary units employed in the two countries. Each country has what is variously termed its "domestic," "local," or "functional" currency. Unfortunately, the domestic currencies of two countries cannot be added together without prior harmonization of their respective values, even though (as in the case of Canada, Australia, Hong Kong, Singapore, and others) the countries use the "dollar" as their official monetary unit.

FOREIGN SUBSIDIARIES

Large-scale business activity usually is most conveniently carried on in the form of corporations. That is true not only in the United States but in practically all of the noncommunist countries in the world. Most accounting problems are the same whether the foreign activities are or are not carried on through corporate form, and there would appear to be little reason for variation in the manner of valuing assets, for example, as between noncorporate and corporate entities. The principal connecting link between the U.S. "parent" corporation and the foreign branch, whether incorporated or not, is the set of reciprocal accounts. Thus, a portion of the outstanding capital stock and retained earnings in the balance sheet of the branch is reflected (but not necessarily in identical amount) in the "investments" section of the domestic parent corporation's balance sheet. Apart from that linkage, the remaining interrelationships are the same whether the foreign branch is or is not incorporated.

ACCOUNTING FOR RECEIVABLES AND PAYABLES

If we assume that sales and purchases of goods are made in various foreign countries directly with the buyers and sellers, rather than through branches, the accounting entries are not different from those made to record similar transactions domestically. Sales are recorded by debits to Accounts Receivable and credits to Sales; purchases are recorded by debits to

Merchandise, Raw Materials, etc., and credits to Accounts Payable. If those transactions are carried on in U.S. dollars (domestic currency), no special accounting problems arise.

On the other hand, purchases and sales are often denominated in foreign currency; that is, they call for remittance in the monetary unit of the foreign country. And there's the rub. The amount of U.S. dollars implied to be paid or to be received changes with each change in the value relationship between the U.S. and the foreign currency, and the amount of any change constitutes what is commonly termed "Foreign Exchange Gain and Loss," an element in current income determination. For example, assume that on date 1 we sell merchandise to a Canadian company for C$1,000, to be paid in 60 days in Canadian funds; on the same date we purchase raw materials from another Canadian company for C$1,000, also payable in 60 days, and calling for remittance in Canadian dollars. Assume that the Canadian dollar is quoted at 85 U.S. cents on date 1, the transaction date, at 95 U.S. cents on date 2, when our next balance sheet is prepared, and at par (US$1.00) on date 3, the remittance date. The following entries may be appropriate to reflect all those facts:

Date 1
(1)

Accounts Receivable—Foreign	850	
Sales—Foreign		850

To record sales in Canada for C$1,000, now worth US$850.

(2)

Raw Materials	850	
Accounts Payable—Foreign		850

Purchase to be paid in C$1,000, currently worth US$850.

Date 2
(3)

Accounts Receivable—Foreign	100	
Foreign Exchange Gain and Loss		100

The current exchange value of our C$1,000 of Canadian receivables is now 1,000 × .95, or US$950, an increase of US$100.

(4)

Foreign Exchange Gain and Loss	100	
Accounts Payable—Foreign		100

Liability increase from Canadian dollar.

Date 3
(5)

Cash	1,000	
Accounts Receivable—Foreign		950
Foreign Exchange Gain and Loss		50

Collection of Canadian receivables at par for exchange gain of US$50 since last revaluation.

(6)

Accounts Payable—Foreign	950	
Foreign Exchange Gain and Loss	50	
Cash		1,000

Payment of Canadian account payable at par with exchange loss of US$100 since last revaluation.

From the journal entries, and their explanations, that have just been presented you should observe that an underlying principle is being employed. The principle is that when an enterprise accumulates either assets or liabilities that must be liquidated in terms of the currency of another country (i.e., monetary assets or liabilities) and such monetary items are required to be reported in (translated into) the monetary units of the former country, the translation should be performed at the most current rate of exchange. Resulting gains or losses are properly treated as elements in current income determination. In short, exchange gains or losses with respect to current monetary items (such as cash, receivables, and payables) arising from changes in exchange rates are to be recognized as they accrue, and they become an element in current income determination.

FOREIGN BRANCH ACCOUNTING

Assume that USCAN Corporation, in Chicago, establishes a semiautonomous branch in Toronto for the purpose of manufacturing and selling complete products. The activities for the first year are depicted in the following journal entries with their explanations. When the events to be recorded affect the accounting records of both Chicago and Toronto, entries for each are shown.

Date 1
Chicago books

Investment in Branch	850,000	
Cash in Bank		850,000

Chicago office sends funds to Toronto for purchase of manufacturing plant, US$510,000, and equipment, US$340,000. On this date the Canadian dollar is valued at 85 U.S. cents, for a total of C$1,000,000.

Toronto books (Canadian dollars)

Cash in Bank	1,000,000	
Home Office Capital		1,000,000

Receipt of funds from Home Office for purchase of building and equipment.

Building (510,000/.85)	600,000	
Equipment (340,000/.85)	400,000	
Cash in Bank		1,000,000

Purchase of plant as indicated.

On Date 2, US$87,000 was subsequently sent from headquarters to the Toronto branch to meet its working capital needs. At that date the conversion rate was 87 U.S. cents for each Canadian dollar.

Date 2
Chicago books

Investment in Branch	87,000	
Cash in Bank		87,000

Cash sent to branch for use as current working capital (exchange rate now 87 U.S. cents).

Toronto books

Cash in Bank	100,000	
Home Office Capital		100,000

Cash received from Chicago, converted into C$1.1494 per U.S. dollar.

On Date 3, the annual branch transactions are recorded as follows:

Date 3
Toronto books

Finished Goods	350,000	
Cash in Bank		100,000
Accounts Payable		200,000
Allowance for Depreciation		50,000

Summarization of all factory costs of production of finished products for the year. (No home office entry needed.)

Cash in Bank	400,000	
Sales		400,000

Branch sales for the year.

Cost of Goods Sold	250,000	
Finished Goods		250,000

Factory cost of goods sold for the year.

Selling and Administrative Expenses   60,000
    Cash in Bank   60,000
Branch expenses for the year.

At year-end the following items are recorded. At that date, the exchange
rate for the Canadian dollar is 90 U.S. cents and the average exchange rate
for the year is 88 U.S. cents:

Date 4
Branch Trial Balance before Closing

	Debit	Credit
Cash in Bank	C$ 340,000	C$
Finished Goods	100,000	
Building	600,000	
Equipment	400,000	
Allowance for Depreciation		50,000
Accounts Payable		200,000
Home Office Capital		1,100,000
Sales		400,000
Cost of Goods Sold	250,000	
Selling and Administrative Expenses	60,000	
	C$1,750,000	C$1,750,000
Sales	400,000	
Cost of Goods Sold		250,000
Selling and Administrative Exp.		60,000
Income Summary		90,000
Income Summary	90,000	
Home Office Current		90,000
Branch office closing entries		

Branch Trial Balance after Closing

	Debit	Credit
Cash in Bank	C$ 340,000	C$
Finished Goods	100,000	
Building	600,000	
Equipment	400,000	
Allowance for Depreciation		50,000
Accounts Payable		200,000
Home Office Capital		1,100,000
Home Office Current		90,000
	C$1,440,000	C$1,440,000

Chicago Entries (Optional)

Cash in Bank (340,000 × .90)	306,000	
Finished Goods (100,000 × .90)	90,000	
Building (600,000 × .90)	540,000	
Equipment (400,000 × .90)	360,000	
Allowance for Depreciation (50,000 × .90)		45,000
Accounts Payable (200,000 × .90)		180,000
Branch Income (90,000 × .88)		79,200
Investment in Branch		937,000
Cumulative Translation		54,800
Adjustment-Exchange Gain		

FOREIGN CURRENCY TRANSLATION

The entries made at the home office (Chicago) under date 4 include paren-thetical notations showing how the amounts are derived. Actually, there's little to explain. We have assumed that at the end of the year (date 4) the exchange rate for the Canadian dollar is 90 U.S. cents, and we have multi-plied most of the balances that are recorded in Canadian dollars by .90 to attain their U.S. equivalents. Also, it was assumed that the average exchange rate for the year was 88 U.S. cents, and that provided the best translation rate for the reported net income (which was assumed to have accrued evenly throughout the year).

Clearly, if we have 340,000 Canadian dollars in a Canadian bank account and are presenting a report in U.S. dollars, we must translate the Canadian amounts into their current U.S. equivalents. If the exchange value of the Canadian dollar, for purposes of conversion into U.S. money, is 90 U.S. cents, then our 340,000 × .90, or 306,000 U.S. dollars. Translation of cash at the current rate of exchange is a widely accepted accounting practice. The same rule applies to translation of other mone-tary items—accounts receivable, accounts payable, and the like. The basic reason for use of the current rate here is that the resultant, translated amount is the amount *most likely* to be available when the monetary items mature.

In certain situations exchange rates have lapsed into wildly fluctuat-ing conditions requiring special consideration. Translation of a foreign cur-rency at the current rate in the belief that you are depicting the real worth when it shows every likelihood of as much as, say, 50 percent deterioration in value before realization is, obviously, not a useful exercise. A possible solution would be to accompany such translation by a special provision, similar to the allowance for bad debts, which charges off against current earnings as much of the item as is likely to be lost overall from deterioration of the foreign currency.

IDENTIFYING A FOREIGN ENTITY'S FUNCTIONAL CURRENCY

The rate of translation of the foreign currency representation of nonmonetary assets depends on the foreign entity's functional currency. The functional currency is the currency of the country where the entity primarily generates and expends cash. One may assume that the Toronto branch purchases materials and incurs labor costs with Canadian dollars. The branch also sells its product and collects its receivables in Canadian dollars. Therefore, the exchange rate between the Canadian and U.S. dollar have little or no economic impact. Accordingly, the Canadian dollar would be the functional currency.

The functional currency of the foreign entity is not always its home country. The Toronto branch could have received its funding from an U.S. bank and sold its product and collected its receivables in U.S. dollars. Now the exchange rate between the currencies would have an impact on the Toronto branch's cash flows and ultimately those of the U.S. company. The Toronto branch's day-to-day operations are dependent on U.S. economic conditions affecting its currency. Similarly, asset and liability fluctuations of the Toronto branch will impact the U.S. company's cash flow. For these reasons the functional currency would be the U.S. dollar. It is even possible to have a functional currency other than the that of the branch or the controlling company (e.g., if the Toronto branch had extensive dealings in China).

If it is determined that the foreign branch's currency is the functional currency, the current rate must be used for translation purposes, and all assets will be translated at the current rate. Additionally, revenues and expenses would be translated on a weighted average basis. However, should the functional currency *not* be the foreign entity's home currency, then the historical rate of translation would be used. That means that all assets other than monetary assets will be translated at historical rates as of the date that the asset was acquired. Revenues and expenses are translated on a weighted average basis except that items that can be specifically traced to an event must use the historical rate, such as the inventory amounts in cost of goods sold or depreciation expense relating to property, plant, and equipment.

ACCOUNTING FOR THE CUMULATIVE TRANSLATION ADJUSTMENT

Translation adjustments result from the process of translating foreign financial statements from their functional currency into the U.S. company's reporting currency. Because different exchange rates are being used for different items (current, historical, weighted average, etc.), the symmetry of the balance sheet (assets = liabilities + stockholders' equity) will not work. Therefore, a translation adjustment is necessary in order to balance the balance sheet. Translation adjustments do not exist in terms of the functional currency and do not effect the cash flows of either the foreign or U.S. company. Because of this, the translation adjustment would not be included in current net income. Instead, the translation is reported as a part of "other comprehensive income."

A

SOLUTIONS TO TESTS

CHAPTER 1

DENTON BREAD CO.
Balance Sheet as of December 31, 20XX

Assets			
Current:			
Cash		$ 9,200	
Accounts receivable (less $500 allowance for uncollectibles)		11,500	
Raw materials inventory (at cost)		5,000	
Miscellaneous supplies		1,000	
Prepaid Expenses		500	$ 27,200
Property, Plant, & Equipment:			
Land (cost)		$ 5,000	
Buildings (cost)	$ 50,000		
Machinery and equipment (cost)	60,000		
	$110,000		
Less: Accumulated depreciation	3,400	106,600	111,600
			$138,800

(Continued)

Liabilities & Stockholders' Equity (*Continued*)

Current liabilities:		
Wages payable	$ 1,600	
Taxes payable	3,000	
Interest payable	200	$ 4,800
Long Term Liabilities:		
Mortgage payable		30,000
Total liabilities		$ 34,800
Stockholders' equity:		
Capital stock, par $10	$100,000	
Retained earnings	4,000	104,000
		$138,800

CHAPTER 2

TARRANT CO.
Income Statement for the Year 20XX

Revenues			
Sales			$5,627,483
Other income			13,680
Total Revenues			$5,641,163
Costs & Expenses:			
Cost of goods sold		$3,980,000	
Selling expenses		592,000	
Administrative expenses		614,250	5,186,250
Income From Operations			$ 454,913
Less: Income taxes			154,000
Income before extraordinary item			$ 300,913
Uninsured flood loss			125,000
Net income			$ 175,913
Earnings Per share of common stock:			
Income before extraordinary item	$2.71		
Extraordinary item (flood loss)	(1.22)		
Net income	$1.49		

TARRANT CO.
Statement of Retained Earnings
For the Year 20XX

Retained earnings at beginning of year	$1,500,000
Add : Net Income	175,913
	$1,675,913
Cash dividends on common stock, $1 per share	100,000
Retained earnings at end of year	$1,575,913

CHAPTER 3

EMPIRE CORP.
Ledger

Cash in Bank				Capital Stock		
(1)	100,000	(2)	1,000		(1)	100,000
		(3)	30,000			
		(6)	10,000			

Accounts Receivable			Retained Earnings		
(5)	60,000			(12d)	13,875

Inventory				Sales		
(4)	50,000	(7)	35,000	(12a)	60,000	(5)	60,000

Store Equipment				Cost of Goods Sold		
(3)	30,000	(8)	125	(7)	35,000	(12b)	35,000

Accounts Payable				Miscellaneous Expenses		
		(4)	50,000	(2)	1,000	(12c)	11,125
				(6)	10,000		
				(8)	125		

Income Summary			
(12b)	35,000	(12a)	60,000
(12c)	11,125		
(12d)	13,875		

(9) EMPIRE CORP.
Trial Balance (before closing)
July 31, 20XX

	Balances	
Account Title	**Left**	**Right**
Cash in bank	$ 59,000	
Accounts receivable	60,000	
Merchandise	15,000	
Store equipment	29,875	
Accounts payable		$ 50,000
Capital stock		100,000
Retained earnings		
Sales		60,000
Merchandise cost of sales	35,000	
Miscellaneous expenses	11,125	
	$210,000	$210,000

(10) EMPIRE CORP.
Income Statement
For the period ended July 20XX

Sales		$60,000
Expenses:		
Merchandise cost of sales	$35,000	
Miscellaneous	11,125	46,125
Net income (and earnings retained)		$13,875

(11) EMPIRE CORP.
Balance Sheet,
As At July 31, 20XX

Assets			Equities		
Current:			Current liabilities:		
Cash in bank	$59,000		Accounts payable		$ 50,000
Accounts receivable	60,000		Stock equity:		
			Capital stock	$100,000	
Merchandise inventory	15,000	$134,000	Retained earnings	13,875	113,875
Store equipment		29,875			
		$163,875			$163,875

CHAPTER 4

BLITZ CO.
Worksheet for the Year Ended December 31, 20XX

	Trial balance		Adjusting entries		Income statement		Balance sheet	
	Debit	Credit	Debit	Credit	Debit	Credit	Debit	Credit
Cash in bank	2,500			(1) 25			2,475	
Accounts receivable	40,000						40,000	
Allowance for bad debts		100		(2) 600				700
Merchandise	40,000			(3) 30,000			10,000	
Plant	100,000						100,000	
Allowance for depreciation		35,000		(4) 4,000				39,000
Accounts payable		20,000						20,000
Interest accrued payable				(5) 1,000				1,000
Income tax accrued payable				(6) 650				650
Bonds payable		25,000						25,000
Capital stock		50,000						50,000
Retained earnings		13,400						13,400
Sales		60,000				60,000		
Uncollectible Accounts exp.			(2) 600		600			
Cost of goods sold			(3) 30,000		30,000			
Selling expenses	10,000		(4) 3,600		13,600			
Administrative expenses	11,000		(1) 25 (4) 400		11,425			
Interest expense			(5) 1,000		1,000			
Income taxes			(6) 650		650			
Net income for year					2,725			2,725
Totals	203,500	203,500	36,275	36,275	60,000	60,000	152,475	152,475

BLITZ CO.
Income Statement, Year Ended December 31, 20XX

Sales		$60,000
Net sales		$60,000
Expenses:		
Cost of goods sold	$30,000	
Selling expenses	13,600	
Administrative expenses	11,425	
Uncollectible Acct expense	600	
	$55,625	
Interest expense	1,000	
Income taxes	650	57,275
Net income (and earnings retained)		$ 2,725

BLITZ CO.
Balance Sheet, December 31, 20XX

Assets			
Current:			
Cash in bank		$ 2,475	
Accounts receivable	$40,000		
Less: Allowance for bad debts	700	39,300	
Merchandise		10,000	$ 51,775
Plant (cost)		$100,000	
Less: Allowance for depreciation		39,000	61,000
			$112,775

Equities

Current liabilities:

Accounts payable	$ 20,000	
Interest accrued payable	1,000	
Income taxes accrued payable	650	$ 21,650
Bonds payable		25,000
Total liabilities		$ 46,650
Stockholders' equity:		
Capital stock	$ 50,000	
Retained earnings, January 1	$13,400	
Earnings retained, 19XX	2,725	16,125	66,125
		$112,775

CHAPTER 5

(1)	Cash	500	
	Sales		500
(2)	Accounts Receivable	600	
	Sales		600
(3)	Cash	196	
	Sales Discounts	4	
	Accounts Receivable		200
(4)	Cash in Bank	5,000	
	Notes Payable		5,000
(5)	Interest Expense	100	
	Notes Payable	5,000	
	Cash in Bank		5,100
(6)	Cash	800	
	Allowance for Depreciation	1,100	
	Retirement Loss	100	
	Machinery		2,000
(7)	Sales-Bad Debts	500	
	Accounts Receivable—Allowance for Bad Debts		500
(8)	Accounts Receivable—Allowance for Bad Debts	120	
	Accounts Receivable		120

(9) Cost of Goods Sold	9,000	
Merchandise		9,000
(10) Insurance Expense	300	
Prepaid Insurance		300

CHAPTER 6

TIPTON CO.
Statement of Cash Flows, Year Ended December 31, 20x2

Cash flow from operating activities:		
Net income		$68,000
Add: decrease in accounts receivable (net)	$ 5,000	
Increase in accounts payable	10,000	
Depreciation	10,000	25,000
Deduct: Increase in inventories	$48,000	
Gain from sale of land	5,000	
Decrease in wages payable	5,000	(58,000)
Cash flow from operating activities		$35,000
Cash flows from investing activities		
Sale of land	$15,000	
Purchase of plant	(50,000)	
Cash used by investing activities		(35,000)
Cash flows from financing activities		
Issuance of capital stock	$50,000	
Cash dividends	(25,000)	
Payment of mortgage	(10,000)	
Cash flow from financing activities		15,000
Net increase in cash		15,000

CHAPTER 7

January 10		
Raw Materials	19,600	
Accounts Payable		19,600

Purchase of 25,000 pounds @ 80 cents, terms 2/10, n/30.

January 19		
Accounts Payable	19,600	
Cash in Bank		19,600

January 20		
Raw Materials	17,640	
Accounts Payable		17,640

January 31		
Accounts Payable	17,640	
Loss from Lapsed Discounts	360	
Cash in Bank		18,000
Work in Process	30,032	
Raw Materials		30,032

Consumption of all but 22,000 pounds with FIFO cost of $17,640 plus $1,568 (which is 2,000 units of the first purchase at 80 cents less 2%).

CHAPTER 8

Straight-line procedure:

	Year 1	
Depreciation	1,700	
Allowance for Depreciation		1,700

	Year 2	
Depreciation	1,700	
Allowance for Depreciation		1,700

	Year 3	
Depreciation	1,700	
Allowance for Depreciation		1,700

	Year 4	
Allowance for Depreciation	5,100	
Cash	3,000	
Loss on Sale	1,900	
Machinery		10,000

Sum-of-years' digits procedure:

	Year 1	
Depreciation	2,833	
Allowance for Depreciation		2,833

COMPUTATION: $1 + 2 + 3 + 4 + 5 = 15$. Depreciation for first year is then 5/15 of $8,500. Second year will be 4/15 of $8,500, or $567 less. The amount declines by $567 each year, leaving a salvage of $1,500 at the end of year 5 if the asset is not retired earlier.

	Year 2	
Depreciation	2,266	
Allowance for Depreciation		2,266

	Year 3	
Depreciation	1,700	
Allowance for Depreciation		1,700

Year 4

Allowance for Depreciation	6,799	
Cash	3,000	
Loss on Sale	201	
Machinery		10,000

Double Declining Balance:

Year 1

Depreciation	4,000	
Allowance for Depreciation		4,000

Year 2

Depreciation	2,430	
Allowance for Depreciation		2,430

Year 3

Depreciation	1,440	
Allowance for Depreciation		1,440

Year 4

Allowance for Depreciation	7,840	
Cash	3,000	
Equipment		10,000
Gain on Sale		840

CHAPTER 9

(1)

Cash in Bank	11,250,000	
Capital Stock Common—Stated Value $2		500,000
Paid-in Capital in Excess of Stated Value		10,750,000

(2)

No Entry. Make memorandum entry for stock split.

(3)

No entry. Unissued stock has no effective financial significance and no basis for entry.

(4)

Treasury Stock Common—Cost	3,000,000	
Cash in Bank		3,000,000

(5)

Cash in Bank	1,750,000	
Treasury Stock Common—Cost		1,500,000
Paid-in Capital—Treasury Stock		250,000

(6)

Capital Stock Preferred	1,000,000	
Retained Earnings	100,000	
Cash in Bank		1,100,000

(7)

Cash in Bank	1,050,000	
Capital Stock Preferred—Par		1,000,000
Capital Stock Common—Warrants		40,000
Paid-in Capital in Excess of Par		10,000

(8)

No entry called for.

Stockholders' Equity:

Capital stock preferred—12%, $100 Par		$ 1,000,000
Paid-in Capital in Excess of Par		10,000
Capital stock common, no par, stated value $1, authorized 3,000,000 shares, issued 2,000,000	$ 2,000,000	
Paid-in Capital in Excess of Stated Value	19,500,000	
Capital stock common—warrants	40,000	
Retained earnings	7,000,000	
	$28,540,000	
Less: Capital stock common in treasury at cost (50,000 shares)	1,500,000	27,040,000
		$28,050,000

CHAPTER 10

March 15

Retained Earnings	200,000	
Retained Earnings Reserved for Possible Fire Loss		100,000
Retained Earnings Reserved for General Contingencies		100,000

April 15

Retained Earnings	500,000	
Capital Stock, Par $5		100,000
Capital in Excess of Par		400,000

To record 10% stock dividend or 20,000 shares at market value of $25 per share.

CHAPTER 11

(1)

Cash	97,000	
Bonds Payable—Discount	12,594	
Bonds Payable—Par		100,000
Common Stock Warrants		9,594

Issue of 100 bonds with warrants attached, each to buy 10 shares of common stock at $5.

(2)

Bond Interest Expense	6,500	
Cash		6,500

Payment of coupon 1 at 13%.

Bond Interest Expense	315	
Bonds Payable-Discount		315

To accumulate one-fortieth of the original bond discount.

(3)

Common Stock Warrants	9,594	
Cash	5,000	
Capital Stock—Par		10,000
Paid-in Capital in Excess of Par		4,594

To record issue of 1,000 shares of common stock at $5 cash plus one warrant per share.

CHAPTER 12

(1)

Raw Materials—Control	100,000	
(Also subledger cards, received column, for each kind of material)		
Accounts Payable—Control		100,000

(2)

Work in Process—Control	97,000	
(Also individual subledger job-cost sheets)		
Raw Materials—Control		97,000
(also subledger cards, issued column, for each kind)		

(3)

Work in Process—Control	364,000	
(Also subledger job-cost sheets)		
Wages Payable		364,000
(and individual employee earnings records)		

(4)

Manufacturing Overhead—Control	643,000	
Service 1	127,000	
Service 2	94,000	
Production 1	236,000	
Production 2	186,000	
Various Accounts	643,000	643,000

(5)

Manufacturing Overhead—Control	127,000	
Service 2	34,000	
Production 1	63,000	
Production 2	30,000	
Manufacturing Overhead—Control		127,000
Service 1	127,000	

(6)

Manufacturing Overhead—Control		128,000
Production 1	64,000	
Production 2	64,000	
Manufacturing Overhead—Control		128,000
Service 2	128,000	

(7)

Work in Process—Control		614,000
(also, subledger job-cost sheets)		
Manufacturing Overhead—Control		614,000
Production 1	348,000	
Production 2	266,000	
	614,000	

(8)

Finished Goods		960,000
Work in Process—Control		960,000

(9)

Cost of Goods Sold		29,000
Manufacturing Overhead—Control		29,000
Production 1	15,000	
Production 2	14,000	
	29,000	

OUR COMPANY
Statement of Cost of Goods Manufactured
Year Ended December 31, 20X1

Raw materials used		97,000
Direct labor		364,000
Manufacturing overhead—actual	$643,000	
Less: Unapplied	29,000	614,000
Total manufacturing costs		$1,075,000
Add: Work in process, January 1		100,000
		$1,175,000
Less: Work in process, December 31		215,000
Cost of goods manufactured		$ 960,000

CHAPTER 13

(1)

Raw Materials	240,000	
Materials Price Variance	4,800	
Accounts Payable		244,800

(2)

Finished Goods	200,000	
Materials Quantity Variance	4,000	
Raw Materials		204,000

(3)

Finished Goods	72,000	
Labor Wage Variance	2,440	
Labor Efficiency Variance	1,200	
Wages Payable		75,640

(4)		
Manufacturing Overhead	140,000	
Various Accounts		140,000

(5)		
Finished Goods ($6,000 × 20 batches)	120,000	
Budget Variance 140,000 − (73,200 + 64,000)	2,800	
Efficiency Variance $20 × (6,100 - 6,000)	2,000	
Idle Plant Variance $8 × 1,900 hours	15,200	
Manufacturing Overhead		140,000

CHAPTER 14

Payback Period: Cost, $41,000, divided by annual net cash flow of $7,000 equals 5.85 years payback period.

Present value at 10 percent: $7,000 times present value at 10 percent of 10-year annuity of $1, or 6.144, is a return on investment of $43,008, which exceeds the minimum requirement of $41,000.

CHAPTER 15

Question 1

When one acquires property by gift, the general rule is that the donee has a cost basis in the property equal to the donor's original cost basis. Therefore, the potential gain due to the sale of the gifted property is carried over to the donee. However, should the original cost of the property exceed its fair market value on the date of the gift, then its cost basis upon resale by the donee would be equal to the lower of the donor's original cost or the fair market value on the date of the gift. Therefore, it is unwise to gift property that has either appreciated or depreciated in value from its original cost basis. Cash does not present such a problem since its cost is always equal to its fair market value. Selling your depreciated property would likely yield a tax deductible loss to the seller. However, one must be mindful of the fact that the sale of *personal use* property at a loss is NOT tax deductible. The sale of property that has gone up in value will generally result in a taxable gain. However, should one acquire property by inheritance, the beneficiary's cost basis for income tax purposes is generally equal to the fair market value on the date of the decedent's death. This would mitigate, if not eliminate, any taxable gain.

Question 2

a. A *deduction* reduces taxable income and thereby produces a tax benefit related to the marginal tax rate. The $1,000 deduction might reduce taxes by $170 or by $500 for different taxpayers. A *credit is* a dollar for dollar reduction of the tax liability and gives essentially equal tax benefit to all affected taxpayers.

b. A deduction is used when Congress wants the benefit to be graduated in the same fashion as the tax is graduated. Congress uses a credit when it wants the dollar benefit to be the same at all income levels.

Question 3

Analysis:		
Cost of old unit		$40,000
− Depreciation		28,000
= Adjusted basis		$12,000
Fair market value of new unit		$50,000
− Cash to be paid		21,000
= Value of old unit		$29,000
Value received for old unit		$29,000
− Adjusted basis		12,000
= Gain realized		$17,000

a. If the old unit is traded in, the gain of $17,000 will be deferred by reducing the basis of the new unit to $33,000. If the old unit is sold the $17,000 of gain will be recognized currently. The gain will be taxed as ordinary income inasmuch as it represents the recapture of prior depreciation deductions.The basis of the new asset will then be $50,000.

b. The adjusted basis would be $33,000 and there would be a loss of $4,000 rather than a gain of $17,000. If the unit were exchanged, the $4,000 loss would be deferred by increasing the basis of the new unit to $54,000. If the old unit were sold, the loss would be recognized currently. Technically, it would be an ordinary loss (business equipment is not a capital asset), but it might be treated as a capital loss depending on certain other gains and losses that were recognized during the year.

c. The gain would be $31,000 (43,000 − 12,000), and all would be recognized this year. $28,000 would be ordinary income (depreciation recapture). The remaining $3,000 of gain would be treated as capital gain or as ordinary income, depending on the nature of the other recognized gains and losses.

CHAPTER 17

(1) Elimination entries on January 1, 20XX:

Capital Stock (90% of Their Company)	45,000	
Retained Earnings (90% of Their Company at date of acquisition)	27,000	
Goodwill	10,000	
Investment in Their Company (at cost)		82,000

OUR COMPANY AND THEIR COMPANY
Consolidated Position Statement
January 1, 20XX

Assets			Liabilities & Stockholders' Equity		
Current (sum)	$ 80,000		Current liabilities (sum)		$ 40,000
Plant (sum, net)	188,000		Minority interests:		
Goodwill			Capital stock (10%)	$ 5,000	
(per journal)	10,000		Retained earnings (10%)	3,000	8,000
			Stockholders' equity:		
			Capital stock	$180,000	
			Retained earnings	50,000	230,000
	$278,000				$278,000

(2) Elimination entries on December 31, 20XX:

(1)

Capital Stock (90% of Their Company)	45,000	
Retained Earnings (90% of Their Company at date of acquisition)	27,000	
Goodwill	10,000	
Investment in Their Company (at cost)		82,000

(2)

Retained Earnings (consolidated)	500	
Goodwill		500

To amortize $500 of consolidated goodwill against consolidated retained earnings.

(3)

(not required)

Retained Earnings (Their Company—since acquisition)	8,000	
Minority Interest (10%)		800
Consolidated Retained Earnings (90%)		7,200

To divide new retained earnings between minority and majority.

(4)

Current Liabilities	5,000	
Current Assets		5,000

OUR COMPANY AND THEIR COMPANY
Consolidated Balance Sheet
December 31, 20XX

Assets		Liabilities & Stockholders' Equity		
Current (sum less $5,000)	$119,800	Current liabilities (sum less $5,000)		$ 35,000
Plant assets (net sum)	182,000	Minority interests: Capital stock (10%)	$ 5,000	
Goodwill ($10,000 less $500)	9,500	Retained earnings (10%)	3,800	8,800
		Stock equity:		
		Capital stock	$180,000	
		Retained earnings ($80,800 plus $7,200 less $500)	87,500	267,500
	$311,300			$311,300

CHAPTER 18

(1)

Income Tax Expense	18,000	
Deferred Tax Liability		18,000

The amount is 30% of $60,000.

(2)

Income Tax Expense	150,000	
Deferred Tax Asset	30,000	
Income Tax Payable		180,000

The amount is 30% of the $100,000 expense that won't be allowed as a deduction until a later period.

(3)

Deferred Tax Asset	12,000	
Income Tax Expense		12,000

The amount is 30% of the $40,000 of rent which we have not yet earned but on which we must pay (prepay) tax.

(4)

Income Tax Expense	5,000	
Deferred Tax Liability		5,000

The amount is 30% of the $150,000 of extra depreciation deducted in the tax return.

CHAPTER 19

(1)

Investment in Your Company Common Stock	450,000	
Capital Stock, par $10		100,000
Paid-in Capital in Excess of Par Value (to balance)		300,000
Cash (for direct acquisition costs)		50,000

To record investment in Your Company stock in exchange for $100,000 par value of Our Company common.

(2)

Current Assets	80,000	
Noncurrent Assets	350,000	
Goodwill (plug)	60,000	
Current Liabilities		40,000
Investment in Your Company Common Stock		450,000

To record dissolution of Your Company.

(3)
Acquisition

Investment in Your Company Common Stock	450,000	
Convertible Bonds Payable		400,000
Cash (for direct acquisition costs).		50,000

To record issue of 40 bonds, par $1,000 each, in exchange for 2,000 shares of Your Company common, recorded at market value of bonds, which coincides with par value.

(4)

Current Assets (appraised)	80,000	
Noncurrent Assets (appraised)	350,000	
Goodwill (plug)	60,000	
Current Liabilities		40,000
Investment in Your Company Common Stock		450,000

To record dissolution of Your Company and recognition of assets at current values plus goodwill, at assumed cost, to balance.

B

SUPPLEMENTARY PROBLEMS

CHAPTER 1

1.1

A. Company begins business on January 1 with 1,000 shares of capital stock. Andrus and Payton invest $7,500 each, in cash, and 500 shares of stock are issued to each. On December 31, after one year of activity, the records show assets and liabilities as follows:

Cash	$ 3,000
Coal inventory	12,000
Taxes payable	1,000
Equipment	5,000
Wages accrued payable	400
Notes payable (short term)	2,500
Due from customers	3,500
Due to suppliers	2,000
Unexpired insurance	250
Rent payable	250
Advances from customers	500
Dividends paid	750

Directions

    a. Prepare a balance sheet as of December 31.

    b. Determine the amount of net earnings for the year.

1.2

As of December 31, 20X0, the accounts of Another Company show the following balances:

Cash in Office	$ 700
Retained Earnings	14,000
Accounts Receivable	25,000
Unexpired Insurance	1,000
Cash in Bank	5,800
Dividends Payable	1,000
Office Equipment	1,000
Interest Payable on Notes	150
Advances by Customers	1,100
Taxes Payable	2,500
Accounts Payable	20,000
Office Supplies	300
Payroll Payable	750
Store Equipment	14,800
Merchandise	45,000
Store Equipment Contract*	2,000
Delivery Equipment	2,500
Capital Stock	50,000
Note Payable (due Jan. 1, 20X3)	5,000
Store Supplies	400

*Payable in four quarterly installments.

Directions

    a. Prepare a balance sheet.

    b. Compute the current ratio.

CHAPTER 2

2.1

On December 31 the accounts of Kelly Corp. show the following balances after one year of operation:

Cash in Bank	$ 1,000
Accounts Receivable	3,000
Land	1,200
Equipment	6,000
Building	12,000
Accounts Payable	1,400
Notes Payable (6 months)	1,200
Capital Stock	24,000
Sales	14,000
Merchandise	13,600
Selling Expenses	1,800
General Expenses	2,000

The merchandise remaining on hand on this date cost $6,500.

Directions

Prepare an income statement and a balance sheet.

2.2

On December 31, after one year of operation, the accounts of Laing Corp. show the following amounts:

Cash in Bank	$ 2,000
Accounts Receivable	6,000
Merchandise	27,200
Land	2,400
Building	24,000
Furniture	12,000
Accounts Payable	2,800
Notes Payable (2-year)	2,400
Capital Stock	48,000
Sales	28,000
Selling Expenses	3,600
General Expenses	4,000

The amount of merchandise represents the total purchased this year; the present inventory amounts to $13,000. Depreciation of building was $1,000, and that of furniture was $1,200. The depreciation has not been recognized in the amounts above.

Directions

Prepare an income statement and a balance sheet.

2.3

The accounts of Tidy Service Co. show the following contents at the end of the year:

Cash on Hand	$ 600
Cash in Bank	5,050
Accounts Receivable	15,500
Allowance Uncollectible Acounts	2,100
Prepaid Insurance	1,000
Land	10,000
Buildings	30,000
Machinery	45,000
Delivery Equipment	6,500
Depreciation to date	15,000
Accounts Payable	6,500
Mortgage Payable	15,000
Capital Stock	60,000
Retained Earnings (Jan. 1)	8,050
Sales	27,500
Office Wages	4,000
Plant Maintenance	2,000
Heat, Light, Power	10,000
Advertising	1,000
Taxes	2,000
Miscellaneous expenses	1,500

Of the total depreciation to date ($15,000), $1,000 has been recorded this year; it is included in the $1,500 of "miscellaneous expenses."

Directions

Prepare an income statement for the present year and a balance sheet as of the end of the year.

CHAPTER 3

3.1

Ann and Alice are granted a charter to operate a cash-and-carry grocery under the name Ann & Alice, Inc. The following data summarize the events of June:

1. Each of the organizers invests $5,000 cash, and 500 shares of stock are issued to each. This money is deposited in the State Bank.
2. Showcases and other fixtures are purchased by check, $1,000.
3. Merchandise is purchased by check, $6,000.
4. Merchandise is received from the Essex Co. on account, $1,000.
5. Freight on merchandise is paid by check, $100.
6. A check for $120 is issued to pay for the installation of the fixtures.
7. The cost of labor used in unpacking and placing the merchandise on the shelves, $50, is paid by check.
8. June rent is paid by check, $150.
9. Wrapping paper and other selling supplies are purchased by check, $50.
10. Flowers are purchased by check, $50, and are given away during the opening.
11. Sales for the month are $4,000, cash, and all receipts are deposited in the bank immediately.
12. Selling and delivery wages are paid by check, $400.
13. The Essex Co. account is paid by check.
14. The cost of goods sold during the month was $2,550.
15. Selling supplies on hand June 30 total $15.
16. Depreciation of the store fixtures is estimated at $10.

Directions

a. Record in skeleton T accounts with the following titles: State Bank, Merchandise, Supplies, Equipment, Essex Co., Capital Stock, Retained Earnings, Sales, Cost of Goods Sold, Selling and Delivery Wages, Misc. Selling Expense, Supplies Expense, Depreciation Expense, Rent Expense, and Income Summary. Make proper entries to summarize Expense and Revenue. Allow 15 lines for State Bank, 10 for Income Summary, and 5 for each of the others.
b. Prepare an income statement and a balance sheet.

3.2

At the beginning of the year the accounts of Della, Inc. have the following titles and balances:

Debit balances

Cash in Bank	$ 2,500
Accounts Receivable	22,000
Merchandise	31,000
Supplies	1,300
Prepaid Insurance	1,450
Land	15,500
Building	30,500
Equipment	10,500
	$114,750

Credit balances

Accounts Payable	527,000
Payroll Payable	2,500
Capital Stock	76,000
Retained Earnings	9,250
	$114,750

In summary form the transactions for the year are shown below:

1. Insurance premiums paid, $1,200.
2. Merchandise purchased on account, $200,000.
3. Supplies purchased on account, $2,000.
4. Sales of merchandise on account, $250,000.
5. Collections on account, $245,000.
6. Payments on account, $205,000.
7. Property taxes for the year paid, $900.
8. Salesmen's services received on a credit basis, $7,000.
9. Payments to salesmen, $6,800.
10. Delivery expenses paid, $5,000.
11. Public utility expenses incurred on a credit basis, $3,200.
12. Maintenance costs paid, $3,000.
13. Depreciation for the year: building, $915; equipment, $1,050.
14. Insurance expired during year, $850.
15. Inventory of supplies at end of year, $3,000.
16. Inventory of merchandise at year-end, $30,000.
17. Income tax due at year-end, $10,000.

Directions

   a. Record the transactions of Della, Inc. for the year in skeleton T
      accounts labeled as follows: All of the titles in the listing above and
      Delivery Expense, Depreciation Expense, Income Tax, Insurance
      Expense, Maintenance Expense, Merchandise Cost of Sales, Property
      Tax, Public Utility Expense, Sales, Salesmen's Services, Supplies
      Expense, Taxes Payable, and Income Summary. Allow 10 lines for
      Cash in Bank and 15 for Income Summary. Enter the balances shown
      in the tabulation as of the beginning of the year, and record the trans-
      actions for the year in those accounts. Number the entries.
   b. Make entries in the T accounts to close them.
   c. Prepare financial statements.

CHAPTER 4

4.1

At the end of the first year of operation the trial balance of the general
ledger of Molly's Restaurant stands as follows:

	Debit	Credit
Cash in Bank	$ 1,000	
Accounts Receivable	4,000	
Land	2,500	
Building	65,000	
Equipment	5,000	
Accounts Payable		$ 8,500
Notes Payable (5-year, 12%)		2,500
Capital Stock		70,000
Sales		50,000
Food Costs	40,000	
Selling Expenses	7,500	
General Expenses	6,000	
	$131,000	$131,000

Additional data:

   1. Specific accounts amounting to $500 are presumably uncollectible.
   2. Estimated life of the building is 40 years; equipment life, 8 years.
      It is assumed that there will be no net salvage in either case.

3. A year's interest is due on the notes.
4. Food on hand, priced at cost, totals $10,000.
5. Accrued salaries: selling, $500; general, $1,000.
6. Estimated accrued tax liabilities, $1,500.

Directions

Prepare worksheet, income statement, and balance sheet.

4.2

After one year of operation, the general ledger of Brown Co. shows account balances as follows before adjusting and closing entries:

	Debit	Credit
Cash in Bank	$ 4,000	
Accounts Receivable	12,000	
Merchandise	54,400	
Land	6,800	
Building	48,000	
Equipment	24,000	
Accounts Payable		$ 5,600
Notes Payable (5-year, 12%)		20,000
Capital Stock		80,000
Sales		58,800
Selling Expenses	7,200	
General Expenses	8,000	
	$164,400	$164,400

Other data:

1. Merchandise on hand December 31, at cost, $26,000.
2. Depreciation of building, $1,200, and equipment, $2,400.
3. Interest accrued for one-half year on notes.
4. Accrued selling salaries, $500, and accrued general salaries, $1,000.
5. Estimated taxes accrued, $2,000.

Directions

Prepare a worksheet and financial statements.

CHAPTER 5

5.1

For the first six months of 20X2 the Milan Co. has planned as follows:

	Jan.	Feb.	Mar.	April	May	June
Sales	$300,000	110%	120%	150%	200%	220%
Purchases	30,000	110%	115%	140%	150%	110%
Miscellaneous expenses	10,000	$10,600	$12,000	$12,000	$14,000	$10,000

January is treated as the base month, and sales and purchases for the other months are expressed as percentages of January figures. On January 1 the cash balance is $15,000. Past experience shows that sales will probably be 50 percent cash and 50 percent credit. Accounts receivable, on the average, are collected 80 percent in the month following sale, 10 percent the following month, and 9 percent in the next month, with an average of 1 percent uncollectible. Credit sales made in October, November, and December of 20X1 were $15,000 in each month. Purchases require a 10 percent down payment with the balance paid in the next month. December purchases require a payment of $10,000 in January. Payments for miscellaneous expenses are paid in the month when the expenses are incurred. When the cash balance falls below $14,000, $10,000 will be borrowed; when the cash balance exceeds $25,000, $10,000 will be repaid.

Directions

Prepare a cash budget for the first six months of 20X2.

5.2

Toledo Co. has regularly followed the practice of recording sales at net prices, using terms 2/10, n/30 (2 percent discount for payments made within 10 days). A change to use of the "gross" method is now contemplated. The accountant is asked to present in journal and ledger form a series of typical transactions recorded under each of the two procedures for purposes of comparison. Following are the transactions chosen; all amounts shown are "gross" amounts:

1. Sales on account, $100,000.
2. Collections within discount period, $70,000.
3. Collections too late for discount, $20,000.

4. Sales returns from customers whose accounts are unpaid, $500.
5. Sales returns from customers whose accounts have been collected, $500; of these, $400 had been collected at net. (Use Customer Advances for amount of credit granted.)
6. Of the uncollected accounts at the end of the period it is anticipated that $9,000 will be collected within the discount period. The discount period has expired with respect to the remainder.
7. The collections are made during the next period as anticipated.

Directions

Journalize and post to T accounts (a) assuming use of net prices throughout and (b) using gross prices.

5.3

The Small Co. begins business January 1, 20X1. Sales on account during the year total $100,000, and collections on account are $85,000. On December 31, one account of $750, that of Jane Doe, is written off as uncollectible. During 20X2, sales on account total $140,000 and collections total $135,000; in addition, $100 is recovered from Jane Doe. At the end of 20X2 it is decided to establish an allowance for uncollectibles on 20X2 business of 2.5 percent, to write off certain accounts of 20X1 not yet collected, $2,900, and to write off against the allowance several charges originating in 20X2 in the total amount of $1,925.

Directions

Make journal entries for 20X1 and 20X2.

CHAPTER 6

6.1

MARIE E. CO.
Comparative Balance Sheets, December 31

	20XX	20X1
Cash in Bank	$ 40,000	$ 50,000
Marketable Securities	20,000	90,000
Accounts Receivable (net)	100,000	300,000
Inventories	500,000	900,000
Current Prepayments	3,000	10,000
Land	30,000	40,000
Buildings	100,000	100,000
Equipment	150,000	200,000
Goodwill	70,000	50,000
	$1,013,000	$1,740,000
Accounts Payable	$ 180,000	$ 467,000
Other Current Liabilities	10,000	34,000
Bonds Payable	—	200,000
Allowance for Depreciation	20,000	33,000
Capital Stock	800,000	1,000,000
Retained Earnings	3,000	6,000
	$1,013,000	$1,740,000

Income statement data for 20X1

Net sales	$ 300,000
Cost of goods sold	180,000
Selling expenses	20,000
General expenses (includes depreciation of $23,000)	40,000
Bond interest	6,000
Federal and state taxes	30,000
Gain on equipment sale (cost, 15,000; depreciation to date, $10,000)	10,000
Write-down of goodwill	20,000
Dividends paid	11,000

Directions

Prepare a cash flow funds statement for 20X1

6.2

From the reports of Amy Enne Co.:

Balance Sheet Data

	20XX	20X1
Cash in Bank	$ 15,000	$ 30,000
Receivables	55,000	100,000
Inventories	100,000	260,000
Equipment	30,000	60,000
Buildings	20,000	40,000
Land	10,000	40,000
	$230,000	$530,000
Accounts Payable	$100,000	$190,000
Mortgage Payable		40,000
Allowance for Bad Debts	1,000	3,000
Allowance for Depreciation	20,000	15,000
Capital Stock	80,000	230,000
Retained Earnings	29,000	52,000
	$230,000	$530,000

Income Statement Data for 20X1

Net sales	$400,000
Expenses	330,000
Taxes	38,000
Total expenses	368,000
Net income	$ 32,000
Dividends paid	$ 4,000

OTHER DATA: Equipment that cost $30,000, and had been depreciated down to $14,000, was sold for $9,000 cash. The loss was debited to Retained Earnings.

Directions

Prepare a cash flow funds statement for 20X1.

CHAPTER 7

7.1

On January 1, Megansett Inc. has on hand 1,400 ounces of X inventories at $3 per ounce. During the year the purchases are as follows:

Date	Quantity, ounces	Cost
Feb. 15	1,200	$3,720
Apr. 20	2,000	6,400
July 10	1,800	5,940
Oct. 15	1,750	6,125
Dec. 30	1,500	5,400
Dec. 31 inventory	3,400	

Directions

Determine the cost of X on hand on December 31 and cost of X sold (1) by weighted-average method, (2) by the FIFO method, and (3) by the LIFO method.

7.2

Sy Hardy was just informed that the entire inventory in his appliance store was destroyed by fire. In order to make an insurance claim, he had to come up with a way of estimating the amount of inventory on hand at the date of the fire. Traditionally, the store achieved a gross profit of 30 percent on sales. Net sales for the period were $540,000. Inventory on hand at the beginning of the period was $147,000, and the business had purchases during the period of $280,000.

Directions

Using the gross profit method, determine the amount of the inventory destroyed by the fire.

7.3

Brewster Stores Corp. records merchandise purchases at net invoice prices and sales at gross prices, although the latter are subject to cash discounts. The merchandise inventory on December 1, including freight costs, is $70,000. On that date accounts receivable total $80,000 and the allowance for sales discounts is $1,800. During December the following transactions involving merchandise accounts occur:

1. Merchandise purchases, at invoice prices, $150,000, terms 2/10, n/30.

2. Transportation and other handling costs paid by check and all applicable to December purchases, $10,100.
3. Sales on account, $180,000.
4. Collections on account, $185,000 less discounts of $5,000.
5. Payments on account, $140,000 net; actual amount paid, $140,900.
6. Merchandise returned to vendors, at gross invoice prices, $5,000, of which $4,000 had been paid for at net prices and $1,000 at gross. The corporation was required to pay freight charges on this return amounting to $680.
7. Sales returns, at invoice prices, $4,000.
8. Purchase allowances, at gross invoice prices, granted by vendors, $1,000.
9. Estimated sales discounts to be taken by customers with respect to account balances on December 31, $2,000.
10. Merchandise inventory on December 31, at net invoice prices and before assigning transportation and handling charges, $35,280. (Free advice: Did you notice that the net $35,280 price of the final inventory is exactly one-fourth of the net cost of purchases for the period?)

Directions

Journalize the above transactions, including entries reflecting a reasonable assignment of transportation charges to the final inventory and to merchandise cost of sales.

CHAPTER 8

8.1

Dunfey Co. purchased a parcel of land, a vacant store building thereon, and some delivery equipment from Strong Co. for a lump-sum price of $125,000; terms, 25 percent in cash and the balance in six months with interest at the annual rate of 12 percent. A qualified appraiser estimated the market values of the assets as follows: land, $22,000; building, $104,500; equipment, $11,000. On the books of Strong Co., just prior to the transfer, the property sold was represented by the following accounts and balances:

Land	$15,000
Building	95,000
Delivery Equipment	28,888
Building—Allowance for Depreciation	31,000
Delivery Equipment—Allowance for Depreciation	18,500

Directions

Make an apportionment of the total cost of the property acquired by Dunfey Co. on the basis of relative appraised values and, using the apportionment, record the acquisition on the buyer's books. Also, give the entries when the balance of the purchase price is paid, assuming the entire transaction falls within one accounting period.

8.2

On April 25, year 1, Spring Co. purchased a secondhand delivery truck for $11,000, cash. On April 29, Auto Repair Service submitted a bill for repairs on the truck for $2,500. The truck was placed in service on May 1. Service life was estimated at 2 1/2 years (30 months) and salvage value at $1,500. The buyer's accounting period is the calendar year.

On February 1, year 2, the old truck was exchanged for a new truck with a list price of $32,000. The vendor granted a trade-in allowance of $7,500 for the old equipment, and the balance of the invoice was paid in cash. At that time the old truck could have been sold on the used-car market for $5,000, cash. Depreciation is recorded by the straight-line method.

Directions

a. Record all entries relating to the delivery truck during year 1, including accrual of depreciation for the year.
b. Record the exchange occurring on February 1, year 2.

8.3

On July 1, 20X0, Bickford Co. purchased a machine that cost $5,000 cash. It was estimated that the machine would have a salvage value of $500 after a useful life of 10 years. Installation costs of $300 were charged to machine repairs expense as of July 1, 20X0. Entries recognizing depreciation were made on December 31, 20X0, and on December 31, 20X1. When the accountant was adjusting the books at the end of 20X1, she discovered the error concerning the installation charge, and at that time it was agreed by the accountant and the management that the probable remaining useful life of the machine, from December 31, 20X2, would be 10 years, with salvage unchanged at $500.

Directions

Record depreciation on December 31 for the year 20X2.

CHAPTER 9

9.1

Cloverdale Inc. was formed on January 1, 20X1. Its attorney was granted 1,000 shares of $1 par value common stock in exchange for his services. At that date, the fair value of the stock was unknown. The attorney's billing rate was $250 per hour, and he spent six hours of time on corporate affairs.

Directions

  a. What would be the journal entry to record the issuance of shares in exchange for legal services rendered?
  b. If the shares had an ascertainable market value of $2 per share, what would be the entry to record the issuance of the shares?

9.2

On September 15, 20X6, Maccarone Inc. purchases 2,000 shares of its common stock on the market at a price of $30 per share. Subsequently, on December 15, the shares are reissued by Maccarone Inc. at $25 per share.

Directions

  a. Make the necessary journal entries to (1) record the repurchase of the shares on September 15 and (2) the reissuance of the shares on December 15.
  b. How would your entries change (if at all) had the corporation reissued the shares at $35.

9.3

Johnson Co. enters into negotiations with John Goodyear with the objective of obtaining Goodyear's services for a period of years as an executive of the corporation. The cash value of Goodyear's services, on the basis of a careful determination, is found to be $60,000 per year. A five-year contract is finally agreed upon. Under it Johnson pays Goodyear $50,000 in cash per year and grants him an option to acquire 2,000 shares of unissued common stock of the company at the end of each year of employment, or within three months thereafter, for a cash investment of $95 per share. The market value of the company's stock at the time of the agreement is made is $100 per share.

Directions

Make summary entries for Johnson Co. for the first year of the contract, assuming Goodyear exercises his option for all 2,000 shares at the end of the year.

CHAPTER 10

10.1

A corporation has outstanding 2,000 shares of preferred stock and 35,000 shares of common stock. Par value in each case is $100 per share, and both classes of stock were issued at par. Successful operation has resulted in retention of earnings in the amount of $550,000.

During a year the following transactions relating to the two stock issues occurred:

January 25. Declared a dividend of $1.50 on the 2,000 shares of preferred.

February 5. Paid the preferred dividend.

February 14. Declared a dividend of $5 per share on common stock in the form of notes due in 60 days without interest.

April 15. Paid the note dividend.

June 5. Declared a stock dividend on common stock of 4 percent of outstanding common stock. The fair market value of the shares was $120 per share.

June 30. Issued the dividend shares (1,400).

October 6. Declared a dividend payable in one-half share of Boston Co. stock for every share of common stock outstanding. The stock cost $5 per share and now has a market value of $15 per share.

October 10. Paid dividend declared on October 6.

November 5. Split common stock two for one with a reduction of par to $50 per share. (Three other quarterly dividends were declared and paid on the preferred shares, but the data are omitted from the above list.)

Directions

Journalize.

10.2

A corporation has retained earnings of $500,000 on December 31, and on that date the directors approve:

1. Declaration of a cash dividend of $100,000.
2. Appropriation of $20,000 to the reserve for bond sinking fund.
3. Issuance of a check for $20,000 to the trustee of the sinking fund.
4. Establishment of a reserve for contingencies, $100,000.

5. Calling and retiring 500 shares of preferred stock (par 100) at the call price of $105.
6. Establishment of a special fund (in a separate bank account) of $50,000 to be used to replace old equipment.

Directions

Give general journal entries to record the transactions. In each case, state the effect upon Retained Earnings, if any.

10.3

Zinfadel Inc. has 10,000 shares of its $200 par value, 7 percent cumulative preferred stock outstanding, and 50,000 of its $2 par value common stock outstanding. In the company's first four years of operation, it paid the following total cash dividends: 20X6, -0-; 20X7, $240,000; 20X8, $280,000; 20X9, $280,000.

Directions

Calculate the dividend to be paid to the preferred shareholders and common shareholders for each of the four years.

CHAPTER 11

11.1

On January 1 a company issues $800,000 maturity amount of 20-year, 12 percent debenture bonds at 90% of face value. Interest is payable July 1 and January 1. Use the straight-line method of premium/discount amortization.

Directions

Make entries for the following dates:

    a. January 1 (date on which the bonds are sold)
    b. July 1
    c. December 31
    d. January 1 of second year

11.2

On September 1 a company issues $2,000,000 maturity amount of 10-year notes at par bearing coupon interest of 12 percent, payable semiannually, on November 1 and May 1. The year ends on December 31.

Directions

Make entries for

    a. September 1

    b. November 1

    c. December 31

CHAPTER 12

12.1

Manufacturing costs in process II during a given month consisted of raw materials, $8,600, labor, $25,800, and overhead, $17,200, in addition to product received from process I consisting of 8,600 units with an average cost of $2 per unit. At the beginning of the month in process II there were 400 units of work in process and these were complete as to process I and raw materials costs and three-fourths complete as to labor and overhead. At the end of the month 500 units remained unfinished in Process II. These were complete as to process I and raw materials costs, and were 80 percent complete as to labor and overhead costs.

Directions

Prepare a schedule showing computation of unit costs of materials, labor, and overhead for the month as well as work in process at the end of the month and cost of product transferred to the next process, process III.

12.2

Following is a summary of the manufacturing activities for a company's first year. The company employs process cost accounting methods with three processes recognized: foundry, grinding, and finishing.

    Open the following ledger accounts: Materials and Supplies, Foundry, Grinding, Finishing, Finished Goods. To the extent that these accounts are affected, enter the following transactions directly in the accounts. Number your entries to correspond with the transaction numbers.

    1. Materials and supplies purchased on account, $35,000.
    2. Materials and supplies issued: foundry, $30,000; finishing, $2,000.
    3. Wages accrued: foundry, $22,000; grinding, $10,000; finishing, $14,000.

4. Company-owned machinery consists of units costing $55,000. Depreciation, at the rate of 10 percent, is charged one-half to foundry and one-fourth each to grinding and finishing. No salvage is anticipated.
5. Insurance expired, $660, is assignable in the same ratio as depreciation.
6. Miscellaneous manufacturing costs incurred all for cash, are foundry, $12,000; grinding, $8,000; finishing, $6,000.
7. All production passes directly from foundry to grinding and on to finishing. At year-end there is no unfinished product in foundry and finishing; the inventory of unfinished product in grinding has a computed cost of $3,000. There were no inventories at the beginning of the year.

Directions

a. Open ledger accounts for Materials, WIP—Foundry, WIP—Grinding, Finishing, and Finished Goods. Enter the numbered transaction data insofar as they affect these four accounts.
b. Prepare a statement of cost of goods manufactured.

CHAPTER 13

13.1

A company records materials at standard costs in the accounts, and it uses a process cost system. Materials records for April show the following information:

| Material | Quantity purchased | Quantity used | | Process | Price | |
		Actual	Standard		Actual	Standard
1	2,100	2,300	2,200	A	$ .52	$ .50
2	4,200	3,500	3,200	A	$1.05	1.00
3	1,800	1,500	1,600	B	2.06	2.00
4	2,000	1,800	1,700	C	.74	.75

Directions

Construct ledger accounts for Raw Materials, Raw Materials Price Variances, Accounts Payable, Process A, Process A Quantity Variance, Process B, Process B Quantity Variance, Process C, and Process C Quantity Variance. Enter the data of the problem.

13.2

A company uses standard costs in accounting for direct labor and employs a job-order plan of accounts. Records provide the following information for September:

Department	Labor hours		Wage rates	
	Actual	Standard	Actual	Standard
1	4,200	4,150	$2.75	$2.50
2	3,758	3,800	3.10	3.00
3	5,640	5,600	2.90	3.00

Directions

Construct ledger accounts for Payroll, Work in Process, Department 1 Wage Variance, Department 1 Efficiency Variance, Department 2 Wage Variance, Department 2 Efficiency Variance, Department 3 Wage Variance, and Department 3 Efficiency Variance. Enter the data of the problem.

CHAPTER 14

14.1

We offer two income options to a prospective executive for our corporation. Option 1 provides that, in addition to annual salary, the officer will be given a bonus in shares of treasury stock at the end of each year. The bonus will amount to $100,000 worth of stock at current market value at the end of the next five years, and it will culminate in retirement with a special bonus of $500,000 in the form of a paid-up annuity (in addition to the regular stock bonus). Option 2 provides the same annual salary, but the bonus will be $150,000 worth of treasury stock each year-end. There will be a special bonus, at the five-year terminal date, in the form of a paid-up annuity of such amount as will make option 2 have the same present value as option 1. Assume a 10 percent discount rate.

Directions

Determine the amount needed at the end of 10 years under option 2 to make option 2 equal to option 1 in present value. (NOTE: The present value of $1, discounted at 10 percent per period for five periods, is .621. The present value of an annuity of $1 per period for five periods, at 10 percent, is $3.791. One dollar invested now at 20 percent per annum will grow to "future value" of $1.611 in 5 years.

14.2

A company is considering purchase of equipment for $60,000, which should produce an increase of $18,000 in annual revenue, an increase in operating costs annually of $9,000, and a reduction of annual labor costs of $4,000. Estimated useful life, with no salvage, is 10 years. Straight-line depreciation will be used for tax purposes, and the company's average income tax rate is 40 percent.

Directions

    a. Determine the approximate payback period.
    b. Determine present value of prospective annual net cash flow, using 15 percent rate. Is purchase justified? (NOTE: Present worth of annuity of $1 per period for 10 periods at 15 percent is $5.019.)

14.3

The estimated costs of in-house production of a component part are:

Materials (all costs of order, receive, store)	$1,250
Direct labor	1,750
Variable overhead (200 percent of direct labor)	3,500
Fixed overhead	2,000
Total cost	$8,500

A reliable manufacturer offers to supply this item, F.O.B. our plant, for $7,000 each.

Directions

Present your recommendation and reasons. (NOTE: Our ratio of profit to sales is approximately 10 percent.)

CHAPTER 17

17.1

The ledger balances of Parent Co. and Sub Co., after closing entries have been made, stand as follows at year-end:

	End of year	
	Parent Co.	**Sub Co.**
Cash in Bank	$ 30,000	$ 8,000
Customers (includes Sub Co. $2,000)	55,000	19,000
Merchandise	62,000	30,000
Investment B Co. stock, cost	60,000	
Land	20,000	6,000
Plant (net)	70,000	33,000
	$297,000	$96,000
Current Liabilities	$ 52,000	$23,000
Capital Stock	160,000	60,000
Retained Earnings	85,000	13,000
	$297,000	$96,000

Parent Co. bought 80 percent of $60,000 outstanding capital stock of Sub Co. at beginning of this year when Sub Co. retained earnings balance was $5,000. At year-end, merchandise on Parent Co. books includes goods that Sub Co. bought for $8,000 and sold to Parent Co. for $10,000, of which Parent Co. at year-end owes $2,000 to Sub Co. During the year, Sub Co. sold land to Parent Co for $10,000 cash. This land originally cost Sub Co. $6,000.

Directions

Prepare consolidated journal entries as of year-end for Parent Co. and its subsidiary, Sub Co. Assume any excess of investment cost over book value represents goodwill.

17.2

Papaco acquired 100 percent of the voting stock of Babaco when the latter was organized and, during the following year, all sales of Babaco were made to Papaco. At the end of the year, Papaco inventories included 25 percent of all goods purchased during the year from Babaco. Condensed income statement data for the year are as follows:

	End of year	
	Papaco	**Babaco**
Sales	$600,000	$240,000
Cost of goods sold	$360,000	$160,000
Other expenses and taxes	120,000	40,000
Total deductions	$480,000	$200,000
Net income	$120,000	$ 40,000

Directions

Prepare journal entries and a consolidated income statement for Papaco and Babaco.

17.3

Use the same income-statement amounts as shown in 17.2. Assume Papaco acquired only 80 percent of Babaco stock, that 75 percent of Babaco sales go to Papaco, and 20 percent of the goods remain in Papaco inventory at year-end.

Directions

Prepare journal entries and a consolidated income statement.

CHAPTER 18

18.1

a. Our Company uses the "allowance for bad debts" procedure in its financial statements and recognizes uncollectibles for income tax purposes only when specific accounts are clearly worthless. At the end of a given year, with credit sales of $500,000, the company makes an adjusting entry to provide 1 percent of gross sales as an addition to the "allowance." During that year, a total of $3,800 in specific accounts receivable were recognized as uncollectible and were charged off (and reported as bad debt "expense") on the tax return. The tax rate amounted to an average of 30 percent. What provision should the company make in its accounts so that the statements will properly reflect the disparity in accounting versus tax treatments? Journalize.

b. Assume that we make cash collections that, for accounting purposes, we consider and treat as "advances" from the remitters but are required to report in full as taxable income. Assume the amount of collections is $100,000. Make the indicated tax allocation journal entry (with 30 percent tax rate).

c. We use the sum-of-years digits depreciation method for tax purposes and the straight-line method for book purposes. In a given year this difference results in taxable income (at 30 percent) of $50,000 less than the pretax income per books. Make the required tax-allocation entry.

CHAPTER 20

20.1

A foreign subsidiary was formed on Venus on January 1, 20X1, when the rate of exchange was $3.00 for 1 "Venny" (V). At the date of formation, the subsidiary:

1. Received a $60,000 equity investment in dollars from the parent company's sale of stock;
2. Received a $240,000 loan in dollars from a U.S. bank;
3. Purchased a parcel of land for 100,000V payable in dollars.

At the end of year 1 when the rate of exchange is 1 V = $4.00 the parcel of land is sold for 100,000 V collectible in dollars.

Directions

a. If the U.S. dollar is the functional currency, record the journal entries to be made on (1) January 1 and (2) December 31.
b. If the U.S. dollar is the functional currency, complete the following partial balance sheet as of year-end:

Balance Sheet

Cash	$
Loan Payable	
Owner's Equity:	
Contributed capital	
Net Income	
Total Liabilities & Owner's Equity	$

c. Prepare the same information as (a) and (b) if the Venny (V) is the functional currency.

C

A P P E N D I X

SOLUTIONS TO SUPPLEMENTARY PROBLEMS

CHAPTER 1

1.1

A. COMPANY
Balance Sheet,
December 31, 20XX

Assets			Liabilities & Stockholders' Equity		
Current:			Current liabilities:		
Cash	$ 3,000		Taxes payable	$ 1,000	
Due from			Wages accrued		
customers	3,500		payable	400	
Coal inventory	12,000		Notes payable	2,500	
Unexpired			Advances by		
insurance	250	$18,750	customers	500	
Noncurrent:			Due to suppliers	2,000	
Equipment		5,000	Rent payable	250	
			Total Liabilities		$ 6,650
			Stockholders' equity		
			Capital stock	$15,000	
			Retained earnings	2,100	17,100
			Total Liabilities		
			& Stockholders' Equity		
Total Assets		$23,750			$23,750

Earnings for the year: Paid out in dividends, $750 + retained, $2,100 = $2,850.

1.2

ANOTHER COMPANY
Balance Sheet,
December 31, 20X1

Assets			Liabilities & Stockholders' Equity		
Current:			Current liabilities:		
Cash in office	$ 700		Dividends payable	$ 1,000	
Cash in bank	5,800		Interest on notes	150	
Accounts receivable	25,000		Customer advances	1,100	
Merchandise Inventory	45,000		Taxes payable	2,500	
Store supplies	400		Accounts payable	20,000	
Office supplies	300		Payroll payable	750	
Unexpired insurance	1,000	$78,200	Equipment contract	2,000	$27,500
Noncurrent:			Noncurrent notes		
Office equipment	$ 1,000		Payable		5,000
			Total liabilities		$32,500
Store equipment	14,800		Stockholders' equity:		
			Capital stock	$50,000	
Delivery equipment	2,500	18,300	Retained earnings	14,000	64,000
			Total Liabilities &		
Total Assets		$96,500	Stockholders' Equity		$96,500

Current ratio is 78,200/27,500 = 2.8 to 1; equity ratio is 64,000/96,500 = 66 percent.

CHAPTER 2

2.1

KELLY CORP.
Balance Sheet,
December 31, 20XX

Assets			Liabilities & Stockholders' Equity		
Current:			Current liabilities:		
Cash in bank	$1,000		Accounts payable	$ 1,400	
Accounts receivable	3,000		Notes payable	1,200	
Merchandise Inventory	6,500		Total Liabilities		$ 2,600
Total Current Assets		$10,500	Stockholders' Equity:		
Long Term Assets:			Capital stock	$24,000	
Land	$1,200		Retained Earnings	3,100	
Equipment (net of dedepreciation)	6,000		Total Liabilities &		
Building (net of depreciation)	12,000		Stockholders' Equity		$27,100
Total Long Term Assets		19,200			$29,700
		$29,700			

KELLY CORP.
Income Statement, Year Ended December 31, 20XX

Sales		$14,000
Expenses:		
Cost of goods sold	$7,100	
Selling	1,800	
General	2,000	10,900
Net Income		$ 3,100

2.2

LAING CORP.
Balance Sheet, December 31, 20XX

Assets			Liabilities and Stockholders' Equity		
Current:			Current liabilities:		
Cash in bank	$ 2,000		Accounts payable		$ 2,800
Accounts			Long Term Liabilities:		
receivable	6,000		Notes payable		2,400
Merchandise			Total Liabilities		$ 5,200
inventory	$13,000				
Total Current			Stockholders' equity:		
Assets		$21,000	Capital stock	$48,000	
Long Term:					
Land	$ 2,400		Retained earnings	4,000	52,000
Building	23,000				
Furniture	10,800				
Total Long					
Term Assets		36,200			
			Total Liabilities &		
Total Assets		$57,200	Stockholders' Equity		$57,200

LAING CORP.

Income Statement, Year Ended Dec. 31, 20XX

Sales		$28,000
Expenses:		
Cost of goods sold	$14,200	
Selling	3,600	
General	4,000	
Depreciation	2,200	24,000
Net income		$ 4,000

2.3

TIDY SERVICE CO.
Balance Sheet, December 31, 20XX

Assets				Liabilities & Stockholders' Equity			
Current:				Liabilities:			
Cash on hand		$ 600		Current:			
Cash in bank		5,050		Accounts payable		$ 6,500	
Accounts rec.	$15,500			Long Term:			
Less Uncollectible Accounts	2,100	13,400		Mortgage payable		15,000	
Prepaid Insurance		1,000		Total liabilities			$21,500
Total Current Assets			$20,050	Stockholders' equity:			
Long Term:				Capital stock		$60,000	
Land		$10,000		Retained earnings		15,050	
Buildings	$30,000						
Machinery	45,000						75,050
Equipment	6,500						
	$81,500						
Allow. for depreciation (combined)	15,000	66,500					
Total Long Term Assets			76,500	Total Liabilities &			
Total Assets			$96,550	Stockholders' Equity			$96,550

TIDY SERVICE CO.
Income Statement, Year Ended December 31, 20XX

Sales		$27,500
Expenses:		
Office wages	$ 4,000	
Plant maintenance	2,000	
Heat, light, power	10,000	
Advertising	1,000	
Taxes	2,000	
Miscellaneous	1,500	20,500
Net income		$ 7,000

CHAPTER 3

3.1

NOTE: To save space, the contents of the T accounts are listed rather than being presented in T form. The account for *State Bank* has the following left-hand (debit) entries: (1) 10,000, (11) 4,000. The right-hand (credit) entries are (2) 1,000, (3) 6,000, (5) 100, (6) 120, (7) 50, (8) 150, (9) 50, (10) 50, (12) 400, (13) 1,000. *Merchandise* debits: (3) 6,000, (4) 1,000, (5) 100, (7) 50. *Merchandise* credit: (14) 2,700. *Supplies* debit: (9) 50. Credit: (15) 35. *Equipment* debits: (2) 1,000, (6) 120. Credit: (10) 10. *Essex Co.* debit: (4) 1,000. Credit: (3) 1,000. *Capital Stock* credit: (1) 10,000. *Retained Earnings* credit: (h) 655. *Sales* credit: (11). Debit: (a) for 4,000. *Cost of Goods Sold* debit: (14). Credit: (b) for 2,700. Selling Expense debit: (10). Credit: (e) 50. *Selling and Delivery Wages* debit: (12). Credit: (d) for 400. *Supplies Expense* debit: (15). Credit: (e) for 35. *Depreciation Expense* debit: (16). Credit: (f) for 10. *Rent Expense* debit: (8). Credit: (g) for 150. *Income Summary* credit: (a) with 4,000. Debits: (b) 2,700, (c) 50, (d) 400, (e) 35, (y) 10, (g) 150, and (h) 655. The *income statement* shows Sales, $4,000, from which are subtracted the list of expenses: Cost of Goods Sold, 2,700; Selling Expenses, 50; Selling and Delivery Wages, 400; Supplies, 35; Depreciation, 10; and Rent, 150, for a total of 3,345, leaving Net Income, $655. The *balance sheet* shows current assets: State Bank, 5,080; Merchandise, 4,450; and Supplies, 15. To the total of 9,545 is added the Equipment, 1,110, to make Total Assets, $10,655. The liabilities and stock-holders' equity consist of no liabilities and Stockholders' Equity made up of Capital Stock, 10,000, and Retained Earnings, 655, for a total (also) of $10,655, Total Liabilities & Stockholders' Equity.

3.2

NOTE: To save space, the contents of the T accounts are listed rather than being presented in T form. The account for *Cash in Bank* has the following left-hand (debit) entries: Bal. 2,500, (5) 245,000. The right-hand (credit) entries are (1) 1,200, (6) 205,000, (7) 900, (9) 6,800, (10) 5,000, (12) 3,000. *Accounts Receivable* debits: Bal. 22,000, (4) 250,000. Credit: (5) 245,000. *Merchandise* debits: Bal. 31,000, (2) 200,000. Credit: (16) 201,000. *Supplies* debits: Bal. 1,300, (3) 2,000. Credit: (15) 300. *Prepaid Insurance* debits: Bal. 1,450, (1) 1,200. Credit: (14) 850. *Land* debit: Bal. 15,500. *Building* debit: Bal. 30,500. Credit: (13) 915. *Equipment* debit: Bal. 10,500. Credit: (13) 1,050. *Accounts Payable* debit: (6) 205,000. Credits: Bal. 27,000, (2) 200,000, (3) 2,000, (11) 3,200. *Payroll Payable* debit: (9) 6,800. Credits: Bal. 2,500, (8) 7,000. *Taxes Payable* credit: (17) 10,000. *Capital Stock:* Bal. credit, 76,000. *Retained Earnings* credits: Bal. 9,250, (c) 16,785. *Sales* debit (*a*) and credit (4) for 250,000. *Merchandise Cost of Sales,* debit (16) and credit (*b*) for 201,000. *Delivery Expense,* debit (10) and credit (*b*) for 5,000. *Salesmen's Services,* debit (8) and credit (*b*) for 7,000. *Depreciation Expense,* debit (13) and credit (*b*) for 1,965. *Insurance Expense,* debit (14) and credit (*b*) for 850. *Maintenance Expense,* debit (12) and credit (*b*) for 3,000. *Public Utility Expense,* debit (11) and credit (*b*) for 3,200. *Supplies Expense,* debit (15) and credit (*b*) for 300. *Property Tax,* debit (7) and credit (*b*) with 900. *Income Tax,* debit (17) and credit (*b*) for 10,000. *Income Summary* debits [all labeled (b)] 201,000, 5,000, 7,000, 1,965, 850, 3,000, 3,200, 300, 900, 10,000, and (c) 16,785. Credit: (*a*) 250,000.

The income statement lists *Sales,* $250,000, followed by the list of expenses shown as debit items in the Income Summary account and Net Income of $16,785.

The balance sheet lists, as current assets, Cash, 25,600; Accounts Receivable, 27,000; Merchandise, 30,000; Supplies, 3,000, and Prepaid Insurance, 1,800. As long-term assets: Land, 15,500; Building, 29,585; and Equipment, 9,450. The total for all assets is $141,935. Under Liabilities and Stockholders' Equity, the current liabilities are Accounts Payable, 27,200; Payroll Payable, 2,700; and Taxes Payable, 10,000, totaling $39,900. The Stockholders' Equity consists of Capital Stock, 76,000, and Retained Earnings, 26,035, a total of 102,035. The Liabilities & Stockholders' Equity total is $141,935.

CHAPTER 4

4.1

	Trial balance		Adjusting entries		Income statement		Balance sheet	
	Debit	Credit	Debit	Credit	Debit	Credit	Debit	Credit
Cash	1,000						1,000	
Accounts receivable	4,000			(1) 500			3,500	
Land	2,500						2,500	
Building	65,000						65,000	
Equipment	5,000						5,000	
Accounts payable		8,500						8,500
Notes payable		2,500						2,500
Capital stock		70,000						70,000
Sales		50,000				50,000		
Food inventory	40,000			(4) 30,000			10,000	
Selling expense	7,500		(5) 500		8,000			
General expense	6,000		(5) 1,000		7,000			
Sales-bad debts			(1) 500		500			
Depreciation			(2) 2,250		2,250			
Allowance for depreciation				(2) 2,250				2,250
Interest			(3) 300		300			
Interest payable				(3) 300				300
Food cost of sales			(4) 30,000		30,000			
Salaries accrued				(5) 1,500				1,500
Taxes			(6) 1,500		1,500			
Taxes accrued				(6) 1,500				1,500
Earnings of stockholders					450			450
Totals	131,000	131,000	36,050	36,050	50,000	50,000	87,000	87,000

4.2

BROWN CO.
Worksheet, Year Ended December 31, 20XX

	Trial balance Debit	Trial balance Credit	Adjusting entries Debit	Adjusting entries Credit	Income statement Debit	Income statement Credit	Balance sheet Debit	Balance sheet Credit
Cash	4,000						4,000	
Accounts receivable	12,000						12,000	
Merchandise	54,400			(1) 28,400			26,000	
Land	6,800						6,800	
Building	48,000						48,000	
Equipment	24,000						24,000	
Accounts payable		5,600						5,600
Notes payable		20,000						20,000
Capital stock		80,000						80,000
Sales		58,800				58,800		
Selling expense	7,200		(4) 500		7,700			
General expense	8,000		(4) 1,000		9,000			
Cost of goods sold			(1) 28,400		28,400			
Depreciation			(2) 3,600		3,600			
Allowance for depreciation				(2) 3,600				3,600
Interest			(3) 1,200		1,200			
Accrued liabilities				(3) 1,200				4,700
				(4) 1,500				
				(5) 2,000				
Taxes			(5) 2,000		2,000			
					6,900			
Earnings of stockholders								6,900
	164,400	164,400	36,700	36,700	58,800	58,800	120,800	120,800

CHAPTER 5

5.1

MILAN CO.
Cash Budget, First Six Months, 20X2

	January	February	March	April	May	June
Cash balance	$15,000	$21,850	$22,300	$21,200	$23,850	$18,835
Receipts (see schedule)	29,850	31,350	34,050	39,900	51,285	60,870
Total cost	$44,850	$53,200	$56,350	$61,100	$75,135	$79,705
Disbursements:						
Purchases of last month	$10,000	$27,000	$29,700	$31,050	$37,800	$40,500
Down payments	3,000	3,300	3,450	4,200	4,500	3,300
Miscellaneous expenses	10,000	10,600	12,000	12,000	14,000	10,000
Total disbursements	$23,000	$40,900	$45,150	$47,250	$56,300	$53,800
Cash balance	$21,850	$12,300	$11,200	$13,850	$18,835	$25,905
Borrowed		10,000	10,000	10,000		
Repaid						10,000
Balance forward	$21,850	$22,300	$21,200	$23,850	$18,835	$15,905

Receipts:

Month	Sales	January	February	March	April	May	June
October	$30,000						
November	30,000	$ 1,350					
December	30,000	1,500	$ 1,350				
January	30,000	12,000	1,500	$ 1,350			
February	33,000	15,000	12,000	1,500	$ 1,350		
March	36,000		16,500	13,200	1,650	$ 1,485	
April	45,000			18,000	14,400	1,800	$ 1,620
May	60,000				22,500	18,000	2,250
June	66,000					30,000	24,000
							33,000
Collections		$29,850	$31,350	$34,050	$39,900	$51,285	$60,870

5.2

a. Net prices

Cash

(2)	68,600		
(3)	20,000		
(7)	9,320		

Accounts Receivable

(1)	98,000	(2)	68,600
(6)	10	(3)	19,600
		(4)	490
		(7)	9,320

Customer Advances

		(5)	492

Sales

		(1)	98,000

Lapsed Sales Discounts

(5)		(3)	400
		(6)	10

Sales Returns

(4)	490		
(5)	490		

b. Gross prices

Cash-same as in (a)

Accounts Receivable

(1)	100,000	(2)	70,000
		(3)	20,000
		(4)	500
		(7)	9,500

Allowance for Outstanding Discounts

(7)	180	(6)	180

Customer Advances

		(5)	492

Sales

			(1)	100,000

Sales-Discounts

(2)	1,400	(5)	8
(6)	180		

Sales Returns

(4)	500	
(5)	500	

5.3

20X1

(1)

Accounts Receivable	100,000	
Sales		100,000

(2)

Cash	85,000	
Accounts Receivable		85,000

(3)

December 31

Bad Debt Loss	750	
Accounts Receivable		750

20X2

(1)

Accounts Receivable	140,000	
Sales		140,000

(2)

Cash	135,000	
Accounts Receivable		135,000

(3)

Cash	100	
Bad Debts Recovered		100

(4)

December 31

Uncollectible Accts Expense	3,500	
Allowance for Uncollectible Accts		3,500
Allowance for Uncollectible Accts	2,900	
Accounts Receivable		2,900
Allowance for Uncollectible Accounts	1,925	
Accounts Receivable		1,925

CHAPTER 6

6.1

MARIE E. CO.
Statement of Cash Flows
Year Ended December 31, 2XX1 (000 omitted)

Cash Flows From Operating Activities:		
Net income [300 − (180 + 20 + 40 + 6 + 30 + 20 − 10)]		$ 14
Add: Increase in accounts payable	$ 287	
Increase in other current liabilities	24	
Depreciation	23	
Amortization of goodwill	20	354
Deduct: Gain on sale of equipment	$ 10	
Increase in accounts receivable (net)	200	
Increase in inventories	400	
Increase in current prepayments	7	(617)
Net cash used by operations		($249)
Cash Flows from Investing Activities:		
Sale of Equipment (15 + 10 − 10)	15	
Purchase of Land (net change)	(10)	
Purchase of marketable securities	(70)	
Purchase of Equipment (net change + 15)	(65)	
Net cash used for Investing Activities		($130)
Cash Flows from Financing Activities		
Capital stock issued	200	

Bond issued	200	
Dividends	(11)	
Net Cash provided by Financing Activities		389
Net Increase in Cash		$ 10
Cash at Beginning of Year		40
Cash at End of Year		50

6.2

AMY ENNE CO.
Statement of Cash Flows
Year Ended December 31, 20X1 (000 omitted)

Cash flows from operating activities:		
Net income		$ 27
Add: Depreciation	$ 11	
Loss on sale of equipment $(14 - 9)$	5	
Increase in accounts payable	90	106
Deduct: Increase in receivables (net)	$ 43	
Increase in inventories	160	(203)
Net cash used in operations		($ 70)
Cash flows from investing activities:		
Equipment sold	9	
Purchase of building	(20)	
Purchase of land	(30)	
Purchase of equipment	(60)	
Net cash used in investing activity		(101)
Cash flows from financing activities:		
Mortgage Issue	40	
Capital stock issue	150	
Dividends	(4)	
Net cash flows from financing activities		186
Increase in cash in bank		15
Cash at beginning of year		$ 15
Cash at end of year		$ 30

CHAPTER 7

7.1

1. Average cost method:

Inventory, Jan. 1, 1,400 oz.		$ 4,200
Purchases, 8,250 oz.		27,585
Total cost to be accounted for, 9,650 oz.		$31,785
Average cost per ton ($31,785 9,650)	$3.2938	
Inventory, Dec. 31, 3,400 oz. @ $3.2938		11,199
Cost of X Sold		$20,586

2. FIFO method:

Total cost to be accounted for (see 1)		$31,785
Inventory, Dec. 31:		
Purchase on Dec. 30, 1,500 oz.	$ 5,400	
Purchase on Oct. 15, 1,750 oz.	6,125	
From purchase July 10, 150 oz. @ $ 3.30	495	12,020
Cost of X Sold		$19,765

3. LIFO method:

Total cost (as above)		$31,785
Inventory, Dec. 31:		
On hand Jan. 1, 1,400 oz.	$ 4,200	
Purchase on Feb. 15, 1,200 oz.	3,720	
From purchase Apr. 20, 800 oz. @ $ 3.20	2,560	10,480
Cost of X Sold		$21,305

7.2

GROSS PROFIT METHOD OF INVENTORY ESTIMATION

Beginning inventory		$147,000
Purchases during the period		280,000
Cost of goods available for sale		$427,000
Less: Estimate cost of goods sold		
Sales during the period	$540,000	
Less estimated gross margin ($540,000 × 30%)	(162,000)	
Estimated cost of goods sold		378,000
Estimated cost of ending inventory		$ 49,000

7.3

(1)

Merchandise	147,000	
Accounts Payable		147,000

Purchases on account, at net, gross = 150,000.

(2)

Transportation Costs	10,100	
Cash		10,100

Paid transportation costs.

(3)

Accounts Receivable	180,000	
Sales		180,000

Sales recorded at gross.

(4)

Bank	180,000	
Allowance for Sales Discounts	1,800	
Sales Discounts	3,200	
Accounts Receivable		185,000

Collections, including prior period accounts.

(5)

Accounts Payable	140,000	
Loss from Lapsed Discounts	900	
Cash		140,900

Payments on account, including $900 in late-payment penalties.

(6)

Accounts Payable (or Due from Vendors)	4,920	
Loss from Lapsed Discounts		20
Merchandise—Returns and Allowances		4,900

Returns, including $980 on which $20 penalty was paid.

(7)

Sales—Returns	4,000	
Accounts Receivable		4,000

(8)

Accounts Payable	980	
Merchandise—Returns and Allowances		80

(9)
End of period

Sales-Discounts	2,000	
Accounts Receivable—Allowance for Sales Discounts		2,000

(NOTE: This is a valid entry under accrual accounting—like Allowance for Bad Debts.)

(10)

Merchandise—Returns and Allowances	5,880	
Merchandise Inventory		5,880

To close returns and allowances (a contra account) to Merchandise, which now has a net balance of (147,000 − 5,880 = 141,120).

(11)

Cost of Goods Sold	70,000	
Merchandise Inventory		70,000

To close out old inventory (FIFO) under first in, first out.

(12)

Merchandise Inventory (35,280 net)	37,975	
Cost of Goods Sold (105,840 net)	113,925	
Merchandise		141,120
Transportation Costs (one-fourth to Inventory)		10,100

To set up end-of-period inventory as $35,280 plus share of transportation cost, which is 10,780/141,120 = 7.639%, or $2,695 for a total of $37,975. The remainder represents an addition to the cost of goods sold.

CHAPTER 8

8.1

	Appraised Value	%	Apportioned cost
Land	$ 22,000	16	$ 20,000
Building	104,500	76	95,000
Delivery Equipment	11,000	8	10,000
	$137,500	100	$125,000

Since the total appraised value is 110 percent of cost, each of such values is 110 percent of its respective cost figure.

Land	20,000	
Building—Cost	95,000	
Delivery Equipment—Cost	10,000	
Cash		25,000
Strong Co., Contract Payable		100,000
To record purchase of assets.		

Interest Expense	6,000	
Strong Co., Contract Payable	100,000	
Cash		106,000
To record payment.		

8.2(a)

Year 1, April 25

Delivery Equipment	11,000	
Cash		11,000
Purchase of delivery truck.		

April 29

Delivery Equipment	2,500	
Accounts Payable		2,500
Costs to make truck available for service.		

December 31

| Depreciation Expense, Delivery Equipment | 3,200 | |
| Accumulated Depreciation, Delivery Equipment | | 3,200 |

To record depreciation for eight months – $13,500 − 1,500 = $12,000 \times {}^{8}\!/_{30}$.

Year 2, February 1

Depreciation Expense, Delivery Equipment	400	
Accumulated Depreciation, Delivery Equipment		400
To record depreciation for one month.		

8.2(b)

Delivery Equipment—Cost	32,000	
Accumulated Depreciation, Delivery Equipment	3,600	
Loss on Retirement	2,400	
Cash		24,500
Delivery Equipment		13,500
To record exchange of delivery equipment.		

8.3

12/31/X2

Depreciation Expense	360	
Accumulated Depreciation		360

To recognize depreciation for one-tenth of the estimated remaining life on $4,500 - 900 = $3,600, × 10% = $408.

CHAPTER 9

9.1(a)

1/1/X1 Organizational & Start-Up Costs	1,250	
Common Stock		1,000
Additional Paid-in Capital, Common		250

Issued 1,000 shares of $1 par value common stock for attorney's services.

9.1(b)

1/1/X1 Organizational & Start-Up Costs	2,000	
Common Stock		1,000
Additional Paid-in Capital, Common		1,000

Issued 1,000 shares of $1 par value common stock worth $2 per share for attorney's services.

9.2(a)

9/15/X6 Treasury Stock, common	60,000	
Cash		60,000

Acquired 2,000 shares of corporation's own stock at $30 per share.

12/15/X6 Cash	50,000	
Retained Earnings	10,000	
Treasury Stock, common		60,000

Treasury stock reissued at price below original cost.

9.2(b)

9/15/X6 No change.		
12/15/X6 Cash	70,000	

Treasury Stock, common		60,000
Additional Paid-in Capital, Treasury Stock		10,000

Treasury stock reissued at price above original cost.

9.3

(1)

Administrative Services	60,000	
Salaries Payable		50,000
Stock Options Outstanding (2,000 @ $5)		10,000

(2)

Salaries Payable	50,000	
Cash In Bank		50,000

(3)

Cash (2,000 × 95)	190,000	
Stock Options Outstanding	10,000	
Capital Stock Outstanding		200,000

CHAPTER 10

10.1

January 25

Retained Earnings (or Dividends)	3,000	
Dividends Payable—Preferred		3,000

February 5

Dividends Payable—Preferred	3,000	
Cash		3,000

February 14

Retained Earnings	175,000	
Note Dividend Payable		175,000

April 15

Note Dividend Payable	175,000	
Cash		175,000

June 5

Stock Dividends Declared	168,000	
Common Stock Distributable		168,000

June 30

Common Stock Distributable	168,000	
Capital Stock		140,000
Additional Paid-in Capital, Common		28,000

October 6

Retained Earnings	91,000	
Dividend Payable in Boston Stock		91,000

(36,400 common @ $2.50)

October 10

Dividend Payable in Boston Stock	91,000	
Boston Stock		91,000

November 6

The 36,400 shares of $100 par value common stock issued and outstanding were split 2 for 1, resulting in 72,800 shares of $50 par value common stock Issued and outstanding.

10.2

(1)

Retained Earnings	100,000	
Dividend Payable		100,000

Decreases Retained Earnings by $100,000.

(2)

Retained Earnings	20,000	
Reserve for Bond Sinking Fund		20,000

Earmarks Retained Earnings but has no effect on total.

(3)

Sinking Fund Trustee	20,000	
Cash in Bank		20,000

No effect on Retained Earnings.

(4)

Retained Earnings—Unrestricted	100,000	
Retained Earnings—Reserve for Contingencies		100,000

No effect on total.

(5)

Preferred Stock	50,000	
Retained Earnings	2,500	
Cash in Bank		52,500

Decreases Retained Earnings by amount of call premium.

(6)

| Cash—Equipment Replacement Fund | 50,000 | |
| Cash Bank (general banking account) | | 50,000 |

No effect on Retained Earning.

10.3

	Preferred dividend	Common dividend	Total dividend
20X6	–0–	–0–	–0–
20X7	$240,000*	–0–	$240,000
20X8	$180,000**	$100,000	$280,000
20X9	$140,000***	$140,000	$280,000

*$140,000 regular annual preferred dividend ($200 par value × 7% × 10,000 outstanding shares) plus the lesser of dividends in arrears from 20X6 ($140,000) or the balance of dividends actually declared ($240,000 − $140,000 = $100,000).

**$140,000 regular annual preferred dividend plus dividends in arrears from 20X6 ($140,000 − $100,000 declared in 20X7 = $40,000).

***Just the regular annual preferred dividend of $140,000 since there were no longer any dividends in arrears.

CHAPTER 11

11.1

January 1

a. Cash ($900.00 × 800 bonds)	720,000	
Unamortized Bond Discount	80,000	
Bonds Payable (at par)		800,000

To record issuance of bond.

July 1

b. Bond Interest Expense	50,000	
Cash (800,000 × .12 × 6/12)		48,000
Bond Discount		2,000

To record payment of interest and amortization of bond discount.

December 31

c. Bond Interest Expense	50,000	
Bond Interest Payable (800,000 × .12 × $^6/_{12}$)		48,000
Unamortized Bond Discount		2,000

To record the accrual of interest and amortization of bond discount.

January 1

d. Bond Interest Payable	48,000	
Cash		48,000

To record the payment of bond interest accrued in the prior period.

11.2

September 1

a. Cash	2,080,000	
Bonds Payable		2,000,000
Bond Interest Expense ($2,000,000 × .12 × $^4/_{12}$)		80,000

To record the bond issuance between interest payment dates.

November 1

b. Bond Interest Expense	120,000	
Cash ($2,000,000 × .12 × $^6/_{12}$)		120,000

To record bond interest payment.

December 31

c. Bond Interest Expense	40,000	
Bond Interest Payable ($2,000,000 × .12 × $^2/_{12}$)		40,000

To record bond interest accrual.

CHAPTER 12

12.1

	Number	Finished equivalents				Cost totals
		Process I	Materials	Labor	Overhead	
Started and finished	8,100	8,100	8,100	8,100	8,100	
In process, finished (1/4 to complete)	400	—	—	100	100	
Started, 80% finished	500	500	500	400	400	
Totals	9,000	8,600	8,600	8,600	8,600	
Costs	—	$17,200	$8,600	$25,800	$17,200	$68,800
Cost per equivalent unit		$ 2	$ 1	$ 3	$ 2	
In process equivalents (units)		500	500	400	400	
Work in process		$ 1,000	$ 500	$ 1,200	$ 800	3,500
Cost of product transferred						$65,300
WIP—Process III	65,300					
WIP—Process II		65,300				

12.2

a.

		Materials and Supplies		
(1)	35,000		(2)	32,000

		WIP-Foundry		
(2)	30,000		(7)	67,080
(3)	22,000			
(4)	2,750			
(5)	330			
(6)	12,000			
	67,080			67,080

		WIP-Grinding		
(3)	10,000		(7)	83,620
(4)	1,375			
(5)	165			
(6)	8,000			
(7)	67,080		v	3,000
	86,620			86,620
v	3,000			

		Finishing		
(2)	2,000		(7)	107,160
(3)	14,000			
(4)	1,375			
(5)	165			
(6)	6,000			
(7)	83,620			
	107,160			107,160

		Finished Goods		
(7)	107,160			

b.   **Statement of Cost of Goods Manufactured**
                    Year Ended December 31, 20XX

Materials and supplies		$ 32,000
Labor		46,000
Overhead:		
Depreciation	$ 5,500	
Insurance	660	
Miscellaneous	26,000	32,160
Total factory costs		$110,160
Work in process, Dec. 31		3,000
Cost of goods manufactured		$107,160

CHAPTER 13

13.1

Raw Materials

(1)	1,050	(1)	1,150
(2)	4,200	(2)	3,500
(3)	3,600	(3)	3,000
(4)	1,500	(4)	1,350

Raw Materials Price Variances

(1)	42	(4)	20
(2)	210		
(3)	108		

Accounts Payable

		(1)	1,092
		(2)	4,410
		(3)	3,708
		(4)	1,480

WIP—Process A

(1)	1,100	
(2)	3,200	

Process A Quantity Variance

(1)	50		
(2)	300		

Process B

(3)	3,200		

Process B Quantity Variance

		(3)	200

Process C

(4)	1,275		

Process C Quantity Variance

(4)	75		

13.2

Payroll

		Dept. 1	11,550.00
		Dept. 2	11,649.80
		Dept. 3	16,356.00

Work in Process

Dept. 1	10,375.00		
Dept. 2	11,400.00		
Dept. 3	16,800.00		

Dept. 1 Wage Rate Variance

1,050.00			

Dept. 1 Efficiency Variance

125.00			

Dept. 2 Wage Rate Variance

375.80			

Dept. 2 Efficiency Variance

			126.00

Dept. 3 Wage Rate Variance

			564.00

Dept. 3 Efficiency Variance is $120 dr.

CHAPTER 14

14.1

PLAN OF SOLUTION: Find present value of option 1 payments, including special bonus at retirement date; find present value of option 2 annual bonus; subtract the latter from the former to find present value of necessary terminal bonus under option 2; finally, convert present into future value of option 2 terminal bonus. Use 20 percent as the discount rate to neutralize growth of annual bonus in option 1.

1. Present value of option 1 annual payments:

    $100,000 × present value of an annuity,
    5 years @ 10% (100,000 × 3.791) $379,100

    To the $379,100 we now add the present value of the
    terminal $500,000 lump sum.

    To do so, we multiply $500,000 × .621 (the present value
    for 5 periods at a 10% discount rate.   310,500

    Option 1 total present value equals $689,600

2. Present value of option 2 annual payments is calculated as
   the present value of a $1, five-payment annuity at 10 percent
   multiplied by 150,000, or $150,000 × 3.791 =   568,650

3. The difference (689,600 − 568,650) $120,950

4. The difference as of five years later, 120,950 × 1.611
   (future value @ 10% for 5 years) $194,850

14.2

a. Payback period is cost of asset divided by average (or other determination of) cash flow: $60,000/10,200 = 5.88 years. The 10,200
   is 18,000 + 4,000 − 9,000 = 13,000, less 40 percent tax on 13,000
   minus depreciation of 6,000, or .4 × $7,000 = $2,800.

b. 10,200 × present worth of 10-period annuity of $1 at 15 percent,
   or 10,200 × 5.019 = 51,193. Acquisition appears unwise, since
   present value of future proceeds is less than the amount that would
   have to be expended now to obtain those proceeds.

14.3

Our variable (differential) cost of manufacture is $8,500 − 2,000, or
$6,500, for a component element in our product. The best bid from suppli-
ers is $7,000. This relationship appears to favor in-house production.
However, our apparent gain of $500 is 500/7,000, or 7.1 percent, which

compares unfavorably with our overall 10 percent profit ratio. This suggests that we might better undertake to expand our regular product output to soak up idle capacity if demand exists at present prices. If not, in-house production on a temporary basis can be justified, assuming no other, more profitable, alternative.

CHAPTER 17

17.1

Consolidating Journal Entries

(1)

Capital Stock-Sub Co. (100%)	60,000	
Retained Earnings—Sub Co. (100%)	5,000	
Goodwill	8,000	
Investment—B Co. Stock—Cost (80%)		60,000
Minority Interest (20%)		13,000

To eliminate intercompany stock equity items as of date of acquisition.

(2)

Retained Earnings—Sub Co.	6,000	
Merchandise—Parent Co.		2,000
Land—Parent Co.		4,000

To eliminate intercompany profit in assets remaining "in the family," referred to as "unrealized."

(3)

Retained Earnings—Sub Co. (13,000 − 5,000 − 6,000)	2,000	
Minority Interest (20%)		400
Consolidated Retained Earnings (80%)		1,600

To allocate realized earnings of subsidiary to minority and majority interests.

(4)

Current Liabilities	2,000	
Customers		2,000

17.2

a. Sales (100% of Babaco)	240,000	
Cost of Goods Sold (100% of Babaco)		160,000
Other Expenses and Taxes (100% of Babaco)		40,000
Merchandise Cost of Sales (Large Co., 75% of Small Co. income)		30,000
Inventory (Large Co, 25% of Babaco income)		10,000

b. Consolidated Income Statement

Sales		$600,000
Merchandise Cost of Sales	$330,000	
Other Expenses	120,000	450,000
Consolidated Net Income		$150,000

17.3

a. Consolidating journal entries (worksheet only):

Sales (75% of Babaco)	180,000	
Cost of Goods Sold (75% of B)		120,000
Other Expenses and Taxes (75% of B)		30,000
Merchandise Cost of Sales—Papaco (80% of 75% of Babaco profit)		24,000
Inventory—Papaco (20% of 75% of Babaco profit)		6,000

b. Consolidated income statement after entries above (000's omitted):

Sales (840 − 180)		$ 660
Merchandise cost of sales (520 − 144)	$376	
Other expenses and taxes (160 − 30)	130	506
Total net income		$ 154
Minority interest 25% of (40 − 6)		(8.5)
Consolidated net income*		$145.5

*PROOF OF CONSOLIDATED NET: It should be equal to the net income of the parent (120) plus 75 percent of the net income of the subsidiary after subtracting "unrealized" profit of $6 = 145.5.

CHAPTER 18

18.1

a. Deferred Tax Asset   360

    Income Tax Expense   360

The amount is 30% of (5,000 − 3,800), deferred because, from the standpoint of the "books" method of recognizing bad debts, the amount reported for tax purposes is understated by $1,200, resulting in $1,200 × 30%, or $360, apparent overpayment of taxes.

b. Deferred Tax Asset   30,000

    Income Tax Expense   30,000

c. Income Tax Expense   15,000

    Deferred Tax Liability   15,000

CHAPTER 20

20.1

(a)	January 1	
Cash	300,000	
Owner's Equity		60,000
Loans Payable		240,000

To record receipt of $60,000 from stock sale and $240,000 from loan proceeds.

Land	300,000	
Cash		300,000

To record purchase of land (100,000 × $3 direct rate)

	December 31	
Cash	400,000	
Land		300,000
Gain on Sale		100,000

To record sale of land (100,000 × $4 direct rate).

(b) **Balance Sheet**

Cash		$400,000
Loans Payable		$240,000
Owner's Equity:		
Contributed Capital	$ 60,000	
Net Income	100,000	160,000
Total Liabilities & Owner's Equity		$400,000

(c) **January 1**

Cash	100,000	
Owner's Equity		20,000
Loans Payable		80,000

To record receipt of $20,000 equity investment ($60,000/3) and $240,000 loan ($240,000/3) when the exchange rate was $1V = \$3$.

Land	100,000	
Cash		100,000

To record purchase of land for 100,000V.

December 31

Loan Payable	20,000	
Exchange Gain on Loan		20,000

To adjust $240,000 loan payable, which is denominated in dollars, to an equivalent amount of V due to change in rate from $1V = \$3$ to $1V = \$4$ ($240,000/4) − ($240,000/3).

Cash	100,000	
Land		100,000

To record sale of Land for 100,000V.

Balance Sheet

	Foreign Currency	Exchange Rate	U.S. Dollars
Cash	100,000V	4.00	$400,000
Loan Payable	60,000	4.00	240,000
Owner's Equity:			
Contributed Capital	20,000	3.00	60,000
Net Income	20,000		100,000
Total Liabilities & Owner's Equity	100,000V		$400,000

INDEX

FINAL EXAMINATION

If you have completed your study of *The McGraw-Hill 36-Hour Accounting Course,* you should be prepared to take this final examination. It is a comprehensive test, consisting of 100 questions.

INSTRUCTIONS

1. You may treat this as an "open-book" exam by consulting this and any other textbook. Or, you can reassure yourself that you have gained superior knowledge by taking the exam without reference to any other material.
2. Answer each of the test questions on the answer sheet provided at the end of the exam. For each question, write the letter of your choice on the answer blank that corresponds to the number of the question you are answering. Or, you may take the exam online at:

   www.mcgraw-hill36-hourcourses.com

3. All questions are multiple-choice, with two to four alternative answers from which to choose. Always select the answer that represents in your mind the *best* among the choices.
4. Each correct answer is worth one point. A passing grade of 80 percent (80 correct answers) entitles you to receive a Certificate of Achievement. This handsome certificate, suitable for framing, attests to your proven knowledge of the contents of this course.
5. Carefully fill in your name and address in the spaces provided at the top of the answer sheet, remove the answer sheet from the book, and send to:

Laura Libretti
McGraw-Hill
Professional Book Group
1333 Burr Ridge Parkway
Burr Ridge, IL 60527

1. A company whose balance sheet shows total assets of $100,000 and total liabilities of $40,000 is worth:

   a. $100,000   *c.* $60,000

   b. $160,000   *d.* Probably none of these

2. If Company A has an accounting net worth of $500,000 with 100,000 shares of common stock outstanding and Company B has a net worth of the same amount but with only 50,000 shares outstanding, the market value of a share of Company B stock will be twice that of a Company A share.

   a. True

   b. Very unlikely

3. The current ratio is the ratio of current liabilities to current assets.

   a. True

   b. False

4. In a balance sheet, all assets are valued at the current fair market values.

   a. True

   b. False

5. In most situations a company's revenues for the period, its net income for the period, and its cash inflow for the period are likely to be three entirely different amounts.

   a. True

   b. False

6. The accountant's concept of the accrual basis of accounting represents a practical compromise between, on the one hand, the cash basis of accounting and, on the other hand, the economist's theory that income accrues as production proceeds.

   a. True

   b. False

7. Under the accrual basis of accounting, revenue (and resulting income) is recognized in the period when:

   a. Cash is collected if the customer pays in advance of delivery of the product

   b. Cash is collected if the customer pays after product delivery

   c. Cash is collected

   d. The goods or services are delivered to new owners

8. An expense is:

    a. Any loss   *c.* Any item of factory overhead

    b. Any amount spent   *d.* A cost incurred to produce for an asset revenue

9. Retained earnings is equal to accumulated net income over the years less dividend distributed.

    a. True

    b. False

10. Bad debts are an operating expense.

    a. True

    b. False

11. Working capital (or net working capital) is the arithmetic excess of cash over bank loan.

    a. True

    b. False

12. Working capital increases when we borrow money from a bank on a short-term loan.

    a. True

    b. False

13.

ESSEX PRODUCTS CO.
Income Statement, Year Ended December 31, 20XX

Sales and other revenues		$320,000
Cost of goods sold	$180,000	
Selling expenses	41,000	
General expenses	62,000	
Income taxes	10,000	293,000
Net income		$ 27,000
Dividends on common stock		20,000
Earnings retained		$ 7,000

NOTE: Depreciation total of $15,000 is included in the expenses listed above.

The "gross margin" of Essex Products Co. for 20XX, as evidenced by the income statement, was:

    a. $ 7,000   *c.* $140,000

    b. $27,000   *d.* $180,000

14. Increases in assets are recorded by:

    a. Debits

    b. Credits

15. Increases in expenses are recorded by:

    a. Debits

    b. Credits

16. Increases in liabilities are recorded by:

    a. Debits

    b. Credits

17. Increases in owners' equity are recorded by:

    a. Debits

    b. Credits

18. Increases in revenues are recorded by:

    a. Debits

    b. Credits

19. A discount that you are allowed to take upon paying a bill before a certain date is properly classified as:

    a. Income

    b. Adjustment of cost of item purchased

20. From the managerial point of view, the more important of the following items of information is the amount:

    a. Of discounts you have "earned"

    b. Of discounts you have "lost"

21. Assume:

Date	Item	Units	Cost
Jan. 1	Initial inventory	10,000	$100,000
Jan. 12	Purchase	12,000	150,000
Jan. 24	Purchase	8,000	120,000
Jan. 31	Inventory	15,000	?

    The cost of the January 31 inventory, using FIFO, is:

    a. $162,500   *c.* $207,500

    b. $185,000   *d.* None of these

22. See question 21. The cost of inventory using LIFO is:

   a. $162,500   *c.* $207,500
   b. $185,000   *d.* None of these

23. See question 21. The cost of the January 31 inventory at average cost is:

   a. $162,500   *c.* $207,500
   b. $185,000   *d.* None of these

24. During a given year our sales total $250,000, our cost of goods sold is $150,000, and our average inventory (at FIFO cost) is $10,000. Our inventory turnover approximates:

   a. 25 times
   b. 15 times

25. See question 24. Our ending inventory amounts to approximately:

   a. 24 days' supply
   b. 17 days' supply

26. X Co. purchased a parcel of land with a building. The toal purchase price was $640,000. The land was appraised for $180,000, and the building was appraised at $540,000. How much would X Co. debit the land account?

   a. $180,000   *c.* $160,000
   b. $213,333   *d.* $480,000

27. The straight-line method of recording depreciation has merit when the depreciable asset renders approximately the same amount of service in each month, year, or other uniform time period.

   a. True
   b. False

28. Because most depreciable assets render more valuable (or less costly) services per period in the earlier periods of useful life than they do in the later periods, some form of increasing-charges depreciation method is generally to be preferred.

   a. True
   b. False

29. If an asset that cost $1,000 has an estimated useful life of five years and probable salvage value of $400, the amount of annual depreciation charge by the straight-line method is:

   a. $280   *c.* $120
   b. $200   *d.* $110

30. See question 29. The annual depreciation for the second year will be the following amount if the sum-of-years' digits method is used:

    a. $200   *c.* $120

    b. $160   *d.* $80

31. If we were to use the declining-balance method for the asset in question 29, the amount of depreciation in year 1 would be:

    a. $400   *c.* $200

    b. $240   *d.* $120

32. Depreciation is a use of cash flow.

    a. True

    b. False

33. **See question 26.** How much should the building account be debited?

    a. $180,000   *c.* $160,000

    b. $213,333   *d.* $480,000

34. Depreciation must be recorded in order to provide for replacement of the asset.

    a. True

    b. False

35. In a balance sheet the account Allowance for Depreciation denotes that the company has reserved funds in an amount at least as great as the balance of that account.

    a. True

    b. False

36. A stock split automatically increases the value of the common stock held by a stockholder.

    a. True

    b. False

37. A stock dividend distributes corporate earnings.

    a. True

    b. False

38. Because of the ambiguity of the term *reserve,* use of the term as the title of an item in the balance sheet is generally discouraged by professional accountants.

    a. True

    b. False

39. When long-term notes (or bonds) are issued at a price above par value, they are said to be issued at a:

    a. Discount

    b. Premium

40. Bond premium represents income to the debtor company at the time of issuance.

    a. True

    b. False

41. Bond discount should be amortized (accumulated) over the life term of the bond issue and thus shown as an addition to the periodic interest expense.

    a. True

    b. False

42. Under so-called "actual" cost accounting procedures, the actual overhead costs of manufactured goods are approximated by use of applied overhead rates that are established on the basis of estimates made at the beginning of the period.

    a. True

    b. False

43. Of the two objectives of cost accounting, (a) the determination of the cost of goods manufactured and (b) the minimization of costs, the latter is likely to be the much more significant to the welfare of the business.

    a. True

    b. False

44. Under a system of standard cost accounting, if we purchase 10,000 pounds of material for $11,000 during a period when our standard cost for that material is $1 per pound, we should record a materials price variance of $1,000 as a credit.

    a. True

    b. False

45. If we consume 8,500 pounds of the material referred to in question 44 to produce 100 units of product with a standard raw material content of 80 pounds per unit, we should record a materials quantity (usage) variance of:

    a. $150 debit   *c.* $500 debit

    b. $550 credit   *d.* $500 credit

46. If we turn out 1,000 units of product today in a department that has a standard direct labor allowance of 5 hours per unit and a standard wage rate of $10 per

hour, the standard cost of the day's output, as far as direct labor is concerned, is $50,000.

a. True

b. False

47. See question 46. If we actually use 5,500 direct labor hours to produce the 1,000 units and if the actual wage rate is $11.00 per hour, our direct labor efficiency variance is:

a. $5,500 debit   c. $5,000 debit

b. $5,500 credit   d. $5,000 credit

48. In a given department the capacity level of operation for a four-week period is considered to be 6,000 machine hours, with departmental fixed overhead of $6,000 and variable overhead of $2 per hour. In the four weeks just past, this department operated for 4,500 machine hours and had fixed overhead of $6,000 and variable overhead of $10,000. The overhead budget variance for the period was:

a. $2,000 debit   c. $1,000 debit

b. $2,000 credit   d. $1,000 credit

49. See question 48. The cost standards for this department provide for 4,300 machine hours for the amount of product actually turned out. The overhead efficiency variance for the period was:

a. $1,700 debit   c. $600 debit

b. $3,400 credit   d. $600 credit

50. See questions 48 and 49. The idle capacity variance for the four-week period was:

a. $1,500 debit   c. $4,500 credit

b. $4,500 debit   d. Zero

51. The essential element of "responsibility" accounting is the assigning of responsibility for costs, as they are incurred, to the persons most immediately in a position to control them.

a. True

b. False

52. Under a system of responsibility accounting, costs that have once been assigned as the responsibility of one individual are never subsequently transferred to another department.

a. True

b. False

53. The term "direct costing" denotes a system in which only the direct costs of material and labor are charged to products.

    a. True

    b. False

54. Under a system of direct costing, fixed costs are known as "period" costs, and they are assigned to products on the basis of predetermined allocation rates.

    a. True

    b. False

55. If the fixed costs for a given period amount to $20,000 and the variable costs are $5 per unit of product, the differential cost of production at 80 percent of capacity (8,000 units) versus production at 60 percent of capacity is:

    a. $10,000   c. $20,000

    b. $14,000   d. Zero

56. See question 55. If we sell our products for cash only, at $10 each, and are able to sell only 6,000 units per period, what percent of bad-debt losses could we afford to incur (and break even on the added sales) if we were to increase our sales to 8,000 units by allowing the new customers to charge their purchases?

    a. 20 percent   c. 50 percent

    b. 30 percent

57. Your accountant presents the following analysis of cost and profit data with respect to a component part:

Comparative Costs

	To make	To buy
Direct materials	$ 50	$ —
Direct labor	30	—
Variable factory overhead	30	—
Nonvariable factory overhead	20	—
General administrative overhead	10	2
Purchasing overhead, nonvariable	10	15
Normal profit margin	50	—
Invoice cost of complete part	—	120
	$200	$137

If your make-or-buy decision is to be resolved on the basis of incremental (differential) costs, the decision should be to:

a. Buy

b. Make

58. See question 57. The unit differential cost of producing the part internally appears to be approximately:

a. $100   c. $50

b. $110   d. $120

59. See question 57. If your make-or-buy decision is to be resolved on the basis of full, or total, costs, the decision should be:

a. Buy

b. Make

60. See question 57. The numbers to be compared in arriving at the decision in question 59 are:

a. $130 and $120   c. $150 and $137

b. $140 and $120   d. $200 and $137

61. You are contemplating purchase of an item of machinery and your accountant provides you with the following data:

Invoice cost of machine, $25,000; installation cost, $5,000; probable useful life, 10 years, with no salvage value.

Benefits from machine: labor cost saving of $10,000 per year.

Operating costs of machine per year: power, $2,000; maintenance, $1,000; depreciation, $3,000; sundry cash costs, $1,000.

The estimated approximate payback period for this machine on the basis of the available data is:

a. 10 years   c. 5 years

b. 6 years   d. 4 years

62. Would acquisition of the machine of question 61 be justified if you decide it must produce a 15 percent (before-tax) rate of return over its lifetime? (NOTE: the present value of $1 per year for 10 years, discounted at 15 percent per period, is approximately $5.02).

a. Yes, by a considerable margin (more than $2,000)

b. Yes, by a narrow margin

c. No, by a considerable margin (more than $2,000)

d. No, by a very narrow margin.

63. See question 62. In order to estimate the probable rate of return to be earned by a new machine, we assume that our cost (assume $30,000) represents the present value, at our effective earning rate, of the future periodic cash flow (assume $6,000 per period). Thus, for each $1 of cash flow we will have to invest $30,000/$6,000 = $5. By reference to compound-interest tables for 10-year periods, we find the present value of $1 per period that most nearly approximates $5. The column in which this amount appears will be headed by the sought-for interest rate. In the present case the rate is approximately:

   a. 5 percent   c. 20 percent

   b. 10 percent   d. 15 percent

64. Consolidated statements automatically contain at least some element of fiction.

   a. True

   b. False

65. The terms "consolidated" and "combined" statements have the same meaning for accounting purposes.

   a. True

   b. False

66. When one company owns sufficient voting stock of another company to be able to exercise a major influence upon the decisions of the other company, the two companies are properly referred to as:

   a. Affiliated companies

   b. Consolidated companies

67. One of the principal tasks to be performed in the preparation of consolidated statements is that of eliminating intercompany items.

   a. True

   b. False

68. Entries for eliminations referred to in question 67 are not made on the books of either the parent or its subsidiaries-they are, essentially, worksheet entries.

   a. True

   b. False

69. The stockholders' equity of Sub Co. stands as follows on the date when Parent Co. acquires 80 percent of Sub Co. common stock for $2,000,000, cash:

   Capital stock, common, par $10 $ 1,000,000

   Retained earnings   500,000

If the other assets of Sub Co. are already reasonably valued in their balance sheet, preparation of a consolidated balance sheet at date of acquisition would probably call for recognition of goodwill amounting to:

a. $500,000   c. $800,000

b. $1,000,000   d. Zero

70. To reflect acquisition of the Sub Co. stock (see question 69), Parent Co. would record a credit to cash and debit(s) to:

a. The various assets held by Sub Co. plus goodwill

b. Intercompany liabilities

c. Investment in Subsidiary

71. See question 70. On Sub Co. books, entries must be made to mirror those made by Parent Co. at date of acquisition.

a. True

b. False

72. The preparation of a consolidated balance sheet commonly requires elimination from Inventories, and correspondingly from Retained Earnings, of the amount of profits (booked by any of the affiliates) resulting from sales among affiliates and upon which the profits have not yet been "realized" through sale to outsiders.

a. True

b. False

73. In the preparation of consolidated income statements the key principle is that sales and expenses representing strictly transactions between affiliates must be eliminated.

a. True

b. False

74. The term *deferred asset,* or *deferred liability,* refers to account balances that now show on the asset side of the balance sheet and will later show up in the income statement as expenses (charges against income).

a. True

b. False

75. The term *deferred liability* refers to account balances that are now shown on the right-hand side of the balance sheet and will later show up in the income statement as credits (additions to income).

a. True

b. False

76. Income taxes have characteristics similar to the various classes of operating expenses and accordingly should be matched, as realistically as is feasible, against the income to which they pertain.

    a. True

    b. False

77. If we, as lessors of machinery, collect rentals in advance for the next year, our accountant should record the receipts as a debit to Cash and should make a credit to:

    a. A revenue account (such as Lease Revenue)

    b. A deferred credit account (such as Deferred Lease Income)

78. See question 77. If we are required to pay income tax this year on the advance leasehold collections, our accountant should record the payment (or accrual) as a credit to Cash (or Taxes Payable) and a debit to:

    a. Income Tax Expense

    b. Deferred Income Tax

79. In the case of certain types of installment sales, the income of which is fully recognized in the books at date of sale but is deferred for income tax purposes until collections are made, tax allocation is accomplished in the period of sale by:

    a. Making credits to a deferred credit account

    b. Making credits to an accrued tax liability account

80. If the depreciation that we record on our books is less than that reported on our tax return and we fail to make tax allocation entries, then our current income will be:

    a. Overstated

    b. Understated

81. The tax allocation entry appropriate for question 80 consists of a debit to tax expense accounts and a credit to:

    a. Deferred income tax credit

    b. Accrued income tax liability

82. If in a given period we record expenses that are not allowable as tax deductions until a later period, we must make appropriate tax allocation entries so that our net income will not be:

    a. Overstated

    b. Understated

83. The term *net assets* means:

   a. Total assets minus total liabilities

   b. Plant assets minus allowances for depreciation

   c. Receivables minus allowance for uncollectibles

   d. The sum of (b) and (c)

84. In the case of an acquisition (purchase), good accounting requires that the acquired assets be recorded at reasonably current (appraised) values and that goodwill (or other intangibles) be recognized in the event that the purchase price exceeds the aggregate appraised values of the tangible assets minus liabilities.

   a. True

   b. False

85. In which of the following situations will the gain or loss realized be deferred for income tax purposes?

   a. gain on sale of a personal residence

   b. loss on sale of a personal residence

   c. gain on exchange of like kind business property

   d. loss on non-like kind business property

86. Goodwill recognized in the process of an acquisition:

   a. Must be kept on the books permanently

   b. Must be amortized over a period of reasonable length

   c. Must immediately be charged off to Retained Earnings

Use the following information to answer the next two questions:

Product K's expected selling price per unit is $36, projected variable cost per unit is $20, and estimated fixed costs per month are $12,000.

87. The break-even point in sales units per month is:

   a. 1,800

   b. 1,500

   c. 1,250

   d. 750

88. The break-even point in dollars per month is:

   a. 36,000

   b. 27,000

   c. 45,000

   d. 25,000

89. Period costs are:

    a. Treated as expenses in the period in which they are incurred

    b. Always directly traceable to products

    c. Costs including direct labor

    d. Costs including factory overhead

    The Spotts Company uses a process costing system. Assume that materials are added at the beginning of the period and labor and overhead are added continuously throughout the process. The company uses the FIFO method. The following data are available for one of its accounting periods:

	Units
Beginning Work in Process (60% complete for labor and overhead)	32,000
Units started	192,000
Units transferred out	204,000
Ending Work in Process (40% complete for labor and overhead)	20,000

90. Equivalent units for materials are:

    a. 212,000 units   c. 224,000 units

    b. 244,000 units   d. 192,000 units

91. Equivalent units for labor and overhead are:

    a. 232,000 units

    b. 192,800 units

    c. 212,000 units

    d. 204,000 units

92. When a company reaches the break-even point in sales, fixed costs equal:

    a. Sales less variable cost

    b. Total costs

    c. Variable costs

    d. Sales

    e. Zero

93. When the break-even point is 800 units and the sales per-unit variable cost is $2, fixed costs are:

    a. $400   c. $1,000

    b. $800   d. None of the above

94. To reach a target net income of $20,000, a firm with fixed costs of $10,000 and a per-unit differential cost between sales and variable costs of $5 must sell:

    a. 2,000 units

    b. 4,000 units

    c. 6,000 units

    d. 8,000 units

Use the following information to answer the next two questions about Alexis Company.

Actual units completed	800 units
Standard labor rate per hour	$10
Standard hours per unit	140 hours
Labor rate variance	$29,000 Unfavorable
Labor efficiency variance	$10,000 Unfavorable

95. Given the above information, the standard labor cost per unit is:

    a. $1,400   c. $4,000

    b. $2,000   d. $8,000

96. Given the above information, the actual hours were:

    a. 80,000 hours

    b. 112,000 hours

    c. 113,000 hours

    d. The answer cannot be determined

97. Which of the following should not be included in manufacturing overhead costs:

    a. Utility bills relating to the factory

    b. Indirect materials used in production

    c. Depreciation of machinery used in production

    d. Advertising costs for the finished good

    e. Indirect labor such as custodial service costs

98. Under the job-order cost system, when factory overhead is applied by a predetermined rate:

    a. Factory overhead is debited

    b. Goods in process is credited

    c. Factory overhead applied is credited

    d. None of the above

99. When the job-order cost system is used, the accounting entry for jobs completed would include:

    a. A debit to Cost of Goods sold
    b. A credit to Finished Goods
    c. A credit to Work in Process
    d. A debit to Finished Goods

100. Materials purchased on account during the month amounted to $175,000. Materials requisitioned and placed in production totaled $159,000. From the following, select the entry to record the transaction on the day the materials were bought:

    a. Materials   159,000
           Accounts Payable   159,000
    b. Materials   175,000
           Accounts Payable   175,000
    c. Work in Process   159,000
           Materials   159,000
    d. Accounts Payable   175,000
           Materials   175,000

Name _____

Address _____

City _____ State-Zip _____

FINAL EXAMINATION ANSWER SHEET: THE McGRAW-HILL 36-HOUR ACCOUNTING COURSE

See instructions on page 1 of the Final Examination.

1. _____	21. _____	41. _____	61. _____	81. _____
2. _____	22. _____	42. _____	62. _____	82. _____
3. _____	23. _____	43. _____	63. _____	83. _____
4. _____	24. _____	44. _____	64. _____	84. _____
5. _____	25. _____	45. _____	65. _____	85. _____
6. _____	26. _____	46. _____	66. _____	86. _____
7. _____	27. _____	47. _____	67. _____	87. _____
8. _____	28. _____	48. _____	68. _____	88. _____
9. _____	29. _____	49. _____	69. _____	89. _____
10. _____	30. _____	50. _____	70. _____	90. _____
11. _____	31. _____	51. _____	71. _____	91. _____
12. _____	32. _____	52. _____	72. _____	92. _____
13. _____	33. _____	53. _____	73. _____	93. _____
14. _____	34. _____	54. _____	74. _____	94. _____
15. _____	35. _____	55. _____	75. _____	95. _____
16. _____	36. _____	56. _____	76. _____	96. _____
17. _____	37. _____	57. _____	77. _____	97. _____
18. _____	38. _____	58. _____	78. _____	98. _____
19. _____	39. _____	59. _____	79. _____	99. _____
20. _____	40. _____	60. _____	80. _____	100. _____

ABOUT THE AUTHORS

Robert L. Dixon, Ph.D., CPA, is Professor Emeritus of Accounting, Graduate School of Business Administration, University of Michigan, where he taught from 1942 to 1974. Previously he taught at Yale and the University of Chicago and held the position of guest professor at MIT, the University of California, and North Texas University.

His nonteaching experience includes public accounting, consulting, and work on the principal committees of the American Accounting Association, American Institute of CPAs, and the National Association of Accountants. He has served as editor of the *Accounting Review*, president of the American Accounting Association, and AICPA Distinguished Visiting Professor. He is the author of two other books and numerous articles in professional publications.

Harold E. Arnett, Ph.D., CPA, CMA, is Professor of Accounting, School of Business Administration, University of Michigan, where he has taught since 1962. Previously he was a research associate at the American Institute of Certified Public Accountants. He has authored many articles and seven books and monographs, served on numerous committees of a number of business and professional organizations, as well as consulted for businesses and business organizations.

Howard Davidoff, Esq., CPA, LLM, is a Professor of Accounting, Taxation and Law, Department of Economics, City University at Brooklyn College, where he has taught since 1986. His nonteaching experience includes an accounting and law practice concentrating on the areas of taxation and wealth preservation. He has authored numerous articles in publications including The CPA Journal, Estate Planning Journal, Taxation For Accountants, Taxation For Lawyers, and the National Public Accountant. He has also authored three books and has written for and taught CPA Review and Continuing Professional Education courses for CPA's.